ELIZABETHAN

GOVERNMENT AND SOCIETY

Photo by Mark Gerson

ELIZABETHAN GOVERNMENT AND SOCIETY

Essays presented to

SIR JOHN NEALE

edited by

S. T. BINDOFF

J. HURSTFIELD

C. H. WILLIAMS

UNIVERSITY OF LONDON

THE ATHLONE PRESS

1961

Published by
THE ATHLONE PRESS
UNIVERSITY OF LONDON
at 2 Gower Street, London WC1
Distributed by Constable & Co Ltd
12 *Orange Street London* WC2
Canada
University of Toronto Press
Toronto 5
U.S.A
Oxford University Press Inc
New York

Printed in Great Britain at
THE CURWEN PRESS LTD
PLAISTOW E.13

Preface

FOR more than four decades Professor Sir John Neale has been associated with London University as teacher and administrator. He began his career at University College in 1919, as an assistant in history under A. F. Pollard. From 1925 to 1927 he occupied the Chair of Modern History at the University of Manchester, when he was called back to University College to become Astor Professor of English History. Here he remained until his retirement in 1956, when the University conferred upon him the title of Emeritus Professor of English History.

Sir John Neale has for a long time presided over his post-graduate seminar in Tudor Studies at the Institute of Historical Research. To this seminar he has attracted scholars and students from many British universities and from countries abroad, especially the United States. It is in recognition of his many services to learning and to commemorate his seventieth birthday, which falls on 7 December 1960, that we, three of his colleagues and some of his other friends, offer this volume as our tribute. The eminent American scholar, the oldest of those friends, Dr Conyers Read, finished his contribution to this volume only a short time before his death on 23 December 1959.

All the contributors have been associated with Sir John Neale, in most cases as students or colleagues; and each was asked to write on an aspect of the period, combining his own researches with one or more of its general themes. There could of course be no question of representing in this book all aspects of Elizabethan studies. We have been concerned rather to illustrate some of the recent trends in Tudor political and social historiography which owe so much to Sir John Neale's pioneer work and inspiration. We have at the same time sought to give a balanced picture of the age from the economic experiments of the early period to the succession struggle at the end. An attempt has also been made to analyse the social structure and its impact upon government, central and provincial; and there are chapters on the propaganda and strategy of the time. Our Irish, Scottish and Welsh contributors have enabled us to include something of the complex story of the relations between the four peoples who occupy these islands.

Sir John Neale, on the eve of his seventieth birthday, is still one of the most active scholars in our midst. To his great work on the Elizabethan parliaments he expects soon to add his contribution to the official history of parliament. We hope that the present volume may show how deeply two generations of Elizabethan historians stand in his debt.

Miss Helen Miller, who compiled the list of Sir John Neale's writings, was also largely responsible for indexing the volume.

S.T.B.
J.H.
C.H.W.

London, 27 September 1960

Contributors

S. T. BINDOFF, M.A.

Professor of History, Queen Mary College, University of London.

MARJORIE BLATCHER, PH.D.

PATRICK COLLINSON, M.A., PH.D.

Assistant Lecturer in Ecclesiastical History, King's College, London.

A. H. DODD, M.A.

formerly Professor of History, University College of North Wales, Bangor.

GORDON DONALDSON, D.LITT.

Reader in Scottish History and Palaeography, University of Edinburgh.

R. DUDLEY EDWARDS, D.LITT.

Professor of Modern Irish History in the National University of Ireland at University College Dublin.

G. R. ELTON, LITT.D.

Fellow of Clare College, Cambridge, and University Lecturer in History.

W. G. HOSKINS, M.A., PH.D.

Reader in Economic History, University of Oxford.

J. HURSTFIELD, B.A.

Professor of Modern History, University College, London.

WALLACE T. MACCAFFERY, A.M., PH.D.

Professor of History, Haverford College.

HELEN MILLER, M.A.

CONTRIBUTORS

† CONYERS READ, A.M., PH.D.

formerly Professor in English History,
University of Pennsylvania.

R. B. WERNHAM, M.A.

Professor of Modern History,
University of Oxford.

C. H. WILLIAMS, M.A.

Professor of History, King's College, London.

Contents

ILLUSTRATIONS

I

In Search of the Queen

C. H. WILLIAMS

IN ONE of his essays Sir John Neale has sketched the way in which the common people of England enshrined 'Good Queen Bess' within the folk memory and thereby transformed the realities of her reign into a myth.[1] Already within her lifetime they began to keep the anniversary of her Accession Day to the peals of church bells calling them to listen to sermons in commemoration of her virtues and achievement. The effects, it may be conjectured, were quickly dissipated by the junketings and the dances around the bonfires with which the festivities of the day were brought to a close. As the years passed, new generations arose for whom the meaning of the festival was blurred: the features of the Queen faded away from them into the obscurity of a past they did not know: her memory became a film of legends: and ultimately lingered in a myth.

There is another side to this typical example of folklore in the making. In the three and a half centuries which have run since Queen Elizabeth I's death there have always been inquiring minds unwilling to be content with the myth. According to their powers they have tried to get behind the legends, seeking to discover what manner of woman this could have been to leave so deep an impression upon her countrymen. They have tried, with varying degrees of success, according to their power, and the resources at their disposal, and their theories of what biography should be, to arrive at what they considered an accurate impression of her character and qualities. A full appreciation of the ways in which a succession of historians have gone in search of the Queen, and a reasoned estimate of what they have accomplished, is far too complex a topic for so short an essay: but an outline of the story is worth attempting. It may well give the reader opportunity for some interesting reflections.

[1] J. E. Neale, *Essays in Elizabethan History*, 9–20.

To bring to life again a figure from the past is never easy: it is more than usually difficult when that figure is Elizabeth I of England. Like all the rulers of her time she spent the greater part of every day in open court, closely watched by an attentive circle of followers. Zealous servants, insincere flatterers, inquisitive diplomats, listened eagerly to every word she let fall, watched intently everything she did. The gossip, the rumours, the speculations she inspired were the stock-in-trade of palace conversations, found a place in private letters, and provided subjects for solemn memoranda dispatched by industrious, and sometimes all too credulous, ambassadors to royal masters eagerly awaiting news from England before they made the next move in their game of diplomatic chess. Much of this miscellaneous material has survived, and it is the responsibility of the historian to assess it at its true worth, for amongst it he may find the clue which will lead him to what he is seeking, the secret of the way in which this woman's mind worked. And yet, what are the standards he may apply to distinguish false witness from true, how is he to sift reliable testimony from that worth less than the paper on which it was written? Baffling, indeed, is the search after this Queen's motives. Her thoughts were her own. She kept no private journal that might be a window into her soul. Even the letters which bore her signature were drafted, more often than not, by the hand of a secretary. What moved her to action, or prompted her to postpone a decision, was her own secret if she cared to keep it so, and her motives none but she could really know. Yet some notion of them the historian must have if he is to make intelligible the pattern of events in which her life was involved.

Nor is this the only problem before the historian. From the moment of her accession until the time of her death Elizabeth I was a phenomenon—it is not too strong a word—in European history. She was at once a crowned monarch and an unmarried woman. To such an unconventional conjunction some of the stiffest problems of the reign must be attributed. The Queen's methods of dealing with them often bewildered her contemporaries. They have not been any clearer to the historians.

Lastly, there is one other fact with a bearing on the historian's difficulties, a fact too often in evidence to be missed. The progress of the Reformation in England, as elsewhere, aroused passions and bred hatreds which were to influence the opinions of men concerning the events and the personalities of the period for centuries. In assessing the historical worth of books dealing with the sixteenth century many modern bibliographies recognize this fundamental cleavage by grouping works according to whether they are by Catholics or Protestants. It is a distinction which should be remembered when conflicting estimates of the Queen are being considered.

Among contemporary descriptions of Elizabeth there is one which may be taken as a starting point for this essay. John Clapham entered Burghley's household as a youth, owed much of his education to him, and spent over seven years in attendance upon him. He must, therefore, have had opportunities for knowing something of the gossip of informed political circles during the later years of Elizabeth's reign. His short essay seems to have been written in haste, as something in the nature of an obituary notice.[1] His description of the Queen is eminently favourable. Her comeliness of person, countenance, speech, and gesture full of majesty were accompanied by many princely virtues. Her disposition and natural gifts of mind and body matched, if they did not excel, those of all other princes of her time. She showed great spirit, tempered with moderation. Affable towards her subjects, she was always careful of her great estate, so that she was at once loved and feared. In her later years she always appeared in public in magnificent apparel, hoping that the eyes of her people, being dazzled by the glitter of her ornaments, would be diverted from the signs of age and decay of her natural beauty. She possessed a rich collection of jewels, many of them given to her by her subjects on her progresses. Temperate in diet, she liked simple fare and drank her wine sparingly, greatly diluted by water. Quick tempered, she was easily appeased, and endured trouble of mind and body stoically. Her bearing in face of attempts on her life indicated a religious resolution, and great constancy in a woman, and rare, indeed, in men, save those of more than ordinary spirit.

Clapham draws special attention to the Queen's proficiency in languages: in Latin, Spanish, French, and Italian she could speak elegantly and answer ambassadors impromptu, while she was not

[1] Clapham's essay, 'Certain observations concerning the life and reign of Queen Elizabeth', was only known to a few specialists before it was edited from two British Museum MSS. by E.P. and Conyers Read, *Elizabeth of England.* The introduction contains a short account of Clapham together with reasons for ascribing the work to him.

ignorant of Greek. She also showed some skill as a translator. Her style of writing he describes as tending towards obscurity largely because of its individuality. She had a moderate skill in singing, dancing, and instrumental music. Concerning her faults Clapham is discreet. As for flatterers, it is certain that she had many too near her, especially Leicester, Hatton, Raleigh, and Essex, and that she too readily listened to them.

In her later years, Clapham asserts, she had the reputation of being very close-fisted, and slow to spend money, but he tempers this accusation by the suggestion that if the rewards she sometimes gave freely had been granted for merit, she would no doubt have won for herself the name of a very liberal prince. He makes the point that in her anxiety not to overburden her subjects, for they had granted her many subsidies and lent her great sums of money, she sold some of her own lands and jewels to support the charges of the Irish war. In conclusion, Clapham rises above his matter-of-fact assessment into a eulogy of a Queen who retained her reputation at home and abroad, even to the last, as a prince feared of her enemies, honoured by her confederates, beloved of her own people: living peacefully and dying happily, to enjoy an immortal crown in Heaven, and to leave a perpetual memory of her name to posterity upon earth.

To this short summary of Elizabeth's qualities may be added a few details from another essay, written some years later. Sir Robert Naunton[1] describes Elizabeth as tall in person, of hair and complexion fair and well-favoured, but high-nosed, of limb and feature neat, and of stately and majestic comportment.[2] These qualities, he suggests, she had inherited from her father rather than from her mother, who was not of royal descent, although she

[1] Robert Naunton (1563–1635) probably wrote his impressions in 1630. They were printed in a very poor text in 1641, and this was reprinted in 1642. A revised edition under the title *Fragmenta Regalia: or observations on the late Queen Elizabeth, her times and favourites*, appeared in 1653. Edward Arber reprinted this 1653 edition in 1870.

[2] The Queen's personal appearance interested foreign visitors to England, as witness the well-known description by P. Hentzner, *Itinerarium* (1612), trans. in W. B. Rye, *England as seen by Foreigners*, 104; the starkly realist one by André De Maisse, *Journal*; Clare Williams ed., *Thomas Platter's Travels in England*, 192, 228; V. von Klarwill, *Queen Elizabeth and Some Foreigners*; and *Cal. S. P. Venet.* vi, 1058–60. Portraits of the Queen have their problems, which are indicated in F. M. O'Donoghue, *A Descriptive and Classified Catalogue of Portraits of Queen Elizabeth* and E. Auerbach, 'Portraits of Elizabeth I' (*The Burlington Magazine*, xcv), 197–205.

Elizabeth I, *c.* 1592

belonged to a noble and very ancient family, that of Boleyn. Sweet tempered, she was beloved of her people, who gave her the name and fame of a most gracious and popular prince. Like other observers Naunton was impressed by the Queen's learning, which was beyond all common belief, allowing for her age and sex. Her intellectual ability was revealed by her rule, which was full of magnanimity, tempered with justice, pity, and piety (the only stain on it being the death of Mary Stuart), and all her deprivations of life and liberty were lawful and could be justified on grounds of necessity. Touching on what he calls her 'frugality' he admits that there are not many instances of her liberality save towards her favourites. Her rewards, he comments, consisted chiefly of leases of offices: in grants of large sums in ready money she was very sparing, for she had heavy expenses to meet. Naunton disagrees with the common opinion that Leicester was absolute and alone in the Queen's grace and favour. In his opinion Elizabeth was absolute and sovereign mistress of her grace, and all those to whom she distributed her favour were never more than tenants at will, standing on no better terms than her princely pleasure and their own good behaviour. To some extent Naunton was inclined to attribute the success of Elizabeth's rule to the nature of her parliaments: the members were grave and discreet persons, not factious and ambitious of fame, 'such as came not to the house with a malevolent spirit of contention, but with a preparation to consult on the public good, and rather to comply than to contest with majesty'. Looking back over the Queen's reign, Naunton ventured on the prophecy that the judgment of history would be that Elizabeth ruled much by faction and parties, which she herself both made, upheld, and weakened as her own great judgment advised.

So far we have been introduced to Elizabeth by those who had little save good to say about her. There were, however, those who had no reason to praise her. They were the Catholic exiles who carried on from the continent during her reign a sustained and powerful attack upon her government. The foundations on which their accusations against her rested were not very strong. They had little direct knowledge of what had been happening in England since they had left the country, and their opinions were formed mainly from the news they gathered from later exiles. In their own special field of theological learning they were adversaries to be reckoned with very seriously, for they were men with acute minds and deep knowledge, wholly dedicated to their mission of opposition to the Reformers, and they were highly skilled in the technique of religious controversy and propaganda. It is fortunate that the abstruse theological arguments, the bitter attacks upon the Reformers, and even the political theory they expounded in so many virulent treatises do not have to be noticed here. Some of their opinions, however, cannot be ignored. The profound conviction many of them held, that England could only be saved by the removal of Elizabeth, led them to attack her position as queen and her reputation as a woman. What they wrote not only affected practical politics, it also coloured the writing of history on the period for many years to come.[1]

The earliest and best known attack upon the Queen was the indirect one delivered by Nicholas Sanders in his account of the early years of the English Reformation.[2] The source of much of the abuse appearing in the writings of the exiles, it was a forceful piece of polemical writing and as an account of the events of the time did not deserve all the hard things said about it by its opponents. It contained, however, one blazing indiscretion which put the work out of court for all loyal subjects of Queen Elizabeth, and brought this history into complete disrepute with Protestant writers. Repeating a story which he is presumed to have found in William Rastell's life of Sir Thomas More—although it may well have been a common piece of defamatory gossip circulating on the continent—Sanders asserted that Anne Boleyn was not only a person of loose morals herself, she was also the daughter of Henry VIII by the wife of Sir Thomas Boleyn. Intended as a convincing argument against Elizabeth's right to the throne, it was used by

[1] From the wide polemical literature of the period the following may be chosen as representative: Nicholas Harpsfield, *A treatise of the pretended divorce between Henry VIII and Catherine of Aragon*, 1556, ed. N. Pocock (Camden Soc. N.S. xxi); Nicholas Sanders, *De origine ac progressu schismatis Anglicani liber*, 1585 (see next note); William Allen, *A true, sincere and modest defence of the English Catholics* . . . Ingolstadt, 1584, and in *The Catholic Library*, 2 vols, 1914; and *An admonition to the nobility and people of England* . . . Antwerp 1588, and ed. I. Mendham, 1842.

[2] N. Sanders, *De origine ac progressu schismatis Anglicani liber* has a confusing history. He began it after his arrival in Rome in 1572, but it was unfinished five years later when he left Spain for Ireland. Some copies circulated in MS. and one came into the hands of Edward Rishton, who added a fourth section which carried the narrative into Elizabeth's reign and published the whole work, Cologne, 1585. This was translated from the Latin by David Lewis, *Rise and Growth of the Anglican Schism*, 1877, with a long introduction in defence of Sanders, and notes to the text. For Sanders in Ireland see below, 328.

other writers, and it did not lessen the passions aroused by the warfare of words waged by the two rival parties.

As long as the period was approached in this way, nothing more could be expected than noisy conflict between two earnest, but angry factions, each convinced of the other's lack of honesty and good faith. If anything approaching a conclusive debate was to be reached there must be some attempt to verify facts. This could only be done by going to documents. By the end of the seventeenth century this truth was beginning to reach men on each side, and a new phase in the writing of sixteenth-century history began with two men who tried to put these ideas into practice.

In 1676 there appeared a French translation of Sanders' *History*. It helped to stimulate Gilbert Burnet to embark upon a full-scale history of the events of the Reformation as he saw them.[1] Sanders had to be refuted because his lies had left a foul and lasting stain, not only on the memory of Anne Boleyn, but also on her incomparable daughter, and Burnet devoted a whole appendix to a refutation of the errors and falsehoods he found in Sanders' book. He went to the documents, and the impressive collections printed in his appendices reveal his industry and the wide range of his researches. It was his intention to continue his narrative on the same scale for the whole of Elizabeth's reign, but as he approached that period he changed his mind, because he did not feel that he had enough information, so his book ended with only a brief outline of the Queen's reign.

Despite his assurance that he knew the duty of the historian was to write impartially, neither concealing the faults of the one party nor denying the just praises that were due to any of the other side, Burnet made his own opinions very clear. It is not likely that a deeper knowledge of the sources would have persuaded him to change the account he gave of Elizabeth's reign, an account not intended to be a full one, but merely a demonstration of 'the unusual happiness of her whole reign, which raised her to the esteem and envy of that age, and the wonder of all posterity'. To Burnet it was wonderful, indeed, that a virgin queen could rule such a kingdom for above forty-four years with such constant success, in so great tranquillity at home, with a vast increase of wealth, and with such glory abroad. It was with real conviction

[1] Gilbert Burnet, *History of the Reformation of the Church of England*, 3 vols. 1679–1715; ed. N. Pocock, 7 vols. 1865.

that he wrote of the happy and glorious days of Queen Elizabeth. One important fact, too, Burnet did sense. It was the remarkable gift which Elizabeth possessed of being able to insinuate herself into the affections of her people. This was, he thought, the main secret of her success. To those who thought she was too theatrical in it, he retorted that it achieved her purpose, since by these little things in her deportment she gained more of the affections of her people than other princes have been able to do by more real and significant arts of grace and favour.

The improved methods used by Burnet were also employed by Charles Dodd.[1] His contribution, too, was a history of the Church in England, his chosen period running from 1500 to 1688. Although he was primarily concerned with the Reformation as a whole in England, he devoted considerable attention to the Queen's reign. His treatment introduced innovations. Like Burnet he worked conscientiously on manuscript materials, many of which he found at Douai, where he had been trained as a priest, and at other Catholic centres on the continent. Like Burnet he recognized the need to produce evidence in support of his narrative, and this he printed in his appendices. At the end of his preface he gave a rudimentary kind of bibliography of the works he had used. They indicate a considerable reading in Protestant as well as Catholic authors. Like Burnet, too, he approached his subject as a strong partisan, writing in defence of his Church. His views of Elizabeth, however, were at variance with those of the earlier Catholic writers. Unlike them, Dodd did not base his criticism of her on mere abuse. He did not think that his case could be established by visiting the wickedness of the parents on the child. Elizabeth's early life and education were not enough to explain the defects he found in her. To the young Queen he was sympathetic, recognizing her physical attractions and speaking well of her intellectual attainments. She showed wisdom in her choice of advisers, but it was they who were responsible more than she for her reputation as an able ruler. Dodd was critical of her character, condemning her vanity, jealousy, insincerity, and duplicity. Despite the criticisms which have been brought against his work, its partisan prejudices,

[1] Charles Dodd (otherwise Hugh Tootel), *The Church History of England from 1500 to the year 1688, chiefly with regard to Catholics*. 3 vols. Brussels (probably London) 1737–42. The work as now used is in a new edition, with considerable additions of documents and notes, by M. A. Tierney, 5 vols. 1839–43.

its careless inaccuracies, and wilful mis-statements, Dodd's more careful approach to the problem of Elizabeth's character is a decided advance on the attempts of earlier writers on the Catholic side. His book was the prelude to a much more sophisticated undertaking by an abler scholar writing from the same side.

John Lingard gained a high reputation, which he thoroughly deserved, for his general survey of English history.[1] The two volumes comprising his narrative from the accession of Henry VIII to the death of Elizabeth contain the results of some of his deepest research, and are considered the outstanding feature of his work. His handling of the intricate problems of that period won approval from Protestants as well as from members of his own Church, largely because his cool and balanced assessment of the problems at issue stood out in such striking contrast to the more obvious partisanship of previous writers from both religious camps. Lingard intended to get at the facts. He told his friend Dr John Kirk that for the reign of Elizabeth it was his wish to compose it entirely, or at least as far as might be, from the original letters and papers.[2] It was a decision in keeping with the ideal he set himself in the preface of his *History*, where he expressed his determination to admit no statement merely upon trust, to weigh with care the value of the authorities on which he relied, and to watch with jealousy the secret of his own feelings and prepossessions.

There was, however, a divided allegiance in his mind which made the fulfilment of so lofty an intention impossible. In a frank letter to Dr Kirk written just after the first three volumes of his work had appeared, Lingard explained what his purpose in writing his history really was.[3] Throughout his work, he told Kirk, he had made it a rule to tell the truth, whether it made for us or against us; to avoid all appearance of controversy that he might not repel Protestant readers; and yet to furnish every necessary proof in our favour in the notes: so that if his narrative were compared to Hume's, for example, it was, with the aid of the notes, a complete refutation, without appearing to be so. This he thought preferable. He continued:

> In my account of the Reformation I must say much to shock Protestant prejudices: and my only chance of being read by them depends

[1] John Lingard, *A History of England from the First Invasion by the Romans to the Revolution in 1688*, 8 vols. 1819–30; an enlarged edn. in 10 vols. 1849, was the last revised by Lingard.

[2] M. Haile and E. Bonney, *Life and Letters of John Lingard*, 194. [3] Ibid. 166.

upon my having the reputation of a temperate writer. The good to be done is by writing a book which Protestants will read. . . . This, however I can say, that I have not enfeebled a single proof in our favour, nor omitted a single fact or useful observation through fear of giving offence to Mawman,[1] as Bishop Milner asserts. Such a thing never entered my mind. Whatever I have said or purposely omitted has been through a motive of serving religion.

Whatever Lingard made of Elizabeth must be considered within the narrow limits of these qualifications. In his estimate of her character Lingard saw no objection to the Protestant view that she was one of the greatest and most fortunate of English rulers, but he found it impossible to decide how much of this was due to Elizabeth and how much to her counsellors. When it came to assessing her personal qualities he had his own opinions, and they conflicted with earlier judgments. For Lingard her greatest weakness—significant as an explanation of the relationship existing between her and her ministers—was her consistent hesitation when it came to making decisions of policy. This trait, he argued, could not be interpreted as a sign of her cautious statesmanship. While her ministers sometimes did attribute it, publicly, to her wisdom, in private they were often exasperated by it, condemning it as folly. Lingard's explanation was that it was due in part to Elizabeth's suspicious nature, which made her distrust the motives of her advisers, but to a greater degree, he thought, to a defect in her make-up, for she showed the same irresolution to take decisions on small personal matters as she did over weightier questions of public policy. His discussion of her relations with her favourites is cautious, but it is not in Elizabeth's favour. His least damaging comment on her behaviour was that she was extremely vain, and that her courtiers were quick to recognize the advantages to be gained by playing up to her weakness, flattering her because she liked it: 'even in her old age she exacted the same homage to her faded charms as had been paid to her youth, and all who addressed her were still careful to express the admiration of her beauty in the language of oriental hyperbole.'[2] Next to her vanity came her parsimony, although Lingard is prepared to admit that this was largely due to the expenses to which she was put by the foreign policy of her ministers.

Lingard had made a notable contribution. He was to be succeeded

[1] Lingard's publisher. [2] *History*, vi, 321.

by an historian who would arouse more and fiercer controversy by his interpretation of the Queen, and indeed of the sixteenth century as a whole. Froude undertook a study of the sixteenth century because he disapproved the attitude of many influential thinkers in England and Europe towards the Reformation.[1] The English Reformers, who for three centuries had been the object of enthusiastic panegyric, were being assailed with equally violent abuse by the High Churchmen on one side and by Liberal statesmen and political philosophers on the other. Macaulay had attacked Cranmer as the basest of mankind. It had become the fashion to speak with extreme severity of the persecution of the Catholics by Elizabeth. Even writers generally favourable to the Reformation described the English branch of it as a good thing done badly. Froude's own opinion—and the longer he worked in the period the more certain he became that it was right—was that the truth was quite otherwise. He considered the Reformation a good thing in itself, and something which in England had been accomplished with peculiar skill and success: it was the greatest incident in English history, the root and origin of the expansive force which has spread the Anglo-Saxon race over the globe and imprinted the English genius and character on the constitution of mankind.

Such opinions, coupled with his forthright statement that he did not pretend to impartiality, brought much ill-informed criticism on his work. It was looked at askance as merely another contribution to Reformation history from the Protestant side, a counterblast to Lingard's challenge. There is some slight justification for the criticism, but it does not dispose of this historian. His own defence to this charge was not without point. He claimed that he had not consciously allowed himself to be influenced by his prepossessions, and he put forward as proof the fact that, as a result of his researches concerning the actions of some of the most distinguished persons with whom he had to deal, he had been compelled to sacrifice prejudices early formed, tenaciously held, and unwillingly renounced. That he was untiring in his effort to get at the facts cannot be disputed. For nearly twenty years he had worked on the history of the sixteenth century, seeking manuscripts in archives, public and private, at home and abroad, often in conditions not conducive to comfort or efficiency. He made

[1] J. A. Froude, *History of England from the fall of Wolsey to the defeat of the Spanish Armada*, 12 vols. 1856–70; rev. edn. 1862–70.

his own transcripts, which, when used, he deposited at the British Museum for any student to examine. That he made slips in copying, and sometimes showed a lack of technique in incorporating material in his text, would be admitted and condoned by any critic save Freeman. It was not lack of industry nor imperfect knowledge of his sources that was open to objection. What, then, is the real criticism of Froude's work?

In one short sentence in the preface to his *History* Froude summed up his work, and provided the key to his method. 'The coming of the Armada', he wrote, 'was the last act of a drama of which the divorce of Queen Catherine was the first.' Drama. It is the word which reveals where Froude stood in the controversy beginning to agitate the minds of some of his contemporaries, as to whether history was a science. Froude gave his answer in a lecture in which he made very clear what he meant by Drama and History. 'Macbeth', he said, 'were it literally true, would be perfect history: and so far as the historian can approach to that kind of model, so far as he can let his story tell itself in the deeds and words of those who act it out, so far is he most successful.'[1] This was the spirit in which Froude approached the sixteenth century. For him the fascination of a study of the past lay in watching the reactions of the individual to events. Like his friend Carlyle, he had cultivated to the highest degree the faculty of seeing through the documents to men. What he saw he turned into literature, and in doing so he showed that history was not propaganda.

The volumes Froude devoted to the reign of Elizabeth are not the best part of his work. In them he carried to the extreme the view he expressed in his lecture, that it was the duty of the historian to allow his characters to speak for themselves, that he should lay the facts before his readers but must not tell them what he himself thinks about those facts.[2] The result was, as his biographer admits, that long and frequent extracts from the dispatches of the Spanish ambassadors waterlog the book and make it too like a series of extracts with explanatory comments. Even so, allowing for this and other defects, Froude did manage to convey a very clear idea of what he thought about the Queen's character and qualities.

[1] J. A. Froude, *Short Studies* (1872): 'The Science of History', 35.

[2] *Short Studies*, 36. Cf. *History*, xii, 503: 'Her [Elizabeth's] character I have left to be gathered from her actions, from her letters, from the communications between herself and her ministers, and from the opinions expressed freely to one another in private by those ministers themselves.'

Beginning his study of her reign with a great admiration for her, as he read more deeply into the sources he found himself reluctantly compelled to change his mind. After working through the private letters which passed between Burghley and Walsingham about Elizabeth, Froude wrote to Lady Salisbury that they had destroyed finally the prejudice that still clung to him, that notwithstanding her many faults, she was a woman of ability. Evidently in their opinion she had no ability at all worth calling by the name.[1] The loose phrasing of a private letter ought not to count too seriously, but even in the *History* itself he committed himself to the caustic comment that if, as is sometimes said, Elizabeth was the greatest English sovereign, one is tempted to suppose that the average stature cannot have been excessive.[2] His change of opinion concerning her brought him up against the vital question: if not Elizabeth, then who was responsible for the undoubted achievement of the reign? Again Lady Salisbury was the confidante of his changing opinions. He would return from Simancas, he told her, more a *Cecil maniac* than ever, for it was becoming ever more clear to him that he was the solitary author of Elizabeth's and England's greatness.[3] While he carried this idea into the *History*, however, he recognized that Elizabeth was Queen, and that the ultimate responsibility for policy was hers. 'Princes', he commented, 'who are credited on the wrong side with the evils which happen in their reigns have a right in equity to the honour of the good.'[4] It was not a complete answer, as his own narrative was to show, and his final solution was a happier one 'Elizabeth was a strange woman: or rather, she was a woman and a man; she was herself and Cecil: and while her acts were the joint result of her own inclinations and Cecil's counsel she gave way among her women and her favourites to her personal humours.'[5]

The attacks on the Queen's personal purity, made by Lingard and others, he rejected outright: but he was a severe judge of some of the less pleasing traits he found in her character: her vanity, as insatiable as it was commonplace: her vacillations and infirmity of purpose: her great dishonesty: her love of intrigue—she could never be simple: and the fact that she never hesitated to break a promise where to keep it was inconvenient. Above all he could

[1] H. Paul, *Life of Froude*, 120. [2] *History*, x, 501. [3] Paul, op. cit. 119.
[4] *History*, xii, 510. [5] Ibid. ix, 275.

not forgive her parsimonious ingratitude to her great seamen. He had no sympathy with her susceptibility to flattery and nothing but contempt for her favourites. They were negligible: Elizabeth kept her intellect for Burghley and Walsingham, and gave her folly to her favourites. As for Leicester, Froude thought him the most worthless of her subjects and his presence about her person a disgrace to her. With her religious opinions he was not unsympathetic: her creed was a perplexity to herself and the world: with no tinge of the meaner forms of superstition, she clung to practices which exasperated Reformers while Catholics laughed at their inconsistency. But Froude did not hold this against her. It was the result of her peculiar temperament and foreshadowed the eventual attitude into which the minds of the laity would subside.[1] On the other hand, Froude was not ungenerous in his recognition of the better qualities he found in Elizabeth. She lived simply, worked hard, and ruled her household with rigid economy. She was free of access to her presence, quickwitted, and familiar of speech with men of all degrees. If she rode, shot, jested, and drank beer, spat and swore round, mouthfilling oaths, well, what of it? It was a rough age, and these were the things her subjects could understand. What was all-important was the fact that, with all her shortcomings, Elizabeth had two great qualities: she disliked political executions, and she was supremely brave.

We have seen that not the least of Froude's merits was his work on original manuscripts carried out with little to help him in the way of printed texts and guides. After 1870, when he had completed his *History*, the position began to change. Students could look forward to the appearance at regular intervals of additions to their resources. From the Public Record Office came volumes of calendars of state papers, domestic and foreign, a steady stream of volumes which led into the Spanish archives at Simancas where Froude had worked, and to diplomatic materials elsewhere. The Historical Manuscripts Commission was to open the priceless store of the Hatfield, Rutland, and other private collections of manuscripts. And there were other treasures too numerous to mention. Partly because of the wide scope of Froude's work, and partly because time was necessary for these new printed materials to accumulate and be assimilated by historians, some time elapsed before any important work appeared to throw fresh light upon

[1] Ibid. vii, 249.

the character of the Queen. Between 1870 and the end of the century there was only one significant attempt to re-interpret her personality. Curiously enough, it was again the work of a priest, but it does not take us back into the polemics of an earlier age. Rather it is the mirror of a very different world.[1]

There is cause for wonder why Bishop Creighton should ever have written it. His biographer says that the Age of Elizabeth was a period in which he had long been specially interested, but he groaned over the way in which its glamour disappeared with increased knowledge. 'As for the Tudors', the bishop once wrote, 'they are awful: I really do not think that anyone ought to read the history of the sixteenth century.' He found it difficult to untangle before a mixed audience the complicated web of motives and intrigue of an age which he felt to be more and more demoralized the better he understood it.[2] But he took the risk. True, it was only a small book, and its author was modest: the objective he had in mind was a sketch of the life of Elizabeth, written as plainly as possible, to illustrate a character rather than to write the history of a time.

Was the bishop contemplating an Anglican Settlement of Elizabeth? After all the time was ripe for it. The vile calumnies cast at her parents had long been bundled into disrepute. They could be ignored. But intelligent Victorians like the bishop knew something about the influence of heredity on character. Was not this the *via media* which would answer all the questions? Thus, in her great qualities of caution and prudence Elizabeth reverted to her grandfather, Henry VII, while from her father she inherited the royal imperiousness and personal charm which always secured his popularity. To her mother she owed her vanity, her unscrupulousness, her relentless and overbearing temper. Anne Boleyn's hardness and coarseness passed to her daughter, in whom they were modified by finer qualities, and were curbed by a sense of duty.

Then there was her education: a governess like the foolish and imprudent woman, Catherine Ashley, little capable of guiding the precocious girl amid the dangers which beset her: we may pity a girl exposed to such temptations, but we must admit that there

[1] M. Creighton, *Queen Elizabeth*, first published in the Goupil series with impressive illustrations, 1896; 2nd edn., with only one portrait of the Queen, 1899.
[2] L. Creighton, *Life and Letters of Mandell Creighton*, i, 288.

was little intuitive modesty in a character which could not resist their grossness. No wonder there was the Seymour affair, in which the tall handsome man made love to Elizabeth in a corrupting way, Elizabeth showing no displeasure at his revolting attentions. If it ended in tragedy it was perhaps worth while, for it taught Elizabeth a lesson on the limitations of human trustworthiness and the inevitableness of personal responsibility, and how dangerous it was to follow her inclinations and indulge her affections: 'what place had love in such matters as these? It was possible for a village maiden: it was an impossible luxury for one who had a shred of claim to the throne of England.' Later on there was to be Leicester, with whom Elizabeth would carry on a flirtation which sorely perturbed her ministers: she had endangered herself before by the coarse affair with Seymour: now she was endangering her position by an unseemly flirtation with Leicester. How Elizabeth would have loved it all, and how it would have confirmed her opinion of bishops!

We must not be unjust to Creighton. If he was a little out of his depth in dealing with the hidden mysteries of Elizabeth's heart, he was on quite solid ground when he was dealing with politics, and his sketch of the Queen's achievements is a skilful piece of condensation and interpretation. He was writing for Victorians, and as one of them he knew the right note to sound: Elizabeth was 'mere English': 'Round her with all her faults the England which we know grew into the consciousness of its destiny . . . There are many things in Elizabeth which we could have wished otherwise: but she saw what England might become, and nursed it into the knowledge of its power.'[1]

On the threshold of the twentieth century this all too cursory survey must be limited. It would be instructive to digress on the interesting questions which were being canvassed in the 1920s, whether the earlier years of the century had seen a reaction from the ponderous biographies of the Victorian Age and the evolution of 'the new biography'; whether the new approach was an art; whether the artist, or for that matter the historian, could ever arrive at truth. These questions have been adequately discussed by experts.[2] Suffice it to notice that there have not been lacking those

[1] Creighton, *Elizabeth*, 307.

[2] H. Nicolson, *Development of English Biography*; André Maurois, *Aspects of Biography*; L. Woolf, *Granite and Rainbow: Essays by Virginia Woolf.*

who have considered that the interpretation of the colourful personalities of history is not the monopoly of the historian, that it needs the disciplined knowledge of scholarship less than it calls for an intuitive faculty for diagnosing human motive, that all that is essential is a lively imagination to bring to life again the vanished memories of bygone days. The technique may vary from the superb self-confidence of Elizabeth's first biographer, who seems not to have hesitated to publish fictitious documents in support of his worthless narrative,[1] to the invention of purely imaginative conversations for historical characters, or the pseudo-scientific presentation of a mass of evidence from which to probe into the medical history and psychological aberrations which will explain why the Tudors were what they were. The literary merits of such works vary: their historical significance is usually slight. It would be invidious to list a numerous selection here, but there is some justification for a reference to one of them as typical of the dangers of such exercises in the impossible.

Hilaire Belloc's contempt for footnotes and references to authorities is characteristic of most of his writings.[2] In his account of Elizabeth, as elsewhere, he made the most controversial statements about her, without providing the evidence from which their accuracy might be judged. His conclusions about the problems of her reign, although he knew they were bound to be challenged, he put forward as sound simply because they were based upon his right understanding of human nature. His intellectual background, and his profound loyalty to his faith, led him to propound an interpretation of the period based largely on a view of Elizabeth's character which takes the reader back to the crude caricature of the days of polemics. Elizabeth was a disaster for England, because of her character. His account of her private life, diagnosed as confidently as if he had been the Queen's own gynaecologist, is the starting point for an interpretation of the period which has, if it has nothing else, the quality of novelty.

To return to the historians. The opening of the new century brought renewed interest in the Elizabethan Age and a greatly increased output of scholarly books and monographs devoted to the history of the period. A survey of that specialist literature

[1] Gregorio Leti, *Historia . . . di Elizabetta regina d'Inghilterra* . . . Amsterdam. 1692. The original edition seems to have been suppressed, but a French translation appeared, Amsterdam, 1694. [2] Hilaire Belloc, *A History of England*, vols. i–iv.

could only be a catalogue, unnecessary and indeed incongruous as the conclusion of an essay concerned only with the Queen. The relevant question is, what difference has all this work made to the interpretation of her elusive character? The answer must be selective, based on some representative examples.

First, it may be said that the later historians have had at their disposal a much wider range of sources, especially for domestic history, than even Froude could have hoped for, and their special studies in all fields yield, as a result, richer and subtler interpretations than could be expected from the earlier historians. Next, while they have not always been concerned with a study of the Queen herself, in the special fields within which they have worked, her figure, nevertheless, persists in breaking in upon them, and the results of their investigations, whatever the problem may be, will generally be found to throw some light on her position and significance.

Speaking very generally it may be said that these studies have led the historians to write with deep and growing respect for the Queen's ability, and the part she played in the shaping of policy, both at home and abroad. Pollard, whose work led the way in the early years of the century, saw Elizabeth as a Queen of the Renaissance, with points of similarity with Catherine de Medici.[1] He was in no doubt about her domination within the council, which she deliberately constituted to retain for herself the greatest weight in determining the issues of its deliberations. The next generation of workers in this field, led by Neale, Conyers Read, and Rowse, agrees in the main with this interpretation. Neale would have us see the same purposeful and calculated artistry behind her encouragement of the pseudo-romantic cult of herself within her court. It is, however, through his profound knowledge of the workings of parliament, based on so much fresh material, that he has been able to improve on Pollard's argument, and on some points has been able to modify his views. His sustained narrative of Elizabeth's dealings with the house of commons has revealed the full implications of the long struggle over Church and prerogative through the reign, a struggle in which, time and time again, Elizabeth brought her unruly puritans to heel, standing firmly between them and the objectives she was determined they

[1] A. F. Pollard, *The History of England from the accession of Edward VI to the death of Elizabeth, 1547–1603*, 1910.

should not attain. Where Pollard had found her sceptical and indifferent in religious matters, holding in common with the ablest rulers of that age that it was foolishness to sacrifice the security of thrones and the unity of states on the altar of disputable dogma, this new parliamentary narrative reveals a very different character, no *politique* guided by expediency, but a Queen of unswerving purpose who could, and did, stand firm on matters of principle.

That Elizabeth could do these things and stand alone, as sovereign responsible for the government of England, does not mean that she lived without advisors. The studies of Walsingham and Cecil by Conyers Read have taught us much about what went on behind the scenes in administration, and no modern historian would seek to deprive Cecil of the credit his indefatigable labours so richly deserve.[1] The work of Rowse in the field of social history, resulting in his admirable picture of Elizabethan England, based on an analysis of the structure of its society, is a powerful reminder of the dynamic forces in the new England which was coming into being, and with which the Queen's claim to greatness must be for ever linked.[2]

It is time to end this survey. Although a theme deserving of more serious study has been sketched very lightly, at least attention has been directed towards some pertinent reflections. It would seem that the protracted search for the Queen has, indeed, been rewarding. Her personality has emerged more clearly as the succession of historians have examined the evidence more intensively until at last that figure the common folk of England in their ignorance had long since transformed into a myth has become for the serious student a convincing historical reality. Much of the credit for such a result is due to the achievement of modern scholarship in breaking free from the shackles of religious bigotry and partisan propaganda. Even today the price of that freedom is ceaseless vigilance: although it is now well established that there are principles and standards which must be respected in any work for which the seal of true scholarship is sought. It is, however, no less true that interpretation of human character and motive is inevitably coloured by the private judgement of the individual

[1] Conyers Read, *Mr. Secretary Walsingham and the Policy of Queen Elizabeth*; *The Tudors: Personalities and Politics in Sixteenth Century England*; *Mr. Secretary Cecil and Queen Elizabeth*; *Lord Burghley and Queen Elizabeth.*

[2] A. L. Rowse, *The England of Elizabeth: The Structure of Society*; *The Expansion of Elizabethan England.*

historian. For this reason there can be no ultimate assessment of Elizabeth's qualities. Even although the essentials of her personality may now find general acceptance there yet remains the chance that even accepted facts may present themselves in a new pattern when seen by fresh eyes. Already a younger generation of students is at work on a variety of problems in Elizabethan history. Not all of them are concerned with the Queen herself, but often their discoveries have a significance, directly or otherwise, for the interpretation of her character. The studies contained in this book confirm this statement. A discerning reader will discover in several of these essays a hint, sometimes more than a hint, that their authors would not willingly accept, at any rate without some modification, conclusions about the Queen which were wholly satisfactory to earlier historians. The problem of striking a balance between the credit due to the sovereign in a personal monarchy such as that of sixteenth-century England, and that which should be divided between the Queen and her ministers, remains a dilemma affecting many problems of the period.

So the search for the Queen will continue. For the time being the historians have had their say. Good manners decree that the woman must have the last word. Does she, perchance, strike nearer to the ultimate secret?

I know the title of a King is a glorious title; but assure yourself that the shining glory of princely authority hath not so dazzled the eyes of our understanding, but that we well know and remember that we also are to yield an account of our actions before the great Judge. To be a King and wear a crown is a thing more glorious to them that see it, than it is pleasant to them that bear it. For myself, I was never so much enticed with the glorious name of a King or royal authority of a Queen, as delighted that God hath made me His instrument to maintain His truth and glory, and to defend this Kingdom (as I said) from peril, dishonour, tyranny and oppression.

There will never Queen sit in my seat with more zeal to my country, care for my subjects, and that will sooner with willingness venture her life for your good and safety, than myself. For it is my desire to live nor reign no longer than my life and reign shall be for your good. And though you have had and may have many princes more mighty and wise sitting in this seat, yet you never had nor shall have any that will be more careful and loving.[1]

[1] Elizabeth's 'Golden Speech' to the parliament of 1601. Text from J. E. Neale, *Elizabeth I and her Parliaments, 1584–1601*, 391.

II

William Cecil and Elizabethan Public Relations

CONYERS READ

ONE of the characteristic attributes of Tudor government was its increasing interest in public relations, that is to say, in the relations between the Crown and its neighbours and the Crown and its subjects, through public channels of communication. The most obvious channel, though by no means the only one, was the press.

Long before the press was readily available the most familiar channels in domestic affairs were the parliament and the courts of law, particularly the justices on circuit and, increasingly, the justices of the peace. Parliament of course met only infrequently and what happened within its walls was not publishable, though inevitably a good deal of it leaked out. The more dramatic episodes must have been spread abroad by the Members when they returned to their constituencies. It is to be noted that during Elizabeth's reign, and even before, Members of Parliament began to keep diaries of proceedings, an indication of increasing interest and increasing desire to remember and record. These diaries indeed supply much of what we know about the Elizabethan house of commons. Unfortunately the peers do not seem to have been given to diaries: at least no example has been found.

The bills passed in parliament and subsequently enacted by the Crown were of course matters of public knowledge. In earlier days manuscript copies were made and sent down to the counties at the end of each parliament to be proclaimed by the sheriffs. From the reign of Richard III the statutes were printed and distributed in that form. Very likely enough copies were printed to supply the Members of the House and perhaps even for limited sale. In any case, statutes not only became widely known but offered a convenient vehicle by which new laws might be explained and justified. The preambles to the statutes became increasingly important. This was notably so of the preambles to subsidy bills—Members of Parliament were naturally eager to justify to their constituents the taxes which they voted. On one notable occasion they even tried to record a royal promise in the preamble, much to the Queen's wrath who perceived its purpose and forced its alteration.[1]

A more direct channel between Crown and country was through royal proclamations, sometimes designed to direct, sometimes to impose, sometimes to explain and justify royal action. Many of these were directed against Roman Catholics, some against puritans. Many of them were economic in character, many were to emphasize laws enacted but not observed. About four hundred and fifty have been preserved, twice as many as in the reign of Elizabeth's father and a little fewer than those issued by her successor in a reign not half as long.

During William Cecil's[2] term as principal secretary he evidently had much to do with drafting these proclamations. We have drafts in his own hand for over a dozen of them.[3] But we can draw no conclusions from these chance survivals. In the great majority of cases drafts of the proclamations are missing. After Cecil became lord treasurer in 1572 his surviving drafts are fewer in number but enough to reveal the fact that he was still playing an active part in their preparation. The last example we have of this is in April 1591, where three separate drafts of a proclamation in his own hand are preserved among his papers.[4] In his valuable essay on the subject Dr Robert Steele observes that during Elizabeth's reign 'the practice of having the proclamations drawn by the law officers of the Crown seems to have become the rule':[5] but he cites no evidence, and I have found very little, to support this view of the matter.

Such evidence as we have about the number of proclamations printed reveals the fact that early in the reign the average edition was five hundred, though in some cases only fifty were printed. There is one example of an edition of seven hundred[6] and several

[1] J. E. Neale, *Elizabeth I and her Parliaments 1559–1581*, 163–4. On at least one occasion Cecil drafted the preamble of the subsidy; B.M. Lansd. 58 ff. 182–7.

[2] To avoid confusion I refer to him as William Cecil throughout his career.

[3] R. Steele, *Tudor and Stuart Proclamations*, nos. 506, 526, 585, 593, 595–8, 609a, 623, 626, 634.

[4] Ibid. no. 832. [5] Ibid. p. xiii. [6] Ibid. no. 638.

instances of a second edition of the same proclamation. Of their distribution we know little or nothing. It would be rash to assume that the procedure outlined a century later in Charles II's reign[1] applied under Elizabeth. A few figures for her reign are, however, preserved of the costs of distribution by special messengers which seem to vary between £16 and £24. To the more important question, who got them, there is no certain answer. Doubtless some copies fell into unofficial hands, as witness Humphrey Dyson's collection. Professor Shaaber, on the basis of rather scant evidence, believes that the publisher sold some of them.[2] In any case, they were posted far and wide. Certainly in all the important centres of population the literate Englishman could read them and the illiterate listen to another man's reading.

Another channel of communication was of course by direct messages from the Queen or her council to the local justices ot the peace, the maids of all work in local government. This was made the more valuable by the common practice of gathering together at the end of law term in Star Chamber all the J.P.s within easy reach to receive a special charge from the Queen, generally delivered by the lord chancellor.[3] On at least three occasions Cecil participated in these assemblies. He first appears in this connection as the author of a speech delivered in Star Chamber by his brother-in-law, Sir Nicholas Bacon, lord keeper, on 15 June 1570, immediately after the posting up, in London, of the papal bull excommunicating Elizabeth. It was a defence of her policy towards the Roman Catholics.[4] Again, on a like occasion in 1573, he was himself the speaker, whether, as he said in his speech, because Bacon was away, or because Elizabeth decided that Cecil could present the matter more effectively, remains in doubt: he was a recognized orator, but so was Bacon.

We have a copy of Cecil's speech in his own hand.[5] It had to do with the puritans.

There are [he declared] in sundry parts of her Majesty's realm, entered into ordinary cures of souls . . . and into places of preaching and reading, a number of persons young in years, but over young in

[1] Ibid. p. xiv *n.* [2] *Some Forerunners of the Newspaper in England*, 37–38.

[3] The similar use of quarter sessions, by means of the charge to the grand jury, is illustrated by William Lambard's own reports of his speeches between 1581 and 1601 to grand juries in Kent, which are preserved at the Folger Shakespeare Library, Washington, D.C. [4] Cecil's draft is in S.P. 12/71/17.

[5] B.M. Cotton MSS. Titus B ii ff. 247 sqq. Printed in Strype, *Parker*, ii, 35 sqq.

soundness of learning and discretion, which, according to their own imaginations and conceits, and not according to the common services of the church . . . have made sundry alterations, but also, by their examples and teaching, have enticed their parochians . . . to conceive erroneous opinions in condemning the whole government of the church and order ecclesiastical and in moving her Majesty's good subjects to think it a burden of conscience to observe the orders and rights of the church, established by law:—a matter so pernicious to her state of government, that her Majesty cannot, for the charge committed to her by Almighty God, but by speedy good means procure the stay of the dangers that must needs follow.

He went on to remind his listeners that the Queen had issued injunctions commanding uniformity and called upon the justices of the peace to see that these orders were obeyed. The speech was well phrased and probably well delivered. Perhaps the Queen charged Cecil with the business because his sympathy with the puritan position was generally assumed. He did not discuss the merits of that position. He simply elaborated upon the necessity for obedience and uniformity. These were basic principles in the political and religious credos of Tudor country gentlemen of all shades of opinion and probably were best calculated to carry weight with the J.P.s, even with those more or less tarred with the puritan brush.

The third instance of Cecil's participation in these Star Chamber gatherings was early in July 1588, just before the arrival of the Spanish Armada in the Channel. On that occasion there were two speakers, Hatton, the lord chancellor, and Cecil. Cecil's speech is preserved among Robert Beale's papers.[1] He dealt with three subjects, all of them matters of considerable concern to well-informed Englishmen in those anxious days: first, Cardinal Allen's published denunciation of the Queen and his call to all good Englishmen to rise against her; second, the adequacy of military and naval preparations to meet the Spanish threat; and third, the mysterious negotiations for peace which had been going on during the spring. Cecil attacked Allen as a 'base companion', a low fellow who had taken upon himself 'Luciferian authority' to set the crown of England upon the head of any person whom the pope and the king of Spain should select. There was nothing about religion, the appeal was to the justices as gentlemen and as

[1] B.M. Add. MSS. 48027 ff. 691*b* sqq.

patriots. As to the preparations to meet the Armada—he declared that the Queen's navy was stronger than ever it had been, and longing to get at the Spaniards. He expressed some doubt whether the Spaniards would venture to attack: if they did, by the grace of God they would get the worst of it. Finally, with regard to the peace negotiations, which had been widely criticized in England, Cecil said that the Spaniard had asked for peace and that the Queen could not refuse to consider any honourable means of peace. But she had met with nothing but trifling and had broken off the negotiations. To those who did not know the inside story of Elizabeth's frantic efforts for peace, the explanation was plausible. Unfortunately there was a very slim attendance of J.P.s to hear it.

On the whole Cecil's performances at these Star Chamber gatherings are impressive. They reveal his understanding of his audience and his careful choice of those arguments most likely to carry weight with them. In all three of them he had to deal with problems in part religious. In all three he avoided religious issues and based his appeal on loyalty to the Crown and obedience to the law. It is a pity that we do not have an adequate report of that part of his speech delivered when the Spanish Armada was in the offing, which dealt with Elizabeth's ability to meet the enemy and overcome him. Certainly Cecil lacked Drake's fine confidence. He knew too much about the inadequacies of the preparations. But he spoke brave words at a time when brave words were called for.

In the ecclesiastical controversies of the reign, government propaganda was usually handled by the churchmen. But there are plain indications of secular prodding, particularly by Cecil in the first decade of the reign. It is certain that the first great defence of the Anglican position by Bishop Jewel was inspired, indeed ordered, by Cecil.[1] He had the manuscript in his hands in May 1561, and released it for publication later in the year. It was published in Latin in 1562, but an English translation, by Cecil's sister-in-law Ann Bacon, appeared later in the same year. Cecil probably also enlisted the services of Dr Walter Haddon to answer the attack of Osorius upon the English Church in 1563. In November 1563 he wrote to Sir Thomas Smith, an old friend and distinguished scholar, then in France:

[1] Conyers Read, *Mr. Secretary Cecil and Queen Elizabeth*, 262.

I wrote to you of late date that Mr. Haddon had written an answer to Osorius's slanderous epistle. I wish you had the sight thereof and the allowance thereof, by some commendatory epistle to be added. If you could by some good means procure it to be well printed in France, without peril of the book, I would send you a copy. Or if you think you can get it printed at Strassburg or Basel by some means from thence. But if you cannot I will send it by some of my own means to Christopher Mount to be printed in Strassburg.[1]

Smith apparently arranged for publication in Paris. An English translation appeared in 1565.[2]

It may have been at Cecil's prompting that Bishop Jewel wrote an answer to the Bull of Excommunication of 1570, though it was not published until 1582.[3] After the excommunication, propaganda against the Roman Catholics was directed not against their theology but against their politics. Cecil was quick to seize upon the identification of Roman Catholicism with treason, and made much of it in response to charges by Catholic powers that Elizabeth was as intolerant of Catholics as they were of heretics. He stressed it, for example, in drafting the instructions for Francis Walsingham when he went to France as English ambassador in 1570.[4]

In the official pamphlet war against puritanism, Cecil seems to have taken no active part. If anything, he was on the other side of the fence. He had befriended in his time most of the puritan leaders and he was probably the man chiefly responsible for the appointment of Walter Travers, a notorious puritan, as lecturer at the Temple. This was to have valuable repercussions, since it brought Travers into direct conflict with Richard Hooker and so produced the greatest of Elizabethan justifications of Anglicanism, Hooker's *Ecclesiastical Polity*.

It is rather surprising that the Crown made no considerable use of the pulpit in its battle with the Roman Catholics. The official *Book of Homilies*, for example, though it passed through several editions in Elizabeth's reign, remained virtually unchanged. After the Rising in the North, a special homily was issued in 1570, dealing with Disobedience and Wilful Rebellion,[5] and this homily was added to editions of the *Book of Homilies* published thereafter.

[1] B.M. Lansd. 102 f. 45. [2] *D.N.B.*, *s.v.* Haddon. [3] *S.T.C.* 14614.
[4] Dudley Digges, *The Compleat Ambassador*, 3.
[5] *S.T.C.* 13679; it added a prayer of thanks for delivery from the rebellion.

But there were no other separate homilies issued to meet specific situations: at least none was published.[1]

Another, less obvious, channel for influencing opinion through the Church was the various prayers published. Perhaps the best example of this is in the prayer of thanksgiving for deliverance from the Parry Plot in 1585. It began by thanking the Lord for the 'establishment of Elizabeth' according to her right, for deliverance of the people that were captive in Babylon out of bondage and for enabling them to enjoy 'the free function of the Gospel'. It went on to thank the Lord for revealing Dr Parry's treasonable intent and to describe his course of action. Obviously this was not intended for the edification of the Almighty but for the English people in the parishes. We have a draft of the prayer corrected in Cecil's own hand.[2] It was probably published.

A particularly beautiful prayer for divine aid against the approaching Spanish Armada, composed by Anthony Martin, a gentleman of the royal household, for use in the chapel royal, was published at the end of Martin's *Exhortation to her Majesty's subjects . . . to defend their country*,[3] and was widely used in other churches. Again, in 1596, a *Prayer of Thanksgiving and for Continuance of good Success of her Majesty's Forces* was published in connection with the Essex expedition to Cadiz. The draft of it, dated 3 July, corrected in Cecil's hand and in what may be Elizabeth's own hand, survives.[4] During the last fifteen years of the reign, prayers issued for special occasions seem to have multiplied. Perhaps the government concluded that publicity in the churches was more effective in that form than in the form of homilies. Cecil was a prolific prayer writer. Drafts of various other prayers intended for public use are preserved among his papers. But none of these appears to have been published.

Two other obvious channels of approach to the people were the drama and the popular ballad, but there is little evidence that they were utilized by the government. As to the drama, in 1559 the Spanish ambassador in London said that Cecil was supplying playwrights with materials for plays making mock of Philip of Spain. This may have been true, but there is no other evidence to support it.[5] On one other occasion Cecil envisaged the possibility

[1] None in *S.T.C.* or in B.M. Catalogue.

[2] B.M. Lansd. 116 f. 29.

[3] *S.T.C.* 17489.

[4] B.M. Lansd. 116 f. 30.

[5] Read, *Cecil and Elizabeth*, 133; cf. Chambers, *Elizabethan Stage*, i, 243–4.

of utilizing the stage. It was in connection with a case in Star Chamber which had to do with the 'cozening of young gentlemen' by one Howe, a broker, and one Easte, a solicitor. They were found guilty, fined, whipped and set up in the pillory at Westminster. In the course of the trial, Cecil remarked that 'he would have those that make plays to make a comedy thereof and to act it with those names'.[1] But there is no evidence that Cecil followed up the idea. In general he shared the puritan dislike of the theatre. It is, however, to be remarked that Shakespeare's *Midsummer Night's Dream*, with its familiar lines on a Virgin crowned in the West, was probably first produced at the marriage of Cecil's granddaughter to the earl of Derby in January 1595, when Elizabeth herself was present.

The ballad was a different matter. It was cheap, in its published form it was often illustrated with pictures, it was anonymous. It could be said or sung at the street corners. Its publication was controlled by government censorship, but a great many ballads, particularly those which criticized governmental policy, were secretly printed and issued without the official licence. It was, in short, a convenient vehicle for the promotion of any cause or the airing of any grievance. Falstaff, in his well-known altercation with Prince Hal just before the affair at Gadshill, remarked, 'An I have not ballads made on you all and sung to filthy tunes, let a cup of sack be my poison'. Shakespeare indeed is full of ballads. King Lear quoted from one of them, Benedict, in *Much Ado about Nothing*, from another; Autolycus, in *A Winter's Tale*, is a ballad-monger par excellence. We get Nightingale, another ballad-monger, in Ben Jonson's *Bartholomew Fair*. The figure was a familiar one in Elizabethan life.

Ballads dealt with all sorts of subjects, from monstrous births to the execution of the queen of Scots. Most of them have disappeared, particularly the political ones. Of twenty-five dealing with the Armada and licensed to appear, only four survive, three of them by Thomas Deloney, the best known of the small number of Elizabethan ballad writers whose names have come down to us.[2] There were few political events of importance in Elizabeth's reign which were not the subject of ballads. At least

[1] Chambers, op. cit. i, 267 *n*, and reference there.

[2] C. H. Firth, 'The Ballad History of the Reigns of the Later Tudors' (*Trans. R.H.S.* 3rd ser. iii), 51 sqq.

four saluted Elizabeth upon her accession. Two more were inspired by the English expedition to France in 1562. The career of Mary Stuart produced a number of Scottish ballads, while an English one dealt with Bothwell and his part in the Darnley murder. The Rising in the North produced no less than twenty licensed ballads of which about half survive. These all supported the Queen's cause. But there were some, unlicensed, which favoured the rebels.

In 1570 the excommunication of the Queen called forth another burst of balladry. The Ridolfi Plot produced a curious one called *The Decay of the Duke*. The execution of Campion the Jesuit, ten years later, produced another spate: three ballads, privately printed, which took the Catholic side, were answered, line by line, in three parodies by Anthony Munday. Three years later the Throgmorton Plot occasioned another, and three years after that the execution of Mary Stuart called forth *An excellent ditty, made as a general rejoicing for the cutting of the Scottish queen*. Curiously enough there are almost none dealing with Leicester's expedition to the Low Countries. Leicester was not a popular figure, but known to be a vindictive one and safer left alone. After the Armada, ballad writers on matters political devoted most of their products to the naval exploits of the English in the war against Spain, though only one of them, Deloney's on the capture of Cadiz, seems to have survived. It is difficult to believe that the government made no use of this admirable propaganda medium. But the evidence is lacking. Of all the balladers whose names are known, none, unless it be Anthony Munday, reveals any political affiliation. No trace of any connection between Cecil and the balladers survives.

Where Cecil was chiefly active was in the preparation of pamphlets designed to explain or to justify official action. It is not easy to follow his activity because virtually all official pamphlets appeared anonymously and generally assumed the form of a letter from one private individual to another. For that reason it is difficult to distinguish between official and unofficial pamphlets, government issues from publishers' ventures, although publication by the Queen's printer establishes a strong presumption of government sanction. As the reign progressed and public interest developed, publishers' ventures became more numerous.

Cecil's first appearance in the public press was not long after the death of Henry VIII. Late in the year 1547 Cecil edited Catherine

Parr's little book, *The Lamentations of a Sinner*. It was evidently popular enough to justify a second edition the following spring.[1] Cecil announced that he had undertaken the work at the earnest desire of the duchess of Suffolk and the marquess of Northampton. It was not quite what its title indicated, for it included a denunciation of the papacy and all its superstitions, condemned the adoration of the saints, emphasized the unique authority of the Bible and in general came as close to the position of the Protestant reformers as a wife of Henry VIII, writing during his lifetime, could safely come. After Henry's death, what Catherine wrote had propaganda value. That was probably why Catherine's brother, Northampton, and the (dowager) duchess of Suffolk, two of the foremost champions of Protestantism at the beginning of Edward VI's reign, appeared as its sponsors. Cecil's introduction did not emphasize its Protestant character. He was content to point out that Queen Catherine[2] was a pious woman who 'eschewed superstition' and embraced true religion. He bade other women follow her example. This was propaganda of the mildest character. Probably Cecil was reluctant to go further until the situation immediately following Henry's death clarified itself. As literature his introduction is negligible. His style is verbose, affected and ineffectual. But Cecil was only twenty-seven at the time and this seems to have been his maiden effort.

We get no more published propaganda from his pen until after Elizabeth's accession. During the first decade of her reign, very little official propaganda, except that of the proclamations, seems to have been attempted. There appear to have been no official published justifications even of the acts of supremacy and uniformity. This official silence may perhaps be explained by Elizabeth's intention to maintain as long as she might an ambiguous position in matters controversial, particularly on the religious issue. Cecil drafted, probably soon after the driving of the French out of Scotland in 1560, a pamphlet entitled 'The Queen's Declaration against Slanders against her', apparently intended to defend Elizabeth from charges that she entertained aggressive designs against her neighbours.[3] But the draft was never finished nor the pamphlet published.

[1] *S.T.C.* 4827–8. Cecil's introduction appears in both editions. There is a MS. copy in the Huntington Library, Ellesmere MSS. 8727.

[2] She died between the appearance of the first and second editions.

[3] B.M. Lansd. 104 f. 49.

In 1562, however, as Elizabeth's troops invaded France and occupied Le Havre, she issued *A Declaration of the Queen, containing the causes which have constrained her to arm certain of her subjects for defence both of her own estate and the most Christian King Charles IX, her good brother, and his subjects.*[1] In essence this was an attack upon the duke of Guise, his slaughter of good Frenchmen, his domination and ruination of the French Crown, his menace to English trade, his hostile intentions towards herself and her realm. It was the first of many declarations which Elizabeth was to issue in defence of her foreign policy. Cecil, who drafted it, evidently did not find it easy to justify English military intervention in the affairs of a neighbour, particularly since his mistress was of no mind to assume the role of champion of the Protestant cause. We have three separate drafts of the 'Declaration', all in his own hand.

The next crisis, arising out of the seizure of the duke of Alva's pay ships in English harbours in 1568, seems to have passed without any official public justification other than that of an unusually long proclamation issued on 6 January 1569.[2] Cecil set forth the official account of the affair in a long memoir, dated 18 January, but it was, apparently, never printed.[3] In the same year came the Rising in the North. I do not find any royal proclamation dealing with that crisis, but while the fighting was still in progress, Thomas Norton, co-author of *Gorboduc* and afterwards notorious as the 'rackmaster' of the Catholics, composed a pamphlet, no doubt officially inspired, addressed *To the Queen's Majesty's poor deceived subjects of the North Country rebellion by the earls of Northumberland and Westmorland.*[4] It was chiefly an attack upon the character of the two earls and, making light of the religious issue, denounced the vices of disloyalty and disobedience. It ran to three editions. Quite possibly also the government in the same year prompted the publication of a new edition of Sir John Cheke's *The Hurt of Sedition*, first published in 1549.[5]

[1] Patrick Forbes, *A Full View of the Public Transactions*, ii, 69 sqq. A draft by Cecil: *Cal. S.P. For.* 1562, 325. The printed Latin version: *S.T.C.* 9187. Also published in French.

[2] Steele, *Proclamations*, no. 632: three folios.

[3] B.M. Cotton MSS. Galba C iii ff. 158 sqq.

[4] *S.T.C.* 18680–2.

[5] Ibid. 5110. The MS. 'Discourse of the traitorous attempts of the earls of Northumberland and Westmorland in 1589 (*sic*)' in the library of Trinity College, Dublin (E.1.10 ff. 153 sqq.) is of unknown authorship and appears not to have been printed.

Shortly after the rising was suppressed, Elizabeth bade Cecil prepare a 'Declaration' in which she denied any 'meaning or intent that our subjects should be troubled by examination or inquisition in any matter either of their faith . . . or for their opinion in any rites and ceremonies appertaining to the Christian religion, so long as they shall in their outward conversation show themselves quiet and conformable'. We have two drafts of this 'Declaration', both of them corrected in Cecil's own hand.[1] It is one of the most effective of all the Queen's manifestoes and an admirable statement of her religious position. Cecil evidently laboured long on it and did a fine job. The style is much better than in most of his writings. One suspects that Elizabeth herself had a hand in its composition, though I have found no evidence of this. 'We will,' the Declaration concluded, 'that beside the ordinary means of publication hereof to be made in all accustomed places in our realm, all curates in their parish churches shall, at such time as the bishops and ordinaries shall think meet and requisite, read these admonitions to their parishioners.' But I find no evidence that it was ever proclaimed or even published. Early in 1570 a book was published in France defending the action of the northern rebels. Cecil attempted a reply to it, under the title, 'Copy of a letter from a gentleman in England to his cousin, a Student in Paris'. We have a manuscript of it in Cecil's hand. It was a poor effort and Cecil never finished it.[2]

The papal bull excommunicating Elizabeth was posted up by Felton in St. Paul's churchyard in May 1570. It called forth at once ballads, proclamations, and vigorous retorts in pamphlet form, probably officially inspired, by Thomas Norton, a grave sermon by Bishop Jewel and a refutation by Bullinger. Cecil attempted a pamphlet on the subject entitled 'England Triumphant', in which he undertook to trace the history of England's relations with the papacy and to show that England had never admitted the papal supremacy.[3] It began with the mythical Brutus of Troy, accepted the legend of Joseph of Arimathea and designated King Lucius of

[1] S.P. 12/66/54; Cecil Papers (Hatfield) 159/9–12; the Hatfield MS. printed in S. Haynes and W. Murdin, *Burghley Papers*, i, 589–93. The conjectural date Feb. 1570 in *Cal. S.P. Dom.* 1547–80, 364, is probably too late in view of the close relation with the proposed Star Chamber speech mentioned above, 23.

[2] S.P. 12/66/55.

[3] S.P. 12/75/58, with corrections in Cecil's hand. A fragment of it, entirely in Cecil's hand, is in B.M. Cotton MSS. Caligula B iv ff. 235 sqq.

Britain as the first Christian king of the west. Cecil's style was as bad as his history. He represented England in the first person, speaking for herself, a device which apparently appealed to him, since he was to use it later in another connection.[1] The whole composition is a tedious, long-winded affair. It was fortunately never finished nor ever printed. It reveals, what became increasingly apparent as time went on, that he had an itching hand for the pen but no marked aptitude in the use of it.

Hard upon the Rising in the North followed the intrigue of Thomas, duke of Norfolk, with Mary queen of Scots. The first phase of this was a project of marriage between Thomas and Mary. It produced the only political pamphlet we have from Francis Walsingham, *A Discourse touching the pretended match between the Duke of Norfolk and the Queen of Scots.*[2] Two separate editions are recorded. It was written sometime in 1569 before Walsingham had any official position in the government but when he was employed by Cecil in secret service. Probably Cecil inspired it. Cecil himself at about the same time produced a discourse entitled 'A Necessary Consideration of the perilous state of this time'.[3] The essence of it was to propose a private association of Englishmen sworn by oath 'to defend the Queen's Majesty's most royal person and the common peace of the realm and to conserve the exercise and continuance of the Christian religion as it is by law established in the realm'. The idea anticipated the famous Association, organized later, against Mary queen of Scots. It revealed Cecil's distrust of the competence of the ordinary machinery of administration to cope with internal disorders, particularly if they sprang from religious differences. Nothing apparently came of it. The memorandum itself ends abruptly, suggesting that before Cecil had finished writing the impracticability of the idea dawned upon him.

The second phase of Norfolk's treasonable practices found expression in the so called Ridolfi Plot of 1571. Cecil drew up an elaborate account of the plot in a discourse entitled 'The Order of proceeding to the knowledge of matters wherewith the Duke hath been charged before he was endited of treason', a copy of which, dated January 1572, is preserved in Cecil's handwriting.[4]

[1] Below, 42–43.

[2] Printed in Conyers Read, *Mr. Secretary Walsingham and the Policy of Queen Elizabeth*, i, 68, and discussed ibid. 63 *n*.

[3] S.P. 12/51/6; cf. Read, *Cecil and Elizabeth*, 453.

[4] S.P. 12/85/11.

Probably it was intended for publication:[1] but there is no evidence that it was published. A pamphlet entitled *Salutem in Christo* was published on the same subject late in the year 1571, by an anonymous author who signed himself R.G.[2] It has been suggested that Cecil wrote this[3], but the only ground is that the Roman Catholic answer to it was directed specifically at Cecil. The style is not his but is rather better than his.

It provoked a retort from the Roman Catholics entitled *A Treatise of Treasons*, published somewhere on the continent in 1573.[4] It was in part a defence of Norfolk, in part an attack upon the Protestant leaders, specifically upon Cecil and his brother-in-law Sir Nicholas Bacon—and was particularly virulent in its attack upon Cecil. One sentence from it will serve to reveal its general tone:

> What child can show a more base, abject and contemptible courage than he [Cecil] whose insolency is intolerable, whilas authority fawneth on him and for every least thwart of his superiority faineth either to be sick for sorrow or lame of the gout and falleth to sighing and sobbing, crouching and kneeling, weeping and whining like a boy and a babe, till his head be stroked and he comforted and called a good son again.

Elizabeth herself was outraged and issued a proclamation telling her subjects to disregard these seditious slanders and to turn over any copies of the book in their possession to the government. Cecil was not amused. For most of his life he was, for a veteran politician, exceptionally sensitive to personal attacks. He tried his best, through English representatives in Scotland, France and the Low Countries, to identify the author, and got different answers from different correspondents.[5] At one time he seems to have contemplated publishing an answer to it, and drew up copious notes on the subject.[6] But nothing came of them.

The decade following the publication of the *Treatise of Treasons* reveals little in the way of government propaganda. Such as there

[1] Kervyn de Lettenhove, *Relations politiques des Pays-Bas*, vi, 187.

[2] *S.T.C.* 11504. Black letter; 7½ pp.; 3 edns.

[3] Cf. entry in B.M. Catalogue.

[4] *S.T.C.* 7601. Walsingham sent Cecil a copy from Paris in January 1573: B.M. Cotton MSS. Vespasian F vi f. 259.

[5] Hist. MSS. Com. *Salisbury*, ii, 46, 58; Lettenhove, *Relations politiques*, vii, 386, 397, 433; *Cal. S.P. Dom. Add.* 1566–79, 444; Digges, *Ambassador*, 336. The attribution to Henry Howard by B. M. Ward, *The Seventeenth Earl of Oxford*, 131, is not supported by the references there given.

[6] *Cal. S.P. Scot.* 1574–81, 554–61.

was took the form of proclamations, some of them against the puritans, one of them against John Stubbs's attack upon the projected royal match with the duke of Alençon in 1579. Stubbs lost his right hand because of that attack and Sir Philip Sidney, who took the same side in a private letter to Elizabeth, lost, for at least a season, the royal favour. But there was no published defence of the match from government sources. Henry Howard, who was at the time making a great play for the royal favour, circulated in manuscript a discourse in favour of the marriage,[1] which may have been prompted by Cecil, who also favoured the marriage and was on very friendly terms with Howard.

During the 1570s, Cecil was much concerned about the invasion of England by Roman Catholic missionaries in a concerted attempt to win the country back to the Roman communion. It was in that connection that he drafted a pamphlet entitled, 'An Advertisement meet for all persons, that is for good subjects to continue in their duties, for wavering subjects to become more constant in theirs and for all unloyal subjects to know their errors and by repentance to recover mercy'.[2] Cecil pointed out the dangers to the state from rebels and traitors and depicted the seminaries as pouring forth missionaries who 'sowed sedition under the cloak of priesthood, aiming to bring the realm not only into a war against strangers but into a war domestic and civil'. He concluded with a declaration that the Queen would not be moved from the general course she had pursued from the beginning of requiring outward conformity, but forcing the conscience of none. The manuscript is undated, but must belong to the late 'seventies, when the missionary invasion was under way but before it had gained menacing momentum. Echoing the sentiments expressed in the 'Declaration' drafted by Cecil some years before, it persisted in the hope that Roman Catholic sympathizers might yet be won by a tolerant attitude towards their beliefs. Perhaps Cecil realized that the hope was a vain one, perhaps he was reluctant to advocate a course of behaviour by English Catholics which smacked of what he would have called Jesuitical casuistry. The pamphlet may thus represent an interesting stage in Cecil's thinking on the subject, or it may have been simply an attempt to

[1] B.M. Harl. MSS. 180.

[2] S.P. 12/73/49; ascribed in *Cal. S.P. Dom.* 1547–80, 391 to Aug. 1570, but clearly of later date.

formulate what he took to be the Queen's position. In any case, though it had more literary merit than most of his work, it was never published.

The missionary invasion reached its peak with the arrival of Edmund Campion and Robert Parsons in June 1580. For over a year Campion eluded capture while he travelled all over England making converts wholesale by his eloquence. He was indeed the most formidable of all the Jesuit preachers. Shortly after his arrival he addressed a letter to the privy council, asking that he might appear before it and debate matters of faith with chosen scholars from the universities. He even suggested that the Queen herself should attend the debate. This challenge was not printed until long afterwards but it was widely circulated in manuscript, and it created such a stir that the government employed William Charke, a puritan divine who had been expelled from Cambridge University for non-conformity, to answer it. Campion replied with his *Decem Rationes*, written in Latin and printed secretly in England. Some five hundred copies were distributed at the Oxford Commencement in June 1581. It was so effective that the government wheeled out its great guns to deal with it, the Regius professors of divinity at both Oxford and Cambridge. An enterprising London publisher proposed to publish an English translation of one of their answers but was apparently prevented by the bishop of London.[1]

Thereafter a great mass of propagandist literature poured forth from pens private and official, Catholic and Protestant. Anthony Munday, at different times an actor and a playwright, and one of the most prolific writers of his time, had a book off the press on *The English Roman life* in 1580, another on the capture of Campion in 1581, and later four other pamphlets on the same subject, some of them running to two editions and two of them dedicated to the earl of Leicester.[2] There were at least thirty pamphlets, for and against, published before 1590. Campion and his works became a *cause célèbre*. We need not follow the controversy nor attempt to distinguish between pamphlets inspired by the government and those which were publishers' ventures. No doubt Cecil took an

[1] R. Simpson, *Edmund Campion*, has a useful bibliography of Campion's writings and the controversial literature which ensued from them.

[2] Eleanor Rosenberg, *Leicester, Patron of Letters*, 233.

active interest in the dispute, but there is no evidence that he participated in it until 1583.

In that year two pamphlets appeared which have been ascribed to him: *A Declaration of the Favourable Dealing of her Majesty's Commissioners appointed for the examination of certain traitors*, and *The Execution of Justice in England*.[1] Both were published anonymously in 1583, the first by an unnamed publisher, the second by Barker, the Queen's printer. The only ground for ascribing the first to Cecil seems to be that it was joined with the second in a Latin translation published in 1584.[2] It was probably written by Thomas Norton, one of the commissioners who examined Campion. Norton had been imprisoned in the Tower late in the spring of 1581, because of indiscreet manifestations of puritanism in and out of parliament. While in prison he was employed by Walsingham to write an account of the torturing of Campion. He sent this to Walsingham on 27 March 1582. The argument in the *Declaration of the Favourable Dealing* followed this account closely. We know, too, that Norton was to be employed later in producing anti-Catholic pamphlets.[3] The gist of the pamphlet was that torture was legal and that its application to Campion was not so severe as to hinder his walking or writing; that it was never applied to extort answers regarding faith, but simply to discover treasonable practices. The statement was probably true in the main and doubtless the application of torture might have been more severe and more indiscriminate than it was. Yet even sixteenth-century Englishmen were uneasy about it, and Catholic pamphleteers made so much of it that the government felt impelled to explain and to justify what had been done.

The second pamphlet was undoubtedly written by Cecil. John Strype said that he had seen a complete manuscript copy of it in Cecil's own hand. This I have not found, but there are parts of it in Cecil's hand scattered through some volumes of the Domestic State Papers at the Public Record Office.[4] His name does not

[1] *S.T.C.* 4901–2. [2] *S.T.C.* 4904.

[3] *Archaeologia*, xxxvi, 109 sqq. There is other material on Norton among the Beale Papers: B.M. Add. MSS. 48023. He died in 1584 and his books and papers passed into the hands of Thomas Wilkes, clerk of the council; a list of them is preserved at Hatfield: Cecil Papers 140/5.

[4] S.P. 12/73/49; 12/153/74; 12/164/85. In a note among the Beale Papers, B.M. Add. MSS. 48063 f. 6, are two short discourses, against which Beale has written a marginal note: 'These two discourses were made by Mr. Dr. Hammond at the

appear, but there are none of the customary devices of camouflage. Published by the Queen's printer, the pamphlet went into a second printing almost at once, and in the following year translations appeared in Latin, French and Dutch.[1] Of all that Cecil ever published, *The Execution of Justice* was the most considerable and easily the most important. It was the official justification of Elizabeth's treatment of the Roman Catholic missionaries and it is the best statement we have of Cecil's own position. Though somewhat verbose and repetitious, it is on the whole well written and well documented. If it does not succeed in vindicating, it at least defines, the royal policy. Space does not serve to examine the pamphlet in detail. Its approach to the problem was a political one, the justification of the persecution being that the missionaries were spreading treason, since every English Catholic who accepted papal supremacy was bound by the bull of excommunication and was thus at least a potential traitor.

The following year came the Roman Catholic answer in Allen's *Modest Defence of the English Catholics*. Robert Parsons, the Jesuit, wrote late in December 1584 that Allen's letter was so convincing that the heretics regretted that Cecil's pamphlet had ever appeared. He went on to say that the earl of Leicester had reprehended Cecil for the writing of it and Cecil had retorted by producing the malignant attack upon Leicester commonly known as *Leicester's Commonwealth*. This was of course nonsense, and it goes to show that Parsons's sources of information were very imperfect.[2] But this much at least was true, Allen's pamphlet was uncommonly good. Cecil got hold of John Stubbs—Stubbs the left-handed as he signed himself—and charged him to compose an answer to Allen. Stubbs had the answer ready in July 1587; at Cecil's direction he submitted it to two civilians for comment and criticism, received their approval and sent the manuscript to Cecil on the 27th. That is the last we hear of it.[3] This is the second instance of Cecil's employment of puritan pamphleteers—first Norton and then Stubbs—in the attack upon the Roman Catholics.

request of the Lord Treasurer before the setting forth of the book called *Justitia Britannica*.'

[1] *S.T.C.* 4903–6; an Italian translation appeared in 1587.

[2] *Catholic Rec. Soc.*, xxxix, 267.

[3] B.M. Lansd. 54 f. 57. Strype endorsed the letter: 'Touching the book in answer to the English Justice, in which he was employed by the command of the Lord Treasurer.' I see no sound reason for questioning Strype's statement, though I have found no evidence to confirm it.

Official accounts were prepared and published both of the Throgmorton Plot of 1583 and the Parry Plot of 1584–5. With the Throgmorton pamphlet Cecil appears to have had nothing to do. We have no indication of the author of the official narrative. It took the form of a letter from a gentleman of Lion's Inn, who signed himself Q.Z., to a friend concerning Throgmorton. No place or printer is named on the title page, but it was fairly certainly printed by the Queen's printer.[1]

The official account of the Parry Plot[2] was probably prepared by the law officers of the crown. Cecil was certainly interested in its preparation. He wrote to Walsingham shortly after the discovery of the plot: 'It were good that the fact of Parry were better published than it seemeth to be by divers busy printers, especially one by one Henry Carr.'[3] Carr was a commercial publisher whose speciality was ballads.[4] At different times he published what he called 'doleful ditties' on the deaths of Darnley and of Sir Philip Sidney. In 1584 he brought forth a pamphlet by Philip Stubbs called *The Intended Treasons of Dr. Parry.*[5] It was no doubt to this that Cecil referred. Certainly Stubbs's account of the Parry Plot was hopelessly inadequate. Somehow or other he had got hold of the letter written to Parry by Cardinal Como and his English version of it is word for word identical with that published later in the official account. It looks a little as though the enterprising Carr, having secured a copy of the Como letter which was the very core of the case against Parry, invited Stubbs to write a brief pamphlet about it. We may have here an early example of a journalistic scoop. Perhaps that accounts for Cecil's irritation. In any case, it reveals that treason plots were becoming subjects for commercial publishing.

Cecil meanwhile had busied himself about the matter. Three days later he wrote to Walsingham: 'This afternoon my Lord of Leicester, Mr Vice Chamberlain and some others do meet in my house to consider of things by me committed this morning to Mr Attorney and Mr Solicitor for publication of the truth of Parry's fact.'[6] It was, perhaps, in cases of high treason, the normal

[1] *S.T.C.* 24050–1; published in Holinshed, *Chronicle* (1587 edn.), iii, 1370 sqq., but without the prefatory letter to the reader; a MS. account of the plot is in S.P. 12/171/86. [2] *S.T.C.* 1934. [3] S.P. 12/177/1.

[4] Shaaber, *Forerunners of the Newspaper in England*, index Carr, H.

[5] *S.T.C.* 23396; reprinted in Shakespeare Soc. Papers, iii (1847), 17–21.

[6] S.P. 12/177/4.

practice to refer publicity to the law officers of the crown, and this may have been the procedure followed in the Throgmorton case, as it was, a little later, in the Northumberland affair. Otherwise I have found no evidence of it.

Not long after the disclosure of the Parry Plot, the earl of Northumberland, who had been charged with treason and imprisoned in the Tower, was found dead in his cell, shot through the heart. Immediately after his death a pamphlet was published in Cologne asserting that he had been put to death by the English government. This pamphlet, originally in Latin, was reprinted in French, German, English, Italian and Spanish. Elizabeth called for an inquiry in Star Chamber. The outcome was an official pamphlet published later in the year under the title: *A True and Summary Report of the earl of Northumberland's treasons declared publicly in the Court of Star Chamber by the Lord Chancellor and others of her Majesty's most honorable Privy Council and counsel learned in the law by her Majesty's special commandment; together with the examinations and depositions of sundry persons touching the manner of the most wicked and violent murder committed upon himself with his own hand in the Tower of London the 20th day of June 1585.*[1] The title reveals the contents. The pamphlet runs to twenty pages and contains an outline of Northumberland's treasons by the attorney general and the solicitor general, and the presentation of the evidence of suicide by Roger Manwood, chief baron of the exchequer. It was ostentatiously official. Cecil's only revealed connection with it was his presence at the Star Chamber proceedings. He is not mentioned as among those who spoke.

Later in the year 1585 Elizabeth decided to support the Dutch rebels in the Low Countries by dispatching a small army in their support. She proceeded to justify her action by a published *Declaration.*[2] It was skilfully composed, beginning with an account of England's long and friendly relations with the Low Countries, and continuing with their occupation by the Spaniards, who established a 'bloody tyranny' of foreigners and robbed the Netherlanders of their ancient liberties under the pretence of maintaining the Roman Catholic religion; with Elizabeth's efforts to dissuade the king of Spain from such a course, the Netherlands' rebellion, her efforts to prevent them from transferring their

[1] *S.T.C.* 19617; printed in Holinshed, iii, 1404.
[2] *S.T.C.* 9188–93; printed in Holinshed, iii, 1414.

loyalty to another prince, and the Spanish retort to her efforts by invading Ireland and plotting against her life and her throne. For all of these reasons Elizabeth had decided to assist the Dutch rebels with armed force, not with the idea of conquest but simply to help the Dutch to recover their ancient liberties and to prevent the Spaniards from invading England from that quarter. An 'Addition' was made to the *Declaration* in the form of an answer to an Italian pamphlet which had charged Elizabeth with ingratitude to the king of Spain, who had saved her life when she had been condemned to death in her sister's reign, and with participation in a plot to murder the duke of Parma, Spanish governor of the Low Countries. The first charge was met by an indignant denial, the second by the assertion that she regarded Parma as a fine man by whose loss she would have nothing to gain. The passage in the 'Addition' about Parma reflects an effort to cultivate his goodwill and, perhaps a hope, which was later explored, of dividing him from his Spanish master.[1]

There can be little doubt that this *Declaration* was the joint work of Cecil and Walsingham. We have no manuscript of the whole pamphlet, but there is at Hatfield a draft of the 'Addition' in a clerical hand, corrected by Walsingham and endorsed by Cecil.[2] It is to be noted that the *Declaration* was prepared some time before being printed in October 1585. A copy of it was carried to Parma by an English agent in August,[3] and Cecil had apparently been working upon it almost a year earlier. He wrote to Walsingham on 12 October 1584:[4]

> Since I came here I looked into a book entitled *De Leone Belgico*, written by Michael Aitzinger, wherein I find, in the 79th page, the Confederation of the Nobility of the Low Countries against the Inquisition which, if I had seen before, I would have followed some form thereof. I would you would see it . . . and if you have not I will send [it] . . . My meaning nevertheless is not now to alter ours. I wish it were in Latin.

On 12 October 1585 Walsingham wrote to Cecil that at the Queen's request he had composed an answer to the Italian pamphlet and that she had approved of his draft, which he was sending

[1] Cf. Read, *Walsingham*, iii, 265–6; L. Stone, *Sir Horatio Palavicino*, 263 sqq.

[2] Cecil Papers 138/155; Haynes and Murdin, ii, 294–6, misdated 1576.

[3] *Cal. S.P. For.* 1584–5, 67.

[4] S.P. 12/173/72; on Aitzinger cf. P. J. Blok, *History of the Netherlands* (trans. Putnam), iii, 507.

to Cecil. He hoped that Cecil would 'make such corrections as he thought meet'.

> I think [Walsingham added] it most expedient that the [Dutch] commissioners here should be made acquainted with the Declaration before it be printed. It may be that there is somewhat contained therein that haply may more prejudice the cause than yield benefit in point of justification. The perusal thereof can no way hinder her Majesty's intent and therefore, in my poor opinion, your Lordship shall do well to acquaint them herewith.[1]

These two letters throw a good deal of light upon the preparation of the *Declaration*. Publication followed later in the year. Dutch, Italian and French versions were also published, all of them by the Queen's printer.

While the *Declaration* was in preparation, Cecil tried his hand upon another pamphlet, evidently designed to deal with English relations with the Low Countries. He called it 'Anglia personata loquens'. All that we have of it is a draft in Cecil's hand running to six folio pages and evidently unfinished.[2] The title reveals the form, the same form he had employed in that other unfinished essay, 'England Triumphant', written some fifteen years before. Cecil's purpose in writing was stated by Anglia speaking:

> I mind to offer some remembrance of my ancient estate in years passed, to notify my present state and condition at this present in such manifest and plain sort as all other countries, being neighbours, shall see my disposition for continuance of peace and commerce and shall also understand how unnaturally by some of my own people, and how unneighbourly by divers of my most ancient confederates, I have been of late years misrepresented, misused and manifestly wronged.

Anglia goes on to praise her country and her Queen, and concludes:

> There resteth now to notify my present state with the house of Burgundy, my next neighbour and my oldest. If I shall speak that I think, the provinces belonging to that dukedom desire rather the amity, conversation and friendship with me England and my people than with any other far or near in the world. And if the Spaniard himself, when he confesseth to the Duke of Burgundy, were asked whether he thinketh that the Fleming, the Brabanter, the Hollander and the Zeelander

[1] B.M. Harl. MSS. 6993 f. 100.

[2] B.M. Lansd. 103 ff. 52 sqq. dated June 1585, a date supported by internal evidence.

would [prefer] to live [under] the English or the Spanish rule, the answer would be very against the Spaniard, if the sword were not used to exact the answer.

At this point, fortunately, Cecil abandoned his essay. Let us hope that he realized what a dreary affair it was, how impotent both in form and substance. He could write straight, factual prose well enough, but when he attempted rhetoric he failed lamentably.

The next crisis which Elizabeth had to face was the Babington Plot, with its revelations of the complicity of the queen of Scots in a conspiracy to murder her. We have at least four printed pamphlets on the subject. The first of them reproduced at length petitions from parliament to the Queen calling upon her to bring Mary to judgment and Elizabeth's replies to these petitions. It took the form of a letter to the earl of Leicester, then in the Low Countries.[1] It was reprinted in the second edition of Holinshed, almost the final entry in that remarkable book, rushed in apparently at the last minute. The dedicatory letter to Leicester is signed R.C. The pamphlet has customarily been ascribed to Richard Crompton, but it was in fact written by Robert Cecil, William Cecil's son. Robert Beale in his 'Notes of the proceedings of the parliament in the cause of Mary Stuart' wrote in his own hand: 'Other notes concerning the parliament. Look in the book published in print by Mr R. Cecil and dedicated to the earl of Leicester.'[2] His authorship is confirmed by personal references in the dedicatory letter which fit him closely, Crompton not at all.

Sir John Neale has pointed out that there is a manuscript copy of the Queen's speeches as printed in the pamphlet, corrected in Elizabeth's own hand, preserved among the Cotton Manuscripts in the British Museum.[3] This must mean that Robert Cecil's pamphlet was prepared under the eye and with the assistance of the Queen herself. It is surprising that we have no inkling of young Cecil's part in the business (he was only twenty-two at the time) from any other source. But the evidence seems conclusive. It was after all only an editorial job. No doubt William Cecil rejoiced at the opportunity to bring his young son to the attention of the Queen and directed his footsteps in the difficult business of getting on with the royal collaborator. Clearly the object of the

[1] *S.T.C.* 6052; printed in Holinshed, iii, 1580.
[2] B.M. Add. MSS. 48027 f. 396.
[3] Neale, *Elizabeth and Parliament, 1584–1601*, 130.

pamphlet was to publicize the fact that Elizabeth was very reluctant to deal with Mary as her parliament required. It was the first step in a course of action which eventually led her to disclaim any responsibility for Mary's execution and to place the blame upon her council. The pamphlet was widely circulated, both in English and in several other languages.[1] The English and French versions were both published by Barker, the Queen's printer. It furnishes an interesting example of Elizabeth's personal participation in government propaganda.

A second pamphlet, also signed R.C. and again ascribed to Richard Crompton, entitled *A Declaration of the end of Traitors*, was dedicated to Archbishop Whitgift. It dealt with Mary's execution and undertook to justify it. A Dutch translation was published later at Middelburg. There is no evidence of William or Robert Cecil's connection with it, nor indeed of government prompting. Professor Shaaber thinks that it was a private venture.[2] A third pamphlet, wrongly ascribed to Maurice Kyffin, also defending the sentence against Mary, appeared in 1587.[3] Finally, there was a pamphlet by George Whetstone, a literary adventurer of some experience, called *The Censure of a Loyal Subject*, dedicated to William Cecil. Two editions appeared, one before Mary's execution, the other, with a foreword by Thomas Churchyard, afterwards.[4]

There is no evidence that William Cecil had any connection with the publication of any of these pamphlets justifying Mary's execution. He did receive, from Robert Wingfield, the keeper of a royal park near Fotheringay, who had been present at the execution, a complete account of it.[5] Probably at Cecil's prompting, Wingfield edited the account for the press, dedicated to Cecil. It was a gruesome story as Wingfield told it.[6] But in view of Elizabeth's outburst against her council and particularly against Cecil for having engineered Mary's death, he probably decided to

[1] Ibid.; only an English and a French version are listed in *S.T.C.* 6052–3.

[2] *S.T.C.* 6055; *Forerunners of the Newspaper in England*, 66.

[3] *S.T.C.* 15098; *D.N.B. s.v.* Kyffin. [4] *S.T.C.* 25334, 25334a.

[5] Cf. *Cal. S.P. Dom.* 1581–90, 395–7; printed in H. Ellis, *Original Letters*, 2nd ser. iii, 113–18.

[6] From the official report of the execution (*Cal. S.P. Scot.* 1586–8, 269 sqq.) Cecil prepared a résumé (Hist. MSS. Com. *Salisbury*, iii, 231–3) probably for the Queen's perusal, omitting a paragraph to the effect that Mary had asked for a priest and been denied. He doubtless realized that Elizabeth would not have liked such a demonstration, on such an occasion, of puritan intolerance.

suppress it. Walsingham worked over another manuscript on the same subject, which bears his endorsement: 'A project of a discourse touching the Scottish Queen.'[1] But this too, and probably for the same reason, was abandoned.

The year following Mary's execution was the year of the Armada. Except for the singularly beautiful prayer for divine aid, nothing in the way of propagandist literature on the subject appears to have been published before the arrival of the Spanish fleet. Cecil prepared a 'Declaration' for the press in June and sent a copy of it to Walsingham on the 24th.[2] His reference to it in the accompanying letter describes its purpose: 'When you shall read it,' Cecil wrote, 'you shall find a purpose to notify the people both all her Majesty's former actions in dealing with Scotland and France and now in the Low Countries, and her present preparation to defend the country, for that her actions are by the enemies abroad published as original causes of the civil troubles in all foreign countries'. One wonders when he found time to write this in the mad frenzy of war preparations. It was, apparently, never published.

The most important of a spate of pamphlets recording the Spanish defeat appeared early in the autumn of 1588 under the title *The Copy of a letter sent out of England to don Bernardino Mendoza, ambassador in France for the King of Spain, declaring the state of England*. It was said to have been found in the chamber of Richard Leigh, a seminary priest 'lately executed for high treason', and it was written as though from a devoted English Catholic whose hopes of deliverance had been blasted by the defeat of the Armada. There can be no reasonable doubt that Cecil was the author. Among his papers in the Lansdowne Manuscripts is a complete draft of the pamphlet in his own hand, a revision of that draft in the hand of his secretary, Henry Maynard, with copious corrections and interlineations in Cecil's hand, and finally a revision of the introductory paragraph in Cecil's hand.[3] The pamphlet as printed follows fairly closely the revision of Cecil's manuscript draft. There are some interesting variations between the first draft and the revised draft, and some between the revised draft and the printed text, but no essential changes. We should perhaps regard the pamphlet as the logical outcome of Cecil's own suggestion in

[1] *Cal. S.P. Scot.* 1586–7, 258–61.
[2] S.P. 12/211/56; with enclosures.
[3] B.M. Lansd. 103 ff. 134–163*b*.

July that Cardinal Allen's virulent attack upon the Queen should be answered 'by some expert learned man, pretending to speak for the English Catholics'.[1] After the Armada, Cecil took on the task himself. In his text he sustained his assumed role well, so well that even to this day the pamphlet is ascribed in the *Short Title Catalogue* to Leigh.[2] Actually Cecil never pretended to be Leigh. He wrote as a Catholic layman lamenting the defeat of the Armada, which he attributed to a faulty estimate of English fighting strength and to an unjustified expectation that the English Catholics would rally to the support of the invader.

After a somewhat exaggerated appraisal of English strength by land and sea, Cecil devoted a large part of the pamphlet to the demonstrated loyalty of the English Catholics, pointing out that good Catholics who remained loyal to their Queen were in no jeopardy of life or limb, contrasting their position with that of the Protestants under Mary or the English victims of the Inquisition in Spain. Speaking as an English Catholic he deplored the activities of those who, professing to be priests, came secretly into the realm to preach treason. He even suggested that the pope might alleviate the lot of the recusants by granting them dispensation to attend the Anglican Church.

Of all Cecil's contributions to the literature of propaganda, this *Letter to Mendoza* was the best. His touch was never a light one, but here he contrived to present a plausible picture of an English Catholic, loyal to his faith, paying tribute indirectly to the English war effort, to the English nobility, to the gallant Queen and most of all to the national loyalty of the English Catholics; at the same time denouncing papal policy and making mock of Mendoza's omniscience and of Spanish invincibility.

Not long after Cecil had finished the *Letter to Mendoza* but before it had gone to press,[3] he received a letter from Sir Henry Wallop in Ireland, enclosing examinations of several mariners from the Spanish fleet who had been taken prisoner on the Irish coast. Taken together they presented a harrowing revelation of the destruction suffered by the Armada in Irish waters. Cecil—it was probably he—at once seized upon the idea of publishing these examinations, translated of course but otherwise unchanged,[4]

[1] S.P. 12/211/15. [2] *S.T.C.* 15412.

[3] Dated 18 Aug. in printed version, registered at Stationers' Co. 23 Oct. Cf. *S.T.C.*

[4] Cf. text in the pamphlet with the originals printed in *State Papers relating to the Defeat of the Spanish Armada* (Navy Rec. Soc.), ii, 219 sqq.

as a supplement to the *Letter to Mendoza*. He had to work fast,[1] and perhaps on that account refrained from transmuting the actual words of the prisoners into his own ponderous prose. Certainly as propaganda the material was much more effective as it stood. Cecil added a summary of Spanish losses in men and ships in the Channel and off the Irish coast. He put the loss in ships at 32, in mariners at 10,185. It was later revealed that the Spaniards had lost 63 ships, almost twice his estimate and approximately half the entire Armada.

In both editions of the *Letter to Mendoza*, the 'Certain Advertisements' were issued under the same cover. Taken together, the two pieces furnish a very convincing picture of the fate of the Armada. But Cecil did not stop at that. On 30 December he wrote to Walsingham: 'At this present I am not free of pain in the right hand but free from other pain though weak and sore in my legs. I send you, translated out of the Spanish, lies which I have termed *A Pack of Spanish Lies*, with the discovery of the same pack in English. I mean to have the same printed in Spanish for the comfort of Don B. Mendoza.'[2] The full title of the resulting pamphlet explains its contents: *A Pack of Spanish Lies sent abroad to the world, first printed in the Spanish tongue and translated out of the original; now ripped up, unfolded and by just examination condemned as certainly false, corrupt and detestable wares, worthy to be damned and burned.*[3] The method employed was to state in parallel columns first the Spanish lie and then the truth. The best passage deals with a report, dated 2 September, from the governor of Rouen, to the effect that he held Drake's chief pilot a prisoner, who reported that the English had been defeated, with 22 ships sunk and 40 captured, and Drake himself in prison. This was answered as follows:

> The governors of Boulogne and Calais can inform the governor of Rouen that the English army fought with the Spanish, chased the Spanish as a brace of grey hounds would a herd of deer. The Spanish ships were beaten, spoiled, burnt, sunk, some in the main seas afore Dunkirk, some afore Flushing and the rest chased away, so as they fled continually afore the English navy . . . without daring to abide a fight . . . Why durst any report that 22 English ships were sunk and forty taken, when in truth there was not one sunk or taken.

[1] They were also printed separately (*S.T.C.* 14257), and Walsingham sent a copy to Stafford in France on 30 Sept.: B.M. Cotton MSS. Galba E vi f. 384.
[2] S.P. 12/219/46; from the postscript in Cecil's hand.
[3] *S.T.C.* 23011; *Somers Tracts*, i, 453 sqq.

The rest was of like character, written with a vigour of style which hardly suggests Cecil's handiwork. He may merely have conceived the idea and furnished the facts. But certainly he, if anyone, should be credited with the pamphlet. The *Pack of Lies* probably appeared early in 1589. Spanish and Dutch versions followed, and probably French and Italian. Doubtless it was intended chiefly for overseas consumption. Quite possibly one of its objectives was to discredit Mendoza, who was in Paris working hard to strengthen the Catholic League and the Franco-Spanish alliance. Throughout Cecil's writings at this juncture he made much of what he called 'Mendoza's mendacities'.[1]

An interesting pamphlet appeared in 1589, entitled *A Short and True Discourse for satisfying all those who speak indiscreetly of her Majesty*.[2] Its title is misleading. In fact it was privately printed by Peregrine, lord Willoughby, and was a defence of his conduct in the Low Countries which had been publicly attacked in a 'Plakkaat' published by the Dutch in April 1589. There is no evidence that Willoughby was prompted by the government.

In the same year Norris and Drake went forth on their ill-fated expedition to Lisbon. It was a private enterprise, but the Queen had a large investment in it. The best account of it, by Anthony Wingfield, was probably written in justification of what was in fact a flat failure.[3] Mendoza in Paris reported it as a Spanish victory.[4] There is no indication of government propaganda in the

[1] Strype asserts (*Annals*, iii, pt. 2, 32) that the Spanish book which Cecil attacked had been brought from Flanders to England by a Spaniard, but does not document the statement; probably he had in mind *S.T.C.* 17131, which had to do with the English expedition to Spain the year following. I have made some search for the Spanish pamphlet which Cecil used. The one which seems to come closest to it, suggested to me by Professor Garrett Mattingly, is entitled: *Relacion del succedido a la Armada de su Majestad que entro en el Canal de Inglaterra hasta a lo que se entendio en Dunquerque los doze y trese de Agosto de 1588 . . . Impressa en Sevilla en Casa de Cosme delare Impressor . . .* The publisher corresponds with the one named in the *Pack of Spanish Lies*. It is only three pages long and it does claim that at a general engagement off Calais Drake was captured, many ships taken, many sunk and many fled to port; but it hardly sustains the details as Cecil set them forth.

[2] *S.T.C.* 7597; the only known copy in England is in the Ogden Collection, University College London Library; a copy in Folger Shakespeare Library, Washington; the *plakkaat* in question is in *Cal. S.P. For.* 1589, 205.

[3] *S.T.C.* 6790; another account in Latin is in *S.T.C.* 18653. Both were published by the same publisher.

[4] *Avis de la victoire du roy Catholique contre l'Anglais en Espagne, contenant la defait de quinze mil hommes et de quarante navires des plus grands, suivant les memoires qu'on a reçu de l'illustrissime ambassadeur Don Bernardino de Mendoza*, Paris, 1589, 11 pages; B.M. 9200 aaa 42. It was this pamphlet which was answered by a Spanish refugee

matter. Practically the only spoils which Norris and Drake had to show for their pains were 80 hulks (transports), most of them Hansa ships, laden with corn and naval stores which had been captured in Lisbon harbour. The Hansa merchants demanded their return. Elizabeth's privy council was faced with an issue of international law which has cropped up in virtually every war since—are neutral ships trading with the enemy lawful prize? Elizabeth herself was for hanging on to anything which could be salvaged from an expedition in which she had suffered considerable financial loss. The privy council thought otherwise and urged her to return the ships to the merchants with 'such goods as are not comprehended within the title of munitions'.[1] The views of the council prevailed and on 27 July it issued an order explaining its position and defining munitions of war, which were to include naval stores, weapons, powder and bullets, copper, lead and match, and, under the head of victuals, wheat and other cereals and bacon.[2] The Hansa merchants were further notified that if they repeated their performance the Queen would confiscate both ships and cargo.

Cecil thought that the Queen should justify her action in a public declaration and Walsingham passed on the suggestion to his brother-in-law, Robert Beale, a trained civilian, directing him to confer on the subject with two other well-known civilians.[3] Beale addressed himself to the task and produced both an English and a Latin version of a declaration which was published under the title: *A Declaration of the Cause which moved the chief commander to take and arrest in the mouth of the river of Lisbon, certain ships*, published in 1589 by Barker, the Queen's printer.[4] It was largely an attack upon the king of Spain, partly a rebuke of German protestant traders for helping the enemy of their faith, partly a definition of contraband of war.[5]

No significant pamphlet seems to have appeared in 1590. Early in 1591 the Emperor Rudolf made an attempt to mediate a peace

from the Low Countries (see p. 48 *n* 1 above) both in Spanish and English: *S.T.C.* 17131–2.

[1] Walsingham to Cecil, B.M. Harl. MSS. 6994 f. 187.

[2] *Acts of P.C.* 1588–9, 447.

[3] Read, *Walsingham*, iii, 351 *n*.

[4] *S.T.C.* 9196–7; a copy of this *Declaration* is in Beale's papers with a draft of part of the Latin version corrected in Beale's hand: B.M. Add. MSS. 48023 ff. 220 sqq.

[5] Cecil prepared a more elaborate definition of the English position on contraband in 1591; B.M. Lansd. 104 no. 30: never printed.

between the Dutch rebels and Spain, which created some alarm in England and called forth from Cecil one of his discourses[1] in which he set down at length reasons why the Dutch should reject the Imperial approach. He sent it to Elizabeth and she approved of it. On 20 February, Windebank wrote to Cecil: 'The Queen, having read herself a good part of the writing, being your Lordship's labour and caused [me] to read the other part, hath willed me to send you word of her great liking thereof, and perceiveth that howsoever your want of health is, your care wanteth not. Only her Majesty seeth not how it may be justified to charge the king [of Spain] with seeking or procuring directly her death and therefore would have that allegation altered, or somewhat mitigated, or else left out.'[2] The passage in the *Discourse* to which the Queen alluded ran as follows: 'He [Philip of Spain] raised wars against the Queen of England . . . adding also procuration to have murdered her sacred person at divers times.'[3] Apparently the copy which Elizabeth read was in Robert Cecil's handwriting. Windebank went on to write: 'Her Majesty knew the hand and [noted] your very good speeches of Mr Cecil for his many good parts of sufficiency to serve her.' Cecil never missed an opportunity to put in a good word for his son.

Two days later Cecil wrote to Thomas Bodley in the Low Countries that he had dashed off ('suddenly made') an answer to the Imperial peace approach 'wherewith her Majesty, being acquainted, she doth so well allow thereof as she hath commanded me with all diligence to send it unto you with intention that you should impart the same to such of the general estates [of the Low Countries] or of the council as you should think capable of such a matter'. Cecil further suggested that the substance of the *Discourse* might be published both in Dutch and in French and 'in sundry other languages'.[4] Bodley did not agree, but Cecil was not to be denied. He wrote again on 21 March that the Queen would be glad to see the *Discourse* printed.[5] Bodley again objected. In the end nothing came of it, though Cecil and Bodley corresponded about it for nearly a year. From the point of view of government propaganda, the incident is interesting as revealing

[1] B.M. Lansd. 103 no. 63, undated, corrected in Cecil's hand; fair copy in Cotton MSS. Galba D viii f. 206.

[2] B.M. Harl. MSS. 6995 f. 32.

[3] B.M. Lansd. 103 f. 183.

[4] B.M. Cotton MSS. Galba D viii f. 92.

[5] Ibid. f. 95*b*.

Cecil's disposition to issue pamphlets even through foreign channels for the promotion of English policy. In September of the same year, when Elizabeth decided to recall the earl of Essex and his army from Normandy, Cecil had a declaration ready for publication on the subject, a copy of which was sent to Essex.[1] It was never used; the Queen changed her mind.

The year 1591 was marked in England by more stringent measures against Roman Catholic recusants, provoked partly by Philip II's all-out attack upon France, but mainly by the policy of Gregory XIV, elected pope in December 1590, who threw all the weight of his office on the side of Philip's purposes against both France and England. As Elizabeth put it, King Philip had the pope 'hanging to his girdle'. This increased severity took form in a proclamation issued in October, directed primarily to the hunting down of the missionary priests by a careful check upon the recusants who gave them shelter and support.[2] In its application it developed into an inquisition into the daily lives of the recusants and made their already lamentable state almost unendurable.

The Catholics blamed this policy upon Cecil. One of them alluded to it as the 'new Cecilian Inquisition'. Camden says that they attributed the offending proclamation to his authorship.[3] There is no evidence that he composed it but probably he did. In any case, a pamphlet defending the Catholic position, written by Robert Parsons, the Jesuit, and published in Latin in November 1591, was largely an attack upon Cecil.[4] An English translation published the next year bore the title: *An Advertisement written to a secretary of my Lord Treasurer*.[5] It followed the line of attack revealed earlier in the *Treatise of Treasons*. Cecil, grown old and patient, was probably less disturbed than he had been twenty years before: at least he has left no comment upon it. So far as he was concerned, its chief interest lies in the fact that it provoked an eloquent vindication of him from his nephew Francis Bacon, not published until much later, but widely circulated in manuscript.[6]

[1] S.P. 78/25/356; a first draft, copiously corrected in Cecil's hand; another copy in a fair hand in B.M. Cotton MSS. Caligula E viii f. 77, endorsed in Cecil's hand: 'Sent to the e. of Essex.'

[2] Steele, *Proclamations*, no. 837.

[3] *Annals* (1635 edn.), 406.

[4] Code, *Queen Elizabeth and the English Catholic Historians*, 49 *n*.

[5] *S.T.C.* 19885; cf. also 10005.

[6] J. Spedding, *Life and Letters of Bacon*, viii, 143 sqq.

Whether sincerely meant or not, this constitutes one of the finest tributes ever paid to Cecil.

The following year brought the first inkling of the so-called Lopez Plot. The story of the plot has been told too often to need repetition. Like the Parry Plot, it turned upon the question whether Lopez, who like Parry pretended to be in the secret service of the enemy in order to facilitate his secret services for the Queen, at last turned traitor. It has been represented as having been discovered by Essex's secret service, scoffed at by Cecil and his son at the outset, but finally demonstrated to be true. The story of the scoffing comes from Anthony Standen, one of Essex's followers. According to him, Robert Cecil, after the first examination of Lopez, rode post haste to court and told Elizabeth there was nothing in it.[1] It may be that Essex exploited the whole affair with the idea of discrediting the official secret service and glorifying his own. The weakness of the case against Lopez is exposed by the lack of confirmatory evidence from Spanish sources, and most scholars now agree that Lopez's guilt was more than doubtful. But in the end Essex won his case. Lopez was tried, found guilty of treason and condemned to death.

In the examination of the conspirators Robert Cecil took an active part, and he expressed himself as in complete accord with the verdict. William Cecil had little to do with the preliminary examinations or with the trial, probably because of ill-health. He did however take complete charge of the publicity. Immediately after the trial he asked William Waad, clerk of the council, to prepare a narrative of the Lopez treason. On 4 March 1594 Waad sent him a manuscript of eleven folios, and two weeks later Cecil himself drew up a shorter report evidently intended for publication.[2] For some reason or other it was not published. Quite possibly Elizabeth herself, still unconvinced, held it up for the same reason that she held up the warrant for Lopez's execution. He was not in fact executed until 7 June.

Later in the year Cecil wrote and published *A True Report of Sundry horrible Conspiracies of late times detected to have (by barbarous murders) taken away the life of the Queen's most excellent Majesty*.[3] A draft of the printed version, copiously corrected in Cecil's hand, is in the Public Record Office.[4] This manuscript

[1] T. Birch, *Memoirs of Queen Elizabeth*, i, 150.
[2] *Cal. S.P. Dom.* 1591–94, 452–3, 462. [3] *S.T.C.* 7603. [4] S.P. 12/250/10.

ends two pages short of the printed version. A manuscript in the Cecil Papers at Hatfield is evidently a second draft with corrections in the hands of Robert Cecil and Sir Edward Coke, the solicitor general, and includes the additional pages of the printed version.[1] Cecil also submitted the draft to Waad, who made further corrections and suggested the addition of two confessions.[2] There can thus be no doubt that Cecil was the author of the official version. Evidently he was at pains to have it checked before it went to press by three men well acquainted with the facts.

At least three other accounts of the plot are extant, one by Francis Bacon, not published until 1657,[3] one in Murdin's Burghley Papers,[4] of unknown authorship, and one still unpublished in the hand of William Waad among Beale's papers.[5] We may wonder whether Bacon's account was inspired by Essex, trying to steal a march on Cecil.

Sir Edward Coke's comment on Cecil's pamphlet, written on a copy of it in the British Museum, is worth noting: 'The Lord Treasurer Burghley thought best to rely principally upon the confessions of the delinquents without any inference or argument. This book was never answered to my knowledge, and this is the best kind of publication.'[6] Curiously enough, this comment has been used to support an argument that Coke was the author. In the light of the other evidence it turns out to be a confirmation of Cecil's authorship along with an approval of his method. It is the only appraisal we have of Cecil as a pamphleteer and goes far to explain why Cecil's style of writing, which certainly lacked the qualities usually associated with political propaganda, commended itself to the Queen and her legally minded counsellors.

The last of Elizabeth's propagandist pamphlets for which Cecil was responsible was *A Declaration of the causes moving her Majesty to send an army to the seas*, published in 1596 just before the departure of Essex upon his famous expedition to Cadiz.[7] It also appeared in Latin, Dutch, French, Italian and Spanish versions. The draft, copiously corrected by Cecil, is preserved among his papers in the British Museum.[8]

[1] Cecil Papers 139/41–8.
[2] Hist. MSS. Com. *Salisbury*, v, 2.
[3] Spedding, viii, 274.
[4] pp. 669 sqq.
[5] B.M. Add. MSS. 48029 ff. 145–184*b*.
[6] Spedding, viii, 274 *n*.
[7] *S.T.C.* 9203–8.
[8] B.M. Lansd. 64 f. 77.

But what was to be his swan song Cecil had written the previous year.[1] Only one copy of it appears to have survived, probably in the hand of Cecil's secretary, Michael Hicks.[2] It is of thirty-eight folio pages and is unfinished. Of Cecil's authorship there can be little doubt, although it bears no traces of his handling. But it is assigned to him in a later hand, the style is his, the references to himself in the text indubitably his. Judging from the style it was intended for publication, probably for publication overseas. But it was never published. The title, added to it in a later hand, is 'A Meditation of the State of England'. In essence it is a hymn of praise of Elizabeth's government and a defence of the Queen against her detractors. In form it suggests dictation from memory. There is some repetition. Some of the facts are wrong, some of them deliberately misrepresented, as when he describes the election of bishops by cathedral chapters with never a word about the royal *congé d'élire*, or treats the surrender of Le Havre in 1563 as a voluntary withdrawal. Like all his extant writings designed for publication, it is propagandist in character.

What a pity it is so. No man alive knew more about the reign of Elizabeth than he did, no man could have contributed more to our knowledge of it than he. In the late afternoon of his life, when he had nothing to gain or lose, he might have told the inside story. But it would not have been true to character had he done so. For critical appraisals we must look to his confidential memoranda to his mistress and the privy council. Publicly he was all for the Queen and her government. When he was young he had constantly tried to make things better, but now that he was very old and very helpless he sat back and contemplated the structure which he had played a large part in creating and found it good. But he laid no public claim to any credit. That all belonged to his mistress and his Queen.

This attitude of mind, which characterized Cecil during the whole course of Elizabeth's reign, was probably the determining factor in the selection of him as her public relations officer par excellence. He did not write very well. As a pamphleteer he cannot bear comparison with the Elizabethan masters of that craft.

[1] It is undated, but more than once in the text Cecil indicated that it was composed in 37 Eliz., some time after the campaign against the Spaniards at Brest (Nov. 1594) and before the appointment of Robert Cecil as secretary (July 1596).

[2] S.P. 12/255/84.

But he had one great virtue which almost all of them lacked. He never sought to display his own cleverness, like Martin Marprelate, or to advance his own interests, like Francis Bacon. He sought only to promote the cause and to serve his mistress.

III

The Making of The Statute of Artificers

S. T. BINDOFF

Among Sir John Neale's specialized studies none can have given him greater satisfaction, or his colleagues more delight, than his unravelling of the tangled problem of the Elizabethan Settlement of religion.[1] For this was a piece of historical detection in which the power to perceive significant details was allied with the imagination needed to interpret them, and its result an approach to the heart of a mystery which even Maitland had failed to penetrate.

To say of the essay which follows that it was inspired by this classic example of the *genre* would be to misuse a word and distort a relationship: but it does at least attempt to apply, however imperfectly, the same form of criticism to another Elizabethan statute, and therein lies its first and chief apology for inclusion in this volume. But its subject-matter may also claim some relevance to that volume's theme. Few acts of any of Elizabeth's parliaments would, if rigorously enforced, have meant so much to the lives and livelihoods of so many of her subjects: their choice of occupation, terms of training, hours of labour and rates of wages, freedom of movement, all these determinants of the 'work, wealth and happiness' of every commoner of the realm were themselves largely determined by 5 Elizabeth caput 4. The practical consequences of the statute have been elucidated in a number of valuable studies.[2] What has not been undertaken, because of an assumed lack of evidence, is an inquiry into its making, and its makers, whether for their own sakes or as guides to its interpretation: and

[1] 'The Elizabethan Acts of Supremacy and Uniformity' (*E.H.R.* lxv), 304–32.

[2] R. H. Tawney, 'The assessment of wages in England by the justices of the peace' (Vierteljahrschr. f. Sozial- und Wirtschaftsgesch. xi), 307–37, 533–64; R. K. Kelsall, *Wage Regulation under the Statute of Artificers*; Margaret Davies, *The Enforcement of English Apprenticeship, 1563–1642*. Cf. Conyers Read ed., *Bibliography of British History: Tudor Period, 1485–1603*, 2nd edn., 239 sqq.

this is the gap in its considerable literature which the following pages, chiefly based upon a scrutiny of the statute itself as the essential but neglected document, are a first attempt to close.

Of the three official texts of the statute (in manuscript in the original act and on the Parliament Roll, and in print in the black letter sessional volume of statutes), the most satisfying historically is the original act preserved in the House of Lords Record Office. This is the bill as it was engrossed for its third reading and afterwards amended, by additions, erasures and interlineations, between then and its receipt of the royal assent.[1] These amendments represent the final stage in the bill's evolution, and they will find an appropriate place in the story: it is the engrossed bill in its pristine state which, as the product of everything done up to and during the second reading, will be subject of this analysis. (Only one of the subsequent amendments, the rewriting of §12, was made in such a way as almost to destroy the clause in its earlier form.) To distinguish it from three earlier versions, the engrossed bill will be called Bill IV.[2]

The first impression made upon the reader is indubitably one of size. Whether he unrolls the nine parchments of Bill IV, stitched end-to-end to form a roll fourteen feet six inches long, or turns the eight large folio pages of print in the *Statutes of the Realm*, he is confronted with a document of massive proportions. Few sixteenth-century statutes—the notoriously large subsidy acts apart—are as big as this one: Bill IV has 38 clauses and well over 8,000 words.[3] To confuse largeness with greatness is temptingly easy: and it is to be feared that the statute owes to its bulk not a little of its fame. The effect is heightened by the preamble, that much-quoted preamble which promises to reduce the chaos of existing legislation 'into one sole Law and Statute, and in the same an uniform order prescribed and limited concerning the Wages and other Order for Apprentices, Servants and Labourers'. If this is

[1] The abridged text in R. H. Tawney and E. Power ed., *Tudor Economic Documents*, i, 338–50, follows the original act and usefully italicizes the additions made after engrossment; but it omits some of the details cited below.

[2] The writer acknowledges with gratitude the help and interest of Mr. M. F. Bond, Clerk of the Records of the House of Lords, in his study of the original act.

[3] Subsidy acts excepted, only three statutes passed between 1547 and 1603 exceed the statute of artificers in length: 1 Edw. VI c. 14 (chantries), 1 & 2 Ph. & M. c. 8 (repeal), and 14 Eliz. c. 5 (vagabonds). Its length may explain an unusual feature of the original act, namely, the numbering of its paragraphs.

what the statute sets out to do, how strong the persuasion, forty clauses later, that this is what it has done. *Si monumentum requieris*, the preamble seems to say, *prospice*. And to doubt this assurance is, in any case, to fly in the face of the guide-books. To its leading native expositor the statute is 'a great labour code' which deals with the problems of the time 'in a statesmanlike fashion': to its outstanding foreign student 'it was one of the most remarkable results of English economic policy' and a unique example of 'an attempt at so thorough a control of the whole industry of a country'.[1] Views have differed, of course, as to its inspiration: it has been called 'the most powerful instrument ever devised, for degrading and impoverishing the English labourer' and 'a classic example of the restrictive legislation which great depressions tend to produce'.[2] Yet all its interpreters have this in common, that they accept the statute as a unitary thing, whose parts cohere in a single grand design. They do this the more readily because, as some of them admit, lack of evidence prevents them from doing anything else.[3] At one in this, they are prone to discern, behind so homogeneous a conception, if not a single mind, at least a like-thinking group. The statute thus becomes more than a monument, it is a monolith.

That it is a document giving some measure of coherent expression to a number of related ideas will not, of course, be denied. The universal obligation to work as a social and moral duty, and the grading of occupations in diminishing order of utility from agriculture to overseas trade; the conception of a fair day's work and of a fair day's wage for it; the value of apprenticeship for civic as well as for technical training; the recognition of the interdependent roles of town and country and the discouraging of both occupational and labour mobility; the acceptance of the claims of birth, education, and property to confer occupational privilege: all these are evident in the statute and help to make it a microcosm of the social thought of its age. But acts of parliament must do more than mirror the *Zeitgeist*: they must convert it into commandments and prohibitions expressed in words and phrases, dates

[1] W. Cunningham, *The Growth of English Industry and Commerce*, 6th ed. ii (1), 27, 39; E. Heckscher, *Mercantilism*, trans. M. Shapiro, i, 226.

[2] J. E. Thorold Rogers, *Six Centuries of Work and Wages*, ed. 1912, 398–9; F. J. Fisher, 'Commercial Trends and Policy in the Sixteenth Century' (*Econ. Hist. Rev*. x), 113.

[3] Fisher, loc. cit.

and figures. When analysed, not simply in its formulation of current notions, but in its conversion of these notions into specific rules of conduct, the statute of artificers falls short of what might be expected in a measure designed to reduce chaos to order and drafted under a single direction and in one co-ordinated operation.

Consider first the order in which its provisions are set out. A legislator who begins by wiping the slate clean (or at least three parts clean) has little excuse for not writing on it anew in rational sequence. How far those who framed the statute were from achieving this end appears from its expositors' enforced habit of replacing its disorder by an order of their own. When Cunningham's reasoned citation of its clauses begins as follows: 7, 22, 7, 8, 10, 11, 18, 10, 31, and Heckscher's 3, 5, 11, 18, 23, 19, it may be inferred that between the numerical order of the clauses and any logical sequence of provisions there is a gulf fixed. Not that the numerical order is without reason: there are groups of clauses which go naturally together. But it is in the hiatuses between these groups, and the separation of other closely related clauses, that there is reflected, not emanation from a single source, but compilation from more than one in successive stages. For even if Tudor draftsmen seldom troubled to re-arrange the clauses of their bills in more intelligible sequence than that in which they originated, it is precisely the persistence of such disorder which implies diversity and independence of origin.

Again, whatever their peculiarities of arrangement, clauses of common provenance might be expected—above all when the watchwords were order and uniformity—to eschew gratuitous discrepancies of form, still more redundancies and contradictions. It would have been natural, for instance, in breaking with the tradition by which all statutes were deemed to have been in operation since the first day of the session which passed them,[1] to name a single 'day of commencement' which would afford reasonable notice to all the Queen's subjects likely to be affected. Clause 1, the repealing clause, does indeed name such a day, 30 September next (the statute received the royal assent on 10 April), and this is repeated in clauses 2 and 5. But there are to be found four other 'dates of commencement' scattered through the statute: Easter next (§2), the Feast of St. John Baptist next (19, 21–23), 1 May next (24), and 'the making of this Act' (38);

[1] M. F. Bond, 'Acts of Parliament' (*Archives*, iii), 210–11.

while elsewhere there is silence on the point. For such variations there seems no better explanation—as there is for the special timetable of the wage-assessment clauses—than individual whim, and hence the twin conclusions, that several hands worked somewhat independently at the production of these clauses, and that their finger-prints were not removed by final polishing. The consequence of this particular diversity must have been, not the good order envisaged in the preamble, but a period of utter, albeit temporary, confusion: for it would have been hard to say, as it still is, what was the law in force between 10 April and 30 September 1563.

Yet even after the dust of transition had settled, all would not have been crystal clear. For the statute, besides saying some things twice, said other things which were contradictory, and yet others which were far from clear. Of its repetitions a good illustration is furnished by clauses 4 and 6. Clause 4 prohibits the ending of service on either side before the agreed term is completed and without a quarter's notice being given. The peculiarity about this otherwise unremarkable clause lies in its relationship to §6, which repeats its provisions (merely extending the list of the courts and jurisdictions competent to hear suits arising) but adds to them one making punishable a refusal to perform compulsory service in husbandry at the wages assessed. Since this form of service is the subject of §5, it seems clear that §4 antedated §5 which, when added, necessitated the inclusion in §4 of the offence thus newly created: the enlarged 4 became 6, but the original and now useless 4, instead of being eliminated, was left in as a 'fossil'. For a case of contradiction, there is clause 10, which forbids a piece- or contract-worker to depart before completing the agreed task. (We may note, in passing, the anomaly that this clause, the counterpart of clause 4 just discussed, is separated from it by several clauses of quite other purport.) The first three-quarters of §10 consists in a long-winded definition of the offence and prescription of the penalty, the remaining quarter in a succinct version of the same thing—but with this difference, that the penalty provided in the first part, one month's imprisonment and a £5 forfeit, appears in the second as imprisonment only. Such, at least, is the effect of the clause in the original act. In the statute as enrolled, however, this clause underwent a change of wording, the only one of significance throughout the document. Where the original act begins the second part of the clause: 'And that no Artificer . . .' (and thus, since the first part has opened identically, involves the repetition), the enrolled statute has: 'And that none other Artificer . . .' This looks like a not wholly successful attempt by the clerk who enrolled the statute to make sense of what appeared to him, as it does to us, an ambiguous addition. But was it ever an addition? Was this second part not the original clause[1] which some legal hand inflated and complicated into the part which now precedes it, an original clause which was then left in, this time not so much a fossil as an appendix?

To show that the statute's boasted homogeneity is not even skin-deep, and that surgical scars abound, is a useful but negative achievement. We must now try to see these things, not simply as flaws in the finished product, but as clues to the successive operations which had produced it. The results of a tedious investigation along these lines, with an indispensable minimum of the reasoning involved, will next be presented. To begin at the end, the six clauses (33–38) which stand last in Bill IV have this in common: they are all qualifications of preceding clauses, and, what is more, of immediately preceding ones. Five (33–36 and 38) are additions to the 'apprenticeship clauses' (18–28) such as are likely to have been made after those clauses had taken shape, and one of them (35) has a 'preamble' of its own which seems to echo an objection raised in debate. The other clause (37) is similarly related to the three 'execution clauses' (30–32), with which, had it been adopted at the same time, it would assuredly have formed a consecutive series. Both their location and their character reveal these six clauses as the last to be added before engrossment. The subtraction of these clauses from Bill IV leaves a bill of thirty-two clauses which we shall call Bill III. This, in turn, concludes with three 'execution clauses' (30–32) which provide for twice-yearly reviews of the working of the statute, for the payment of allowances to the magistrates responsible, and for the recovery and allocation of forfeitures. The interdependence of these clauses argues strongly for their being of common and simultaneous origin. But their location at the end of Bill III is probably to be explained, not by their addition to a previous bill, but by their having retained the final position which they already occupied in it: the reason for this will be mentioned later.[2]

[1] Cf. the similar clause in §2 of 6 Hen. VIII c. 3.

[2] Below, 75.

They are preceded by the longest sequence of clauses closely related in subject matter, the 'apprenticeship clauses' (19–29). At first sight this section of the statute is so coherent as to admit of no doubt that it, at least, was drafted and put together in a single operation. Yet nowhere is scrutiny more rewarding. To begin with, the identity of subject is more apparent than real. True, all these clauses deal with apprenticeship, but they do so in varying ways and from different standpoints. Four topics may be distinguished: (i) the making obligatory of a seven years' apprenticeship for the future exercise of any craft (§24); (ii) the restriction of apprenticeship in certain crafts to the offspring of the socially qualified (19–23) and, by contrast, its throwing open in others to all comers (25); (iii) the compulsion upon certain persons to be apprenticed if required (18, 28, 29); (iv) the maintenance in certain crafts of a numerical proportion between apprentices and journeymen (26) and a proviso to this rule (27). A review of these provisions shows not only that they seek to manipulate the system of apprenticeship for different ends—here to debar people from some crafts, there to drive people into others—but that even their order is not a logical one. Other discrepancies are evident, notably different 'dates of commencement', which further weaken the initial impression of unity.

The same process of dissection being applied to the statute as a whole, when carried out on this section, suggests that, in origin, it consisted of three, or perhaps four, clauses only (an 'eligibility' clause later suppressed, and the present 18, 28 and perhaps 29) and that the remaining clauses are an addition. Of the original clauses, 18 and 28 exhibit an affinity (and a discrepancy) which are best demonstrated by bringing them, in extract, together:

XVIII. And for the better Advancement of Husbandry and Tillage, and to the intent that such as are fit to be made Apprentices to Husbandry, may be bounden thereunto, Be it enacted by the authority of this present Parliament, That every person being an householder, and having and using half a Plough Land at the least in Tillage, may have and receive as an Apprentice any person above the age of ten years, and under the age of eighteen years . . .

XXVIII. And be it further enacted, That if any person shall be required by any householder, having and using half a Plough Land at the least in Tillage, to be an Apprentice, and to serve in Husbandry, *or in any other kind of Art, Mystery or Science before expressed,* and shall refuse so to do . . . [he shall be compelled to do so by the justices of the peace, if they judge him suitable.]

That these are twin clauses, indeed Siamese twins, with—to stretch the metaphor—one head in the form of the 'preamble' to clause 18, cannot reasonably be doubted. How and why did they come to be separated? Only by the surgical interposition of clauses 19–27. But they were not only sawn asunder, one of the two underwent a further, a grafting operation, which was a clumsy performance. To clause 28, originally confined, like 18, to husbandry, there was added a phrase extending its scope to other crafts. This phrase, italicized in the extract above, had the effect of reducing the start of clause 28, if read literally, to near-nonsense by making it confer upon any holder of half-a-ploughland the power of compulsory apprenticeship to any craft whatever! It is this intruded phrase, added at the same time as clauses 19–27, which explains why these clauses had to precede and not follow 28, why, that is, they had to be wedged between clauses 18 and 28: for without them there the new reference in 28 to crafts 'before expressed' would have been meaningless.

If this deduction is correct, it tells us not only that clauses 18 and 28, once consecutive, were separated, but that what came to part them was inserted as a whole. The significance of this second point lies in the seeming paradox that these clauses exhibit some discrepancies themselves. Thus, whereas the first five of them (19–23) show a strong family likeness, setting out the qualifications for apprenticeship to certain crafts in an ordered sequence, and having in common a date of commencement, the Feast of St. John the Baptist next coming, peculiar to them, another clause which in subject-matter (the qualifications for apprenticeship to country weavers supplying clothiers) belongs to this series is found separated from it (being 25), has no date of commencement, and is unique in providing for registration and for a cumulative penalty of 20*s*. per month. Yet, despite its air of an independent afterthought, this clause can scarcely have been added after the insertion of clauses 19–27, since it would then have taken its place, not among them, but among the later apprenticeship clauses, from clause 33 onwards. It follows from this, and from similar clues, that the inserted clauses were first put together from assorted materials and then wedged, as a whole, between the original ones, the original 'eligibility' clause, if there was one, disappearing in the process. It is less easy to determine whether clause 29 was the third or fourth of the original clauses or the tenth and last of the added ones. Since it limits compulsory apprenticeship to persons under twenty-one this clause must always have stood after 28, the clause creating that status: and its position is therefore consistent with either view. So, perhaps, is its content, although we may reflect that its purpose could have been effected in six words by writing, in 28, 'That if any person under the age of twenty-one years shall be required'. The point is, in any case, of no great importance.

The remainder of Bill IV, that is, everything preceding the apprenticeship clauses, also presents, on first inspection, a unitary appearance. Unlike all that follows, which is new legislation, clauses 2–18 are chiefly concerned with re-enacting, here and there in modified form, large parts of the old and thus seem to flow logically from the preamble and clause 1. This common characteristic, and their leading position, serve to identify them as the substance of an original bill (Bill I) of this nature: and their arbitrary arrangement is, in part at least, attributable to their piecemeal derivation from the ancient statutes. Yet this will not explain all of them or all of their peculiarities. Two, we have already seen, are wholly or partially fossilized relics of a yet earlier bill,[1] which may also have contributed the two other clauses (14, punishing assaults by servants on masters, and 17, providing compulsory employment for unmarried women) which are not traceable to the older legislation. If these clauses reveal an alternative source of material for Bill I, others are suggestive of its subsequent expansion. Take, for instance, §2. In prescribing a minimum term of one year for labour-hirings, this clause echoes a provision first heard of in the Statute of Labourers of 1351[2] and thus far blends naturally with the others. But §2 applies the one-year rule, not as its fourteenth-century precursors had done, to husbandry, nor yet, as might have befitted the first item of a comprehensive labour code, to all occupations, but solely to twenty-nine enumerated crafts.[3] This is peculiar in itself: but it is made more so if clause 3 is also brought into the reckoning. This clause compels a person to serve, if called upon, in the trade to which he has been brought up: but its application, too, is limited,

[1] Above, 60–61. [2] Sect. 2 of 25 Edw. III St. 2.
[3] Increased in the statute to thirty-one: below, 65.

both by a long list of exemptions, and by its restriction to 'any of the said Arts, Crafts or Sciences', that is, to the twenty-nine listed in §2. It is therefore in these twenty-nine trades, but in no others, that employers are given first call on trained workmen and employment is stabilized by yearly hirings. Both provisions are entirely consonant with two of the presumed objects of the bill, to check labour mobility and reduce unemployment: so much so that one cannot help wondering why they were not made universal.

The first hint of an answer springs from a recollection that there were twenty-nine crafts listed in §2 of the engrossed bill (Bill IV) and that two more—tailors and curriers—were to be added afterwards, making the total in the statute thirty-one. If the twenty-nine could become thirty-one at the final reading, it is likely that this number had itself been reached by a similar growth earlier. Can we not almost see the list growing, either in the House or in committee, as different Members suggested fresh trades for inclusion? And would it not, in the process, have become just the kind of list it is, an unordered procession in which pewterers march between tanners and bakers, glovers between brewers and cutlers, and butchers, cooks and millers bring up the rear? How many trades were thus added, or when, cannot be known: but the more that were, the fewer there must have been in the original clause. It is thus possible that the significance of this clause, as drafted, lay less in its revival of an earlier rule than in the particular trades to which this rule was to be applied. To that extent its similarity to the clauses which follow it is deceptive and its place at their head something of an anomaly. The same considerations apply to §3, which, being restricted by reference to §2's list of trades, was presumably drafted with it. We shall find, when we come to consider the most likely source of these two clauses, that it is one which they share with certain of the apprenticeship clauses.[1] That being so they are to be thought of, not as founder-members of Bill I, but as recruits drafted into it, probably at the same time as these clauses. Their position would then be easily accounted for: they would have been tacked on to the file, not at the rear where the apprenticeship clauses were falling in at the same time, but at the head. Little wonder that they look out of place, if they were not meant to stand there.

[1] Below, 93 *n* 2.

This consideration of clauses 2 and 3 has already raised the major problem posed by Bill I, its treatment of compulsory service. A statute which, as we have been taught to believe, rests on the principle of the 'universal obligation to work' might have been expected to impose that obligation upon all citizens and in respect of all occupations. Indeed, it is widely believed (and the belief goes back a long way) that this is what the statute of artificers in fact does. But the compulsions introduced by the clauses in question (3, 5, 17, 28, 29) fall far short of a general power to compel any person to work at any trade. The nearest approach to this is found in §17, which renders unmarried women aged between twelve and forty liable to serve at the discretion of the J.P.s. (Does this clause reflect a female employment problem arising from the dissolution of nunneries and the decay of great households?) But over males—and the existence of §17 implies that the word 'person' used elsewhere signifies 'male person'—the statute wields no such general power: neither the compulsory apprenticeship of §28 nor the compulsory service of clauses 3 and 5 is applicable to other than specified occupations, that is husbandry and the enumerated crafts. More noteworthy still is the fact that §6, which furnishes the sanction for clauses 3 and 5, does not make it an offence to refuse to serve but only to 'refuse to serve for the Wages that shall be limited, rated and appointed, according to the form of this Statute'. And if the statute thus limits the compulsory power, how much more narrowly must Bill I have done. For, granted what has been said about it, all that Bill I provided by way of compulsion was service for men and apprenticeship for boys in husbandry (by §5 and §28 unamended) and service for unmarried women (§17). In so far as these provisions embody the obligation to work, they do so by directing all unemployed males into agriculture and all unemployed females into some form of menial service. Here is no novel attempt to organize the labour market, but simply the shovelling of its refuse along a couple of well-worn paths. Only when these clauses came to be amended and expanded would they begin to assume the character of a system of labour direction: and whatever the statute ended by achieving in that field it did not set out to achieve but acquired on the way.

To these indications that clauses 2–17, as we now have them, were, like the apprenticeship clauses, the product of addition and amendment must be added those which characterize Bill I as a clumsy and careless compilation. This impression, already created by the survival within it of the two 'fossils', is strengthened by a consideration of its initial items, §1 and the preamble. Clause 1 is a repeal clause, but a repeal clause of an unusual kind. It neither specifies the statutes which it partially repeals nor defines the extent to which it repeals them. It provides merely that 'as much of all the Estatutes heretofore made, and every branch of them, as touch or concern the hiring, keeping, departing, working, wages, or order' of workpeople shall be repealed from 30 September following, 'and that all the said Statutes, and every branch thereof, for any Matter contained in them, and not repealed by this Statute, shall remain and be in full force and effect'.[1] It is plausible, but unconvincing, to attribute the lack of enumeration to the belief that the statutes concerned were dead letters not worth that effort: for in the years before 1563 there had been some attempt to enforce them.[2] A more matter-of-fact explanation is that the bill was put together in haste, that there was not time to prepare the customary recital in detail of acts or parts of acts repealed, and that the omission was not rectified later. Since haste is more likely to have prevailed at the end than at the beginning of the operation, this in turn prompts the question whether §1, instead of being, as it is instinctive to assume, the first to be settled and drafted, may not have emerged later. Was the bill originally designed, not to supplant, but to supplement, the statutes already in force, as nearly all of them had done in their day, and the decision to repeal them arrived at only as the new bill took shape? Clause 1 would then have been, not the premise, but an afterthought, an afterthought occurring too late to be translated into detail. It is a possible but, as we shall see later, unlikely explanation of the shortcomings of this clause.

We turn, finally and briefly, to the preamble. Like the introduction to a book, the preamble of a statute may be written at any time during its composition: but we may be certain that this one does not, save in one particular, post-date Bill I. The reason is this. The aims set forth in it—to codify existing law, especially with regard to wage-assessment, in order to promote employment,

[1] One revealing consequence of the uncertain scope of the repeal clause was that 12 Ric. II cc. 3–9, in many respects the 'basic' acts of the series concerned, were to be repealed by 21 Ja. I c. 28 as though then still in force. [2] Below, 83–84.

foster agriculture, and adjust wages to prices—are subserved by the first seventeen clauses of Bill IV. Conversely, the purport of the remaining twenty-one, and above all of the apprenticeship clauses, is ignored by the preamble save for its mere inclusion of the word 'apprentices', and even this, to judge from its mentions both there and in §1, seems to be an addition, and a careless one at that.[1] If any doubt lingers that the apprenticeship clauses were an addition to a bill (with an appropriate preamble) in which apprenticeship was a small matter, and that their addition was not matched by any revision of its preamble, that doubt will hardly survive the realization that what its historian has called 'one of the important new departures of the act', the national regulation of apprenticeship, passes altogether unnoticed in the preamble.[2]

At the close of an analysis made possible only by the survival, in the document examined, of traces of its compilation, from diverse materials and in various stages, it is scarcely necessary to observe that these things have survived only because no skilled hand was given the opportunity of polishing them out of existence. The time for that would have been after Bill IV, containing thirty-eight of the final forty clauses, had taken shape, but before it was engrossed: after engrossment only minor touching-up was possible. Why nothing more effective was done will appear later.

So much for what is to be deduced from the bill itself. Now to the Journals of Lords and Commons for light on its passage through parliament.

By the early years of Elizabeth's reign the reading of bills three times, no more and no less, had become standard practice in both houses of parliament. At a time when a reading was literally a reading aloud by the clerk of a manuscript, three of them was the least number necessary for the proper consideration of a bill. At its first hearing the bill would be a novelty to most Members, and although on occasion debate might arise spontaneously (and the bill even be rejected at once), the House would normally need to digest the bill before dealing with it. Thus it was the second

[1] Thus the preamble speaks of the wages of apprentices, who of course received none.

[2] Davies, *Enforcement of Apprenticeship*, 1. The alternative title, statute of apprentices, adopted by Adam Smith and still in use, e.g. by Lipson, reflects the importance of these provisions of the statute, despite their omission from the preamble.

reading, some days or even weeks later, which occasioned the principal debate and which settled the bill's future. A bill which was accepted, with such amendments as could be agreed upon, was then ordered to be engrossed, or copied out fair on parchment: and it was from this copy that the clerk, again after a lapse of some days, read the bill for the third time. Any further amendments were made on this copy as erasures, interlineations or, if necessary, added slips of parchment. Finally, the bill was put to the vote and, since it had already passed its main test, was usually carried. The engrossed copy was then carried to the house of lords—we have assumed that the bill started in the Commons—and the procedure, without the engrossment, was repeated there, any amendment made in the Lords being afterwards submitted to the Commons for their acceptance. When all was agreed, the engrossed bill returned to the Lords to await the royal assent at the close of the session, given by the pronouncing of the formula 'La Roigne le veult' (and usually by its inscription at the head of the bill), which thus became the original act to be copied out on the parliament roll as the legally valid instrument.

To this procedure there was already beginning to be made, by 1558, an addition which, exceptional at first, would rapidly become customary and finally indispensable. This was the committing of a bill. As it developed into a necessary stage in bill procedure, committal became the reference of every bill, after its second reading, to a group of Members, the 'committees', for scrutiny and amendment: and the third reading came to include a 'report' of what changes, if any, they recommended. But in the early years of Elizabeth's reign committal was still both exceptional and elastic. Few bills were committed at all, so that committal betokens some 'hitch' which could not be dealt with in the House. Thus if two bills on the same topic were introduced, or one brought in when a similar one was pending, committal might be resorted to after the first reading with the object of reducing them to one: or if at a second or third reading substantial amendment was called for, the bill would stand committed. A piece of procedure thus still abnormal was also doubtless still informal. Where later the 'committees', elected by their fellow-Members, had their names entered in the clerk's journal, at this formative period the clerk wrote down only one name, that of the Member entrusted with the bill, around whom those with objections or proposals to make would coalesce into a committee: to the clerk all that mattered was that he should know who had the bill, of which there was probably but this one version.

With this procedure in mind let us see what the two Journals of 1563 have to say about the passage of the artificers bill. The six relevant entries in the Commons Journal are:

16 Jan.	1.	The Bill touching Servants to serve their Masters. —The Master of Rolls.
24 Feb.	1.	*nova*. The Bill, of many Articles, for Servants of Artificers and Husbandry (*sic*).—Mr. *Sekford*.
3 Mar.	1.	The Bill for the Orders and Wages of Servants of Husbandry and Artificers.—Mr. *Crofts*.
22 Mar.	2.	The Bill touching Servants of Husbandry, Artificers and Labourers.
2 Apr.	2.	The Bill for Artificers, Labourers, Servants and Apprentices.—*Ingrossetur*.
6 Apr.	3.	The Bill touching Artificers, Servants of Husbandry, Labourers and Apprentices.—*Jud'm*. Sent to the Lords by Mr. Comptroller.[1]

From the Lords Journal we learn that the bill was read by the Lords on three successive days, 6, 7 and 8 April. At the third reading a proviso was added, which was sent to the Commons for their acceptance. The Commons Journal is silent about this, but the proviso itself, stitched on the engrossed bill, records its adoption. The bill, thus agreed, was among those which received the Queen's assent on 10 April.[2]

In the house of lords, then, the bill had a rapid and, the proviso apart, unhindered passage. It may, indeed, be wondered how, or even whether, the Lords endured the tedium of hearing recited, three days running, a bill which by then took about two hours to read: if they did, perhaps its soporific quality mitigated the ordeal. But the bill which thus cleared its three noble hurdles in grand style had struggled over its gentlemanly obstacles with patent difficulty. Between its first and last readings in the Commons there had stretched six weeks; it had been committed, not once, but

[1] *C.J.* i, 62*b*, 66*b*, 67*a*, 70*a*, 71*b*, 72*a*; entries checked with MS. Journal, House of Lords Record Office.

[2] *L.J.* i, 614*b*, 615*b*, 616*b*; entries checked with MS. Journal, House of Lords Record Office.

twice; and, most striking of all, it appears to have been given, not one first and one second reading, but two of each. These are assuredly not the signs of swift, smooth progress: they are the skid-marks produced by sharp brakings.

The journey had begun on 16 January 1563, the second business day of the session, with the introduction of the bill 'Touching Servants to serve their Masters'.[1] This bill was committed after its first (and only) reading to no less official a Member than the master of the rolls: that could mean only one thing—it dealt with matters upon which official proposals were pending. The fate of this bill is thus an indication that the artificers bill was in preparation.[2] In preparation, but assuredly not yet drafted: for that would make the six weeks which were to elapse before its introduction hard to explain. (By the same reasoning it is unlikely to have been a bill shelved by the dissolution of the previous parliament.) This new bill was put together, then, not before but during the early weeks of the parliament, a circumstance which enabled its framers to incorporate in it some parts of the bill which it superseded. That they did so, in the shape of clauses 4, 10, and perhaps 14 and 17, has already been deduced. These, the only survivals of that bill, suggest that it dealt generally with the master-servant relationship; such a bill would have been appropriately committed to the chief legal luminary in the House. It was presumably also under his sponsorship that on 24 February there was introduced the official bill, a bill, as the clerk noted, 'of many Articles'. Our Bill I, it consisted of between eighteen and twenty-one clauses, contained some five thousand words, and can hardly have occupied less than an hour in the reading.[3] Its principal features have been noticed already: preamble and repeal clause were already there, followed by re-enacting clauses, the borrowings from its precursor, and the provision for compulsory service and apprenticeship in husbandry: whether the three 'execution clauses', perhaps in unamended form, brought up the rear it is impossible to say—hence the doubt as to the bill's length.

Among its provisions we might guess, even if we had no reason to believe, that those most likely to excite attention were

[1] For a tabular summary of the various readings: see over.

[2] For an earlier one: below, 90.

[3] An estimate arrived at by practical experiment, and by comparison with the other indications of the time consumed by readings: cf. J. E. Neale, *Elizabethan House of Commons*, 370.

THE READINGS OF THE BILL

Unofficial Bill 16 Jan.		Bill I 24 Feb.		Bill II 3 Mar.		Bill III 22 Mar.	Bill III 2 Apr.	Bill IV 6 Apr.
		Preamble		Preamble		**Preamble**	Preamble	**Preamble**
		1		1		**1**	1	**1**
						2*	**2***	**2**
						3	**3**	**3**
		2		2		**4**	4	**4**
		3		3		**5**	5	**5**
1		**4**		4		**6**	6	**6**
		5		5		**7**	7	**7**
		6		6		**8**	8	**8**
		7		7		**9**	9	**9**
2*		**8**		8		**10**	10	**10**
		9*		**9***		**11***	11*	**11**
	Committed to Cordell	**10***	Committed to Seckford	**10***	Committed to Croft	**12***	12*	**12**
		11*		**11**		**13**	13	**13**
?3		**12**		12		**14**	14	**14**
		13		13		**15**	15	**15**
		14		14		**16**	16	**16**
?4		**15**		15		**17**	17	**17**
		16		16		**18**	**18**	**18**
						19	**19**	**19**
						20	**20**	**20**
						21	**21**	**21**
						22	**22**	**22**
						23	**23**	**23**
						24*	**24***	**24**
						25	**25**	**25**
						26	**26**	**26**
						27	**27**	**27**
		17*		17		**28**	**28**	**28**
		18		18		**29**	**29**	**29**
		?**19**		19		**30**	30	**30**
		?**20**		20		**31**	31	**31**
		?**21**		21		**32**	32	**32**
								33
								34
								35
								36
								37
								38
							(Commons proviso)	**39**
							(Lords proviso: 10 April)	**40**

* Unrevised form of final clause.
Clauses in heavy type were read at these sittings.

its wage-assessment and compulsory service clauses. That wage-assessment was already included, although not susceptible of proof (and it was possible at one stage of this inquiry to believe the opposite), appears on reflection almost a certainty. Apart from the genesis of the bill,[1] two points, one general and one particular, favour this presumption. The first is that a bill consolidating the labour laws of the last two centuries was little likely to ignore their *fons et origo*, the control of wages. The second is the position occupied by the clauses concerned, or their successors, in the bill. Numbered 11 to 13, they are placed centrally among the clauses constituting Bill I, a most unlikely place for an addition. Once installed there, however, they could have undergone amendment, even drastic amendment, without being displaced: and it is their amendment, not their addition, which is in question.

How do we know that they were amended? The internal evidence which elsewhere makes this possible is here either lacking or inconclusive: one of the three clauses (12) was afterwards almost wholly rewritten and its earlier contents obliterated, and traces of revision in the others afford little basis for theorizing. Evidence must be sought in the Journal, and it proves to consist of two small, but precious, items. There is, first, the committal of Bill I after the reading of 24 February: again, as on 16 January, it is committal after first reading, and again it is committal to a Member holding important legal office, this time to Thomas Seckford, one of the masters of requests. If this points to another hitch, and a hitch calling for official manipulation, the other piece of evidence reveals both the cause of trouble and the agency of its removal. On 3 March the clerk recorded a further reading of the bill: but this reading he numbered, not '2', but '1'—and this was no slip of the pen, for the second reading, nay the two second readings, still lay in the future. For this 'second first' reading of 3 March (as for its counterpart on 2 April) there is, among a number of possible reasons, only one which fits all the circumstances: it is that between 24 February and 3 March Bill I had acquired substantial new matter which, if it were to achieve parity with the rest, had to be read to the House.[2] (Minor amendment

[1] Below, 83–88

[2] The writer has, he believes, considered all possible alternatives (including the obvious one that the bill was too long to be read at a single sitting and so had to be spread over two) and has abandoned them as not consistent with all the facts.

would not have made necessary this departure from routine: it could have been taken at a second reading.) Thus it was only this new matter which the House heard on 3 March, not the whole bill (for then parity would have been lost), although the clerk, adhering to formula, entered it as a reading of the bill. Yet, even as he did so, he spoiled the effect of normality by adding to his previous description of the bill the two words: 'and Wages'. Would he have done so unless the proceedings he thus recorded had concerned, chiefly if not solely, this part of the bill? And since these proceedings were the outcome of Seckford's committee, which in turn had arisen from the reading of 24 February, can we doubt that what had chiefly troubled the House that day was the wage provisions of the bill? There was, surely, little else to quarrel over. Compulsory service and apprenticeship, these were, it is true, to raise difficulties, but, so it appears, at the next stage, not at this: and, these apart, the provisions of Bill I seem strikingly uncontroversial. But the wage-provisions were evidently another matter. Unfortunately, it is another matter, too, to say why they were—a matter largely of speculation. For what we have before us is not the clauses which provoked criticism on 24 February, but those clauses after they had been amended to meet that criticism (or even, in the case of §12, as later rewritten in deference to further criticism). Thus the question: what was objected to in the original clauses? resolves itself into the question: what do the present clauses reveal, not only of those objections, but of any concessions to them? Do these clauses bear any trace of challenge and response?

Clauses 11 to 13 laid upon the justices of the peace in the shires, and the magistracies in the towns, the duty of annually compiling and continuously enforcing a set of wage-rates for every occupation practised within their jurisdiction, under penalty of a £10 fine for evading this responsibility. The duty (although not the penalty) was an old one: first imposed in 1390, it had in theory been lifted only during one or two short intervals since. But it had long since ceased to be discharged with any regularity, and to the justices of 1563—of whom there were upwards of a hundred in the house of commons[1]—it would appear, not an old, familiar burden, but a strange new one. True, that generation of justices had come to expect little else from a central government whose ardour for new

[1] Norah M. Fuidge, 'The Personnel of the House of Commons, 1563–1567' (London Univ. M.A. thesis, 1950), table I.

forms of social regimentation brooked no doubts whether or how they could be applied: to that extent the artificers bill was merely another straw added to the mounting load. But might it not have appeared (until the next one followed) one straw too many? If it did, then the answer, short of removing, would be to ease, the fresh burden. Changes were, we know, to be made to the wage-clauses even after the bill was engrossed.[1] Are there traces of earlier ones? The questing eye is caught in §11 by a concluding provision that justices may keep an assessment, once made, either wholly or partially in force beyond its year's term. Coming immediately after the firm and elaborate arrangements for yearly assessment, this cannot but appear something of an anti-climax, something of an escape-clause: which is, of course, what—to look ahead for a moment—it was often to turn into.[2] Again, one of the 'execution clauses' (31) grants justices an allowance of five shillings a day, up to a limit of three days at a time, for duties arising from the statute. As the clause itself reminds us, they had long been entitled to such allowances, which were as old as the Ordinance of Labourers itself and had first been made statutory in 1390.[3] None the less, their confirmation has something of the look of a *douceur*.

Such provisions, we may reflect, might prudently have been written in to the bill at the outset: and, even if added after 24 February, they would in themselves hardly account for the 'second first' reading of 3 March. Casting about for some greater object of contention, we may remind ourselves that local assessment was only one of the methods of wage-control handed down from the past: there was another, that of a statutory, country-wide assessment, which was, indeed, still nominally in force under the act of 1515. May there not have been a demand for its continuance so that the responsibility, even the odium, of holding down wages might be borne at the centre? and does the requirement (a new one) in §11 that local assessments should come into force only by the direction of the privy council perhaps represent a concession to that viewpoint? Again, there could well have been a conflict of opinion as to which should be made a punishable offence, the taking of higher wages, or the giving of them, or both. The first

[1] Below, 78–79. [2] Kelsall, *Wage Regulation*, 7–9.

[3] Bertha H. Putnam, *The Enforcement of the Statutes of Labourers, 1349–1359*, 44 sqq.

had always been an offence since the Ordinance of Labourers: but the second, although made so by fourteenth-century legislation, had twice since then been exonerated and had not been punishable for fifty years before 1563.[1] It may be that in these, or in other so far unsuspected ways, the provisions of Bill I differed from those adopted, and that their revision was also the work of Seckford's committee. But for the present the matter must stand adjourned with no further conclusion than that between 24 February and 3 March the wage-assessment clauses underwent substantial change of an indeterminable nature.

In the guise of a 'second first' reading of the bill, then, the new or amended clauses were read on 3 March, and Bill I became Bill II. How the changes were received it is impossible to say. What is clear, however, is that the bill ran into fresh difficulty. So much might be conjectured from the fact that the Commons did no other business that morning, for the reading of the new matter would not in itself have taken long. But what turns conjecture into near-certainty is that after this reading the bill was committed for a second time, its 'committee' being Sir James Croft, knight of the shire for Hereford and a future comptroller of the Queen's household. The reason for this further committal is at first hard to discover. Only when it is coupled with another episode, equally puzzling, do both yield up their secrets. The question, what caused the committal of 3 March? is only to be answered at the same time as the question, why were there to be (apparently) two second readings of the bill, on 22 March and 2 April? The answers, it is suggested, are as follows.

The reference of the bill to Croft's committee arose from dissatisfaction with another part of it, the provisions for compulsory service and apprenticeship in husbandry laid down in clauses 5, 6, 18 and 28. To these that committee both made amendments and added eleven new clauses, the present 2, 3 and 19–27. Thus when on 22 March the House again considered the bill—which we may call Bill III—it consisted of two parts: there were the twenty-one clauses which had taken shape by 3 March (Bill II) and the eleven new ones. To Bill II the Commons could, and did, give a second reading that morning, and we may presume that it passed without trouble: even so, the reading must have consumed upwards of one

[1] Imposed by 12 Ric. II c. 4, the penalty for giving higher wages than those assessed was repealed by 4 Hen. V St. 2 c. 4 and again by 4 Hen. VIII c. 5.

hour. But the new clauses the House was hearing for the first time, and they would require two readings to 'catch up' with Bill II. Even if time had allowed—and these clauses would have required half-an-hour to read once, or a full hour twice—the House could not have been expected to debate without notice what was equivalent to a new bill. Thus the 'first second' reading of 22 March consisted of the second reading of Bill II and the first reading of the new clauses. Ten days later, on 2 April, the new clauses were read a second time, and the clerk followed his own precedent of 3 March both in recording this as a further reading of the bill as a whole and in recognizing its increased scope by adding to its title, for the first time, the words 'and Apprentices'.

The reader who has come so far will (it is to be hoped) recognize in this version of what took place the counterpart of conclusions already reached by dissecting this part of the bill.[1] Bald and perhaps not wholly convincing as they may have appeared, these conclusions now acquire the verisimilitude of attachment to facts, dates and persons. For it was the compulsory service and apprenticeship clauses which came under fire on 3 March and were referred to Croft's committee. That committee not only amended them but added to them a further eleven, of which nine were inserted towards the end of the bill (19–27) and two towards its beginning (2 and 3). The unity of the nine clauses, as the product of a single operation, is witnessed by their introduction together between the previous clauses, where they had to go if the simultaneous extension of §28 to 'any other kind of Art, Mystery, or Science before expressed' was to make sense: while the community of the nine with the two will be demonstrated in connection with their origin.[2] It is, however, unity, not uniformity, which prevails among these eleven clauses, and this because they did not wholly reconcile—and so continue to reflect—the differing viewpoints of the 'committees' responsible for them or of groups within the House whose opinions they expressed. Within this section of the bill, as throughout the bill as a whole, there are to be discerned the labours of different hands and the preoccupations of various minds.

On 2 April these new clauses received their second reading and thus the bill as a whole (Bill III) reached that stage of procedure. This was the opportunity for the House, profiting by ten days' notice, to debate these clauses and to add to them itself. Whether

[1] Above, 62–64. [2] Below, 93 *n* 2.

amendments were made we cannot say, but the six new clauses added are to be found in their expected position at the end of the engrossed bill: that five of them concern apprenticeship testifies to the interest in this, now the principal subject of the bill. To qualify for inclusion in the engrossed bill, these six clauses (and, of course, any amendments made to the others) would have needed to be read twice running, and this helps to explain why the proceedings again occupied an entire morning. They closed with the motion for engrossing: with its passing the bill entered the home straight.

That was on a Friday. On the following Tuesday morning the engrossed bill (Bill IV) was read. Engrossment had been a formidable task, and it is less surprising to discover that it was done, in roughly equal amounts, by two hands than that the clerks who did it seem to have worked, not at the same time, but one after the other.[1] Urgency there must have been, for when the bill came up for the third reading it wanted but four days to Easter: such urgency indeed as not to admit of the thorough revision which the bill cried out for. Yet, despite its now portentous length, and the obligation to read every fresh amendment three times, despite too the reading of two other bills the same morning, Bill IV underwent a number of further changes: the House might be thin but it was still keen. Unlike those so far discussed, most of these final amendments are indicated in a readily accessible summary of the statute,[2] and need therefore not be dilated upon: the majority are in any case textual changes of minor interest. The addition, in §2, of tailors and curriers to the crafts covered by the one-year rule was, we have seen, probably the last of a series of additions,[3] as was that of occupation in London's grain-supply to those exempting from compulsory service in husbandry (§5).[4] In §11 the date for the compilation of the first wage-assessments was altered from six weeks after Easter (that is, 23 May) to 10 June 1563, doubtless because of the protraction of the parliamentary session, and in §24 the *terminus a quo* of obligatory apprenticeship was fixed at 1 May 1563.

[1] This is suggested by the fact that the change of hand occurs within a clause (20) and not between clauses, and by the absence of any indication that the membranes were cut where the clerks' work joined.

[2] *Tudor Economic Documents*, i, 338–50. [3] Above, 65.

[4] This last insertion well illustrates the unforeseen changes of meaning apt to be produced by such alterations: cf. *Tudor Economic Documents*, i, 340.

Three of the changes are of greater moment: an amendment, a rewriting, and a proviso. The amendment, to §24, limited the obligatory apprenticeship introduced by that clause to 'any crafts ... now used or occupied within the Realm of England or Wales'. These words were to have a potent future: they would serve the turn of all who desired to restrict the scope of the statute, and it is tempting, but probably fallacious, to see in them the first blow struck for economic liberalism. The clause rewritten was 12. The original clause of this number in Bill IV was, save for its last two lines, literally cut out and replaced by a freshly-stitched parchment slip bearing a clause written in a different hand. The new clause inflicts a penalty of £10 upon any resident justice failing to take part in a wage-assessment session. Since the sum itself occurs, not in the new clause but in the two lines left of the old, it cannot have been the size of the penalty which underwent alteration, but the circumstances in which it would be incurred: and we may guess that the change was made to protect justices from being mulcted unfairly. The new clause may well echo earlier restiveness.[1] The proviso is one of two stitched to the foot of the bill, the other, safeguarding the rights of high constables, being the proviso originated in the Lords. The Commons' proviso rendered any servant or apprentice illegally withdrawing from service and moving into another shire liable to arrest and imprisonment by writ of *capias* directed by the justices of the one shire to the sheriff of the other. This extension of the competence of the justices beyond the shire-boundary, although not without precedent,[2] is of considerable interest, not least because it seems to have been an afterthought. The neighbouring shire was no longer to offer even a partial escape from the grip of the labour-code: and the Elizabethan workman was to be taught, as long before the slave of imperial despotism had known, that 'to resist was fatal: and it was impossible to fly'.

Thus reinforced the great bill obtained, on the morning of 6 April, the blessing of the Commons. With its swift passage through the Lords and receipt of the Queen's assent, it became, on Easter Eve 10 April 1563, the statute of artificers.

A statute hitherto accepted as unitary in form and content has been resolved, by analysis, into its two components, an initial bill

[1] Above, 75. [2] Cf. 1 Edw. VI c. 1 §2.

of some twenty clauses, and the additions (twenty clauses more) and amendments made during its passage. The omelette being thus unscrambled, the processes which went to its making have next been retraced. What remains to be attempted is an allotment of responsibility for the finished product, and this if possible not simply in terms of 'government' and 'house of commons', but in the sense of individuals or groups within each. This will involve a welcome shift of attention, from the statute and Journal on which it has been so rigidly focused, to other documents and episodes of which the proceedings in 1563 were largely the outcome.

To begin with the governmental side: it is customary to regard both the statute of artificers, and the economic and social measures which accompanied it in 1563, as the culmination of efforts made by Elizabeth's government from the beginning of her reign. There is evidence for this view, both in the parliament of 1559, and during the next four years; but this evidence is both fragmentary and easy to misunderstand, and to elucidate the policy which it exemplifies calls for its re-examination and re-arrangement in intelligible sequence. First in this sequence, as well as perhaps in intrinsic importance, stands the document usually entitled, from one of its two endorsements, 'Considerations delivered to the Parliament 1559'.[1] This remarkable, indeed unique, paper presents, in twenty-four (really twenty-three, since the figure '15' is omitted) numbered paragraphs a comprehensive programme of social and economic regeneration, much of which is to be achieved by the enforcement of old legislation or the passage of new. In what circumstances, and by whom, this was compiled has never been established. Written in a so far unidentified, and probably unidentifiable, hand, and in a language which, while vigorous and colourful, has few idiosyncratic features, it cannot on internal grounds be attributed with any confidence to a known individual; while its ascription to Cecil, which rests chiefly, if not solely, on the location of the only known copy among his papers at Hatfield, cannot be given much weight. Conservatively, even reactionarily paternalistic in outlook, and wide-ranging in its scope, the 'Considerations' give the impression of being an aggregate of similar, but different, opinions, and one is tempted to ascribe

[1] Hatfield MS. 152/96–99*b*, of which, with the permission of the Marquess of Salisbury, I have used the microfilm copy deposited in the B.M.; the version in Hist. MSS. Com. *Salisbury*, i, 162–5, is full and reliable.

them, not to a single person, but to a group addressing its mind collectively to the problems concerned.

Such a group was in being on the eve of the parliamentary session of 1559. Among a number of committees appointed by the privy council on 23 December 1558 was one 'For consideracion of all thinges necessary for the Parlyamente'.[1] Interest in this committee, of which otherwise nothing is known, has hitherto been confined to its possible role in preparing the ecclesiastical measures of the session. Whatever this role may have been—and Sir John Neale himself regards it as a minor one, while the names of the members (which include those of two Catholic judges soon to be demoted) surely point in the same direction—it can scarcely be regarded as having exhausted the committee's wide terms of reference. For, easy as we find it to overlook them, there were other things besides the settlement of religion to be considered in the session of 1559: and when, in the course of that session, the 'Considerations' make their appearance, may we not, without being fanciful, connect them with a committee specifically charged with such 'consideration'? The membership of that committee (lord keeper, judges, serjeants and law officers, with two experienced administrators, Sir Thomas Smith and Richard Goodrich) is certainly consonant with its collective authorship, at least after the removal as *ex officio* members, on 22 January 1559, of the two chief justices, Browne and Saunders. Who but highly-placed lawyers were competent to recommend statutes for confirmation or revision? Who better than Sir Thomas Smith to suggest new ones or than Richard Goodrich to put the proposals in correct religious perspective? Of the aptitude of the lord keeper to head the committee something will be said later.

If the 'Considerations' were literally 'delivered' to parliament, that is presumably to the house of commons, we may infer that this did not happen early in the session, and in all likelihood not before the adjournment of 24 March. Apart from hints in the document itself,[2] what is most suggestive of this is a distinct change in the character of the business dealt with there. Between the opening of parliament (25 January) and its adjournment, there

[1] *Acts of P. C.* 1558–70, 28.

[2] One such is the request, in §16, that the Queen should not grant export licences, which is more likely to have followed than preceded the bill on that subject passed by the Commons on 22 March: *C. J.* i 58*b*.

were few attempts at economic legislation of any kind and only one or two which could conceivably have been inspired by the 'Considerations'.[1] This is, of course, nothing to wonder at: it reflects the preoccupation of everybody concerned with the great problem of Church and State. But during the five weeks following the resumption on 3 April, these other matters came into their own. In that time nine bills of economic interest were introduced in the Commons. They met with varying fortunes: two (apprentices and artisans' fish-days) got no further than a first reading, and three (labourers, flax and hemp, and wine licences) no further than a second, while of the remainder three (iron mills, shipping in English bottoms, and customs) passed and one (export of corn) was rejected.[2] It is hard to believe that this increase of economic-mindedness in a House which had thus far manifested little owed nothing to official encouragement. If the government did point the way, the days following the resumption would have been peculiarly opportune, since the House was then 'marking time' until the new bills of supremacy and uniformity could be introduced: to engage it in some 'matters of commonweal' would help to take its mind off 'matters of state'. This is therefore the point at which the delivery of the 'Considerations' can be fitted in most aptly and where they are most likely to have called forth the bills which began to make their appearance from 7 April. Of none of these bills do we know anything beyond the titles given them in the Journal: but it appears that five of the nine dealt with matters included in the 'Considerations', the remainder with subjects not touched upon there. If the 'Considerations' were in any sense a governmental programme, they did not monopolize the field but rather acted as a catalyst accelerating activity beyond their own range.

Of the subjects of these bills, the two which chiefly interest us, labourers and apprentices, had both appeared in the 'Considerations', the first in the form of a proposal to confirm the statutes of 1388 and 1390 (including wage-assessment by justices of the peace) and to add to them a new 'testimonial' system, the second in a proposal to raise the minimum property qualification of an apprentice's father to 40*s.* a year freehold or, for a merchant's

[1] These were the bills (i) for avoiding of French wares and wines; (ii) for tanners and leather; and (iii) to bring artificers to dwell in market towns: ibid. 53*b*, 54*a*, 54*b*, 55*a*, 55*b*, 56*b*, 57*b*, 58*a*, 58*b*. [2] Ibid. 59*a*, 59*b*, 60*a*, 60*b*, 61*a*.

apprentice, to £10. On 7 April a bill 'touching Order for Men Servants and Women Servants' was read for the first time. Its implied omission of wage provisions, and the fact that it was at once committed (the parallel with the corresponding bill in 1563 will be noted), argue strongly against its having been an official bill based upon the proposal in the 'Considerations'. Its 'committee' was Sir Anthony Cooke, a leading Member and father-in-law to both Cecil and Bacon, and the result was its disappearance in favour of a new bill. This, the bill 'for good order of Servants of Husbandry and Artificers, and their Wages', was read for the first time on 21 April: since it included wage-provisions (although of what nature we cannot say) and was not committed, we may presume that it was officially sponsored. It was read again on 25 April, but that is the last heard of it; since its second reading had not been followed by an order for engrossment, it may have been abandoned, either because of opposition, or simply because of the imminence of dissolution. It had, in any case, got a stage further than its counterpart, the 'Bill for taking and having of Apprentices and Journeyman', which was read for the first time on 18 April, was committed to Sir Nicholas Arnold, and is not heard of again.

Whatever the government's interest in these abortive bills of 1559, their failure faced it with alternative lines of policy. It could either attempt to enforce such statutory controls as it had, even though they were out of date, or it could forego controls until a new parliament enabled it to revise them. A third possibility—which, as we shall see, the government appears to have followed—was to oscillate between the two. The clearest example of a disposition to use existing powers dates from the spring of 1560. On 25 April 1560 the justices of the peace of Northamptonshire, assembled in general sessions at Northampton, drew up a wage-assessment for various categories of workpeople in the shire. In compiling the first shire-assessment for—so far as is known—more than a century, the J.P.s adhered closely to the system (in regard to categories of workers, the assessment of wages with and without meals, the division of the year at Michaelmas, Easter and harvest, and the penalty for non-compliance) prescribed by the latest of the labour statutes then in force, that of 1515:[1] but their wage-rates were uniformly somewhat higher than the maximum rates authorized by that act. This makes it almost certain that they were

[1] 7 Hen. VIII c. 5.

acting on the authority of the privy council: they were certainly acting with the knowledge of the lord chief justice, at whose suggestion at least one of the rates was fixed.[1] The uniqueness of this episode, which has no known parallel during these years, suggests that it was an experiment on the lines proposed in the 'Considerations', but without any new statutory basis. If so, there is, as we shall see, reason to believe that by the following year the experiment had been abandoned. To explain why, we should need to know whether, or how far, the Northamptonshire assessment was enforced, and with what result: and nothing of this sort is known. But it is not difficult to imagine that enforcement, if attempted, proved difficult or impossible. The advance on the maximum rates of 1515 certainly appears incommensurate with the concurrent rise in prices: yet even these modest increases would have had, on a strict reading of the statute of 1515, no legal foundation.

But the circumstance most likely to have given the Northamptonshire experiment the appearance of a false start was the decision, taken within the next few months, to restore the coinage. It is possible that the state of the currency had already influenced proceedings on economic matters in the parliament of 1559. For if, as enlightened opinion would have it, currency debasement lay at the root of most, if not all, economic ills, was it not there, rather than in new laws, that remedial action should begin? In such action parliament could, of course, have no share, since the mint was a branch of the prerogative: this is doubtless why the 'Considerations' are silent on the point. But it would have been strange if, when wage-control was under discussion in a House which included the author of 'The Discourse of the Commonweal', no-one had mentioned, first, the rise in prices, and then the state of the coinage. The government had, in fact, taken the first official step towards reform with the issue of a commission of investigation on 4 February 1559. How far this fact was known, indeed whether the commission was timed to meet or forestall parliamentary criticism, we cannot say. But those who did know may well have set more store by this move than by the prospect of new wage-assessments. That the Queen and her advisers believed, or professed to believe, in the efficacy of currency reform to bring

[1] Bertha H. Putnam, 'Northamptonshire Wage Assessments of 1560 and 1667' (*Econ. Hist. Rev.* I), 124–34.

down prices appears from the proclamation of 27 September 1560, by which, after eighteen months of preparation, the impending recoinage was announced. This listed among its objectives 'the relief and comfort of all that be herewith oppressed', and 'speciallye of Pensioners, souldyers, and all hyred servantes, and other meane people that lyve by any kynde of wages, and not by rentes of landes, or trade of merchaundyse'.[1]

If the summer of 1561 thus found the country beginning to enjoy, for the first time in nearly twenty years, the boon of a sound currency, it also saw the first attempt to grapple afresh with a wide range of other economic and social problems. What may have been a first, and abortive, project is represented by a draft commission to selected J.P.s in every shire to enquire into the execution of certain statutes, accompanied by 'articles and instructions' setting out elaborate arrangements for the presentment and indictment of offenders by representatives of every hundred and parish. The statutes to be inquired into were those concerning usury, tillage, regrators and forestallers, apparel, retainers and liveries, clerical non-residence, pluralities and leases, nonlawful games, and the provision of horses.[2] It was perhaps as a simpler alternative to this scheme that there was dispatched, in the course of the same summer, a new list of statutes for the justices to attend to, backed this time by a council letter, not a special commission. These, the 'sertayne penall statutes to be enquiring off' mentioned in William Tyldesley's well-known letter to Cecil of 3 September 1561,[3] can be enumerated as follows: alehouses, apprentices, archery, plays and games, rebellion, regrators and forestallers, tillage, victuals and wood, wines, vagabonds, retainers, robberies, slanderous tales, highways, and preservation of grain.[4] In his letter Tyldesley, an official at Windsor Castle who lived at Burnham and was a Buckinghamshire J.P., gave a frankly despondent account of its reception and prospects in his own and one or two neighbouring shires.

A comparison of the fifteen subjects named in 1561 with those

[1] *Tudor Economic Documents*, ii, 196.

[2] B.M. Harl. MSS. 589 ff. 310–15; corrected in Cecil's hand. Professor Putnam mistook this for the council letter: loc. cit. 127 *n* 2.

[3] *Tudor Economic Documents*, i, 334–8.

[4] The writer has not found a list of the statutes circulated in 1561; the list given is taken from a later one, which appears to consist of the list of 1561 with additions: B.M. Lansd. 105 ff. 187–190*b*.

recommended for attention in the 'Considerations' shows four in common: apprentices, tillage, vagabonds and wines. The most significant omission is that of any of the statutes of labourers, upon which, after the failure to legislate in 1559, a revived wage-assessment system would have to rest; and this is the more striking in that apprenticeship, the other topic mentioned in the 'Considerations' which had given rise to an unsuccessful bill in 1559, was included.[1] It is hard to believe that a council which in 1561 still believed in the utility of assessing wages would have omitted it from the programme. Fifteen months before an effort had been made in one shire to revive the system, but it seems to have been neither copied nor persisted in. Is not the likeliest explanation that the attempt had failed, and that it was adjudged not worth repeating, at least until the effects of currency reform had shown themselves?

But Tyldesley appended to his report on the penal statutes something which purports to be, and has been taken for, a set of wage-assessments and other labour regulations drawn up by the Buckinghamshire justices.[2] If it were so, it would be hard to reconcile with a waning of interest in the system. The appendix is, however, almost certainly not a record of decisions made. It begins by stating that the justices had assembled themselves by the Queen's special command, but not when or where they did so; and it does not even name the shire concerned. It is written, as is the letter itself, in Tyldesley's hand, and is endorsed, by Cecil, 'Mr. Tyldesley', which scarcely accords with its being an official report; and there is no reference in the letter to any such special meeting of the justices. But the conclusive argument against its acceptance as a record of *res acta* is the nature of certain of the orders which it contains: for some of these, like the penalty of a year's imprisonment or presentation before the council for giving wages higher than those assessed, there was no clear authority in statute law, while others, notably the enforcement of attendance at common prayer, did not lie within the competence of justices of the peace.[3] In the light of all this we must conclude that what Tyldesley sent to Cecil was simply a draft of his own devising. He

[1] The statute cited was 7 Hen. IV c. 17.

[2] So entitled in *Tudor Economic Documents*, i, 334, and so treated by Professor Putnam, loc. cit. 127 sqq.

[3] By the act of uniformity, 1 Eliz. c. 2 §§16, 20, proceedings for non-attendance at common prayer were to be heard before justices of assize.

may well have known of the assessment made the previous year in neighbouring Northamptonshire and, on receipt of the council's instructions to enforce the penal statutes, have been moved to compile both an assessment and such other regulations as he judged necessary to deal with social and religious indiscipline in his own shire. There is nothing to suggest that his initiative was either prompted by the council or followed by any action on its part.

On the contrary, the case for revising the labour laws before attempting to enforce them is likely to have been strengthened by another departure of 1561. This was the distribution throughout the shires, in addition to the list of penal statutes, of an 'abbreviate' of statutes, to such good effect as to warrant its re-issue the following year.[1] If, as is probable, this extended to the statutes of labour, the scrutiny which this involved could scarcely have failed to clinch the argument for revision. Something else may also have played its part—the council's determination to improve the tone of the commissions of the peace by reducing their size. It was in June 1561 that Cecil drafted a letter (which Bacon lightly amended) to the justices of assize foreshadowing this reduction and calling for recommendations for deletion.[2] Temporarily withheld as premature, this instruction was implemented in the following autumn, with the result that the new commissions issued in February 1562 show a marked reduction in size.[3]

The parliament which was to give the country its new statute of labour, although not summoned until November 1562 and not opened until January 1563, had been in prospect since the previous summer.[4] Its principal object was to finance military intervention in the French religious war, but its subsidiary one, laconically described by Cecil himself as 'reviving of some old laws for penalties of some fellonyes',[5] was to embrace the largest output of social legislation so far achieved in one session. What the government's intentions were likely to be with regard to labour-control may

[1] R. Steele, *Tudor and Stuart Proclamations*, no. 565. Professor Putnam appears to be in error in identifying this 'abbreviate' with the list of penal statutes.

[2] S.P. 12/17/100–1.

[3] A. H. Smith, 'The Gentry of Elizabethan Norfolk: Office-holding and Faction' (London Univ. Ph. D. thesis, 1959), 73–74.

[4] Notes by Cecil, ?Aug. 1562, include 'parlament summoned ageynst allhallowtyd': S.P. 12/24/37*b*.

[5] T. Wright, *Queen Elizabeth and her Times*, i, 121.

be inferred from its experience since 1559. Belief that the wage-problem would disappear with the reform of the coinage must have worn pretty thin, and although there might be other grounds for legislation, its heart and core would be, as ever, the control of wages. This, in turn, meant cutting the Gordian knot formed by the two strands of a national maximum wage-level and local maxima which tended to surpass it, a feat only to be performed by the sword-stroke of repeal. Something, too, was likely to be done about apprenticeship, although probably only of a modest and confirmatory kind. But above all, the indications point to a measure conceived in the spirit of the past, a past in which the problems of a relatively simple and predominantly rural society could be met by correspondingly simple and agrarian-minded regulation.

From this sketch of governmental policy between 1559 and 1563 we turn to the question: who, in this respect, was the 'government'? It is a question to which historians have had, for close on half a century, but one answer: William Cecil. This extension to the economic field of the omnipotence already conceded to Cecil in the politics and diplomacy of the reign[1] was largely the work of Professor Lilian Knowles, whose appraisal of Cecil's economic statesmanship[2] seems to have lulled her successors into the comfortable belief that everything not otherwise explained could safely be attributed to him. It would, of course, be absurd to deny Cecil a share, even a considerable share, in economic policy-making: but that his influence was as paramount and pervasive as has come to be supposed is open to serious question. In the case under discussion, for instance, it will be readily granted that his authorship of the 'Considerations', if it were established, would by itself imply prime responsibility for the measures which followed that far-reaching programme. But there is no proof that the 'Considerations' owed more to Cecil than preservation among his papers, along with much else which certainly cannot be ascribed to him; nor is there anything to connect him with the bills introduced in 1559. The Northamptonshire wage-assessment of the following spring may have owed something to him (for he was a Northamptonshire man), although its only hint of influence from above is a mention, not of Cecil, but of Chief Justice Catlin. In the restoration of the coinage in 1560–61, as in the campaign of the following

[1] Above, 13. [2] Cunningham, *Industry and Commerce*, 6th ed. ii (1), 53–84.

summer to enforce penal statutes, Cecil was certainly prominent: but, as has been suggested, neither of these necessarily implies enthusiasm for labour-control, to which both were, in a sense, alternatives.

To see Cecil's hand in most of these things is to reckon in probability, not to deduce from evidence. Moreover, once it is accepted that other names besides his are worth considering, more than one spring to mind: that, for instance, of Sir Thomas Smith, a member of the committee of December 1558, and a man of ripe experience and economic acumen.[1] But if any single claim is worth setting against Cecil's, it is that of his brother-in-law and fellow-councillor, Sir Nicholas Bacon. In general Bacon may be thought at least as likely as Cecil to have concerned himself with these problems at the outset of the reign, and he cannot well have had less time for them than a Secretary who was straightway submerged by a torrent of other business. But it is pointers, not possibilities, which are to seek, and there are some turned in Bacon's direction. Whatever the committee of December 1558 produced was produced under Lord Keeper Bacon's eye: and if it included the 'Considerations' their debt to him may range from general oversight to at least part-authorship. The proposals to foster education, and in particular the education of noblemen and gentlemen; to restrict entry to the profession of law; to punish bankrupts and perjurers; and to give every shire its own sheriff; all these have a Baconian ring, and the first of them was to inspire an enlightened memorial from Bacon to Cecil in the following year.[2] The remainder is less suggestive of him (although the commercial proposals, and especially the proviso for the status of London aldermen and sheriffs, put us in mind of his close links with the city);[3] but it is just these differences of interest and outlook which suggest a committee origin.

In the parliament of 1559, as in that of 1563, Bacon presided as lord keeper. Apart from his speeches to the assembled Houses which in 1559 contained no clear allusion to such matters, he could not participate directly, as Cecil could, in the business of the

[1] Mary Dewar, 'The Career and Writings of Sir Thomas Smith, 1513–1577' (London Univ. Ph.D. thesis, 1956).

[2] B.M. Add. MSS. 32379 ff. 26 sqq.; cf. J. Hurstfield, *The Queen's Wards*, 25–26.

[3] Before becoming lord keeper he lived in Noble Street, Foster Lane; his younger brother James, a merchant, was elected alderman in 1567 and appointed sheriff in 1568: *D.N.B.*

Commons, and there is no hint of any initiative in them by the Lords. But between this parliament and the next Bacon may well have contributed towards what was to be, in the field of labour legislation, the capital decision of 1563, the decision to codify. Among his reforming interests the task of simplifying and publicizing statute law took a leading place. May we not therefore see his hand at work in the 'abbreviate' issued in 1561 and 1562? What the scope of that enterprise was we do not know, but if it included the statutes of labour it cannot have failed to reveal, or at least to confirm, their chaotic state and so to strengthen the twin arguments, the one against their enforcement, at a time when prices, and with them wages, might be expected to fall, and the other in favour of their drastic overhaul as need and opportunity arose. It was the second of these which Bacon must surely have been forecasting when, in his speech at the opening of the parliament of 1563, he invited his hearers to consider, 'if there be not too many laws for one thing, and those so large and busie, that neither the Commons can understand the same, nor yet well the Lawyer, which would be brought into some briefer and better Order, and there Executed'.[1]

Of individual responsibility for the preparation and management in the House of the resulting bill there is scarcely a trace. Whereas the hand of Cecil is evident enough in some of the other measures,[2] the Secretary's sole allusion to the artificers bill is so puzzling as to provoke suspicion that he was not *au fait* with its progress.[3] The grounds for Bacon's connection with it are purely inferential. Relieved of his judicial duties, within three weeks of the opening of the session, by the appointment of a commission to hear cases in his absence,[4] Bacon (unlike Cecil) was free to devote himself to business in parliament, where his prominence in the great matter of the succession may have been matched by care of less spectacular items.[5] Was it by coincidence that the first two committees on the artificers bill were headed by Sir William

[1] D'Ewes, *Journal*, 60*b*. [2] Conyers Read, *Cecil and Elizabeth*, 270–5.

[3] 'There is also a very good law agreed uppon for indifferent allowances for servants' wages in husbandry' (Cecil to Smith, 27 Feb. 1563: Wright, *Elizabeth and her Times*, i, 126). On that date the artificers bill had been read once only and was in the hands of Seckford's committee: to call it 'agreed upon' reflects either optimism or ignorance. Wright dates the letter correctly.

[4] *Cal. Pat.* 1560–63, 621–2.

[5] Including, no doubt, the act 5 Eliz. c. 18 declaring the authority of the lord keeper to be the same as that of the chancellor.

Cordell, who as master of the rolls was Bacon's subordinate colleague in chancery, and Thomas Seckford, master of requests, another law officer moving within the lord keeper's sphere of jurisdiction? If it was Cordell who was responsible, in the eyes of the House, for the drafting of the 'official' bill of 24 February, he may well have performed that task under Bacon's supervision. There are features of the statute, if not of the bill, which may reflect this relationship: who but the lord keeper could have made his own court the clearing-house of wage-assessments?[1] And in conclusion we may wonder whether, without the help of an interested lord keeper, the bill would have survived its scrambling passage through the Lords or the unavoidable lack of royal scrutiny which, it seems, doomed four other belated bills.[2]

Enough—perhaps too much—has been said in support of Bacon's claim to be considered the 'author' of the artificers bill of 24 February. For of much greater importance than that is the fact that neither Bacon, nor Cecil, nor any royal councillor, can make a similar claim in respect of the additions and amendments which were to transform that bill into the statute: the credit for these must go unmistakably to the house of commons. It was that body which, in the course of five readings and two committals, took the provisions laid before it and expanded and refined them to twice their number and many times their sophistication. The fact is of undoubted importance: but it should not be found surprising. For has not Sir John Neale buried, once and for all, the legend that the Commons of 1563, or of any of Elizabeth's early parliaments, was the instrument for passing or rejecting, with no more than a token of independence, whatever bills the councillors in its midst promoted or disfavoured? This, he has demonstrated, was far from true even of those 'matters of state' which the Queen sought to guard most jealously. How, then, should it have been true of a 'matter of commonweal' which all agreed was a proper object of parliamentary initiative?

The Commons' manhandling of the official bill, and the resulting

[1] By clause 11 wage-assessments were to be submitted to the lord chancellor or lord keeper and by him brought before the privy council for approval before their publication.

[2] Neale, *Elizabeth and Parliament, 1559–1581*, 128. On the morning of 10 April, the day of prorogation, Cecil sent Smith a list of bills which he expected to receive the Queen's assent that afternoon (B.M. Lansd. 102 f. 33); if this list was the same as that in B.M. Lansd. 145 ff. 184–184*b*, it included the artificers bill but omitted 9 public and 17 private bills which did receive assent.

changes in it, took place in three discernible stages. There was the argument, at the first reading on 24 February, over the wage-provisions, which provoked the first committal; then came the debate of 3 March on compulsory service and apprenticeship, and the drastic overhauling of this part of the bill through its second committal; last came the readings of 2 and 6 April, at which further additions and changes were made. Of no one of these episodes, of course, is there a scrap of direct evidence: and lacking its guidance we cannot penetrate more than a step or two into the obscurity which surrounds them. Of the first the little there is to say has already been said.[1] It was, surely, the country gentlemen who were most likely to bristle at the wage-clauses: town magistracus were more accustomed to assessing wages and urban workers to being told what they should earn. But we can only guess at the amendments which were made and hence at the objectives of attack.

With the compulsory service and apprenticeship clauses we can do better. The nine new apprenticeship clauses were the largest and most significant addition made to the bill at any stage. They expanded and amended the two or three clauses of the official bill in three main ways: first, by developing the traditional 'eligibility' rule into a system of graded occupations, each with its appropriate means-test; second, by extending to all occupations the element of compulsion which the official bill had confined to agriculture; third, and most notably, by making the seven-year term universal. That these novel provisions of the statute should have originated not, as has always been assumed, with the government but with the House is a fact of great significance both in itself and in its implications. For not only does it put the credit for them where that rightly belongs, it also illustrates the greater competence of the House than of the Queen's ministers to legislate on such a topic, and the different outlook which it manifested. The apprenticeship clauses of the official bill had been chiefly directed to extending that status to agriculture, and in that they were well suited to a bill which was traditional, that is to say, agrarian, in character. The corresponding clauses of the statute, by shifting the emphasis from agriculture to industry and trade, and in particular by depriving the first of that monopoly of compulsory apprenticeship with which the official bill had sought to invest it, asserted the

[1] Above, 74–76.

claims of these growing branches of the country's economy to share in the assumed benefits of national regulation. In line with these changes was the simultaneous extension of the compulsory service clause to a wide range of occupations: in a time of labour scarcity the land was not to be allowed first claim on all surplus labour.

At this stage of the bill's evolution we may guess that it was the businessmen in the House, were they the rank-and-file of burgesses viewing the subject in a local context, or the bigger men seeing it in wider if no less self-interested terms, who dominated the scene. A stray allusion made fifty years later to the presence of outside experts at the committees on the bill may either reflect a fact of which there is no contemporary evidence or imaginatively credit the past with a practice which had only come in later.[1] It would scarcely have been necessary in the House of 1563, with its phalanx of provincial burgesses and its dozen or so merchants, among them such notables as John Marsh, governor of the Merchant Adventurers, alderman Lawrence Withers, John Gresham, and Stephen Hales, brother of the turbulent clerk of the hanaper (who also sat). Such men commanded the *expertise* needed to tailor the system of apprenticeship to the national cloth. But which of them applied it to the task in hand, and to what particular effect—that, alas! it is beyond our power to say. For even though it is possible to trace the origin of certain of the new clauses (with the aid of their idiosyncratic date of commencement, the Feast of St. John Baptist next) to the only surviving draft bill of this session which can thus be linked with the artificers bill, this draft bill too is by an unknown member.[2]

In the final stage, when at two readings six further clauses were added and many amendments made, it must have been the 'die-hards' among all groups of Members who, in a House rapidly thinning after a gruelling session, remained to put the finishing

[1] In Tolley's Case, 1615: *Tudor Economic Documents*, i, 381–2.

[2] S.P. 12/27/212–19. This cannot be identified with any bill recorded in the Commons Journal. Besides the features linking it with the new apprenticeship clauses, this bill is the most likely source of §§2 and 3 of the statute. Its preamble denounces the proneness of apprentices with 'mercers, woollen and linen drapers, haberdashers, grocers, cappers, skinners, tailors, hosiers, weavers and fullers', to forsake those occupations for merchandising: this list of trades bears a close resemblance to those occurring early (and thus presumably originally) in the list in §2, and suggests that the motive of this clause, and §3, was to deter apprentices and workers in these trades from becoming merchants.

touches to a bill in which they could by then feel a proprietary interest. For it was a much changed bill from that which they had heard for the first time nearly six weeks before. Originally designed to codify, but not substantially to change, the legislation of the past two centuries, that bill had been given a 'new look' by the House under whose scrutiny it had to pass. Whatever truth there is in the criticism that the statute of artificers was out of date before it was passed, that criticism attaches first and principally to the royal councillors, Cecil, Bacon, Cordell or any other, who gave it so markedly antiquarian a flavour. But the statute was by no means a mere anachronism, and whatever it had which was new and forward-looking it owed to the house of commons.

IV

Place and Patronage in Elizabethan Politics[1]

WALLACE T. MacCAFFREY

THE political history of England in the sixteenth century is given continuity by the consistent efforts of the successive Tudor monarchs to assert, to maintain, and to expand royal authority in the realm. But the particular pattern which sovereignty assumed was determined by the differing characteristics of the individual rulers, whose successive reigns gave a marked but uneven rhythm to the tempo of Tudor politics. In a society which lacked the continuing momentum of party within the political world at large, and of bureaucracy within the government itself, a new monarch might by his own will radically alter the political milieu.

Since the battle of Bosworth (perhaps since Tewkesbury) a series of such innovations had occurred. Henry VII had opened the doors of political opportunity to a wider range of men than before, particularly to the landed gentry. His son continued this policy, and after 1529 vastly expanded the rewards and opportunities open to the successful politician. These monarchs went far in altering the qualifications for a political career. The factious war-lords of the fifteenth century had required the brutal skills of the armed retainer, half-soldier, half-gangster: now it was the suppler skills of the courtier, suave and persuasive, or the administrator, clear-headed and literate, which were in demand. At the same time there occurred what might be called the 'nationalization' of politics. The person of the monarch became the focus of a single, national political world with centripetal force powerful enough to draw into its orbit all rivalries, personal, local, or dynastic. Thus, centralization of political life accompanied a new

[1] The writer is indebted to the John Simon Guggenheim Memorial Foundation whose Fellowship made possible the research on which this study is based.

sophistication in the political arts and a striking growth in the number of their practitioners. The revolutionary change of the Henrician Reformation added another ingredient. Unwittingly Henry introduced that very diversity of opinion which he so abhorred. How virulent and how fast-growing the bacillus of religious disputation could be was to be vividly illustrated in the reigns of Henry's son and his elder daughter. The polarization of English politics into bitterly-opposed ideological camps was yet a century away, but from the mid-sixteenth century ideology became an increasingly disturbing element in English political life.

At Elizabeth's accession she and her ministers had to face not only these changing circumstances but also some very immediate and pressing problems. The chaotic decade since the death of the Queen's father had seriously disordered the English political scene. Quite apart from the careening course of religious policy, the absence of a strong royal personality had turned the political world into an arena where no prizes (not even the Crown) were out of reach, but where there was no security for the life, liberty, or property of the contestants. Mary had eliminated the worst of this disorder, but had failed to achieve commanding control over the political scene. Hence, among other problems demanding solution by the new government, the restoration of a sure centre of political gravity was imperative.

The firm grasp of the new Queen was speedily felt, but it was more than a decade before the tremors of uncertainty receded. A weary Cecil, worrying over the succession problem in 1564, wished the Queen would so act 'that either by her marriage, or by some common order, we poor subjects may know where to lean and adventure our lives with contentation of our consciences'.[1] Only after the crisis of 1569–72 did politics assume the shape which they were to retain as long as the Elizabethan generation survived —until the mid 'nineties. But the stability of the middle Elizabethan years rested on a foundation quite different from that of the Henrician monarchy. Elizabeth's government was, in the strictest sense, monarchical. All decisions depended ultimately upon the pleasure of the sovereign lady. Only the uncertain boundaries of constitutional tradition or the spasmodic recalcitrance of parliament could hinder that imperious will; and the authoritarian and paternalistic tradition of the state made very wide the scope

[1] T. Wright, *Queen Elizabeth and her times*, i, 173.

of royal intervention. Yet, paradoxically, Elizabeth and her ministers were as sensitive to every nuance of public feeling, every tremor of discontent, within the limited range of the politically active classes, as any modern democratic government is to the reactions of its electorate. For the fateful weakness of this fragile regime was its lack of coercive power. The absence of either a professional army or a paid bureaucracy left it without the final arbiters of forceful compulsion.

Hence the Elizabethan monarchy, outwardly a system of power of majestic simplicity, in fact rested on a curiously complex foundation, its maintenance requiring the most assiduous practice of the arts of political persuasion. The stability of the system demanded the arduous and constant wooing of the body politic. Those conventions of the late medieval world which presumed obedience to constituted authority as a fact of nature were skilfully exploited by a government which made obedience to the sovereign a cult, preached by parson, poet, and magistrate alike. Elizabeth herself, well-endowed for the role of goddess-queen, gave a glowing vitality to the myth by the whole-hearted exercise of her immense talents. Above all, the Queen and her ministers showed uncommon skill in tailoring the difficult but inescapable decisions of the reign to the views and interests of the dominant groupings in English society.

But the monarchy rested also on the substantial pillars of its capacity to reward and to advance its supporters. It secured men's loyal service not only by appeals to their moral sense or through the wiles of the royal charmer but also by offering them material advantages. By the expert sharing of those gifts of office, prestige, or wealth at its command, the government could secure the continuing goodwill of the politically pre-eminent classes. To apply the term 'patronage' to this process is perhaps confusing unless it is given special definition. Clearly it cannot be used in its Hanoverian sense. The Georgian statesman used patronage to establish a working arrangement between Crown and parliament. Agreement between the Crown (or its agent) and a small group of leading politicians could bring order to the whole political scene. And the system had the additional virtue of dissipating the vapours of discontent: the fluidity of its operation gave the disappointed office-seeker of today hope for better things in the inevitable re-grouping of forces tomorrow.

The Tudor situation was at once freer and more rigid. The Crown was far less restrained in its decision-making capacity, but it had to reckon constantly on the possibility of violent resistance. The discontented politician, instead of resorting to the pacific manœuvres of parliamentary intrigue, might be tempted into conspiracy and treason. Already in 1565 an embittered Norfolk was writing to Cecil, mournful that the Queen thought so little of him, resentful of a suit denied, and ending with the sulky declaration that 'Her Highness hardly thinks anything well bestowed on me, be it never so small'.[1] Sir Henry Percy, approached by the Ridolfi conspirators, had initially rejected them, saying that if he were well used in England, he would not move actively for Mary. But when he saw his hopes of the earldom of Northumberland go glimmering, he quickly switched sides.[2] Only unsleeping vigilance and, when necessary, unhesitating use of force crushed the successive conspiracies against the Elizabethan regime.

But a broad preventive policy was also adopted. By wide distribution of favour the Crown and its ministers sought to link to themselves the interests and the hopes of the great majority of the English governing class. They strove to keep down the number of those whose discontents or disappointments under the existing order would draw them towards the nuclei of treason within the realm. It was a patronage which aimed not at the adherence of a party or a faction but at the goodwill and confidence of a whole class. It was the policy urged upon the Queen in 1579, 'That you gratify your nobility and the principal persons of your realm to bind them fast to you with such things as have heretofore been cast away upon them that in time of need can serve you to no purpose, whereby you shall have all men of value in your realm to depend only upon yourself'.[3]

The politically active class of the late sixteenth century was virtually the first generation of that compact yet flexible 'aristocracy' which in another hundred years would elbow aside the monarchy and in the eighteenth century would enjoy a golden age of uncontested power and privilege. Under Elizabeth it was still in its hesitant infancy. Numerically it was small: Burghley's working lists give us some clue to its size. He counted no more

[1] S. Haynes and W. Murdin, *Burghley Papers*, i, 442.

[2] Hist. MSS. Com. *Salisbury*, i, 536. [3] Haynes and Murdin, op cit. ii, 340.

than a hundred names among the inner core of county notables, peers and gentlemen, in a paper drawn up in 1579.[1] A more generous estimate, which included, roughly speaking, all county tax-payers assessed at £20 a year, or more in land, listed above 800 names.[2] Another relevant figure is the total number of justices of the peace in England and Wales, about 1,500 in the year 1587.[3] If we allow for younger sons and for those other aspirants just ready to enter the political lists, we arrive at a total of about 2,500.

This was a political society of which most of the members knew one other directly or indirectly and were almost all personally known to the leading ministers. The importance of that great magnet, the court, in drawing gentry from all over England into a common social circle cannot be over-estimated. Parliament performed a similar function as a social nucleus. These men shared a new conception of politics as a career. The more ambitious saw before them not only the hope of personal success but also the alluring possibilities of lasting family fortune and consequence. The example of a Russell, a Paulet, or a Clinton showed the path to permanent lodgment in the ranks of the élite. Secondly, the connection between local politics and national became more and more evident. Perceptive men saw how their local aspirations might be promoted, their local consequence inflated, by the right kind of court connection.

The range of expectation, the bounds of hope, were as varied as in any fairly sophisticated political society. Inherited place had, of course, much to do with the matter. At the apex of society the sixty-odd peers enjoyed the largest natural advantages. True, the Tudors were apt to treat them with a certain coldness, even suspicion, and only rarely admitted them to the innermost circle of power about the throne. But Elizabeth was a jealous guardian of their privileges and dignity and offered them ample occupation as military commanders, lords lieutenant, ambassadors of honour, and magistrates. Their privileges were large, and they moved in an atmosphere of almost reverential respect in a society which

[1] B.M. Lansd. 683.

[2] 'Principal gentlemen in the shires from collectors' rolls of 1581': B.M. Lansd. 32 no. 27; Burghley once scolded collectors of the subsidy for under-assessing gentlemen: 'If any in commission of the peace assess themselves under £20 they may look to receive the disgrace to be put out of the commission:' F. C. Dietz, *The Exchequer in Elizabeth's reign* (Smith College Studies in History, viii, no. 2), 76.

[3] B.M. Lansd. 91 (*c.* 1587).

self-consciously glorified hereditary rank. Their political ambitions were for the most part limited in scope and conventional in method. Few could be found to lend active support to the somewhat half-hearted ventures of Norfolk, Arundel, or the northern earls; fewer still to join in Essex's ill-advised attempt. They were more concerned to preserve or augment their interests by the conventional methods of marriage or royal favour. A royal servant, reporting on Shrewsbury's expectations whilst that nobleman was custodian of the queen of Scots, wrote: 'I think this would content him: £200 land in fee-farm and that it would please Her Majesty to bestow the reversion of such offices as he hath upon his children as Queen Mary did to him after his father's death.'[1] The Earl well represented the timid conservatism of the majority of his order.

Certain prizes were the perquisites of the nobility—the Garter, ceremonial embassies to foreign royalties, but above all the lord lieutenancies. These last were an assurance and an outward sign of that regional pre-eminence which was perhaps dearest of all to the English nobleman's heart. The seventh earl of Shrewsbury grieved bitterly when the Queen confirmed his late father's lieutenancy of Nottinghamshire to him but withheld that of Derbyshire.[2] The earl of Derby irritably complained of 'directions for matters in this county [Lancashire] wherein I am not writ unto, as I ever was when my father was alive; I must marvel at it'.[3] In fact neither Lord Derby nor his fellows had much cause for complaint; the government, in distributing lieutenancies, paid attention to noble sensibilities and conformed its arrangements to the facts of social geography.

Next below the peers in social rank and not unlike them in outlook were the greater gentry of the counties, those wealthy, established families whose local leadership was recognized and whose possessions were equal to their pretensions—Mores, Harringtons, or Holleses; Cromwells, Gawdys, or Spencers. Here again was a group likely to be preoccupied with its traditional perquisites: knighthoods, deputy-lieutenancies, the commission of the peace, the shrievalty, the knighthood of the shire in parliament. The heads of such families were not obliged to seek high place at court, but it was important for them to keep open their lines of

[1] Hist. MSS. Com. *Salisbury*, ii, 446.
[2] P. R. O. Talbot MSS. (Longleat) Transcripts, letter 133.
[3] Hist. MSS. Com. *Salisbury*, iv, 411; cf. ibid. v, 340; vi, 294.

connection. This could be done either by securing a minor post at court (one which did not require regular attendance) or by placing a younger member there. He could at once serve the family interest and pursue his own career. The gentlemen pensioners came increasingly to be filled with men of this type.[1]

Naturally the greediest and most restless were those with the least in hand and the most to wish for—the great army of younger brothers, or the jostling crowd of lesser gentry, men with little patrimony or none at all, either threatened with the loss of status or desperately anxious to attain it. For them politics was a career in a much more urgent sense than for their luckier fellows. The opportunities for making a living open to them were limited. A soldier's life offered little but short-term service at small pay. Walsingham, writing of an applicant for an Irish presidency in 1575, said: 'If he lived in any other country than this, where martial men presently bear no price, he should not have been so long kept underfoot.'[2] (It was not until late in the reign that the Low Countries and Ireland gave increased scope for a professional military career.) The navy held out little more opportunity to an untrained gentleman. Of the two learned professions, the Church was probably somewhat in disrepute among the higher classes and in any case offered its prizes only to those of considerable learning, while the law required a formidable and special erudition and commanding talent. Again, trade, although possible, demanded special capabilities, and probably, the right connections. For the young man of good birth, poor estate, and average talents a political career was the obvious choice. He viewed entrance into the Queen's service not as a bold bid for fame and fortune but as a prosaic and workaday matter of making a living. The minority, endowed with administrative talents, would win the favour of Burghley or some other great minister and move on to the solid respectability and substantial rewards of an official career. A still smaller group, gifted with poise, wit, and a comely person, would catch the Queen's eye and might then aspire to riches, possessions, title, even to a place in the circle of sovereignty. But these glittering prizes were for the very few and but fool's gold to many of them.

One other political type deserves passing mention—the man of conviction, for whom office or influence meant the chance to

[1] Gervase Holles, *Memorials of the Holles Family* (Camd. Soc. 3rd ser. iv), 94–95.
[2] A. Collins, *Sidney Papers*, i, 70–71.

advance an ideal. New to the English scene, he was no favourite with the Queen; but Walsingham, the second Lord Bedford, Huntingdon, Knollys, or at a lower level, Beale, Hales, or Morice, are examples of the single-minded Protestant idealist.[1] And for a surprisingly large proportion of the politically minded, some tinge of austere Protestant feeling was an integral feature of their outlook.

In the context of monarchy the types later familiar to a parliamentary regime are already apparent. The established magnate for whom politics is a secondary but essential part of life; the daring aspirant, soaring for the greatest prizes; the plodding placeman seeking a secure living; the zealot, the dedicated agent of the Divine Will—all join the cast on the political stage. This was the clientele whose goodwill was a major preoccupation of the Elizabethan political managers. On their co-operation as its servants, paid or unpaid, depended both the political stability and the effective functioning of the Elizabethan state.

From the beginning of the reign Elizabeth and her ministers carefully husbanded their resources of patronage in a manner strikingly in contrast with the preceding twenty years. The last half-dozen years of Henry VIII's reign had seen a notable burgeoning of political opportunity and a great expansion of the rewards of success. Monastic spoils were available for the founding of family fortunes at the same moment that the King reversed earlier policy and began a generous distribution of new titles. Edward VI's reign provided unmatched opportunities for consolidating these gains by a grander spoliation of the Church and rapid promotion in the peerage. Elizabeth, while protecting the interests of the Edwardian *arrivistes*, kept a firm and economical hand on the distribution of new royal favour. Even for a Dudley there was a limit to the royal bounty. An element of dignity and restraint was restored to the political scene when it became clear that the sovereign would not easily yield to the importunities of suitors and that the government's resources would be expended shrewdly and only in return for value received. This perhaps meant a narrowing of opportunity for the political aspirant, but it restored a sense of proportion to the political scene. Under these conditions

[1] e.g. Hales to Cecil, Mar. 1565, urging George Bromley as attorney to the duchy of Lancaster to 'win the hearts of a great many Protestants who are now discouraged [but] will take hope if they hear a Protestant lawyer beareth some authority in Westminster Hall': B.M. Lansd. 9 no. 8.

men were less likely to panic for fear of losing what they had or to gamble desperately for great prizes at long odds.

This principle of economy was applied in the management of the entire stock of royal patronage. The fund was not, all told, an immense one, and with careless management it could have been, as under the Stuarts, all too easily dissipated. Of what did it consist? Perhaps greatest in outward consequence were the grants of honour—peerages, the orders of chivalry, knighthoods. Of more practical importance were the offices at the Crown's disposal, posts in the court and household, the administrative and legal branches of government, the military establishment, the Church and the administration of royal lands. Third came a more miscellaneous category, the whole range of special favours in the gift of the Queen, exemptions, annuities, monopolies, farms, leases, and gifts.

Of grants of honours not much need be said. The first two Tudors had been sparing in the creation of titles, but Henry VIII in the last few years of his reign had suddenly raised up a nursery of new noble houses, and the circumstances of Edward's reign had enabled this group to advance and proliferate. Elizabeth returned to the older Tudor policy, and by the infrequency of her creations[1] made each peerage a gift doubly to be prized. Like a modern gem monopolist she maintained the value of the commodity by enforced scarcity, and without cost to herself increased the value of the assets at her disposal. If some were disappointed in their hopes, a larger number were kept free of the rather dangerous envy excited by the profligate bounty of James I. Knighthood remained an inexpensive but useful token of royal favour. Although granted by the Queen to a substantial number of English gentlemen, this honour remained scarce enough to retain dignity. There were perhaps no more than 300 knights in the early 1580s.[2] Country gentlemen of substantial estate and proven loyalty, Crown officials, soldiers and sailors, and London merchants of great fortune were the chief recipients of this distinction, which thus remained the honourable badge of a distinguished minority, a symbol of success in the categories of activity most approved by contemporaries.

[1] Elizabeth created thirteen peers, promoted three, and restored four.

[2] Calculation based on Lansd. 32 no. 27 and E 163/14/8 (Liber Pacis, 1580). Knighthood was not invariably a reward, since the law required all those with £40 p.a. freehold to accept knighthood. It is not easy to know how often this was enforced under Elizabeth.

More utilitarian was the great array of offices at the Crown's disposal, varying in consequence and in reward from the chancellorship of England down to a gunnership in the Tower of London. To the government they represented the staffing of the public services. But, as in nineteenth-century American politics, patronage and public service were inextricably mixed together. Medieval government had left as one of its heritages the conception of a professional, organized civil service. But since its civil servants had been in large part clerics, holding benefices in the Church, there was no clear idea of a regular salary paid from public funds. More powerful was the lingering notion of personal service to the monarch. In this older view, a royal official entered into a general obligation of obedience in which neither service nor reward was specified. Both lay at the monarch's pleasure; the servant was expected to perform such varied tasks as the sovereign commanded and to accept such reward, regular or occasional, as the latter pleased to grant him.

Hard-working devotion to the royal service was a marked feature of Elizabethan public life and an important source of strength to the government. But the Queen's servants, however conscientious, expected reward and recognition from the sovereign and were not backward in demanding them. Sir Henry Sydney, who loyally bore two great offices, the presidency of Wales and the deputyship of Ireland, through many years, voiced a common sentiment in a letter of 1582. Called upon to resume the Irish deputyship he hesitated, claiming reward (title, land, or fee-farm) for past service in order 'that it may be known and made apparent to the world that Her Majesty hath had gracious consideration of his service past and for his better encouragement hereafter'.[1]

The practice of the Elizabethan administration mingled confusedly the notion of a professional, paid public service with that of personal service to the monarch. Most royal servants enjoyed a fixed annual fee, but in many cases it was hopelessly inadequate. Probably many of these fees had been fixed in the previous century or earlier and, like other aspects of Elizabethan administrative practice, took no account of economic changes. Secondly, a great many royal servants, although nominally assigned to specific posts in the household or one of the public offices, in

[1] Collins, *Sidney Papers*, i, 285.

fact performed quite other tasks, as the Queen or privy council directed. The floating and indefinite nature of their assignments involved them in diplomatic, fiscal, judicial, or ceremonial tasks as need dictated. From the government's point of view this arrangement provided a reservoir of servants of many-sided competence, from the official's it meant burdensome, sometimes costly tasks to perform, but also opportunities for wider reaches of connection, of influence, and perhaps of profit. There was, of course, a considerable, and growing, group of royal servants who had special professional competence. The lawyers, ever more important, not only at Westminster, but in the regional councils and in the fiscal offices, stand out. The navy board contained a nucleus of professional sailors; a smaller group of professional army men were to be found in the ordnance office and in the provincial garrisons. But beyond these two groups professional expertise was little in demand.

Much the largest but the least important category of royal servants comprised the minor functionaries who performed the routine tasks of the household or the government offices. Most of these men were clerks, messengers, waiters, attendants, guards, and so on, who needed little training to carry out their tasks. Exceptions were the artists and artificers of the royal household or military technicians, such as gunners. Opportunities for advancement were limited for this group, but nevertheless such service offered a secure and respectable livelihood and a modest prestige.

Among the royal servants how many held posts which could be classified as sinecures? The concept, as we meet it later, does not seem yet to have clearly emerged. The very informality which pervaded all offices of government confuses and deceives the modern observer. Sinecures proper, offices without functions or duties, seem not to have existed, although there were many posts of an archaic character with functions increasingly irrelevant to the needs of the time, and it is very hard to draw a line here. Performance by deputy was, however, very common. Often the patent of appointment includes a clause explicitly allowing this.[1] The practice was widespread in every branch of the royal service; the Crown's concern was in direct proportion to the importance of the office. Little attention was paid to the myriad local offices, often held by men of importance but invariably exercised by

[1] For patents: E 403/2452–3.

deputy. But at a higher level explicit royal consent was necessary. Robert Beale, aged and ill, wished to appoint a deputy to his clerkship of the council of the north in 1595: the Queen was willing to allow a deputy, but only one approved by the attorney general and judges and confirmed by the privy council.[1] The practice of course added substantially to the number of those who depended on royal service as a means of livelihood.

The entire range of offices and benefits at the disposal of the Crown[2] may be divided into seven classes, of which one, Church livings, will be excluded from this essay. The others can be labelled, rather arbitrarily, as court, central administration, judiciary, regional administration, military and naval service, and royal land administration.

The court comprehended the chamber, the household, the gentlemen pensioners, and the yeomen guards, and accounted for at least a thousand persons. It was divided, on the one hand, into an élite of peers, knights, ladies and gentlemen, and, on the other, into a mass of household servants, guards, hunting or stable attendants, and artificers. The line of division between the two was a sharp one, and advancement across it uncommon in Elizabeth's time. In 1567 the élite numbered about 175 men and a dozen women. The men included household officers, gentlemen in attendance, and nearly sixty members of that exclusive club, the gentlemen pensioners.[3]

Under the heading 'central administration' comes a mingled array of offices, some ancient, others of Tudor creation. Treasury, court of wards, and the miscellaneous secretariat of the government, in the secretaries' and the seals' offices head the list. The treasury comprehended the ancient bureaucracy of the exchequer, the mint, and the partially absorbed fiscal offices of Tudor creation. Besides a staff of about 65 at Westminster it employed an array of customs officials, receivers, and surveyors throughout the country numbering about 200.[4] The court of wards counted perhaps a dozen or so on its central staff and 45 feodaries in the country.[5] The secretariat included the principal secretaries, about a dozen

[1] Hist. MSS. Com. *Salisbury*, v, 195; vi, 387–8; cf. B.M. Lansd. 68 no. 107.

[2] List of Crown offices, *c.* 1588: S. P. 12/221.

[3] Subsidy roll of the household, 1567: E 179/69/82. The élite (other than noblemen and knights) are distinguished by the appellation 'Mr'.

[4] B.M. Lansd. 171 f. 314*b*.

[5] J. Hurstfield, *The Queen's Wards*, 221 sqq.

senior clerks, and some thirty post-riders and messengers under the master of the posts.

Among the regional administrations the duchy of Lancaster was a miniature treasury with some forty officials, and the palatine earldom of Chester, with another dozen, a smaller department of the same kind. The councils of the marches and the north were both establishments of some size. Besides the lord presidencies the choicest plums were the councillorships, seven for each council. Wales had a separate judiciary as well as a secretariat and legal counsel, the north a secretary only. Together they counted about 75 officers.[1]

The judiciary had, of course, a special status because of its largely professional personnel. From the point of view of patronage it offered limited opportunities available only to lawyers, but no branch of government enjoyed such imposing prestige or generous salaries. The organization of roughly thirty-five professional officers was nearly hierarchical, from the chancellor, through the judges, learned counsellors, masters in chancery, and Queen's serjeants. About fifteen attendant officers paid by the Crown served them.

The military services, partly embraced within the scope of central administration, also included establishments all over the country. Their personnel was a mixture of amateurs and professionals. In 1579 Burghley reckoned up a list of some 45 lords and gentlemen who were fit by experience for captaincies at sea and nearly sixty who could undertake military commands on land.[2] The admiralty's permanent administrative staff of about a dozen, its board of administrators, and its big supply establishments at Greenwich and Portsmouth present a more modern appearance. The land forces still lacked central control. The master of the ordnance had a staff of about a dozen assistants plus more than a hundred gunners and nearly twenty armourers, but otherwise the establishment was composed of gentlemen amateurs. Within England the greatest military post was that at Berwick, whose governor was at once military commander, civil governor, and diplomat, with some hundreds of men under his command. The other garrisons, usually numbering no more than a dozen men, were scattered in the coastal fortresses each under its own captain. In the late 1580s there were about thirty-five of these local commands. A considerable supply

[1] B.M. Lansd. 25 no. 39. [2] Ibid. 683.

personnel was attached to both naval and military forces, some of it drawn from the supply departments of the royal household. Such officials were necessarily men of special experience and with commercial connections.

The last category, that of land administration, comprised a small army of bailiffs and stewards of manors, constables of castles, keepers of houses, parks, or game, and foresters, who supervised the Crown's landed estate in every county of England and Wales and amounted to more than 600 persons. The consequence of these offices to their incumbents was certainly greater than the few pounds a year received for their duties; and the Crown had here its best opportunity for spreading wide its net of favour.

In sum, the Crown was able to dispose of about 1200 places worth a gentleman's having and as many again of humbler consequence. Allowing for a considerable amount of pluralism, especially among the minor keeperships and stewardships, there must have been at least a thousand gentlemen-placemen at any given moment in Elizabeth's reign. We need only compare this with our estimate of the number of the politically active in the realm to perceive how large a proportion of them depended in some measure on royal patronage for a living.

A contemporary expressed a grand maxim of Elizabethan politics when he wrote: 'My good lord, advancement in all worlds be obtained by mediation and remembrance of noble friends.'[1] Through the great courtiers who stood closest to the throne, suitors, great and small, pressed their hopeful applications to the Queen. At the best this made for a frenetic atmosphere of pushing competition; at the worst it might have degenerated into a chaotic scramble for favour in which all considerations of political common sense and administrative efficiency would have vanished. Something like this was to happen in James I's time. Under Elizabeth, however, a rough system, a pattern of order at least, emerged. The Queen's own wisdom provided the basis for it. By refusing to limit her confidence to a single favourite, she kept open a number of channels to her bounty; and she made it plain that in return for that bounty she expected hard work and loyal service. In this way a destructive, even dangerous, competition among the magnates for the royal confidence was avoided (at least until the appearance of that unappeasably ambitious courtier, Essex); moreover, a

[1] Ibid. 57 no. 47.

centre of stability was provided by the emergence of a single, dominant figure as patronage minister. One of Burghley's earliest biographers spoke of the Queen's 'never resolving anie private suit (or grant) from herself, that was not first referred to his consideration; and had his approbation before it passed'.[1]

This did not mean that Burghley was the sole channel through which royal favour flowed; although he may have very nearly become that in the last years of his life when almost every leading contemporary of his was dead. But before then the recommendations of Leicester, Hatton, and Walsingham certainly carried weight with the Queen, and if more of their correspondence survived we should have a better idea of their relative positions. The favour of lesser courtiers, men such as Heneage, and of the gentlemen and ladies in attendance upon the Queen, was certainly worth having; and even the humbler household servants could do their friends an occasional good turn. But no one enjoyed the confidence of the sovereign in so large a measure as Burghley, and no one was as well placed to guide the flow of patronage. Other councillors and courtiers could initiate suits and advance them, but increasingly Burghley's approval of vital details or conditions could make or mar the value of the Queen's bounty.

In part his supremacy rested on the offices he occupied himself—the treasurership and the mastership of the wards. These departments included a large proportion of the government's appointments—clerks, customers, surveyors, feodaries, receivers, stewards, and so on. Some were directly at the disposal of the treasurer or master of wards; in most other cases he could expect to be consulted by the Queen before a place was filled. But Burghley was also the friendly, indeed almost paternal, correspondent and confidant of the English aristocracy in general. To cite but a few instances—Sir Arthur Champernowne asks Burghley's good offices in furthering his daughter's marriage; Lady Elizabeth Russell takes counsel with him over her wayward son Hoby; the countess of Westmorland thanks him for his assistance to that fallen house; Edward Zouche asks for a loan of £200; Lord Talbot is grateful for his intervention with Shrewsbury, angry over his son's accumulated debts.[2] Burghley's friends included not only such

[1] F. Peck, *Desiderata Curiosa*, i, lib. i, 22.

[2] Hist. MSS. Com. *Salisbury*, ii, 64, 112 (Champernoun); iii, 183 (Westmorland); B.M. Lansd. 10 no. 38 (Russell); 21 no. 39 (Zouche); P.R.O. Talbot MSS. Transcr., letter 109.

pillars of the regime as Bedford or Huntingdon, but also Protestant malcontents like the Greys and adherents of the old faith like the Cornwallis family. He kept up friendly correspondence with such dissidents as the countess of Westmorland or Lord Morley and had their thanks for substantial favours done.[1] Among his correspondents, and beneficiaries, are numbered most of the magnates of the reign—Huntingdon, Bedford, Knollys, Shrewsbury, Cobham, Warwick, Hunsdon. Hatton declared that he owed the chancellorship to Burghley.[2] Such men had an independent relationship with the Queen, but the lord treasurer's key position at the exchequer increasingly forced them to turn to him for the fulfilment of their suits to the Queen. Her grants of fee-farms, leases, monopolies, licences to export, and so on, could only be profitable if Burghley approved the particular terms and conditions which made the grant valuable.[3]

Although in all this Burghley somewhat resembled the head of a great eighteenth-century connection, and although he did not escape the stigma of partisanship or faction, he used his immense resources, at least until the 1590s, not to build up a Cecilian party but to secure the loyalty of the great English families for the Elizabethan establishment in state and church. How wide his influence was is clear from the record. Burghley's voice was heard in the choice of officials in the household, the council of the north and the council of Wales; in the ordnance and in the army; he was involved in the appointment of new serjeants at law and justices of the peace. In 1588 he was busy drawing up a list of those eligible for new peerages; the chief justice turned to him to solicit a knighthood for his son-in-law. In the appointment of bishops his choice was decisive.[4] His authority waxed with the years and with the disappearance, one after another, of potential rivals, until in the 1590s 'old Saturnus' stood in lonely but unquestioned predominance.[5]

We turn now from the management of patronage to its enjoyment. The political aspirant's problems did not end with the

[1] Hist. MSS. Com. *Salisbury*, ii, 96 (Morley); ibid. viii, 541 and B.M. Lansd. 9 no. 3, 33 no. 80 (Cornwallis). [2] Haynes and Murdin, *Burghley Papers*, ii, 588.

[3] e.g. Hist. MSS. Com. *Salisbury*, i. 488.

[4] B.M. Lansd. 34 no. 23, 61 no. 59 (household); 18 no. 92, 33 no. 8 (North); 63 no. 32 (Wales); 29 no. 12 (serjeants); 69 no. 32 (knighthood); 104 no. 23 (peers); Hist. MSS. Com. *Salisbury*, ii, 213; vii, 147 (bishops).

[5] Collins, *Sidney Papers*, i, 331.

sealing of his patent: he had his office (or other favour), but he must now begin to look about for ways of exploiting it. Immediately at his disposal, of course, were the salary, the perquisites, and the allowances attached to his office. But these were only the foundations on which he hoped to build his prosperity. Looming far larger in his calculations were the extra-official profits of the office—that indeterminate but ceaseless flow of gratuities, *douceurs*, and reciprocal favours which the Elizabethan office-holder accounted the principal part of his reward for service. The amounts of these profits we can only surmise; but we may guess that in almost all cases they were substantially larger than the salary. Thus the salaries themselves need not hold us long. All Elizabethan royal servants thought that they were underpaid, and most of them probably were. Approximately 400 royal servants received an annual fee of £20 or more; above half of these received less than £50, 71 between £50 and £100 and 77 between £100 and £200; a tiny minority of about twenty had more than £200, nine of them more than £300. Officials of public offices—treasury, courts, military services, and regional councils—were better paid than the 179 household officers included in this total, since the great majority of fees over £50 went their way.[1] These figures must be compared with incomes arising outside the royal service. When we realize that most country squires did not receive much more than £50 in cash each year, and few of them more than £100,[2] while even the greater gentry had only a few hundreds at the most, it is clear that some Elizabethan civil servants were decently though not handsomely paid. This could not be said of many courtiers; even with free board and lodging, living expenses must have been high. Clothes, ornament, and servants all loomed large in a courtier's budget in an age and setting which placed a premium on personal magnificence.

The large and intricate problems posed by private exploitation of public office lie beyond the scope of this survey. All we can do here is to observe that part of the iceberg above water—the formal and public opportunities for profit or power which the office-holder might hope to obtain from the Crown. His principal source of profit (publicly acknowledged or privately arranged) lay in the sale of either influence or service. Influence was the more

[1] Figures derived from S.P. 12/221.
[2] Cf. W. K. Jordan, *Philanthropy in England, 1480–1660*, 330 sqq.

valuable, especially if one were placed high enough—near the Queen or one of the great councillors; service, vended in one of the executive or judicial departments, brought perhaps a steadier income. Posts to which regularized fees from the client were attached were naturally more saleable than those which conferred only non-transferable personal influence.

The careers of the brothers Stanhope serve to illustrate the gruelling conditions, the ample opportunities, and the magnificent rewards of life in the highest court circle. Of the four younger brothers of the Nottinghamshire squire, Sir Thomas Stanhope, one, Edward, made a successful career as a civil lawyer; another, also named Edward, did equally well as a member of the council of the north. The other two entered the court. The assiduous efforts of their mother, and of their aunt the duchess of Somerset, secured Burghley's sympathetic interest. The lord treasurer's backing gave them an introduction to the court and a toe-hold there, but it remained for the young men to do the rest for themselves.[1] It was a long and tedious business. John, the elder brother, probably entered the court in 1571 and Michael joined him in the following year. Sixteen years later, John, attached to the chancellor, Hatton, could lament, in making suit to his patron, how small his rewards had been. Although he had never been absent from court for more than six weeks, he enjoyed neither fee, pension, nor wage. Seven years ago he had, through Hatton's means, derived some small benefits,[2] and within the last three years he had had at least one favour in the form of an assignment of the Queen's interest in a seventy-year lease made her by the bishop of Durham, worth about £80 a year.[3] It was probably through Hatton's intercession that in March 1588 he received a grant for life of the manor of Chelsea at a rent of 200 marks.[4] The chancellor's death in 1591 would have have been a worse blow, had the earlier connection with Burghley not proved durable. Already by 1590 Stanhope was much in the confidence of the Cecils, particularly of Robert and, more important still, was very favourably regarded by the Queen herself: he was using this influence for the benefit of the new earl of Shrewsbury, seeking regrant of the late earl's offices to the son.[5] Solid reward came in

[1] B.M. Lansd. 14 no. 88, 16 no. 41, 33 no. 3, 38 nos. 32–33.
[2] H. Nicolas, *Memoirs of the life and times of Christopher Hatton*, 475.
[3] P.R.O. Index 6800 (Signet Docket Book, March 1575). [4] Ibid. March 1587–8.
[5] E. Lodge, *Illustrations of British History* (1838 edn.), ii, 432, 435.

the same year with Stanhope's appointment as master of posts. That promotion marked the turning-point in his career: thenceforward he was inside the charmed circle. Active in all kinds of business, public and private, he became a central figure for any who had suits to press or favours to seek. His own advance was unchecked: he became treasurer of the chamber, vice-chamberlain, privy councillor, and under James I a peer. And with honour went profit: in his heavy purchases of Crown land and his numerous leases we glimpse a great fortune in the making.

Michael Stanhope rose more slowly. A groom of the privy chamber in 1587 and already a purchaser of royal land, he had enough influence by 1590 to be useful to the earl of Shrewsbury, to Lord Keeper Puckering, and to his own eldest brother, Sir Thomas. He is to be seen, in his correspondence,[1] travelling with the Queen on progress, watching over the interests of Puckering, and keeping that anxious dignitary, reluctantly held in London by business, in touch with court affairs. In the Cecil correspondence of the 1590s Michael Stanhope is omnipresent, the busy and trusted agent of Sir Robert Cecil, advancing to knighthood, estate, and a good marriage. He left no male heir but his daughters made highly satisfactory marriages.

The Stanhopes' story is an uncommon one; most successes were much more modest. As an example of moderate achievement in the Elizabethan court circle we may take Henry Middlemore. He began political life in the service of Sir Nicholas Throgmorton in 1559, but transferred to royal service and survived his patron's downfall.[2] An annuitant from 1569, a groom of the privy chamber from at least 1577, he was a much-travelled agent of the government, and one of some consequence, in both foreign and domestic business.[3] Besides his court appointment and his annuity he had had from the Queen by 1590 two grants of concealed lands, the right to oversee licenses and collect forfeitures for not bringing bow-staves into England, a licence to export beans and peas, and a searchership in the port of London.[4] Save for the last, these were speculative benefits: the beans could be exported only when the

[1] B.M. Harl. MSS. 6995 f. 103.

[2] P. Forbes, *A full view of the public transactions*, i, 114, 425; Hist. MSS. Com. *Salisbury*, i, 146. He attended Lord Lincoln to France in 1557.

[3] E 179/69/93; for annuity: E 403/2452–3.

[4] B.M. Lansd. 64 nos. 55, 60; Nicholas, *Hatton*, 300; Hist. MSS. Com. *Salisbury*, ii, 135, 323.

price reached a certain level (which, he maintained, they never approached), the other grants required some investment before they would yield profit. Middlemore claimed (whether truthfully or not we cannot know) that he had sold no less than £3500 worth of his own land during his years of service.

Even so limited a success as Middlemore's was open to only a few. The court circle was small, stable in membership, and highly exclusive: to all but a few the door was hardly even ajar. But there were other opportunities, more prosaic but far from negligible, open to those who could not aspire to the privy chamber. Not the least of these was the perquisite of food and lodging which service in the court carried with it. The deficiencies of Elizabethan administration were never more apparent than here; repeated, increasingly desperate, attempts to limit its beneficiaries were unavailing. To the end of the reign courtiers went on not only eating and drinking at the Queen's expense but feeding their servants and families as well. A survey of 1593 lists 133 household officers in the court, attended by no less than 160 of their own servants, from the seventeen waiting upon the treasurer of the household down to the four servants shared by the five yeomen of the pantry.[1]

Then there were various types of royal favour of a more or less routine character. A very common one was a lease of royal land on special terms: among grantees of such leases are to be found not only the great ones of the court but such humble royal servants as cooks, yeomen, or porters. The lease (sometimes in possession but more commonly in reversion) was granted without payment of a fine, enabling the recipient to sublet, probably to the sitting tenant, collecting the fine himself and reaping a handsome profit.[2] Sometimes a courtier was able to obtain a lease (or renewal of a lease) for a friend on the same favourable terms, doubtless often for a consideration. Such transactions were more or less straightforward, but beyond them lay the vast twilight realm of speculation in royal leases as a dubious, but profitable, form of real-estate business.[3]

Another common form of royal bounty was the pension or annuity, sometimes in addition to salary, sometimes in lieu of it. About 350 persons were receiving annuities in 1573;[4] some were

[1] B.M. Lansd. 64 no. 68.
[2] For detailed examples: Hist. MSS. Com., *Salisbury*, ii, 135, 311.
[3] For a revealing example: ibid. 134. [4] E 403/2362 (4).

retired servants of the Crown; some in such special categories as war veterans; but a large proportion were serving courtiers already on the Crown pay-roll. Prime favourites naturally headed the list: Buckhurst with £200 a year, Howard of Effingham with the same. Dudley had had £1000 a year charged on the customs since the beginning of the reign; Hatton was to be granted £400 a year in 1576.[1] Some of the annuities went to younger sons; Sir Henry Radcliffe, brother to the earl of Sussex, had £50 annually until he was given regular employment as captain of Portsmouth. For some courtiers the annuity was a handsome addition to salary: Sir Robert Constable's £46 13*s*. 4*d*. per annum equalled his wages as a gentleman pensioner, and Sir George Howard, master of the armoury, had 200 marks (£133 6*s*. 8*d*.) a year beyond his salary of £30.[2] But the number and size of annuities reflected the economy of the Queen's government: the general level was low, rising only rarely above £20 to £30 a year. Annuities were negotiable, the market value depending on the life expectancy of the holder. In 1561 Sir George Howard sold half of his £200 annuity for £500 cash and the cancellation of a £600 debt; in 1602 Nicholas Hilliard, the miniaturist, sold a £40 annuity for £120. In some cases the sale took the form of the surrender of an old patent and issuing of a new one for the same sum, but with a new beneficiary.[3]

The indirect yield of an office included that to be derived from its sale. The subject is an obscure one, but there can be no doubt that sale of office was common and that the government was quite aware of it. Thus Thomas Wilkes, who had a patent as Queen's printer, wrote quite frankly to Burghley in favour of its purchaser who was not receiving value for money since his rights were being invaded by other printers.[4] The patent rolls are full of regrants in which a former holder surrenders his patent of office to a new patentee by agreement. Sometimes a patent is granted jointly to the incumbent and a partner, the patent being issued with right of survivorship to the latter, an arrangement worth while only when the incumbent was of advanced age or failing health. Not infrequently a father was able to pass his office to a son in this fashion: Peter Osborne, treasurer's remembrancer, thanked Burghley for securing him the reversion of his office, 'which will be the stay of

[1] E 403/2452–3 (Hatton); B.M. Lansd. 4 no. 53 (Dudley).
[2] E 403/2452–3. [3] E 403/2453.
[4] Hist. MSS. Com. *Salisbury*, ii, 187.

his house, his wife, and children after him'.[1] The treasury affords other examples of official dynasties in the Fanshawes, remembrancers of the exchequer for over a century, and the Neales, successively auditors of the exchequer through Elizabeth's reign and beyond.

Such transactions imply the treatment of an office as a piece of property. The Six Clerks of chancery could write of 'our offices, being our freeholds for terms of our lives'.[2] But the operative phrase here is the last: so long as no grant extended beyond a lifetime, the government retained control of the situation.[3] (Reversionary grants did not violate this principle, since the office still ultimately reverted to the Crown.) A brisk traffic in office was permitted, but the Crown was careful not to lose ultimate control of the appointment of its servants. No transfer of office could take place without the issue of a new patent, which implied the Crown's consent. Moreover, there is evidence that the Crown deliberately discouraged the accumulation of quasi-hereditary offices in noble families. Few noblemen could hope to inherit the whole clutch of offices acquired by their fathers, however much they might desire it. Even those favoured by the Crown could hope for no more than to be allowed a choice from the paternal accumulation.[4] We may conclude that, if the Elizabethan government was prepared to accept trade in offices as a part of the political scene, at least under the Cecils this was not allowed to detract seriously from the efficiency of government and was rarely allowed to become a source of hereditary dynasties of office-holders.

More casual but sometimes more bounteous were the occasional cash gifts of the Queen to a favourite.[5] These could be generous in size and prompt in payment. Lady Scudamore of the chamber had £400 in 1591 and another £300 in 1594; Nicholas Hilliard, the miniaturist, had £400 in 1592 and John Somer, the clerk of the privy seal, £100 in 1580. But, in a fashion characteristic of the Queen's somewhat niggling generosity, many such gifts were charged, not against regular resources, but against an irregular source of income. Ralph Lane, an equerry of the royal stable, was

[1] Ibid. 171. [2] B.M. Lansd. 76 nos. 23–27.

[3] The judiciary, appointed during good behaviour or at the royal pleasure, were outside the system of sale altogether.

[4] E.g. Hist. MSS. Com. *Salisbury*, vi, 287 (Knollys), 286 (Hunsdon); *11th Rep., Savile*, 122; Lodge, *Illustrations*, ii, 432 (Shrewsbury).

[5] The examples which follow: E 403/2559.

given the handsome gift of £1000 in 1583—to be paid out of recusant fines as they came in; Lady Hunsdon was given £160 out of forfeited cloths, Sir Thomas West £1000 out of the Crown's moiety of forfeitures in court. The goods or lands forfeited by recusants were the objects of frequent suits,[1] and it is refreshing to find Sir Philip Sidney declining to have any part in this sordid traffic.[2] The evidence does not warrant firm conclusions about royal cash gifts, but we may guess that they were neither numerous nor large and that the conditions of payment often made them less attractive than they at first appeared.

The bolder and shrewder men who looked for sources of income more regular in flow and more stable in character were likely to focus their attention upon the other form of profit to be derived from a royal office, namely, the sale of its services to the public. The principle that the client should pay for these services was clear enough; what was not so clear was how much should be charged, who should collect the money, and how it should be divided. True, in the older and more important offices, these matters were fairly well regulated. The clerks of the privy seal divided profits with the lord privy seal according to fixed schedules.[3] In 1587 each clerk of the privy seal was receiving about £50 per annum from fees paid by the public. The Six Clerks of chancery (reputed each to have a yearly income of 1000 marks, or more than £650)[4] likewise had established rules, and those of the star chamber were regulated by the privy council in 1585.[5] But there remained a large area where custom offered only uncertain precedents or where the crassest opportunism prevailed. Elizabethan office-holders showed uncommon ingenuity in ferreting out such possibilities of profit.

A good example is provided by a proposal of 1582 in which Richard Cavendish sought the right to make out all writs of supersedeas issuing out of common pleas. Tracing the history of these writs, he noted that they had been originally issued by all of the 300 or 400 clerks or attorneys of that court until the seven prothonotaries and exigenters limited the right to themselves. But these in turn had had to yield when the three inferior judges of the

[1] Hist. MSS. Com. *Salisbury*, ii, 356–7.
[2] Nicholas, *Hatton*, 214.
[3] P.R.O. Index 6800 for annual tabulation of fees.
[4] B.M. Lansd. 64 no. 82, 76 nos. 23–27.
[5] Ibid. 43 no. 7.

court elbowed their way in, and the profits were now shared among ten officers. All this had been done without royal authorization. Cavendish argued that the Crown would serve both the public's and its own interests by taking these fees into its hands and then farming them out—to himself, of course.[1] Cavendish was only following in the footsteps of Leicester, who already had the lease for making writs of covenant and alienation fines in the same court at a rent of about £2300 a year.[2] Grants of this type were attractive but risky. The Crown was a hard bargainer; the costs of collection were high; and in almost every case there was a tangle of vested interests to be encountered. In 1578 William Killigrew, groom of the privy chamber, sought to lease the seals of common pleas and queen's bench, the fees from which then yielded gross to the Crown about £1900 a year.[3] Against this were various charges: one-seventh of the gross receipts to the lord chief justice for office supplies; £100 to the prothonotary; and other smaller sums to the keeper of the common pleas seal. On top of this a comptroller had been appointed in 1565, with a fee of 8*d*. per £, whose function it was to keep a register of the writs. All this reduced the Crown's net income to about £1500. The public was not very well served since out of term time these writs were issued in a casual way in attorneys' offices in Fleet Street. Killigrew, on the usual grounds of better public service and royal profit, received the lease for £1653 a year, but at the cost of buying off the comptroller and lesser officials and providing the supplies himself. In 1582 he claimed to have lost £136 on this operation; but he held on and was still the lessee in 1597.

Another advantage of office-holding in the executive and judicial branches of government was the secondary patronage which it conferred. Around all these offices there buzzed a swarm of attendant functionaries, clerks, ushers, and messengers. Some were provided for in the official lists, paid by the Crown, and appointed by the Queen or by the senior officer whom they served, many others were privately employed by the various officials, while a third group were hangers-on of uncertain status and irregular income. Thomas Fanshawe,[4] the queen's remembrancer, was allowed eight clerks and employed four privately.

[1] B.M. Lansd. 25 no. 17; cf. M. Hastings, *The Court of Common Pleas in Fifteenth Century England*, 102. [2] B.M. Lansd. 21 no. 78.

[3] Ibid. 25 nos. 67, 100, 101, 102, 104, 105; 35 no. 14; 83 no. 79.

[4] Ibid. 40 no. 27.

The chief justice of common pleas[1] had as many as twenty-four offices within his grant; the master of the rolls[2] disposed of fourteen places. The council of Wales was officially limited to eighteen clerks; there were in fact above one hundred in attendance in 1591.[3] To the officials disposing of this petty patronage it was both burden and privilege; employees had to be paid in some fashion, probably to the diminution of their master's income,[4] but the official became in his small way a giver of good things and a man of prestige. The government irritably but ineffectually resisted this blurring of public and private service, which drew into its administrative ranks a large and inchoate group of hangers-on, dependent upon the public service for their income but outside effective government supervision.

Beyond manipulations and inflations of administrative processes and personnel which offered, ostensibly at least, financial advantage to the Crown and greater efficiency to the subject there stretched a murkier province where naked favouritism on the Crown's part was jostled by unashamed opportunism on the suppliant's. Here we find the simplest forms of royal favour, such lavish gifts as Dudley's £1000 annuity or the grants of land made to him and Essex. Here there could be no pretence of equivalent public benefit. It was unabashed favouritism of a kind uncommon in Elizabeth's reign, but all too familiar in James I's. Gifts of this kind, even far smaller ones, were reserved to the few, but they stimulated the imagination of lesser courtiers. Any reader of Lord Burghley's correspondence is struck by the fertility of courtiers' imaginations, ceaseless in invention of new devices whereby the Queen might be served, the commonwealth benefited—and the suitor enriched.

A great favourite with such suitors was the monopoly, the sole right to manufacture or distribute some particular commodity, including the remunerative licensing of artificers or dealers in it. Speculative from the grantee's point of view, from the government's monopolies were fiscally tempting and perhaps economically justifiable, but politically they were foolish since they contravened the very purpose of patronage. For every contented

[1] Ibid. 23 no. 70. [2] Ibid. 143 no. 211. [3] Ibid. 67 nos. 103–4.

[4] Thus Hatton paid his principal servants by assigning them the profits of various functions of his offices of chancellor and treasurer of first fruits: B.M. Lansd. 69 no. 79.

patentee the government could count a crowd of angry subjects, victims, real or fancied, of the patentee's privileges. It was to make this discovery, belatedly, in the parliament of 1601. Grants of monopoly were increasingly numerous in the last fifteen years of the reign. Whatever the economic justification for these patents, the bulk of them went to courtiers—Bryan Annesley, gentleman pensioner; Thomas Cornwallis, groom-porter; Edward Darcy and Michael Stanhope of the chamber; Richard Drake of the stables; Sir Thomas Wilkes, clerk of the privy council; Sir Jerome Bowes, ambassador to Russia, to name but a few.[1] Most of the grantees were hardly in the first rank of political importance—Sir Walter Raleigh perhaps being the outstanding exception; grants of monopoly, speculative and costly to exploit, were not prizes sought by the star players in the political game.

An interesting variation on the monopoly was the export license, a grant of exemption from the trade laws which banned certain types of exports. The patentee sold his license, usually in small lots, to exporters. The beneficiaries of these much coveted patents were often of the highest political rank. Hunsdon, for instance, had a license to export 20,000 cloths (probably undressed) in 1589; he still had not disposed of 14,000 of these cloths in 1595. This princely bounty was accorded only to a few great noblemen and favourites—Huntingdon, Burghley, Walsingham, Sussex, Raleigh, Bedford.[2] But licenses to export contrary to statute were extended to lesser courtiers in a more humble way. Simon Bowyer, gentleman usher, had the right to buy and sell 500 sarplers of English wool annually for ten years; Henry Middlemore, the groom of the privy chamber mentioned above, had license to export 10,000 quarters of beans and peas annually for twelve years when the price was not above a certain level. Arthur Bassano, one of the Queen's musicians, had a license to export calf-skins.[3]

The farms of the royal customs were potentially among the greatest of royal grants. The largest of the farms, that of the London import customs, went to a London businessman, Thomas Smyth. Royal councillors shared in some of the lesser ones; Walsingham had the outport farm; Leicester (and later Essex) that

[1] W. H. Price, *The English Patents of Monopoly* (Harvard Economic Studies, i), apps. B, C, D, F, G. Courtiers, of course, frequently brought in businessmen as partners in the exploitation of these grants.

[2] For a detailed example: B.M. Lansd. 72 no. 23.

[3] Ibid. 22 no. 35, 62 no. 67; Price, op cit. 149.

of sweet wines; Hatton, French wines; and Raleigh, overlengths. But the sums involved in these farms are small in relation to the total customs revenue, and none of these farms had a very long history. The bestowal of them was a great token of royal favour, but they were not richly profitable to the farmers. Walsingham defaulted on his rent; Leicester leased his to Thomas Smyth on terms which brought him about £750 a year.[1] Among the small ulnage farms names of courtiers are uncommon, although an obscure name may veil the interest of some courtier. One clear case is that of two gentlemen pensioners, George Delves and William Fitzwilliam, who leased the ulnage (that is, the official inspection) of new draperies in 1578 for about £60 a year. Fitzwilliam, at least, made a modest success of the venture.[2]

The Queen's lands, her richest asset, were also an object of courtiers' fondest longings. But here again, as with its customs revenues, the Crown was cautious. Outright grants of land do not seem to have been numerous, even to prime favourites, but the evidence is not easy to interpret and much work remains to be done on the subject. What supplicants most eagerly sought was a grant of fee-farm. In effect such a grant was a perpetual lease at a nominal rent, profitable to the recipient if he kept it, a marketable asset if he wished to raise cash.[3] From the Crown's point of view such a grant meant a sacrifice of future possible fines or increased rent. Consequently the grants seem not to have been numerous and in values rarely exceeding £100 a year. The recipients were largely men of major political consequence—Warwick, Nottingham, Sir Henry Knollys, Sir Edward Horsey, Lord Cobham, a diplomat like Robert Bowes, or long-standing courtier like John Baptist Castillian, groom of the privy chamber. Essex was very uncommonly favoured by the grant in 1592 of a dozen parks, fee-farm in socage, with the right to dispark. The freedom which socage tenure afforded from the court of wards, and the right to sell valuable timber, were instances of unusual royal regard.[4]

Attractive to courtiers, though abhorred by subjects, were the notorious patents for concealed lands. Here the patentee was entitled to seek out land owing but not paying rent or other

[1] F. C. Dietz, *English Public Finance, 1558–1641*, 312 sqq.

[2] B.M. Lansd. 71 no. 53; Mary E. Finch, *The wealth of five Northamptonshire families, 1540–1640* (Northants Rec. Soc. Publ. xix), 119–20.

[3] Hist. MSS. Com. *Salisbury*, i, 488.

[4] B.M. Lansd. 69 no. 73.

obligations to the Crown. The vast real-estate transactions following the Dissolution, the endless uncertainties of late-medieval titles, and the universal desire to escape the clutches of the court of wards provided a promising field for such adventurers. The rewards varied but usually included at least half of the annual value of such lands as might be discovered. Sir Edward Dyer was a great speculator in this kind of venture although allegedly with dubious success.[1] Burghley looked after the interests of the exchequer carefully; the costs of investigating titles were high; and the victims of this kind of inquisition were likely to fight back. And more important by far than the disappointments of hopeful politicians were the issues of policy raised by this kind of patronage. Here was approached the dangerous borderland where the claims of patronage met those of public policy. In the history of personal monarchy the sacrifice of the latter to royal caprice or the interests of scheming favourites was all too common: under Elizabeth it was at least infrequent. Generally the Queen's good sense and Burghley's watchfulness prevailed. But the pressures grew throughout the reign as more and more aspirants streamed into the political arena, and there are signs at the end of the reign that the barriers of royal and ministerial resistance were beginning to yield.[2]

We have been concerned thus far with the politician pursuing his career at court or in the royal administration and in the kinds of patronage which interested him. But there was a class of patronage which, while appealing to all, was especially attractive to the less active players in the game. No less important in the balancing of the government's political accounts, these gentlemen amateurs in the shires were the magnates, titled or untitled, who sought royal favour in order to augment or maintain an existing position of prestige, wealth, or influence. For them royal favour was valuable for local purposes; it shored up their consequence among their neighbours, vested them with formal authority, and often gave them the disposal of minor but locally important patronage. The importance of lord lieutenancies, deputy-lieutenancies, and shrievalties to peers and the greater gentry has already been touched on. There was yet another type of local office which was gratifying to their pride and profitable to their pockets. All over England and

[1] Ibid. 73 no. 37; Hurstfield, *Queen's Wards*, 39–41. [2] Cf. ibid. pts. iv, v.

Wales the Crown owned castles, houses, manors, parks, forests, and chases, some part of the ancient demesne, others belonging to one or another of the great honours and franchises accumulated since the fourteenth century. The castles were frequently in decay, the houses little used, the parks never visited by royalty. But supervising these scattered properties was a host of stewards, bailiffs, foresters, porters, constables, walkers, palers, or keepers. To each appointment was attached a small fee. In many cases the functions were minimal; in all cases, a deputy could carry out the necessary duties. But the anxious scramble for such posts is a token of their significance in the eyes of suitors.

These local appointments were often of prime importance in establishing beyond questions the grantee's local pre-eminence. Sir Robert Sidney's steward expressed this point of view in a letter to his master. Referring to negotiations over the Sidney interest in the Queen's park of Otford, he declared: 'But to your lordship, being a Kentish man, the footing you have in Otford and the honor of Otford is of more value than any money, seeing your house of Penshurst holds of it.' And again the same steward told Lord Buckhurst that his master esteemed Otford Park as 'of great value, not for the profit but because it was of Her Majesty's gift and of reputation in his own country, which I was assured he would never sell'.[1] The same consideration provoked a bitter struggle between the earls of Rutland and the Markhams over rights in the forest of Sherwood. The earl evidently regarded the lieutenancy of the forest as hereditary property and was affronted by the attempt of Markham to acquire various stewardships and keeperships within the forest during the Rutland minority. Markham felt no less strongly that his family's standing was bound up with these woodland stewardships. In 1582 he wrote to Burghley pleading for a grant in perpetuity of the walks of Billow and Buckland in Sherwood, wherein his house stood, declaring flatly that 'wanting this I shall not be able to seat my succession in Nottinghamshire'.[2] Derby was concerned over the very petty office of bowbearer of Bolland Forest. The office itself was inconsequential and the earl referred to the incumbent as a man mean enough for such a charge, but the office had belonged to the earl's

[1] Collins, *Sidney Papers*, ii, 167, 181–2.
[2] B.M. Lansd. 27 nos. 7, 8, 9; 34 no. 41; Hist. MSS. Com. *Salisbury*, ii, 227; vii, 121, 302, 483.

father and grandfather and adjoined his own lordships and lands.[1]

To local prestige these offices added material advantage. The hunting alone, in a park or chase, was worth much in an age when gentlemen exchanged compliments in the form of fat bucks. (Sidney was prepared to pay double the rent for Otford if he could have the hunting included.[2]) The perquisites of a forest were also of some value; the keepers of the walks of Waltham forest had each twenty loads of wood yearly;[3] the foresters of the New Forest pasturage rights, from which the lord warden's share alone was £15 a year.[4] Offices of this kind were negotiable also. The Careys of Hunsdon, father and son, patentees of Ampthill park, for which they had £4 a year in fee, sold their life interest for £250.[5] If the office involved the charge of a habitable house, the recipient acquired a free residence as well. Of much greater material value, however, were the stewardship or bailiwick of a manor or some other unit of land administration. As the representative of the lord of the manor (the Crown in this case) the steward had extensive rights. He (or his agent) presided over the court, collected admission fines, granted enfranchisements and leases, enforced suit of mill, and in many ways regulated and controlled the lives of the tenants. The opportunities for profit were numerous, depending upon the inventiveness and lack of scruple of the steward. We may gain some hint of what a stewardship or keepership could produce by some examples from the Border. Here local officers had arduous and sometimes dangerous duties to perform and the Crown wanted to be sure of efficient service. The keeper of Riddesdale enjoyed the demesnes and the court profits of his jurisdiction to the extent of 500 marks (£330) a year. The keeper of Tynedale had £300 a year; and the captain of Bewcastle £400 from similar sources.[6] A vigorous and shrewd steward in more peaceful regions, once he secured the necessary leases from the Crown, might hope for rewards of similar magnitude.

The imposing stability of the Elizabethan regime depended upon a number of conditions, among which the successful distribution of patronage must be numbered. Most of the important gentlemen of England became beneficiaries of the Crown, bound to it by the

[1] Ibid. iv, 465.
[2] Collins, ii, 162.
[3] B.M. Lansd. 30 no. 51.
[4] Ibid. 56 no. 35.
[5] P.R.O. Land Revenue 1/97.
[6] Hist. MSS. Com. *Salisbury*, v, 65.

interest of favours received or hoped for. Probably no one, not even the great favourites, had all he hoped for, but the number of malcontents who felt altogether excluded from these good things was small.

Viewed as a system of political patronage, Elizabethan government nevertheless manifests certain defects. It lacked adequate safeguards against a free-for-all scramble for spoils. In some measure Burghley's ceaseless supervision staved off the worst abuses, but this was a protection which waned with the ageing statesman's health and strength. The nature of the prizes encouraged a reckless competition among the players. They were, first of all, too small; too few offices provided adequate salaries, and the incumbent was driven to increase his income by any means open to him. Second, the terms of appointment were in many cases ill-defined; the fees and profits attached to an office were all too often only hazily known, either to Crown or patentee, and this encouraged the office-holder to exploit his opportunities, often to the detriment of both Crown and subject. Third, the private exploitation of political advantage created a vast 'black market' in which political influence and favour were increasingly bought and sold. Like most black markets it raised prices; the heavy costs of political success made each participant more ruthless in the exploitation of whatever advantage he possessed. The frenetic and reckless character of Elizabethan political life was thereby increased proportionately.

Lastly, the poverty of the Crown drove it to make unwise concessions to suitors for favour or place. Grants of monopoly or exemption, or farms of revenue, were tempting to the Crown because they offered an augmentation of income for no outlay. But grants of this speculative type encouraged the recipient to more and more reckless proposals and, once in possession of a patent, to unabashed exploitation of its possibilities. The results were angry resentment on the part of subjects, a tangle of litigation, and sullen disappointment among the recipients. Only the sense of responsibility and the political shrewdness of both the monarch and her chief minister prevented the kind of demoralization which set in with the next reign.

Yet, in judging the regime as a whole, high praise must be given for the transformation of English political habits which was accomplished during these years. By the end of the reign Englishmen were turning away from their bad old habits of conspiracy and treason—of the resort to force as the final arbiter in politics. Under the tutelage of Burghley and his royal mistress they had learned the peaceful, if sometimes corrupt, habits of a new political order. They had mastered the subtler arts of persuasion and manipulation. When Englishmen next took arms one against another it was not for personal or family ambitions or feuds, but in defence of the principles of lawful government as each side conceived them.

V

John Field and Elizabethan Puritanism

PATRICK COLLINSON

THE STORY of John Field is that of a man who led a movement which failed, and whose role was largely anonymous or clandestine. Hence he is so little known to Elizabethan historiography that it was possible for a succession of writers, mistaking the evidence of a single document, to style him 'minister of Wandsworth', which he never was,[1] and for a modern authority to dismiss him as 'a London preacher',[2] which, though true, is as adequate a description of Field as to say that Francis Place was a Charing Cross tailor. For, during the 1570s and 1580s, Field's influence on the evolving puritan movement was constant and sometimes decisive; and a study of his career reveals the strength and the weakness—as well as the inherent conflicts—of the reformist sector of the Elizabethan Church.

His cause was the further reformation of the Church of England according to the presbyterian platform: the establishment of 'pure' —that is, non-liturgical—worship, and of a reformed ministry and discipline. Field and his contemporaries could not know that the measures for the settlement of religion undertaken by Elizabeth and her early parliaments and convocations embodied a final form of constitution for the Church of England or that they determined the place of the English Church in divided western Christendom. A reformed doctrinal confession had been grafted on to a Church which had renounced the Roman obedience (but preserved, within the limits imposed by the act of supremacy, a Catholic ministry and order), and which was bound by the act of uniformity to the

[1] e.g. P. Heylyn, *Aerius Redivivus* (1670), 273; Athony à Wood, *Athenae Oxonienses* (1813), i, 535.
[2] W. H. Frere, *The English Church in the Reigns of Elizabeth and James I, 1558–1625*, 179.

use of a liturgy which was essentially Catholic, although accommodated in some places to Protestant doctrines. Our sense of the inevitability of these arrangements has given us too rigid a conception of an Elizabethan Church 'Settlement' and obscured until recently its partly circumstantial origins.[1] Yet few Englishmen and no sincere Protestant could have regarded as 'settled' a Church reformed in doctrine but only partly in ceremonies and not at all in discipline. The concept of an insular Anglicanism, Reformed and Catholic, had not been generally assimilated, even at the end of the reign. By Field it was attacked as 'a certain kind of religion, framed out of man's own brain and fantasy, far worse than that of popery (if worse may be), patched and pieced out of theirs and ours together'.[2]

Field was one of the extreme puritans who laboured confidently to complete what they regarded as an interim settlement by making a clean sweep of all the 'popish dregs' yet remaining in the Church. Besides the displacement of bishops by a hierarchy of presbyterian synods, and of liturgical worship by an austere form of public prayer resembling the Scottish 'Book of Common Order', their schemes, to be successful, would have necessitated far-reaching changes in the structure of politics and society which neither the Queen nor the majority of her subjects desired. Field was the man chiefly responsible for devising the means by which this handful of fanatics proposed to accomplish what would have been the most drastic revolution in English history. Its agencies were to be pulpit and press, patronage, suit and petition, and parliament. The campaign was managed by a disciplined organization which not only conducted the public agitation for reform but privately practised presbyterianism within its own membership. Field's importance as the instigator and co-ordinator of much of this activity was recognized shortly after his death by Richard Bancroft, later archbishop of Canterbury, who in 1593 publicly exposed the pattern of puritan subversion from the letters and papers of the puritans themselves:

> This John Field . . . whilst he lived was a great and chief man amongst the brethren of London, and one to whom the managing of the discipline

[1] J. E. Neale, 'The Elizabethan Acts of Supremacy and Uniformity' (*E.H.R.* lxv), 304–32; *Elizabeth I and her Parliaments, 1559–1581*, 51–84.

[2] Field to Anthony Gilby, 4 Aug. 1572: Camb. Univ. Library MS. Mm.1.43 (Baker 32), pp. 442–3. This collection will be subsequently referred to as Baker MS. 32.

(for the outward practice of it) was especially by the rest committed. So as all the letters that were directed from the brethren of other places, to have this or that referred to the London assemblies, were for the most part directed to him.[1]

Although the cause failed, its effect was not entirely lost. The pamphleteering, the national agitation organized in a great public cause, the appeal to parliament and the early connection between that appeal and the claim to free speech in the house of commons: all pointed forward to the puritan revolution of the seventeenth century.[2]

Field's origins and early history are obscure. By the evidence of an ordination certificate which appears to be his, he was born in London in 1545. He was at Oxford in the 'sixties, and later referred to the Jesuit John Howlet, who entered Exeter College in 1564, as 'a scholar in my time';[3] but the details of his university career are indistinguishable from those of his contemporaries of the same names.[4] He was perhaps the John Field who proceeded B.A. in 1564 and M.A. in 1567.[5] His ordination certificate describes him as a Bachelor of Arts of Christ Church. On 25 March 1566 Field was ordained priest by Bishop Grindal of London.[6] About a year before, he had secured as patron the earl of Warwick,[7] the elder brother of the earl of Leicester, a circumstance which perhaps facilitated his ordination at the uncanonical age of twenty-one.

The weeks which followed may well have had a decisive influence on the genesis of his militant puritan outlook. The day after his ordination, thirty-seven London ministers—the first significant and organized group of nonconformists—were suspended at Lambeth for their refusal to wear the vestments prescribed by the Prayer Book rubric and Archbishop Parker's

[1] R. Bancroft, *A survay of the pretended holy discipline* (1593), 369.

[2] P. Collinson, 'The Puritan Classical Movement in the Reign of Elizabeth I' (Lond. Univ. Ph.D. thesis, 1957).

[3] J. Field, *A caveat for Parsons* (1581), epistle.

[4] A. Wood, *Athenae*, i, 535.

[5] *Register of the University of Oxford*, ed. C. W. Boase and Andrew Clark, ii (3), 255.

[6] Ordinations register, bishop of London, 1550–77 (London Guildhall Lib. MS. 9535/1) f. 124*b*. I owe this reference to Dr. H. G. Owen.

[7] Caspar Olevian, trans. J. Field, *An exposition of the symbol of the apostles* (1581), dedication to Warwick; petition from the parishioners of St. Mary Aldermary to Leicester, 1585: *A Seconde Parte of a Register, Being a Calendar of Manuscripts under that title intended for publication by the Puritans about 1593*, ed. A. Peel, i, 135 (misdated).

'Advertisements'.[1] Their vacant pulpits were at once supplied by young and unbeneficed preachers who had not at first been called upon to conform. But these 'godly young men', among whom Field was surely numbered, were shortly afterwards cited before the archbishop and silenced, whereupon Field seems to have returned to Oxford.[2] In January 1567 we have the first letter from his hand: an elegant Latin epistle written to John Foxe, the martyrologist, from Broadgates Hall. Evidently he was much influenced at this time by Laurence Humphrey, the puritan president of Magdalen and a leader of the anti-vestiarian movement.[3] By the spring of 1568 Field had returned to London and after preaching for some time in the church of Holy Trinity, Minories, he became curate of the neighbouring parish of St. Giles, Cripplegate.[4] He is named in the parish books as minister in 1570, when he was living 'at Goodman Swanne's without Cripplegate'.[5] By then he was married (nothing is known of his wife Joan) and his seven children were subsequently baptized in the parish of St. Giles: among them Theophilus (who was to become a Laudian Bishop of St. Davids), in 1574, and Nathan, the future dramatist, in 1587, only a few months before his father's death.[6] By November 1571 Field had his own house in Grub Street, where John Foxe came to live at about the same time.[7]

The neighbourhood of Cripplegate and the Minories was a hot-bed of puritanism and even of sectarianism. As a royal peculiar, the Minories church was exempt from the bishop's jurisdiction, and the parishioners themselves appointed and supported their ministers and preachers, who were always radical puritans.[8] Stow tells us that the first puritans, 'unspotted Lambs of the Lord . . . kept their church in the Minories, without Aldgate',[9] and the

[1] M. M. Knappen, *Tudor Puritanism*, 196–7.

[2] Thomas Wood to William Cecil, 29 March 1566: Herts. Rec. Off. Gorhambury MS. viii/B/143 f. 2*b*; *Correspondence of Matthew Parker* (ed. John Bruce, Parker Soc.), 278.

[3] Field to Foxe, 26 Jan. 1567: B.M. Harl. MSS. 416 f. 185.

[4] H. G. Owen, 'The London Parish Clergy in the Reign of Elizabeth I' (Lond. Univ. Ph.D. thesis, 1957), 519, 611.

[5] Francis Hall to Field, 13 Sept. 1569: B.M. Harl. MSS. 416 f. 189.

[6] R. F. Brinkley, *Nathan Field, the Actor-Playwright* (Yale Studies in English, lxxvii), 2–3, 7.

[7] Field to Anthony Gilby, 22 Nov. 1571: Baker MS. 32 p. 445; *D.N.B.s.v.* Foxe.

[8] E. M. Tomlinson, *A History of the Minories, London*; Owen, loc. cit. 517–24.

[9] *Three Fifteenth Century Chronicles* (ed. J. Gairdner, Camd. Soc. N.S. xxviii), 143.

names of those who preached there in 1569 and 1570 are sufficient to establish a connection between the parish and the separatism of those Londoners who, already partially estranged from their parish churches, were meeting in Plumbers' Hall and other places to use the forms of prayer of Knox's Geneva congregation and of the 'privy churches' of Mary's days.[1] Among the preachers of this semi-sectarian connection, Field began, not later than 1570, to attend regular meetings which seem to have been intentionally modelled on the *classis*, or local conference of ministers of reformed church order. Twenty years later, an erstwhile member of the group named the preachers who in about 1570 had been 'of the brotherhood', 'stood so much upon reformation', and met twice a week in their houses by rotation: they had all at some time preached in the Minories. Field and a young curate of All Hallows, Honey Lane, named Thomas Wilcox were the conveners of the group.[2] This London conference was to have an unbroken existence at least until Field's death in 1588, and with strengthened membership would provide the nerve-centre for a presbyterian movement extending into most of the English counties south of the Trent.

It was almost certainly this group which in the summer of 1572, and towards the end of the parliamentary session of that year, launched the anonymous *Admonition to the Parliament*, the first popular manifesto of English presbyterianism.[3] Field and Wilcox of Honey Lane were the authors: Wilcox contributed the trenchant 'Admonition' itself, Field the more scathing and brilliant 'View of popish abuses yet remaining in the English Church' appended to it, while Field seems to have been the manager of the whole enterprise.[4] These two tracts advanced far beyond the rather superficial objections which until then had been voiced against the Queen's Church. The mere excising of a vestments rubric—the 'shells and chippings of Poperie'[5]—was not enough. 'We in England are so far off from having a Church rightly reformed, according to the prescript of God's word, that as yet we

[1] A. Peel, *The First Congregational Churches, 1567–81*; C. Burrage, *Early English Dissenters*, i, 79–93; ii, 9–18; Owen, loc. cit. 521; Tomlinson, op. cit. 166, 220.

[2] Deposition of Thomas Edmunds, 13 Oct. 1591: Star Chamber 5 A 49/34; Owen, loc. cit. 518–19.

[3] Repr. in *Puritan Manifestoes* (ed. W. H. Frere and C. E. Douglas, Church Hist. Soc. 1907, repr. 1954), 5–55.

[4] A. F. Scott Pearson, *Thomas Cartwright and Elizabethan Puritanism*, 59; *Seconde Parte of Register*, i, 89.

[5] Field to Gilby, 22 Nov. 1571: Baker MS. 32 p. 445.

are not[1] come to the outward face of the same.'[2] The very foundations of a Reformed Church, a 'sincere' ministry and ecclesiastical discipline in the Calvinist sense, were yet to be laid. Two years earlier Thomas Cartwright, the theorist of the presbyterian movement, had said much the same in the polite Latin of the Lady Margaret divinity lectures in Cambridge.[3] Yet, by the degree of popular interest and official displeasure which it aroused, the 'Admonition', rather than Cartwright's lectures, may be said to have launched the presbyterian attack on the Elizabethan Settlement. In mid-June 1572 Field and Wilcox were arrested and in October they were sentenced to a year's imprisonment. In their confinement they entertained a stream of visitors of the ultra-Protestant faction and overnight became popular heroes.[4]

Field and Wilcox gave the signal for a succession of presbyterian manifestoes. The 'Admonition' had been largely a destructive document, anti-anglican rather than positively presbyterian, although founded upon certain Calvinist principles as to the nature of the Church. The elaboration of a presbyterian constitution for the English Church was left to other tracts which appeared from clandestine and foreign presses between 1572 and 1577: the anonymous *Second Admonition*, the *Ecclesiasticae disciplinae . . . explicatio* of Walter Travers, which Cartwright translated as *A full and plain declaration of ecclesiastical discipline*, and Cartwright's own salvoes in the Admonition Controversy with John Whitgift.[5] Although it is often stated that puritanism entered its 'presbyterian phase' in 1572, the 'Admonition' was a product of circumstance, reflecting the exasperated mood of Field and his immediate circle more than a general swing to presbyterianism in the puritan movement. After the dissolution of the parliament of 1571 Field, with some older puritan leaders, had been subjected to special examination by the High Commissioners, perhaps with the aim of uncovering the organization behind the campaign for moderate puritan reform which had been launched in that session. Required to signify his assent to the disputed ceremonies specifically, as well as to the Prayer Book and Thirty-Nine Articles, Field had joined

[1] In 2nd edn. 'scarce'. [2] *Puritan Manifestoes*, 9.

[3] Scott Pearson, op. cit. 26–30.

[4] Inner Temple Lib. Petyt MS. 538/47 f. 481; Bishop Sandys to Burghley, 5 Aug. 1573: B.M. Lansd. 17 no. 43 ff. 96–97.

[5] *The Works of John Whitgift* (ed. J. Ayre, Parker Soc., 3 vols.); D. J. McGinn, *The Admonition Controversy* (Rutgers Studies in English, v).

with others in offering 'a kind of agreement' to the bishop of London. This peace proposal included a polite refusal to wear the vestments which led to Field's suspension from preaching. By January 1572 he was reduced to school-teaching, to his sorrow and vexation:

I sigh and sob daily unto God that I may have a lawful entrance to teach the flock of Christ.... And I await when the Lord will give me a place, a flock, a people to teach. I study for it and employ my whole travail unto it; and nothing is more grievous unto me than that, through the over-much tyranny of those that should be my encouragers, I am compelled instead to teach children, so that I cannot employ myself wholly unto that which I am bent most earnestly.[1]

Field's bitter and doctrinaire opposition to bishops dated from this time. Early in 1572 he was adopted by the parishioners of the Minories as their curate,[2] but it is unlikely that he obtained a licence to serve there. The last hope for Field, as for other inflexible nonconformists, lay in a bill debated in the house of commons in May 1572 which would have authorized the bishops to licence nonconformist deviations from the Prayer Book.[3] It was the failure of this attempt to exclude the puritan ministry from the operation of the act of uniformity which had provoked the printing of the 'Admonition', a declaration of war, not against the Queen, who was really responsible, but against the bishops who were her instruments in enforcing conformity. For the next eight years Field held no licence to preach. Indeed, the occasions on which he preached in parish churches were hardly more than incidents in the career as a revolutionary on which he now embarked with a zeal violent even for a Calvinist of the first generation. Admitting sole responsibility for the 'bitterness of the style' in the 'Admonition', he told Archbishop Parker's chaplain: 'As God hath his Moses, so he hath his Elijah.... It is no time to blanch, nor to sew cushions under men's elbows, or to flatter them in their sins.'[4]

Wilcox, for his part, was no Elijah. Most of his published works were concerned with the cultivation of individual piety and show him to have been one of the first of the puritan pastoral casuists.[5] He corresponded copiously with his many patrons, and more

[1] *Parker Corresp.* 381–82; *Seconde Parte of Register*, i, 82; Field to Gilby, 10 Jan. 1572: Baker MS. 32 p. 447.

[2] Tomlinson, op. cit. 220.

[3] Neale, *Elizabeth and Parliament, 1559–81*, 297–304.

[4] *Seconde Parte of Register*, i, 89.

[5] *The works of ... Mr. Thomas Willcockes*, ed. John Burgess (1624).

especially with their wives, but we are told that his letters contained 'little but godly, plain and necessary exhortations for the exercise of godliness'.[1] Ten years after their collaboration in the 'Admonition', Field led the London conference in debarring Wilcox from preaching and in witholding his stipend, penalties for some undisclosed moral offence. The friendship ended in mutual recriminations, Wilcox suggesting that he 'had perhaps concealed as great infirmities of Field's 'and Field rebuking him for despising the censure of the brethren. 'If God hath made you an instrument to seek for the advancement of Christ's sceptre', Field told him, 'kiss it your self and be subject unto it.'[2] Field was as careful as Wilcox to make friends among the influential Protestant gentry, but he did this less as a spiritual physician than as one with his eye to the main chance. From prison he sent collections of the first and second 'Admonitions' and other pamphlets to ladies of his acquaintance, each inscribed with eight lines of doggerel, which began:

Read and peruse this little book,
with prayer to the Lord
That all may yield that therein look
to truth with one accord.[3]

Later he was to present a copy of another of his works to the foundress of Sidney Sussex College with the inscription: 'To the right honourable and my very good Lady the Countess of Sussex: stand fast: truth shall prevail.'[4]

Propaganda and organization: these revolutionary arts were instinctive to Field and from the early 'seventies he was to use them to construct from the somewhat incoherent dissent of the puritan clergy a purposeful and militant movement. As a propagandist, he had served his apprenticeship in collecting information for Foxe's *Acts and Monuments*;[5] by 1571 he had his own connections with the press and his own methods of procuring inflammatory material

[1] The 17th-century puritan antiquary Roger Morrice's 'Chronological Account of Eminent Persons', Dr. Williams's Library, Morrice MS. ii. 417 (2 & 4), 517 (4), 617 (2 & 4).

[2] R. Bancroft, *Daungerous positions and proceedings* (1593), 118–19.

[3] R. Hooker, *Works*, ed. Keble, Church and Paget, i, 152 *n*; F. Paget, *Introduction to the Fifth Book of Hooker's . . . Ecclesiastical Polity*, 47–48.

[4] Philippe de Mornay du Plessis, trans. Field, *Treatise of the Church* (1579): B.M. C.60.b.2.

[5] Below, 146.

for publication. He informed 'Father' Anthony Gilby of Ashby-de-la-Zouch, a revered puritan of the older generation, that 'had there not been wiser men' than he, he would have printed one of Gilby's pamphlets which had come into his possession, together with a tract of Thomas Sampson's authorship: 'Howbeit, upon the advice of the brethren it is stayed.' Two months later, he told Gilby of his own unsolicited translation of another of Gilby's tracts from Latin into English, presumably for publication: 'I hope you will not be angry with Mr. Wood for sending it unto me, since it is yet at your commandment.'[1] In later years, Field was not always so scrupulous.

His letters to Gilby show that in 1572 Field was urging the puritan leaders to unite more closely in a formal system of conferences approximating to the synods of presbyterian organization. In August he wrote from prison, appealing to Gilby to consider how best to defend the cause against the repression of the bishops. His own remedy was that 'as of late there was a conference, so it might again be renewed, everyone submitting their judgement to the mighty word of God'; and that this conference should prepare a formal doctrinal statement. 'The same I write to you,' Field added suggestively, 'I write to others.'[2] His intention was that Gilby and his other correspondents should communicate these letters to the conferences of preachers in their own districts. Most puritan ministers were already organized in the local associations for the exercise of 'prophesying' which, with episcopal approval, had been set up in many market towns in the early years of the reign and by the early 'seventies were to be found in most of the dioceses of the province of Canterbury.

The principal function of a prophesying was to educate a preaching ministry through the agency of the better clergy of the district. The main proceedings consisted of sermons preached on a select text by three or four of the company under the presidency of a moderator, and before the other members of the exercise and, in most cases, a lay audience. But the public preaching was followed by private 'censure' and conference among the ministers alone, and that by a dinner where there might be some discussion of matters of common interest. This part of the day's proceedings enabled the ministers of an area roughly equivalent to the rural

[1] Field to Gilby, 22 Nov. 1571, 10 Jan. 1572: Baker MS. 32 pp. 445, 447.
[2] 4 Aug. 1572: ibid. pp. 443–4.

deanery to play some part in the government of their churches. The prophesyings, derived from continental experiments in church order, introduced some element of Reformed discipline into the over-centralized episcopal government of the Elizabethan Church. Most of the exercises, in fact, owed their existence to the initiative of local puritan leaders and some became platforms for the dissemination of puritan propaganda. Yet few of these associations were presbyterian or even tended towards presbyterianism. Their orders were sanctioned by the bishops, who in some dioceses bound the whole clergy to attendance and invested permanent moderators with powers of discipline. Where these moderators exercised the bishop's delegated authority, the prophesyings were an experiment in reformed or 'reduced' episcopacy and not a presbyterian conspiracy. Their leaders had no reason to share Field's doctrinaire hostility to bishops. Field's main task after the publication of the 'Admonition 'was to win support for the cause of extremism in these moderate circles.

The leaders of early Elizabethan dissent accepted a reformed episcopacy as a legitimate form of church order and believed that only a difference in inessentials divided them from those who held authority in the Church. Laurence Humphrey, Thomas Sampson, Thomas Lever, Anthony Gilby, these 'fathers' of English Reform had been the contemporaries and friends of some of the bishops both at the universities and in exile. They represented an early and more latitudinarian stage in the Reformation, while the 'Admonition' spoke for a less tolerant generation which followed Theodore Beza's Geneva in proclaiming new dogmas, especially on the question of church government.[1] Bancroft was probably mistaken, therefore, when he reported that the decision to publish the 'Admonition' had been taken at a conference held in London in May 1572 and attended by Gilby, Sampson and Lever.[2] It is more likely that a conference with this representation concerned itself only with the bill to obtain toleration for nonconformity which was brought before parliament that month, and that it was the failure of this moderate programme which gave the extremists their opportunity. What is certain is that the 'Admonition' and the conduct of the presbyterian faction were alike condemned by

[1] N. F. Sykes, *New Priest, Old Presbyter*, 42–44; G. Donaldson, 'The Relations between the English and Scottish Presbyterian Movements to 1604' (Lond. Univ. Ph.D. thesis, 1938), ch.i. [2] *Survay of the discipline*, 54.

most of the older puritan leaders, including Humphrey and Sampson. Thomas Norton, their representative in the early Elizabethan parliaments, speaks for them all: 'Surely the book was fond, and with unreasonableness and unseasonableness hath hindered much good and done much hurt.'[1] These veterans now lost their claim to march in the van of the reformist movement. Field and his friends led what was essentially a new puritan movement, which attracted many of the young men now entering the ministry from the expanding universities, and especially from Cambridge, where the doctrines of Cartwright had become the watchword for a younger generation in revolt.

Conscious of the youthfulness prevailing in the presbyterian faction and of its isolation from what was still the main stream of the reformist movement, Field exerted himself to recruit some at least of the older men. In a letter to Gilby of August 1572 he condemns the bishops in violent terms and contrasts 'our misery, their cruelty, our religion, their superstition, our duty, their negligence'. For too long the godly have exercised restraint 'for hope of amendment in some and peace with all'. Now that the bankruptcy of this policy stands revealed, they must speak the truth fearlessly. Conferences must be organized to maintain unity —a presbyterian unity—on the questions in controversy. 'For otherwise it cannot but come to pass that our churches by mutual dissentions shall be quite overthrown.'[2] Having ranged all bishops with Antichrist and concluded that the established Church lacked even the 'outward face' of a Reformed Church, Field followed a consistent course in calling for a formal presbyterian organization of the puritan churches. At this time he proposed to translate the 'Admonition' into Latin and to circulate it among the conferences for subscription, and with Wilcox he did compose and distribute a private 'Confession of Faith'.[3] Dissuaded in 1572 from the perilous step of making this a public declaration of the faith of the puritan churches, in 1574 the London presbyterians still cherished the idea of a 'confession of our faith, that it may well appear to the world what we are in deed'.[4] Futher evidence of the same trend may be seen in Field's ratification of the 'order of Wandsworth', the

[1] Norton to John Whitgift, 20 Oct. 1572: Inner Temple Lib. Petyt MS. 538/38 f. 65.

[2] 4 Aug. 1572: Baker MS. 32 pp. 443–4.

[3] Ibid.; *A parte of a register* (1593), 528 sqq.

[4] Laurence Tomson to Gilby, 4 April 1574: Baker MS. 32 p. 448.

precise nature of which remains obscure, but which must imply the establishment of some kind of local presbyterian organization.[1] In some churches puritan ministers were encouraged by Field and others of the London conference to seek appointment by the processes of congregational election and presbyterian ordination.[2]

Yet Field was no separatist and had no intention of calling out a gathered church of the godly few. Only a national Reformation, imposed by law on the whole Church, could satisfy him. It follows that his renunciation of the established discipline of the Church could only be justified by an early triumph of the presbyterian cause. This was not an unreasonable expectation in 1573, when Field and Wilcox were 'esteemed as gods' by the London populace[3] and a popular lampoon, written at about this time, implored Matthew Parker that 'as Augustine was the first, so Matthew might be the last' archbishop of Canterbury.[4] Field had powerful friends, even among privy councillors,[5] and it was with difficulty that the archbishop persuaded the council to issue a proclamation calling for obedience to the established order and prohibiting possession of the 'Admonition' and other presbyterian tracts.[6] Even then, scarcely a pamphlet was surrendered, although the tracts were in the hands of many London merchants and country gentlemen.[7] The truth was that episcopacy had few defenders.

It was the Queen, in spite of optimistic puritan rumours to the contrary,[8] who set herself resolutely against the anti-episcopal drift. A further proclamation in October 1573, in which Elizabeth's hand is clearly discernible, castigated bishops and magistrates for their negligence in suppressing nonconformity.[9] This was followed

[1] Bancroft, *Daungerous positions*, 67; cf. Scott Pearson, *Cartwright*, 74–82; Collinson, 'Classical Movement', 140–3.

[2] *Seconde Parte of Register*, ii, 69–70.

[3] Bishop Sandys to Burghley, 5 Aug. 1573: B.M. Lansd. 17 no. 43 ff. 96–97.

[4] Part of the title of *The life of the 70th Archbishop of Canterbury presentlye sittinge Englished* (1574), ascr. to John Stubbs.

[5] *Seconde Parte of Register*, i, 91; Sandys to Burghley, 30 April 1573: *Puritan Manifestoes*, app. iii, 153.

[6] R. Steele, *Tudor and Stuart Proclamations*, i, no. 687; cf. Inner Temple Lib. Petyt MS. 538/47 f. 479.

[7] Sandys to Burghley, 2 July 1573: *Puritan Manifestoes*, app. v, 154–5; list of Norfolk gentlemen in possession of the tracts: Camb. Univ. Lib. MS. Ee.ii.34 no. 4, f. 3.

[8] Laurence Tomson to Gilby, 19 May 1573: Baker MS. 32 p. 448.

[9] Steele, *Proclamations*, no. 689.

by council action: special commissions were set up to make a general enquiry into puritan disobedience, and to require subscription from suspected persons to articles defining the law of the Church on the questions in controversy.[1] The proceedings which followed delayed the development of English presbyterianism by ten years. In many dioceses puritan preachers were deprived or suspended, and in Northamptonshire the moderators of the prophesying were forced to leave the county. In London many puritans gave way and subscribed, while the recalcitrants, clergy and laity, were sent to prison, where at least four had died before April 1574.[2] Cartwright escaped a warrant for his arrest by fleeing to the Palatinate.[3]

Nothing is known about Field during these critical months. On 2 October 1572 he and Wilcox had been sentenced to a year's imprisonment by the lord mayor and aldermen of London. 'Sundry letters from noblemen'—Leicester and Warwick—had secured their removal from Newgate to Archdeacon Mullins's house, but in June 1573 they were threatened with banishment under the act of uniformity and in October they were informed that their release was impossible without special order from the council.[4] Yet by the end of the year Wilcox was free; in December he visited puritan centres in the midlands and by early February was back in his own house in London.[5] Of Field there is no trace, no letters, no published works, no evidence that he was preaching: he reappears only in July 1575, at the burning of two Dutch anabaptists in Smithfield.[6] In the winter of 1573–74, Gilby received his London news from Wilcox, so that Field may have been lying low in the country or have even joined Cartwright abroad. In 1574 some major manifestoes of English presbyterianism appeared from Michael Schirat's press at Heidelberg, and Field, rather than Cartwright, was the man to supervise the printing.[7] He was later

[1] *Acts of P. C.* 1571–75, 140, 171; *Seconde Parte of Register*, i, 93–97.

[2] Collinson, 'Classical Movement', 160–72.

[3] Scott Pearson, *Cartwright*, 121.

[4] *Seconde Parte of Register*, i. 91; *Puritan Manifestoes*, 153; *Acts of P. C.* 1571–75, 90, 93; Inner Temple Lib. Petyt MS. 538/47 f. 480.

[5] Wilcox to Gilby, 21 Dec. 1573, 2 Feb. 1574; Baker MS. 32 pp. 441, 439.

[6] *Seconde Parte of Register*, i, 105; John Stow, *Annales* (1631), 680.

[7] Scott Pearson, *Cartwright*, 135–47; A. F. Johnson, 'Books Printed at Heidelberg for Thomas Cartwright' (*Library*, 5th ser. ii), 284–6; P. Collinson, 'The Authorship of *A Brieff Discours off the Troubles Begonne at Franckford*' (*Journ. Eccles. Hist.* ix), 188–208.

to translate a collection of divinity lectures by a Heidelberg doctor, Caspar Olevian, the only work of his published in England.[1]

By 1577 Field was back in his 'poor house in Grub Street',[2] when Bishop Aylmer complained that he was preaching 'God knows what' in private houses. Aylmer recommended that with Wilcox and other notorious puritans he should be exiled to the 'barbarous countries' of the north midlands, there to wear out his zeal on the papists.[3] If the bishop's advice had been taken, Elizabethan dissent might have had a very different history. But Field remained in London, doubtless protected by his powerful friends.

The London presbyterian conference was still active and claimed a final authority among all the puritan conferences in deciding questions of doctrine and conscience. In 1577 it clashed with Cartwright himself. Under the influence of the liberal Calvinism of the Palatinate, Cartwright had begun to teach that it was better to conform and wear the vestments than to be deprived of the liberty to preach doctrine which he would state publicly in his *Rest of the second reply* against Whitgift. But for Field and other members of the London conference this was the thin end of a dangerous wedge. Strengthened by the presence of deprived ministers from Norfolk and Northamptonshire, they had written for Cartwright's opinion on the matter, but when they received it they at once condemned him for setting himself 'against the Church and the brethren'.[4] In the following year, the London conference was drawn into the plans of a group of puritan government officials for establishing Calvinist orders in the congregation of the Merchant Adventurers at Antwerp. Henry Killigrew and William Davison followed the correct presbyterian procedure in communicating their need of a preacher to the conference, and it was Field who canvassed and nominated suitable candidates. Eventually, Walter Travers was appointed and later he received a presbyterian ordination in the Netherlands. In 1580, when he returned to take up a lectureship at the Temple and to rejoin the London conference, his place was taken by Cartwright. The Antwerp congregation

[1] *An exposition of the symbole of the Apostles . . . gathered out of the catechising sermons of Gasper Olevian Trevir* (1581).

[2] Jean de l'Espine, trans. Field, *An excellent treatise of christian righteousness* (1578), epistle, dated 2 Nov. 1577.

[3] John Strype, *Historical Collections . . . of John Aylmer*, 36–37.

[4] *Parte of a register*, 401–8; *Seconde Parte of Register*, i, 136–43.

later exerted some influence on the development of presbyterianism in England itself.[1]

As secretary of the London conference, Field was the natural intermediary between 'the brethren of England' and Calvinist leaders in other states. In July 1582—a difficult time for presbyterians north of the Border—he wrote to assure John Davidson, a leader of the extreme presbyterian group in Scotland, of the concern of the English puritans. A similar message arrived from the Huguenots at La Rochelle. A few months later, Davidson told Field: 'It is no small comfort, brother, (as ye and I have divers times spoken in conference) to brethren of one nation to understand the state of the brethren in other nations; and therefore let us practise it as occasion will serve.' His letter offered the help of the Scottish Church in procuring a petition from the king and the general assembly to Elizabeth on behalf of the English puritans, a suggestion which was 'liked by the brethren in England'.[2] Such episodes remind us that, in its origins at least, English puritanism, far from being the insular phenomenon which it is sometimes represented, was part of an international revolutionary movement. Bancroft reports that the puritans made regular collections of money 'for their brethren that travail for them beyond the seas' —probably in France—and delivered them to Field and to Richard Culverwell, a mercer of Thames Street, who had many links with the French Protestants.[3]

Although the London conference continued and maintained links with 'the brethren' in the country and overseas, the presbyterian element in the puritan movement was almost wholly submerged in the years after 1574. Parker's repression of the presbyterians culminated in the exposure of what turned out to be a wholly bogus puritan 'conspiracy' and there was a revulsion of feeling against the archbishop in the privy council. In 1575 Parker was succeeded by Edmund Grindal, an old Marian exile who was sympathetic to all but the most divisive puritans. This was the period of closest co-operation between the bishops and the puritan

[1] S.P. 15/23/442 and S.P. 15/25/68, 71, 74, 78, 98, 116, 117; B.M. Add. MSS. 6394; Scott Pearson, *Cartwright*, 171–87; *D.N.B. s.v.* Travers.

[2] 1 Jan. 1583: R.M. Gillon, *John Davidson of Prestonpans*, 262–3; cf. Donaldson, 'Presbyterian Movements', 157–9, 295–6.

[3] *Tracts Ascribed to Richard Bancroft* ed. A. Peel, p. xxix; Culverwell's will, P.C.C. 9 Windsor.

clergy in the prophesyings. In Grindal's early years, the air was full of projects for the adaptation of episcopacy to reformed ideas. At the same time, the growing menace of Counter-Reformation Catholicism had strengthened the plea of the moderates for unity among loyal Protestants at any price: according to Thomas Norton, bishops and puritan preachers were agreed to 'join together against the papists, the enemies of God and of her Majesty, and not spend themselves in civil wars of the Church of God'.[1] The origins of English presbyterianism had been largely shaped by circumstances, and the movement lost ground at a time when most nonconformists enjoyed 'a goodly space of quietness'.[2]

Field appeared to adapt himself to the prevailing atmosphere. Doubtless he shared the common view that the danger of Catholic subversion now overshadowed even the evils of English prelacy: moreover, the bishops would not gain from a crusade against popery, while the puritans could hardly lose. To assault the 'Bishop of Rome' and his agents was obliquely to attack the English prelates, who in common opinion made a poor contribution to Zion's defence in comparison with the godly preachers. There is no reason to suppose that Field ever abandoned the extreme views which he had expressed in 1572—the 'Admonition' was reprinted in 1578—but in the later 'seventies he devoted his main energies to translating from French works of Protestant apology in that language. These were published with dedications addressed to some of the great patrons of English Reform which stridently called for a more forthright Protestant policy and the elimination of all papists and sectaries. In 1577 Field dedicated his translation of Jean de l'Espine's *Excellent treatise of christian righteousness* to Lady Elizabeth Tyrwhit, once the Queen's governess and perhaps still an influential lady at court. The year 1579 saw the printing of two collections of Calvin's sermons, one dedicated to the earl and countess of Bedford and the other to the earl of Huntingdon.[3] In the same year appeared a translation of Philippe de Mornay's *Treatise of the church* with a dedication to Leicester and an epistle directly appealing to the earl to lead an anti-Catholic crusade: it was the immediate occasion of Robert Parsons's *Brief discourse why Catholics*

[1] *Seconde Parte of Register*, i, 190–1.
[2] Josias Nicholls, *The plea of the innocent* (1602), 9–10.
[3] *Thirteene sermons entreating of the free election of God in Jacob, and of reprobation in Esau; Foure sermons, with a briefe exposition of the lxxvii psalme.*

refuse to go to church (1580), a manifesto of Catholic recusancy prefaced with an epistle to the Queen which included a personal attack on Field, 'a strange brainsick fellow, whom Newgate possessed for a long time for his fantastical opinions'.[1] In this epistle Parsons argued that the puritans were a greater danger to the peace and unity of the kingdom than the papists; he provoked more than one puritan reply, including a savage attack from Field on the 'crafty underminings' of 'these parasitical papists' in his *Caveat for Parsons*, published in 1581 and also dedicated to Leicester. In the same year, Field presented Leicester's brother and his own patron, the earl of Warwick, with his translation of Olevian's Heidelberg sermons, and in the preface renewed his attacks. In September 1581 he acted as notary for the disputations in the Tower with the Jesuit Edmund Campion, and subsequently edited the official account of these conferences.[2]

Field's new respectability had won its reward in July 1579, when Leicester successfully petitioned the university of Oxford to grant him a licence to preach. Lord Norris and Sir Francis Knollys, on whose behalf Leicester had written to Oxford, had hopes of placing Field in a town lectureship at Henley.[3] But, in spite of Aylmer's continued hostility, he does not appear to have left London. In 1580 he preached in the church of St. Martin Orgar,[4] and by the following year he had become the parish lecturer of St. Mary Aldermary, where he remained until his suspension in 1585. In November 1581 he declared his gratitude to Leicester, 'since not only I but the whole Church do owe thankfulness unto you as the instrument both of my peace and liberty and of the poor blessing it enjoyeth by my preaching'.[5] But it was not only papists who angered Field, and he went on to rebuke Leicester for patronizing stage-plays: during his time at the Aldermary, too, he took advantage of an accident in a Paris Garden bear-pit to

[1] *Brief discourse*, Sig. F vi.

[2] *A true reporte of the disputation . . . held in the Tower of London with Ed. Campion, Iesuite, the last of August, 1581,* and *The three last dayes conference held in the Tower with Edmund Campion Jesuite, the 18.23 and 27 of September 1581 . . .*, published together, 1583.

[3] *Reg. Univ. Oxford*, ii (1), 149; Eleanor Rosenberg, *Leicester, Patron of Letters*, 253.

[4] St. Martin Orgar vestry minutes and churchwardens' accounts (London Guildhall Lib. MS. 959/1) f. 44*b*. I owe this reference to Dr. H. G. Owen.

[5] 25 Nov. 1581: Brinkley, *Nathan Field*, 148–9.

denounce the growing popularity of the Southwark plays and shows on the Sabbath.[1]

Prolific author and translator though Field was, the works which appeared under his own name probably represent the least part of his propagandist activity at this time. As he wrote in the preface to a posthumous translation by a fellow-minister: 'I am easily drawn ... to put to my helping hand in the furtherance of any profitable work. ... And this is the cause that this godly work ... was by me egged forward to be published to all that fear God.'[2] Field was an inveterate collector and publisher of anything which he thought might help the cause or 'profit the whole Church of God'. When papers of John Knox were lent to him, after Knox's death, by Mrs. Anne Prouze of Exeter, who as Mrs. Locke had been a close friend of the Scottish reformer, he promptly published a sermon which he found among them and only informed the owner by way of a dedicatory epistle. In this he declared that no private person had the right to reserve the common heritage of the whole Church and begged Mrs. Prouze to supply him with any other Knoxiana which she might still possess or could procure from others.[3] He was especially anxious to trace Knox's letters, which contained 'an whole History of the churches where he lived'. Perhaps we owe it to Field's persistence that there was preserved the famous correspondence from Knox to Mrs. Locke which casts so much light both on the character of the writer and on the history of the Scottish Reformation. Anne Locke's second husband had been Edward Dering, a popular preacher who had died of tuberculosis in 1576 at the height of his fame.[4] Field informed his widow that he preserved 'many of the writings, labours and letters of that worthy and godly man ... and gather them in daily, as I can get them of his and my good friends:'[5] hoping that they would increase the posthumous reputation which Dering already enjoyed through his celebrated sermons on the Book of Hebrews. Dering's surviving works were constantly reprinted, both separately and in collections.[6] Two of these tracts have prefaces which

[1] *A godly exhortation, by occasion of the late iudgement of God, shewed at Paris-garden, the thirteenth day of Ianuarie* (1581).

[2] Peter Viret, trans. John Brooke, *A faithfull and familiar exposition upon the prayer of our Lorde* (1582), epistle.

[3] Knox, *Works*, ed. D. Laing, iv, 91–94.

[4] Scott Pearson, *Cartwright*, 82–83, 115–17; Kent County Rec. Off. Dering MS. C1/1, 2.

[5] Knox, *Works*, iv, 92–93.

[6] *S.T.C.* 6676–6733.

seem to be of Field's writing,[1] and it may well be that he was the editor of the collected works of Dering as we have them in late Elizabethan editions.[2]

We shall never know how many anonymous and posthumous writings were 'egged forward' to the press by Field, but we can be certain that he had a hand in most, if not all, of the many tracts printed by Robert Waldegrave, the puritan printer *par excellence*, which are of the nature of presbyterian party manifestoes.[3] We know that it was Field who by some means got hold of Beza's letter to Lord Glamis in denunciation of diocesan episcopacy, and published it in 1580 as *The judgement of a most reverend and learned man from beyond the seas concerning a threefold order of bishops*.[4] Of another important presbyterian tract, the *Brief and plain declaration*, written by William Fulke in the early 'seventies, but only printed in 1584 by Waldegrave, Matthew Sutcliffe wrote: 'When John Field contrary to his mind did publish the pamphlet called *The learned discourse*, [Fulke] was offended with him, and if he had lived would have confuted the same himself.'[5] Where a manuscript which he edited had no direct bearing on the puritan cause, or had been written years before, it was Field's practice to couple it with a topical preface, carrying the familiar appeal for further reformation. He chose the eve of a parliament—whether the session of 1571 or 1581 is not clear—to publish Dering's *Sermon preached before the Queen's Majesty*, in order, as he explains in the preface, 'that things amiss may be reformed, and true religion sincerely advanced, and against this time especially, because that a Parliament is instant and at hand; wherein . . . known abuses shall be removed and many unprofitable strifes ended'.[6]

Besides what he actually put through the press, Field was responsible for amassing the 'register' of evidences of the puritan controversy which today forms our most important source for the

[1] *A sermon preached before the Queenes Majestie*, epistle attached to undated edns. (*S.T.C.* 6699b, 6701) and as one of *Two godly sermons* (1590 and later edns.), initialled 'I.F.'; *XXVII lectures or readings upon part of . . . Hebrews* (1576 and later edns.).

[2] Cf. edns. of ?1590, 1597, 1614, *S.T.C.* 6676–8; C. H. Cooper, *Athenae Cant.* i, 357.

[3] W. J. Couper, *Robert Waldergrave, King's Printer for Scotland*; W. Pierce, *An Historical Introduction to the Marprelate Tracts.*

[4] Donaldson, 'Presbyterian Movements', 154.

[5] Scott Pearson, *Cartwright*, 273.

[6] Epistle to an undated edn., initialled 'I.F.'

history of the movement.[1] Among the resolutions sent down to the conferences from a general presbyterian assembly held in London in the winter of 1586–87 were instructions that cases of the oppression of the bishops and their officers 'especially towards the ministers' were to be 'registered and gathered'.[2] This was no new procedure in 1587, as the copious material in the register from about 1565 shows. There are altogether some two hundred and fifty documents in the register, amounting in manuscript to six hundred and fifty closely-written folios and in print to five hundred and fifty-four pages. They span the years 1565–89 and represent almost every county where puritan preachers were to be found: a striking memorial to the extent and efficiency of the Elizabethan presbyterian organization. We have the testimony of a member of the London conference that it was Field who kept this 'register of all acts and proceedings in his day'.[3] Some of the items are addressed to him or bear his endorsement,[4] and there is evidence that he was the compiler of a contemporary catalogue of the register which survives.[5] Field's project of a register of the sufferings of the puritans was an imitation of Foxe's *Acts and Monuments*, which was a history of 'great persecutions and horrible troubles . . . gathered and collected' from the original sources with which the successive editions of the 'Book of Martyrs' were inflated. Field had begun his literary career as one of Foxe's assistants in tracing information, and it was no doubt in this school that he had learned both the value of such material as propaganda and the technique of collecting it through an organized chain of correspondents.[6] The *Brief discourse of the troubles begun at Frankfort* was the first puritan work in the same vein, and Field almost certainly took a leading part in gathering and publishing these original records of the

[1] Partly printed, by Schilders at Middelburg or Waldegrave at Edinburgh ?1593, as *A parte of a register . . . written by divers godly and learned in our time, which . . . desire the reformation of our Church in discipline and ceremonies*; largely remaining in MS. as 'The seconde parte of a register' and 'Old loose papers', Dr. Williams's Library, MSS. Morrice A and B, and calendared as *A Seconde Parte of a Register*, ed. A. Peel (1915).

[2] *The Presbyterian Movement in the Reign of Queen Elizabeth as Illustrated by the Minute Book of the Dedham Classis, 1582–1589* (ed. R. G. Usher, Camden Soc. 3rd ser. viii), 92–93.

[3] Deposition of Thomas Edmunds: Star Chamber 5 A 49/34.

[4] *Seconde Parte of Register*, i, 219; ii, 219, 238, 239.

[5] B.M. Harl. MSS. 360 ff. 86*b*, 87*b*.

[6] Francis Hall to Field, 13 Sept. 1569, endorsed by Foxe: B.M. Harl. MSS. 416 f. 185; cf. J. F. Mozley, *John Foxe and his Book*, 141.

troubles of the Marian exile.[1] The project was continued in the puritan historical register. 'If it will anything help the common cause, I pray you then, use your discretion', wrote an East Anglian puritan in sending Field an account of his troubles.[2] Many of the documents in the register were circulated in manuscript to support the claims of puritan petitions and bills: there is evidence that they were passed from hand to hand in the house of commons itself.[3] It may have been Field's intention to publish a puritan 'Book of Martyrs' from the material in the register, but it was not until five years after his death that a selection of the documents appeared from a foreign press as *A part of a register*, while the bulk of the collection has remained unprinted.

In the first of the Marprelate Tracts, Martin warns the prelates that he keeps 'a register' of their misdeeds. 'You shall not call one honest man before you, but I will get his examination . . . and publish it. . . . Secondly all the books that I have in store already of your doings shall be published.'[4] Although Field was dead before the first of these brilliant libels appeared, and although serious puritan opinion condemned the tracts for their frivolity, Martin's warning indicates that his plan of campaign closely resembled that of Field's register. Moreover we are told by a contemporary witness that *The Epistle*, the first of the tracts, was written from 'some such notes as were found in Master Field's study',[5] while John Udall of Kingston admitted having shown part of the same tract to Field.[6] While the extent of Field's implication in the Marprelate affair will never be known, there is no doubt that Martin was born from a tradition of puritan libelling which Field had done much to establish and which derived in part from the appeal to history of the *Acts and Monuments* and the register, and in part from the polemic of the *Admonition to the Parliament*.

The 'goodly space of quietness' which had marked Grindal's early years ended with the succession in September 1583 of John Whitgift, who in the early years of the presbyterian movement

[1] P. Collinson in *Journ. Eccles. Hist.* ix, 199–201.

[2] Dr. Williams's Library, MS. Morrice B II f. 91*b*.

[3] J. E. Neale, *Elizabeth and Parliament, 1584–1601*, 229–30; cf. the private papers of an Elizabethan puritan M.P., Sir Edward Lewkenor: B.M. Add. MSS. 38492.

[4] *The Marprelate Tracts*, ed. W. Pierce, 81–82.

[5] E. Arber, *An Introductory Sketch to the Martin Marprelate Controversy*, 94.

[6] B.M. Harl. MSS. 7042 f. 4*b*.

had made himself the champion of Anglicanism against the puritan challenge. Acting on royal instructions, he now initiated an energetic campaign for conformity. The whole clergy were required to subscribe their assent to the Royal Supremacy, to the Prayer Book as containing 'nothing in it contrary to the word of God' and to the Thirty-Nine Articles as 'agreeable to the word of God'.[1] No puritan could conscientiously fulfil the second of these requirements and some approached the other two with misgivings. The penalty for non-subscription was suspension from the ministry and ultimately, for incumbents, deprivation of their livings. This challenge stimulated afresh the extremist, anti-episcopal wing of the puritan movement and Field emerged, from the comparative retirement of the past ten years, to lead it.

The *modus vivendi* between bishops and puritan preachers which had marked the Grindalian episode had been under fire from both sides in the years immediately before Whitgift's elevation. In 1576 the exercises of prophesying were suppressed by the Queen's order and the archbishop who rose in courageous defence of them placed under suspension.[2] This setback was followed within a few years by the deaths of most of the 'fellow-travelling' bishops of Grindal's outlook and the rise of a new generation of prelates who shared Whitgift's abhorrence of puritanism. In some dioceses the bishops were still willing to wink at the prophesyings under another name, but elsewhere the puritan conferences were forced to become voluntary and unauthorized associations. Unlike the prophesyings, their orders were presbyterian[3] and their meetings secret. In East Anglia, where bishops Freke of Norwich and Aylmer of London aligned themselves with factions hostile to puritan preaching, every puritan was faced with the constant threat of silencing or deprivation. In 1582, extraordinary conventions of preachers were held at the churches of leading puritan ministers—John Knewstub's Cockfield in Suffolk and Richard Rogers's Wethersfield over the Essex border—and at Cambridge.[4] These and perhaps other meetings of a similar character elsewhere led to the establishment of clandestine conferences resembling the presbyterian *classes*, in

[1] J. Strype, *The Life and Acts of John Whitgift*, i, 229–32.

[2] *The Remains of Edmund Grindal* (ed. W. Nicholson, Parker Soc.), 376–90.

[3] Cf. the Norwich orders drawn up during the vacancy of the see in 1575: J. Browne, *History of Congregationalism in Norfolk and Suffolk*, 18–20.

[4] Bancroft, *Daungerous positions*, pp. 112–13; Essex Rec. Off. Quarter Sessions Rolls 84/34, 43.

which the puritan ministers of convenient circuits met monthly to discuss their troubles and to regulate the affairs of their churches. The minute-book of one such conference, formed by the preachers in the neighbourhood of Dedham in Essex, has survived and sheds much light on the development of this practical presbyterian movement.

It was at about this time, apparently, that the London conference began to make definite plans for the establishment of a working system of presbyterian assemblies.[1] The East Anglian leaders informed Field of developments in their country and may even have taken their instructions from him. Of the secret meeting at Cockfield, a Suffolk preacher wrote: 'I hope all things were so proceeded in as you your self would like of. . . . I suppose before this time some of the company have told you by word; for that was permitted unto you.'[2] It was Field who suggested a general meeting to follow at Cambridge, and in Suffolk it was thought that this might 'easily be brought to pass, if you at London shall so think well of it, and we here may understand your mind'.[3] It may have already been regular practice, as it certainly was a year or two later, to hold synods at the two universities in July, at the time of the graduation ceremonies—at Stourbridge Fair time (September), too, at Cambridge—and a general assembly in London during the days of the St. Bartholomew Fair. These occasions provided cover for the unusually large assemblies of puritan ministers. In this way the *classes*, synods and assemblies of a presbyterian Church of England were already roughly sketched out. Yet it took Whitgift's general assault on nonconformity to stir this embryonic organism fully into life. Field's correspondence with the country leaders had grown occasional: when he wrote to Gilby in February 1581, some of his London news was more than a year old.[4] In the summer of 1583 an Antwerp correspondent congratulated Field on the establishment of presbyterian assemblies, but added: 'I will tell you that which is true: you have begun this course too late.'[5] Field himself confessed to the ministers of the Dedham conference that he had been 'strongly drawn of late not to be so careful, diligent and zealous in God's causes as I was wont; this unhappy time of looseness and liberty gaining upon me and

[1] Deposition of Thomas Edmunds: Star Chamber 5 A 49/34.

[2] Oliver Pig to Field, 16 May 1582: Bancroft, *Daungerous positions*, 112–13.

[3] Ibid. [4] Field to Gilby, 28 Feb. 1581: Baker MS. 32 p. 446.

[5] Bancroft, *Daungerous positions*, 73.

choking those good things which I thank God I was wont to feel in greater measure'. But conference and correspondence became an urgent necessity after October 1583. While Edmund Chapman of Dedham urged Field to call a 'general conference for unity', Field told Chapman: 'You are wise to consider by advice and by joining together how to strengthen your hands in this work. The Lord direct both you and us, that we may fight a good fight and finish with joy. Amen.'[1]

'This work,' this 'good fight': Field's attitude to the subscription struggle was characteristic and exceptional. Most moderate puritans looked no further than their own parishes, where they hoped to occupy their pulpits quietly and to be allowed the discreet use of some nonconformist practices. Faced with the test of subscription, they at first refused, but hoped that they would later be permitted to make a modified, conditional subscription and that the tolerance of earlier years would return. These hopes were well-founded, for a policy found few defenders which silenced hundreds of zealous preachers at the very time when the country stood in mortal danger of Catholic subversion. In the later months of 1584, Whitgift was forced by the pressure of opinion in the council and the court to give way, and to allow the majority of the ministers to subscribe with reservations. Of three to four hundred non-subscribers, only a fraction were deprived of their livings or permanently suspended from preaching.[2] These were, as Whitgift himself termed them, the ring-leaders,[3] whom the general demand for subscription had served to identify, and who were now singled out and called up to the High Commission to answer to a new schedule of inquisitorial articles.[4] Field himself, who had somehow contrived to continue as lecturer at the Aldermary throughout 1584, was suspended by the High Commissioners on 4 March 1585,[5] and so far as we know never preached openly again. In 1586 he was included in the puritan register in a short list of ministers and preachers who still stood suspended or deprived.[6]

For as long as the issue was uncertain, Field seems to have been

[1] *Dedham Minute Book*, 95–96.
[2] Collinson, 'Classical Movement', 419–34, 457–62.
[3] Whitgift to Burghley, 29 May 1584: B.M. Lansd. 42 no. 43 f. 105.
[4] Strype, *Whitgift*, iii, app. iv, 81–87.
[5] *Seconde Parte of Register*, i, 283–4; the two petitions from parishioners to Leicester of the same time (ibid. 135, 284) are misdated by the editor.
[6] Ibid. ii, 262.

as determined as the archbishop himself that the outcome should not be a return to latitudinarian tolerance, partly because such a settlement would isolate the presbyterian minority from the more numerous moderates, but also perhaps because he saw in the archbishop's extreme demands an opportunity to discredit the bishops once for all. Subscription would certainly be refused by hundreds of clergy who were no fanatical opponents of episcopacy but who habitually omitted parts of the Prayer Book or ignored its rubrics. If these ministers continued to resist even a modified subscription, a general revulsion of Protestant opinion against Whitgift and his suffragans might follow, opening the way for the overthrow of episcopacy itself. If, on the other hand, the ministers subscribed, even with reservations, it might later be claimed, even against the presbyterians—as in fact it was by 1585—that they had abandoned their position. 'I am sure the greater part, yea even of your forwardest men, subscribed.'[1]

By early December 1583 Field had prepared a statement on the unlawfulness of subscription of which a version was probably sent out to the conferences. Like other tracts in circulation at the same time it listed the particular errors in the Prayer Book, but unlike them it insisted more on the generally Catholic spirit of the Anglican liturgy; so that, even if every fault were explained away or excepted, the 'general inconveniences' of the book remained insurmountable. The liturgy by its length alone left little time for preaching—and on that subject Field professed to find 'a deep silence throughout the whole book'—while to subscribe to the threefold, Catholic ministry of the Ordinal, which was contained within the Prayer Book, was plainly impossible. Field concluded that the most tolerable of conditional subscriptions was 'vain and frivolous.... Might we not as well and better subscribe to Æsop's fables?' He warned the bishops 'to take heed whereunto they urge us' and the people 'to consider that we have cause to refuse and admonish our fellow ministers to beware of subscription'.[2]

This was not the attitude of most non-subscribers. Indeed, Chapman of Dedham confessed 'some dislike of both parties for

[1] John Udall, *The State of the Church of England*, ed. E. Arber, 21; cf. the preface to Thomas Rogers, *The English creed* (1587).

[2] Three versions of Field's views are extant: S.P. 12/164/11; Dr. Williams's Library, MS. Morrice B 11 ff. 94–96, printed in part, *Seconde Parte of Register*, i. 284–6; and 'the general inconveniences of the Book of Common Prayer', ibid. i, 256–7.

their hot and violent manner of proceeding, either seeking by all means to conquer and deface the other'.[1] While the puritan ministers throughout the province of Canterbury searched for a common policy and circulated a variety of forms of answer to the articles,[2] the great influence of the London conference was exerted to persuade them to refuse subscription in any form. When a group of Sussex non-subscribers, who came to Lambeth to present their case in December 1583, were inclined between one day and the next to withdraw their conditional subscription, bishop Young of Rochester remarked: 'It seemeth they have been with some in London since they went hence. If I were as you, I would not care with how few such I were acquainted.'[3] In the early months of 1584, while most of the puritan ministry still resisted subscription, Whitgift complained of a conspiracy in their 'disordered flocking together... from divers places and gadding from one to another', which argued 'some hope of encouragement and of prevailing'.[4] Petitions to the archbishop and the council from the suspended ministers and from groups of gentlemen on their behalf flowed into London, closely followed by delegations of the ministers and their patrons. Field was doubtless active in engineering much of this agitation, as in spreading the rumour that the cause of subscription would soon be abandoned, which, complained Whitgift, 'is spread abroad in every place, and is the only cause why many forbear to subscribe'.[5] A group of Lincolnshire ministers who were pressed by their archdeacon to subscribe replied that they had heard in London that they would be restored to their pulpits without subscribing. The archdeacon reported that many of them held copies of a letter from Field to the corresponding secretary of the movement in Lincolnshire, exhorting them to 'stand stoutly to the cause, affirming the same not to be theirs but the Lord's'. Those who had already subscribed were told that they had 'made a breach' and henceforth would be 'branded men' who would do no good in the Church.[6] Field may have written in these terms

[1] To Thomas Cartwright, 4 Nov. 1584: *Dedham Minute Book*, 81.

[2] The puritan register alone contains over twenty forms of answers and limited subscription and the papers of the Dedham conference many more.

[3] Dr. Williams's Library, MS. Morrice B II f. 46*b*.

[4] To the privy council, 4 Feb. 1584: Inner Temple Lib. Petyt MS. 538/52 f. 8–10*b*.

[5] To Sir Christopher Hatton, 9 May 1584: B.M. Add. MSS. 15891 f. 123.

[6] John Barefoot, archdeacon of Lincoln, to Whitgift, 1 June 1584: Hist. MSS. Com. *Bath*, ii, 24–26.

to every county. 'Weaklings, led by the masters of that faction,' was a Lichfield prebendary's opinion of the non-subscribers.[1]

There is no knowing what the outcome for the Church of England might have been had parliament met in the early months of 1584, with hundreds of pulpits silenced, the radical Protestant gentry in an uproar, and everyone at court, with the exception of Sir Christopher Hatton and the Queen herself, opposed to Whitgift's policy.[2] By the time parliament was called in November, the archbishop had lowered his demands and the majority of non-subscribers had been re-admitted to their charges upon some form of limited subscription: a settlement which Field had striven unsuccessfully to prevent. But even so, this parliament was bombarded with petitions for the relief of the small number of preachers who still stood suspended, and for the reformation of the ministry. These petitions were accompanied by the first instalments of a great 'survey of the ministry' on which the puritan conferences in many counties were now engaged.[3] The survey was an examination of the Church, parish by parish, which set out to prove how many of the clergy were unfitted for their callings, and so to strengthen the plea for more preaching and less persecution of the godly ministers. The Commons, spurred on by letters from the country conferences,[4] were wholly in sympathy with this clamour and sent up the substance of the puritan complaints to the house of lords in a grand petition of sixteen clauses. The effect of this was to demand the abandonment of the archbishop's attempt to reduce the Church to conformity and the adoption of a familiar programme of moderate puritan reform, which had already been rejected on more than one former occasion. But as always, these efforts were made futile by the personal intervention of the Queen, who stated plainly that 'as she found it at her first coming in', so she intended to maintain the state ecclesiastical.[5]

The large number of puritan gentlemen who sat in this parliament—many of them for shires[6]—and the enthusiasm with which

[1] Herts. Rec. Off., Gorhambury MS. VIII/B/143 f. 45.

[2] Cf. Whitgift to the Queen, 12 April 1584 (B.M. Cotton MSS. Vespasian C XIV. ii. f. 224) and to Hatton, 9 May 1584 (B.M. Add. MSS. 15891 f. 123).

[3] Most of the surveys are preserved in the puritan register: *Seconde Parte of Register*, ii, 88–184.

[4] Examples are in B.M. Add. MSS. 38492 ff. 37–38*b*, 68–69.

[5] Neale, *Elizabeth and Parliament, 1584–1601*, 75.

[6] R. C. Gabriel, 'Members of the House of Commons, 1586–87' (Lond. Univ. M.A. thesis, 1954), 10, 18–19.

they received the puritan petitions are no doubt a measure of the fears and passions aroused at a climax in the cold war against the Counter-Reformation. But we must also recognize in the composition and humour of this parliament the fruit of activity by the organized puritan movement, and especially by Field and the London conference. We have little means of judging to what extent organized puritanism had been capable of influencing the parliamentary elections of 1584. Yet on the eve of the next parliament the Dedham conference advised Field to take note of the boroughs which were represented in the house of commons and to use his best means to secure the election of godly members who would advance God's cause. 'Confer amongst yourselves how it may best be compassed. You are placed in the highest place of the Church and land to that end.'[1] When parliament assembled in November 1584 the conferences held fasts and prayer meetings, timed according to Field's directions, and sent up representatives to a general assembly for which the London conference provided the venue.[2] Thomas Fuller reports (without stating his evidence) that these delegates attended 'all day at the door of the Parliament House, and some part of the night in the chambers of the Parliament men, effectually soliciting their business with them'.[3] The correspondence of the puritan conferences shows that there were two sessions of the assembly, one before and the other after Christmas, corresponding to the two sessions of this parliament.

The object of the petitions before the parliament of 1584 was to make the Church safe for puritans and to promote a learned, preaching ministry. There is no reason to suppose that more than a small minority of the puritans were such fanatical presbyterians as to hazard the failure of this moderate programme on a presbyterian bill overturning the entire ecclesiastical establishment. When a presbyterian Member, Dr. Peter Turner, tried to procure the reading of the Geneva 'Form of Prayers' and an enacting bill, he found almost no support from a House which a few days later gave its full backing to the petition of sixteen clauses. Field and the London conference, with some of the Scottish presbyterian leaders then in England, were probably behind this move, but it was

[1] *Dedham Minute Book*, 58.

[2] Ibid. 40–42; Bancroft, *Daungerous positions*, 75; *Survay of the pretended holy discipline*, 366.

[3] *Church History of Britain* (1845), v, 83.

certainly not endorsed by the country conferences. On the eve of the next parliament, Dedham was concerned because some of the London brethren proposed to demand 'a full reformation and to accept of none if they had not all', and decided to advise London that a moderate reformation should be accepted if it were offered.[1] There were many in the Dedham conference who held that presbyterian discipline was not an essential mark of the Church, that prelacy was not necessarily 'antichristian', and that the ministers were bound to offer a 'reconciliation' to the bishops and to accept their government, if only to preserve the unity of the Church. The only practical alternative to a *modus vivendi* with the bishops, they pointed out, would be to 'erect discipline, which we desire, that we may proceed by the order thereof appointed and laid out by the word of God'.[2]

To 'erect discipline', that is, to set up presbyterian church government secretly, within the Church of England: this was the 'grand design'—to use Fuller's phrase—with which Field and other presbyterian leaders were now increasingly occupied. Their first concern was to prepare a constitution to be approved by the puritan assemblies, a 'book of discipline', such as already defined the systems of church order of other Calvinist churches. But to compose such a document and to have it subscribed would bring the puritan churches to the brink of separation from the established Church. Behind this new and critical development lay the influence of a score of leading Scottish presbyterians, including Andrew and James Melville and John Davidson, who were refugees in England from an episcopalian reaction north of the Border. Soon after their arrival in London in June 1584 some of these Scottish ministers had conferred with English puritan leaders,[3] and during July others of them visited the two universities and took part in the usual puritan synods of that month. The secretary of the Oxford conference, Edward Gellibrand of Magdalen, informed Field of profitable meetings in which the delegates had discussed how far they should wait for the state to take the initiative in establishing a presbyterian reformation—an obvious reference to the English, as well as to the Scottish situation.[4] Some of the Scots,

[1] *Dedham Minute Book*, 59.

[2] Ibid. 81, 97–98; John Rylands Lib., English MS. 874 ff. 33–34.

[3] Donaldson, 'Presbyterians Movements', 183.

[4] James Melville, *Autobiography and diary* (Wodrow Soc.), 219; Bancroft, *Daungerous positions*, 73–74.

including James Melville and Davidson, spent the winter of 1584–85 in London, and they no doubt influenced the general assembly which was meeting at the same time. One of the offences for which Field was suspended from preaching in March 1585 was resorting 'to the Scottish ministers, being three of them, and sometimes they come to his house'.[1]

The first draft of the English book of discipline may be found in the book which Dr. Turner proffered to parliament in December 1584. This was the Geneva liturgy, extensively revised and recently reprinted by Waldegrave,[2] which contained the form of government for a single congregation, John Knox's at Geneva. But Field and his friends had pasted in the back cover a loose leaf,[3] which briefly defined a polity of conferences and synods and so adapted the book to the needs of a national presbyterian Church. Turner's book provided the basis for the full-scale book of discipline on which the theorists of English presbyterianism were now engaged. The authors of the *Disciplina Ecclesiae*[4] or, as the seventeenth century knew it, the *Directory of Church-government*,[5] were Walter Travers and, probably, Thomas Cartwright. Field's function was to hasten the work, to inform the conferences of its progress, and finally to send out copies of the completed text. By July 1585 the first draft must have been complete, for Field told Travers that he wanted it 'read over with as much speed as could be', so that instructions could be given to the conferences for putting it in practice.[6] This suggests that Field had already received requests like that from Suffolk, which asked him for 'the several grounds and demonstrations for the holy discipline, which we are sure you have in readiness'.[7] Field told Travers that if the brethren agreed to circulate the conferences with fair copies of the discipline and instructions for action, he would 'wholly employ' himself in that service.[8] In November, Gellibrand of Oxford sent Field an urgent request for the book. But meanwhile it must have been agreed

[1] *Seconde Parte of Register*, i, 284.

[2] W. D. Maxwell, *John Knox's Genevan Service Book*, 75; Bancroft, *A sermon preached at Paules Crosse* (1589), 62.

[3] An example is in B.M. C. III. b. 6.

[4] In two parts: *Disciplina ecclesiae sacra Dei verba descripta* and *Disciplina synodica ex ecclesiarum quae eam ex verbo Dei instaurarunt usu synodis atque libris de eadem re scriptis collecta, et ad certa quaedam capita redacta;* printed, F. Paget, *Introduction to the Fifth Book of Hooker's Ecclesiastical Polity*.

[5] Eng. trans. with this title, 1644; repr. in facsimile by P. Lorimer, 1872.

[6] Bancroft, *Daungerous positions*, 76.

[7] Bancroft, *Survay of the discipline*, 366.

[8] *Daungerous positions*, 76.

that Travers should revise the text. In January 1586 Gellibrand was again asking Field to send him the discipline, 'which Master Travers promised to make perfect, when it is finished. We will put it in practice and try men's minds therein as we may.'[1]

In the event, repeated revisions of the discipline seem to have delayed its dispersal until early in 1587, when copies were distributed from a general assembly which had sat in London to direct the puritan campaign in the parliament of 1586–87.[2] Attached to the book of discipline was a form of subscription to its contents, probably composed by Field.[3] The conferences were to subscribe the discipline 'as agreeable to God's Word', if necessary with the exception of doubtful points; to promise to work for its establishment by petition to the Queen, privy council and parliament 'and by other lawful and convenient means to further and advance' it; and to undertake to practise it, so far as the law of the land and the 'peace of our present state of our Church may suffer and not enforce to the contrary', a safeguarding clause on which the issue of a prosecution would later depend. In particular, the ministers were to promise to follow a uniform order in their preaching and ministry—presumably an approximation to the Geneva liturgy—and to observe the discipline in convening the conferences and assemblies of the Church: meeting every six weeks in local *classes* of not more than ten members, every half year in provincial synods and at the general assembly annually, at parliament time, and on any other occasion when it might be summoned.

The welcome accorded to the book of discipline varied from county to county. In some places, the puritans seem to have subscribed the articles of approbation and, where meetings of the ministers had hitherto followed no formal order, to have distributed themselves in *classes* of the prescribed size and set up provincial synods. In Northamptonshire, for example, the ministers divided themselves between three conferences, which sent delegates to a provincial meeting in Northampton.[4] Yet when a general assembly met in Cambridge in September 1587, most conferences had sent no reply to the London articles, while others

[1] Ibid.

[2] Collinson, 'Classical Movement', 561–9, 577–8.

[3] Versions in *Dedham Minute Book*, 92–93 and Lambeth Palace Lib. MS. 113; fragments in B.M. Harl. MSS. 6849 f. 222 and Star Chamber 5 A 49/34.

[4] Bancroft, *Daungerous positions*, 76; deposition of John Johnson: Star Chamber 5 A 49/34.

had registered doubts, and all action was deferred.[1] The Dedham conference repeatedly put off consideration of the book, having already ruled before they received it that to subscribe their opinion in such a matter was 'not safe in any respect'.[2] There is no evidence for the frequently quoted statement of Daniel Neal that there were five hundred subscribers to the book of discipline. The probability is that it was rejected or indefinitely deferred by the majority of the members of the conference movement. A decision of the Cambridge assembly of September 1587 to circulate a printed text[3] was never implemented, and the book was still undergoing revision at assemblies which met in London and at Cambridge in 1589.[4] Field's attempt to impose a presbyterian uniformity on English puritanism had plainly failed.

Although it is sometimes stated that the book of discipline was 'prepared for Parliament',[5] there is no evidence that the puritans ever contemplated putting the presbyterian system before parliament in such a systematic and detailed form. In spite of the limiting clauses which were inserted in the articles of approbation to preserve a shadow of legality, there is no doubt that the discipline was intended for immediate practice. Nevertheless, there was one final attempt to employ the authority of parliament to establish a presbyterian Church of England. A new parliament met at the end of 1586, and in November petitions for the relief of suspended preachers and for the reform of the ministry once more came into London from many counties. The survey of the ministry, complete for at least thirteen counties or portions of counties, was summarized and attached to a massive 'General Supplication'.[6] A general assembly met in London and presumably communicated these documents to sympathetic Members of the house of commons.[7]

Under cover of this barrage, the presbyterian leaders intended once more to bring the Geneva 'Form of Prayers', newly revised, before parliament. On this occasion, they had the assistance of a

[1] John Strype, *Annals of . . . Queen Elizabeth's Happy Reign* (Oxford, 1824), iii (2), 477–9.

[2] *Dedham Minute Book*, 61–67; John Rylands Lib. English MS. 874 f. 10*b*.

[3] Strype, *Annals*, iii (2), 478.

[4] Depositions of Thomas Stone, Thomas Barber, William Perkins: Star Chamber 5 A 49/34.

[5] P. J. Hughes, *The Reformation in England*, iii, 202.

[6] *Seconde Parte of Register*, ii, 70–87.

[7] *Dedham Minute Book*, 60–61, 92–93, 98.

small organized party within the House. Five Members, including Peter Wentworth, were later stated to have made plans before parliament met for preferring the Geneva liturgy and a bill to establish it, preparations in which Field and others of the clerical party must surely have shared. The great matter of Mary queen of Scots prevented any action before Christmas, but on 27 February Anthony Cope, one of the group of five, rose to bring before the attention of the House the 'Form of Prayers'[1] and an enacting bill, which, if carried, would have authorized the Geneva liturgy as the only legal prayer book of the Church of England.[2] More than that: the bill proposed to make 'utterly void and of none effect' all 'former laws, customs, statutes, ordinances or constitutions' which in any way defined the religious practice or ecclesiastical organization of England. Cope's collaborators followed him in speaking to this drastic measure. It says much for the extremes to which Protestant feeling was running on the eve of the Armada, and something, too, for the lobbying by presbyterians inside and outside parliament, that the Commons heard these speeches out and, in calling for the bill to be read, overrode the Speaker himself. At this moment the Queen acted. She confiscated both the documents then before the House and Turner's bill and book of 1585, thus provoking Wentworth's celebrated oration on the privileges of the house of commons. Cope and his fellow-conspirators were committed to custody, and three privy councillors were charged to make set speeches in the House against presbyterianism.

These events proved once and for all that, so long as Elizabeth lived, the most masterly tactics which Field and his parliamentary friends could devise would not achieve the establishment of presbyterianism by public authority. It was doubtless at the close of this parliament that Field told a wavering brother: 'Tush, Mr. Edmunds, hold your peace. Seeing we cannot compass these things by suit nor dispute, it is the multitude and people that must bring the discipline to pass which we desire.'[3] All hope now rested on the covert practice of presbyterianism: these were the months when the book of discipline was circulated to the conferences.

A general assembly at Cambridge in September 1587 came

[1] A revised text printed by Richard Schilders in Middelburg in 1586.
[2] *Seconde Parte of Register*, ii. 212–15; for partly corrected text: S.P. 12/199/2.
[3] Deposition of Thomas Edmunds: Star Chamber 5 A 49/34.

within a hair's breadth of advocating separatism, when it decided to refer to the conferences and to other reformed churches overseas the motions that the brethren should cease to communicate with unlearned ministers, should withold recognition from the bishops and repudiate the unlawful episcopal discipline, and should base their ministries on the true, presbyterian discipline.[1] At a synod in Warwickshire in the spring of 1588 it was ruled that 'the faithful' ought not to communicate with unlearned ministers; that since the calling of bishops was unlawful, the godly could not be ordained by them or accept deprivation from them unless 'compelled by . . . civil force'; and that the discipline was to be taught to the people and that 'men of better understanding' were to be persuaded to embrace and practice it 'so far as they shall be well able, with the peace of the Church'.[2] In Northamptonshire, some ministers renounced their orders and received a new ordination from the brethren of the conferences.[3] Presbyterian elderships were secretly established in some parishes.[4]

Unless the Church of the Elizabethan Settlement was no true Church, these decisions were a denial of all that the puritans had hitherto stood for. The hope of a national reformation was now abandoned for a sectarian separation. Field had said that 'the people' were to bring the discipline in. But how many presbyterians were there among the people of England? Presbyterianism could not hope to stand unless it stood united with its discipline strengthened by the authority of the civil magistrate. Only a minority, even of the puritan ministers, would follow the extremists in their complete renunciation of the ministry and discipline of the Establishment. Richard Rogers of Wethersfield, certainly one of the hotter spirits, noted in his diary 'the variety of opinions' about church government among the learned, confessing his own 'unsettledness therein', and later observed that the question of communicating with unlearned ministers 'doth still spread further undissolved'.[5] And now, while the puritans floundered in perplexity 'and men's minds

[1] Strype, *Annals*, iii (2), 477–9.

[2] Bancroft's translation of the *Acta* of this synod: B.M. Harl. MSS. 6866 f. 321*b*; *Daungerous positions*, 86–87; cf. the examinations of participants: Star Chamber 5 A 56/1.

[3] B.M. Harl. MSS. 6849 ff. 220, 222*b*; Star Chamber 5 A 56/1, 27/33; Bancroft, *Daungerous positions*, 113–14.

[4] Collinson, 'Classical Movement', 710–16.

[5] *Two Elizabethan Puritan Diaries*, ed. M. M. Knappen, 98–99.

wavered this way and that way',[1] the political tide turned decisively against them.

The great patrons of puritanism were dead or dying; the defeat of the Armada had for the time allayed those extravagant fears of popery which had sheltered the puritans for so long; while the mischievous libels of Martin Marprelate disgraced the whole puritan cause and gave its enemies their opportunity. Confident of the Queen's favour, Whitgift, Hatton and, among the High Commissioners, Richard Cosin and Hatton's chaplain, Richard Bancroft, now undertook the systematic exposure and repression of organized puritanism. One by one, in 1589 and 1590, the known ring-leaders of the movement were examined before the High Commissioners and their studies searched for incriminating evidence. Among the papers which fell into the hands of the authorities were some at least from Field's files, including at least fifty letters from more than twenty correspondents in the country conferences, which Bancroft later used in his published exposures of presbyterian subversion. The register, however, escaped Bancroft's vigilance. The evidence gathered by these means was employed in the prosecution of nine ministers, including Cartwright, first before the High Commission and then in the Star Chamber, the aim being to prove judicially that the presbyterian movement had been seditious in manner and intent. Although it was clear by 1592 that this exemplary prosecution had failed in its main purpose, its effect was to drive the organized puritan movement so far underground that only occasional glimpses of it can be caught in the decade before its revival at the accession of James I. Many puritans were driven into the congregationalist separatism of the Barrowist movement, while many more conformed and reserved themselves 'to a better time.'[2] Very few found the presbyterian position of the 'church within the Church' to be any longer tenable.

Whether the course of events would have been the same if John Field had remained at the centre of the organization is a matter for mere speculation, for Field was buried at St. Giles, Cripplegate, on 26 March 1588.[3] There are very few references to him in puritan documents for some months before that, and we may guess that illness had removed him from active leadership of the movement

[1] Nicholls, *The plea of the innocent*, 31–32.
[2] Ibid. 35.
[3] Brinkley, *Nathan Field*, 5.

even earlier.[1] With the death of Field, the London conference ceased to give the decisive lead which had always been the mainspring of the presbyterian movement. When the Northamptonshire conference suggested preparing a new survey of the ministry for the parliament of 1589, Walter Travers, who had taken Field's place as London corresponding secretary, 'seemed nothing to mislike' the suggestion but thought that there was too little time to complete the survey before parliament met.[2] What if Field had lived? There are some hints, such as the impatient remark to Thomas Edmunds already quoted, and the possibility of a connection with Martin Marprelate, that in the last year of his life, Field was moving into a more extreme position out of exasperation with the repeated failure of the puritans to make any headway in parliament. Like some in the midlands, he may well have come to the conclusion that an established Reformed Church of England was no longer realizable. It is at least possible that he was about to use his remarkable powers of organization to lead out a presbyterian secession from the Church on a larger scale than the sectarian separation of the Brownists and Barrowists.

John Field was one of the most brilliant revolutionaries in an age of revolution, although neither his own generation nor posterity has appreciated the scope and significance of his career. In a state with the political structure of a France or a Scotland, and perhaps even in England under any sovereign but Elizabeth, he might have emerged as one of the statesmen of sixteenth-century Calvinism: the Melville, or even the Knox, of a thoroughgoing English Reformation.

[1] His will was made on 1 Feb. 1588: P.C.C. 38 Rutland.
[2] Deposition of John Johnson: Star Chamber 5 A 49/34 f. 8.

VI

The Elizabethan Merchants of Exeter

W. G. HOSKINS

The first meeting of the Chamber, the governing body of Exeter, after the accession of Queen Elizabeth I, took place as usual in the ancient Guildhall that still stands in the High Street of the city, though it lacked in the autumn of 1558 its now-familiar renaissance portico. Of this assembly of twenty-four men, including the mayor, all but one were merchants. The single exception was Robert Chafe, an ecclesiastical official connected with the cathedral, a skilful and learned lawyer, 'a man of very good condition being of great modesty and gravity, very friendly and loving to all men', who was twice to be chosen mayor of the city—in 1568 and again in 1576.[1]

John Buller, as mayor, presided over this first Elizabethan assembly, but the father of the house was old William Hurst, now in his seventy-sixth year. He had been mayor as far back as 1524 and three times since, and three times had represented Exeter in parliament. He had come to the thriving city, the son of a South Devon yeoman, as long ago as 1497 and so could look back over sixty years in its streets, and to more than forty years of service on its governing body. Around this venerable figure on the benches of the Guildhall sat not a few prosperous men who had been his apprentices in their youth. Even at that great age, his fifth mayoralty—in 1561—had yet to come and he had another ten years of life ahead of him.[2]

[1] Exeter city records, Book 55 (known as John Hooker's Commonplace Book), which contains a number of biographies of mayors written by Hooker from his personal knowledge. He was chamberlain of the city from 1556 until his death in 1601.

[2] William Hurst is traditionally said to have died (in 1568) at the age of ninety-six, which would have made him eighty-nine at the time of his last mayoralty. The records show, however, that he was admitted to the freedom of the city by

The city governed by this assembly was one of the largest and wealthiest in Elizabethan England. It was the social and cultural capital of a large province, a cathedral city, an industrial town, and a busy port. In wealth and population, among the provincial towns, it ranked after Norwich, Newcastle and Bristol, and was the most important city between London and Land's End.[1] Yet it was very small in extent. A man could walk comfortably around the entire circuit of its walls in twenty minutes or so, for it was less than a mile and a half around. The entire area enclosed by these walls was but ninety-three acres, though to that one must add, by the year 1558, small suburbs outside all four gates which carried houses along the road in a ribbon development for possibly a couple of hundred yards in each direction. The extra-mural suburbs consisted almost entirely of working-class houses, except for a few merchant-houses outside the West Gate in the principal industrial and commercial quarter. But the great majority of the merchant-class lived within the walls, in one of half a dozen small, rich, central parishes, and in one or other of only half a dozen streets.

The merchant-class was similarly small, compact, and closely inter-related by marriage. We can get a rough idea of its total size in a given generation from the number of admissions to the freedom of the city, a necessary qualification for all who practised as merchants whether they had been apprenticed in boyhood to an Exeter freeman or had come to the city from elsewhere as grown men. In the last quarter of the sixteenth century the number of merchants and mercers admitted to the freedom amounted to 104.[2] We may reasonably assume that the average business-life of a merchant was not much above 25 to 30 years, so that at any given time there may have been about a hundred merchants in the city.

apprenticeship in 1504–5, probably at the age of twenty-one, so making his birth-date about 1483. This gives a more likely, though still remarkable, chronology for his public career.

[1] For the ranking by wealth of English towns in the 1520s see W. G. Hoskins, 'Provincial Towns in the Early Sixteenth Century' (*Trans R.H.S.*, 5th ser. vi), 4–6. Since that time Coventry and Salisbury had both greatly declined, leaving Exeter in undisputed fourth place among the provincial towns.

[2] The occupations of new freemen are not regularly stated in the records until 1575. The terms 'mercer' and 'merchant' were practically inter-changeable at Exeter, as is abundantly clear from the records. I am indebted to Mr R. A. MacKinley, the keeper of the Exeter city records, for the use of his valuable lists of the freemen, as yet unpublished.

Such a figure is clearly only approximate, but it will not be far wrong: at its worst it serves to give us an order of magnitude.

The total population of the city in this generation was between nine and ten thousand—about two thousand families at the most. Of these, then, one family in every twenty was a merchant-family[1] and belonged potentially to the governing class. From these alone, with very few exceptions, were chosen the mayors, sheriffs, and members of parliament for the city. The choice, indeed, was even finer, for within this small class there were closely-knit dynasties of the wealthiest merchants related to each other, often more than once over, by marriage. The fifty Elizabethan mayors—there were two mayors in some years because of early deaths—were chosen from twenty-six different families. But in this narrower field, too, marriages had united Hursts, Martins, and Peters, or Periams and Blackallers. In this way we are reduced to perhaps a score of ruling families in the Elizabethan city and this oligarchic rule carried over well into the seventeenth century.[2]

In the smaller town of Leicester, the Elizabethan mayors were also drawn from twenty-six different families: but Leicester had just about one-third the number of families as Exeter,[3] so to that extent its choice of mayor was far less oligarchic. At Norwich, by far the largest and richest of provincial cities, the forty-seven Elizabethan mayors were drawn from twenty-nine different families. Here, with a total population of well over three thousand families, the field of choice was even narrower than at Exeter. The larger the town, the more oligarchic was its government likely to be in the sixteenth century. Yet there was a wider choice at Norwich as between occupations. Whereas at Exeter only four of the fifty mayors were chosen from outside the ranks of the merchants, at Norwich the non-merchant groups provided thirteen out of forty-seven mayors, drawing upon worsted and dornix weavers, a butcher, a baker, a saddler, a scrivener, and a goldsmith.[4]

[1] This estimate of an 'upper class' amounting to five per cent of the total population agrees substantially with the conclusions of Professor MacCaffrey, arrived at by an entirely different method, in *Exeter, 1540–1640*, 249, 250.

[2] For more examples of merchant family alliances see MacCaffrey, op. cit. 254–6.

[3] It had 591 families in 1563, say about 650 families during the later Elizabethan period.

[4] For Norwich, see B. Cozens-Hardy and E. A. Kent, *The Mayors of Norwich, 1403 to 1835*.

At Bristol, the second richest provincial city, the choice of mayor was more widely made. Of the eighteen mayors between 1558 and 1576, eight were not merchants, tanners and brewers being conspicuous in the list. After 1576, however, the merchants predominated heavily. Out of the next twenty-eight mayors only three were not merchants, and Mr McGrath has shown that in the seventeenth century the key positions of mayor, sheriff, and chamberlain were all held by merchants.[1] Mayors were chosen also from a much wider range of families than at Norwich or Exeter. No fewer than thirty-eight different families are represented in the mayoral list from 1558 to 1603. Bristol was, for some local reason, the least oligarchical of the large provincial cities, though it was becoming more so in the last quarter of the century.

The merchant class at Exeter, as in all the larger provincial towns, was recruited to a considerable extent from outside—not only from the surrounding countryside but from such distant parts as Wales, Cheshire, Worcestershire, or Suffolk. Younger sons of ability for whom there were no bright prospects at home would naturally tend to move to a thriving commercial city like Exeter; but their biographies by John Hooker make it clear that their destinies often depended upon some human accident and not upon any inhuman calculation of economic prospects. 'The girl at the door of an inn' is as important in this respect as the account-book, perhaps more so.

So it was that Thomas Prestwood the elder, who died in the autumn of 1558, had come to Exeter from his native city of Worcester exactly thirty years earlier. His father, 'conceiving a good hope of him by reason of his pregnant wit and forwardness sent him to London, where he bound him apprentice unto a rich and wealthy merchant under whom he prospered and did very well. And upon occasion, being a traveller for his master and in his affairs, he came to this city [Exeter] and in course of time he became acquainted with the widow of one John Bodley of this city. She . . . having found favour in his sight, he made his master acquainted therewith and with his good favour he followed his former suit to the widow and obtained and married her. And then,

[1] P. McGrath, *Merchants and Merchandise in 17th-century Bristol* (Bristol Rec. Soc. xix), pp. xxv–xxvi. I am greatly indebted to Miss Elizabeth Ralph, the city archivist of Bristol, for preparing for me a list of the Elizabethan merchants of Bristol and their occupations. There is no complete printed list for this period.

leaving his master, he remained and dwelled in this city, and followed the trade of merchandise wherein he had been brought up, and did prosper very well and increased unto good wealth and riches . . .'[1]

Thomas Prestwood followed a familiar pattern in marrying a rich widow. So did Thomas Bodley, the grandson of John Bodley, when he married the widow of a wealthy Totnes merchant in the summer of 1586, within four months of her husband's death. Nicholas Ball of Totnes, then one of the richest little towns in England, had made a fortune in a short space of time 'specially by trading for pilchers', and much of this fortune passed by the marriage of his widow to Bodley. The Bodleian Library is founded in part at least upon the humble pilchard.

The marriages of Prestwood and Bodley illustrate a general thesis: the influence of rich widows upon economic progress. In an age when men generally died young, the supply of active and wealthy widows was a noticeable feature of society. Many an enterprising young man in the sixteenth century owed his ultimate success to this simple biological fact.

Thomas Richardson, a merchant dealing principally in wines, mayor in 1566–7, had come to Exeter from Cheshire, through some personal relationship which is not made clear by Hooker. 'By means of one Michael Lymett of this city, apothecary, he was brought to this city and served under the said Lymett. When he came to ripe years and was married, he kept a wine tavern and was a merchant adventurer for wines, and following that trade in good order and diligently he attained to good wealth and nobility, and did not only serve this city by retail but also all the gentlemen in the shire of Devon by the tuns and hogsheads, with whom he was in great credit and favour. He was of very good conditions and qualities, given to all good excercises and a good companion for any gentleman or honest man, whether it were shooting, bowling, or any other pastime. And albeit he were very honest, friendly, and courteous to all men, so would he not receive wrong at any man's hands, neither would he give his beard for the washing. He had passed and borne all the offices of the city, in every of

[1] Hooker, Commonplace Book, loc. cit. The city records show Thomas Prestwood admitted by fine to the freedom in 1528–9, and chosen for the Twenty-Four on 27 September 1534. He was mayor in 1544–5 and in 1550–1, and sat in parliament as the member for Exeter from October 1549 until April 1552.

M

which he used and behaved himself very well . . . for which he was well respected both in town and country.'

Simon Knight, mayor in 1570 and again in 1579, was Somerset born, of good parentage. 'His father having many other children brought him to this city and bound him apprentice unto a merchant named John Morgan, after whose death he served under Mr William Hurst, who, having a good liking of the towardness of the young man did employ him both at his side and beyond the seas, and he did so well follow his business that he prospered very well and was of good wealth and hability, and was at length twice mayor of this city. [He] did very well in the first, but in the latter he was so encumbered in litigious and troublesome matters that in following of them he was the more remiss in public matters . . . [But] well thinking of himself and standing in his own conceit to be wiser than others, and also for his too much jesting of other men, he was much blamed and the less liked.'

Though the Elizabethan merchant class was liberally recruited from outside, more often than not from the younger sons of good families, it contained also a solid core of second-generation mercantile families. Such were the Periams, the Midwinters, Blackalls (or Blackallers), Martins, and Spicers. Some successful merchants failed to find successors in trade: their eldest sons either moved out to a country estate or withdrew their money from trade to use it in other ways: we shall return to this point later. But a few merchant-families continued into the second, and occasionally into the third generation. Of these, the Periams were perhaps the most notable. The first of them in the city, William Periam, was the son of a franklin in the nearby parish of Broadclyst. He had been admitted to the freedom of the city as a capper in the same year as William Hurst (1504–5) and had flourished exceedingly, making most of his early fortune at least in the tin trade and dying a rich man. He was followed in business by his second son, John Periam, who was chosen mayor in 1563 and again in 1572. He was a zealous Protestant and had assisted Lord Russell during the Catholic rebellion of 1549 in the West 'with money and other necessaries to his great comfort'. As a consequence of this, he was obliged to spend several years abroad during Mary's reign, by which he lost nothing, for he became the chief governor of the company of English Merchants in Antwerp. He was apparently an unlikeable man, for Hooker, though a good Protestant and therefore well disposed to Periam on religious grounds, speaks of him with modified approval as 'a very worthy man in many respects, and had many good parts in him'. Nevertheless, he made a good mayor of the city. 'His government was upright. A great favourer of the poor man's cause, an upright judge in all causes of law depending before him, severe against the wicked and lewd persons who received at his hands according to their deserts, and friendly and loving to the good and honest, and them he defended against all enemies . . . As he lived, so he died virtuously, godly, and in years, whose memory deserves not to be forgotten.'

The Periams were perhaps a quick-tempered lot. Hooker tells us of William Periam, mayor in 1532, that 'he was but a plain dealing man, but rough and soon offended if he was abused and with wrongs he would not lightly lay up . . .' He remained a peasant for all his business acumen and wealth. And the temper of his son is revealed to us in his will. He had left 'to Jasper Horsey to fynde at one of the Universities £30'. In a codicil a few months later he tightened his bequest: 'Jasper Horsey only to have his legacy if he stand bound to be at one of the Universities there to study Divinity and so to be of the ministry'. A few days later, there was a row. Young Jasper was evidently not amenable to the dictates of old Periam. To the will was added: 'This I write 22 May 1573. Forasmuch as Jasper Horsey went from the house on Whitsunday morning very ungratefully and uncourteously not saying farewell to me or any of all the household, whereas he had been sufficiently brought up as I take it v or vi years, I having in remembrance this his ungratefulness give him only 40 shillings with his apparel and his books and nothing else, so god bless him.'

John Periam was a great believer in education. His own father, rough as he was, had caused him 'to be brought up in knowledge and learning', later putting him as apprentice to a merchant. His own eldest son, William, he sent to the High School in Exeter and thence on to Oxford, where he became a fellow of Exeter College, apparently at the age of seventeen, in 1551. William Periam turned to the law, in which (surprisingly) Devonians had always shown unnatural abilities, and eventually became a judge (1581) and sat on the commission for the trial of Mary queen of Scots. Down in Devon he had his country seat at Fulford, a few miles outside Exeter, not far from his younger brother, John, who had ceased also to have any interests as a merchant and lived, for the latter part of his life, as a country gentleman.

Once admitted to the freedom of the city, by apprenticeship or by fine, the merchant set up in business for himself. No Exeter merchant was substantial enough to own a whole ship, or even half a ship. The great majority joined with half a dozen others to fill a ship with cargoes. Harry Maunder (died 1564) owned 'half a quarter of a barke called the Dragon, of Topsham', valued at £8. George Hunt (died 1565) owned half a ship called the *George*, valued at £30. And the ships of the late sixteenth century were generally very small. Of the 123 ships that entered the port of Exeter in the year 1597–8 no fewer than 96 were of less than thirty tons. The average ship belonging to the port of Exeter was one of twenty to thirty tons. The largest in that year were the *Dolphin* of Exmouth (100 tons), the *Endeavour* of Topsham (80 tons), and the *Rose* of Exmouth (70 tons). A typical sort of ship was the *Robert* of Topsham, of only twenty tons, which came in from St. Malo in Brittany with a cargo shared among eleven Exeter merchants; or the *True Meaning* of Kenton, of thirty tons, which came in from Bordeaux with a cargo of twenty-four tuns of Gascon wine shared between two Exeter merchants and one from Tiverton.

Even at the end of the century, too, the range of the Exeter merchant's trading activities was not great. Of the ships entering the port in 1597–8, nearly one-half were engaged in the coasting trade, mainly from Wales with coal, from London with mixed cargoes, and from other Devon ports. Of the fifty ships coming in from foreign ports, Brittany sent the most (18), and the 'salt ports' of western France were second with 16. Other French ports (Rouen and Bordeaux) accounted for four more. So three ships out of every four in Exeter's foreign trade came from or went to France. Of the rest, five ships entered from Newfoundland (mainly with salt fish), four came in from Middelburg or Danzig, and three from Madeira or Portugal. The merchants of Exeter were certainly not as adventurous and wide-ranging as those of Plymouth. Their trade with France was a long-established one and they felt little desire, apart from Newfoundland, to open up new lines of country. What they could not get from France, and to a limited degree from a few other foreign ports, they relied upon getting through the re-export trade from London. There was, at the end of the sixteenth century, the beginning of wider interests. By about 1600 a small trade with Ireland and with the Baltic had been developed, and we can detect the beginnings of the trade with Holland which was to become the greatest of all the Exeter trades during the latter half of the seventeenth century. There was, indeed, a more considerable trade with Spain than might appear from casual references in the port books. This trade was stopped for years by war, but it is significant that in 1580, for example, the biggest 'adventure' that William Chappell was engaged in was in Spain, where he had £322 owing to him. From Spain, when political conditions permitted it, came Spanish wool and Bilbao iron.

The inventories of Exeter merchants' personal estates tell us a good deal more about their trading activities than we could gather from the port books or custom accounts. Nearly every merchant at this period carried on a retail business through a shop on his premises. The list of people who owed money to Harry Maunder at his death in 1564 is probably typical of most merchants' businesses. There were 112 debtors, of whom no fewer than 75 owed small sums ranging from one penny to twenty shillings. These, and probably others, are clearly retail customers. Other debtors owed several pounds and are identifiable as wholesale buyers. Such are Thomas Richardson, the vintner, who owed £18 9*s*. 8*d*., and Philip Yard of Exeter, also a vintner, who owed £9 6*s*. 8*d*. for sack.

Harry Maunder had an extensive business in Spanish iron, supplying numerous smiths in the city and for a dozen miles around. But besides wine and iron, he dealt in an extraordinary miscellany of commodities: the 'shop book' speaks of canvas, calico, figs, coal, tin, linen cloth, hops, grindstones, mustard mills, vinegar, raisins, dowlas, saffron, alum, playing cards, shirts, and woollen cards, while in the shop and warehouse we find many other commodities, such as brass, brown paper, soap, wax, kerseys, yarn, thread, silk, nails, buttons, parchment, lead, pepper, ratsbane, and Heaven knows what else.

Much went to other shopkeepers and to country gentry. The Elizabethan merchant covered the whole range of trading, rather indiscriminately, from direct import from overseas or London and the coastal ports, down to pennyworths of things sold in the shop. There is some indication, however, that by the early seventeenth century the keeping of a shop was regarded as beneath the dignity of a big merchant, and he was beginning to leave that to others. When John Periam, in the third generation of the family (1616), left £1000 to be lent to five Merchant Adventurers of the city, trading beyond the seas, he stipulated that they should not be shopkeepers by retail.

The only inventories of personal estate to survive are those in the court of orphans records among the city muniments.[1] This court was set up in 1563 to safeguard the interests of widows and orphaned children where a citizen died leaving children under age. Hence the value of many estates is less than it would have been had the head of the family lived to his full term of years. On the other hand, it may well be argued that death in the forties or fifties was a common feature of sixteenth-century life and to that extent these records are more truly representative of the economic facts of merchant life than those drawn from men who all died of old age. A table of twenty-seven merchants' estates for the period 1564 to 1618 is therefore as instructive as any (Table 1).

The average merchant estate was one of £1913 gross (that of John Aplyn, 1594). This compares very closely, as we might expect, with the average personal estate of a Bristol merchant (over a somewhat wider period) which Professor Jordan puts at £1921. In the same period, the average (median) personal estate of a London merchant was £7780,[2] about four times that of Exeter or Bristol men. About one-third of the Exeter merchants left personal estate valued at £3000 or more.

It will be observed from the table opposite that there is often a considerable gap between the gross personal estate and the net estate. This gap is accounted for in two ways: by the money owing at the time of death by the dead man, and by the debts due to him which the executors write off as 'doubtful', or more usually, 'desperate'. The proportion of 'desperate debts' to the whole debt owing to the merchant's estate is often remarkably high. In some instances they were greater than the 'good debts'. An outstanding example is that of the rich merchant William Martyn, who died in 1609. The good debts amounted to nearly £1542, and the

[1] The entire contents of the Exeter probate registry were needlessly destroyed in an air-raid of May 1942, while the inventories preserved (if that is the correct word) at Somerset House are still inaccessible to students.

[2] W. K. Jordan, *Philanthropy in England*, 376. The average personal estate for a provincial merchant at this period was £1,428: ibid. 336.

desperate debts to over £2633. William Spicer (1604) was owed £300 in good debts, but a further £662 of debts were written off as 'desperate'. No uniformity is observable in this respect.

TABLE I. *Exeter Merchants' Estates, 1564–1618*

Name	*Date*	*Gross Personal Estate*	*Net Personal Estate*
Harry Maunder	1564	£556	£360
Edmond Whetcombe	1565	£791	£710
Edward Lymett	1571	£509	£382
John Bodley	1572	£156	£146
Thomas Prestwood	1576	£905	£662
William Chappell	1580	£2378	£2265
Thomas Chappell	1590	£3266	£3225
Richard Swete	1591	£1485	£708
John Follett	1591	£255	£135
Richard Mawdytt	1592	£356	£277
Richard Reynolds	1592	£2086	£1473
John Aplyn	1594	£1913	£1592
John Spurway	1595	£1074	£862
Walter Horsey	1597	£2670	£2464
Richard Beavis	1603	£3492	£3063
William Spicer	1604	£3825	£2916
David Bagwell	1604	£675	–£102*
John Trosse	1605	£236	£166
Thomas Cooke	1606	£3000	£1716
Alexander Germyn	1608	£986	£551
Robert Parr	1608	£3976	£2223
John Plea	1609	£827	£713
Thomas Snowe	1609	£2032	£1818
William Newcombe	1609	£2174	£2037
William Martyn	1609	£6381	£4401
Thomas Mogridge	1617	£5189	£4343
John Lant	1618	£7317	£4664

* David Bagwell died young at St. Malo. His debts amounted to £777, exceeding his assets at that time.

Sometimes the desperate debts are less than one-tenth of the whole; in other cases they are as much as two-thirds of the whole debt due to the dead man's estate. Much must have depended upon whether England was at war with the country where the debtors lay; but it is also clear from many inventories that a high proportion of 'desperate debts' were purely local.

The variation from one inventory to another is so great, and must so often arise from accidental circumstances at the time, that an average proportion of bad debts to good is probably rather meaningless. All we can note is that the Elizabethan merchant had

TABLE II. *Good Debts and Desperate Debts, 1565–1617*

Name	*Date*	*Good Debts*	*Desperate Debts*	*Total Debts Due*
Edmond Whetcombe	1565	£230	£81	£311
William Chappell	1580	£902	£113	£1015
Thomas Chappell	1590	£957	£21	£978
Richard Beavis	1603	£256	£193	£449
William Spicer	1604	£300	£662	£962
Alexander Germyn	1608	£257	£270	£527
Robert Parr	1608	£1958	£1310	£3268
John Plea	1609	£350	£38	£388
Thomas Snowe	1609	£696	£52	£748
William Martyn	1609	£1542	£2634	£4176
William Tothill	1609	£201	£95	£296
Thomas Mogridge	1617	£1186	£410	£1596

to reckon with the serious possibility that a considerable proportion of the money owing to him at any given time was going to be difficult to collect, and that a considerable residue might have to be written off as beyond hope of realization. The estimate of 'desperate debts' was probably a rather subjective one also, and might be considerably amended before the estate was finally wound up. We see this in the case of Richard Swete (1591), where the original estimate at the making of the inventory was of £295 3*s.* 11*d.* in desperate debts. In what seems to be the final reckoning, the figure had been reduced to £46 8*s.* 5*d.* Executors probably tended to take an extremely conservative view of debts outstanding as a precaution against arousing optimistic hopes in the widow, but hoped for better things eventually.

We also notice the great variation in the sums of ready money kept in merchants' houses at any particular time. This is largely a reflection of the opportunities for investment and also perhaps of the enterprise, or lack of it, manifested by different men of wealth.

The second smallest sum of ready money was left by one of the wealthiest merchants in the city. This was Thomas Prestwood, the son of the Thomas Prestwood already referred to. The inventory of his personal estate does not reveal his true wealth, for he had put a great deal of money into real estate—both farms in the countryside and houses in the city. His total personal estate was therefore comparatively small—only £905, less than half the average. In such cases as this the inventories can be quite misleading about a man's true wealth.

TABLE III. *Ready Money in Merchants' Houses*

		(*nearest* £)
Harry Maunder	1564	£69
John Bodley	1572	£20
Thomas Prestwood	1576	£25
William Chappell	1580	£192
Thomas Chappell	1590	£1303
Richard Swete	1591	£566
Richard Beavis	1603	£410
Thomas Mogridge	1617	£914

Thomas Prestwood senior had built up a substantial merchanting business, but then, Hooker tells us, 'in his later age by little and little he gave over his trade of merchandise and employed his wealth in purchasing of lands and in building of houses, especially within the city, which do yet remain as goodly ornaments to beautify the same.[1] He died in good age and left his lands and possessions to his only son Thomas Prestwood . . . who, beginning where his father left, did not much follow the trade of merchandise in which also he was trained up, but lived rather as a gentleman by his lands . . .' This is why there was so little ready money in the house at his death in 1576, and why also his shop—for he still continued to live in a merchant's house in the High Street—contained nothing but a few oddments worth less than four pounds in all. When Thomas Prestwood the elder died in 1558 he possessed

[1] The house illustrated in the plate facing p. 176 was built by Thomas Prestwood the younger in 1567. It is a superb example of an Elizabethan merchant's house. Though it escaped the heavy attacks of the German vandals in 1942, it may not escape the more persistent threat of importunate motorists, for whose dubious benefit it may be destroyed.

the manors of Butterford, Tynacre, and Venny Tedburn, and farms in a dozen other parishes, besides a tin-blowing mill and a fulling-mill, and eight large houses in the city of Exeter. His son Thomas inherited this estate, was styled gentleman, and divided his time between a large town house in the High Street of Exeter and his 'mansion house' of Butterford, some thirty miles away in the South Hams.

William Chappell, who died in the early months of 1580, 'was brought up in the trade of merchandise and by the same he grew to good wealth, and giving himself to purchasing of lands he in a manner gave over his trade'. Hooker here gives a slightly false impression, for there is a very marked difference between the financial affairs of Thomas Prestwood (1576) and William Chappell (1580). Prestwood's inventory shows very little ready money, the shop abandoned to the storage of junk, and very small debts due to the estate. William Chappell's inventory also shows a shop containing nothing but oddments, but a larger sum of ready money (nearly £200), and very considerable trading interests. More than forty per cent of his large personal estate took the form of trading debts due to him, and another twenty per cent was wrapped up in 'adventures abroad', most of it 'in the Isles' and in Spain.

Merchants' wills and inventories tell us little or nothing about their real estate, which in some instances was substantial. At least half a dozen Elizabethan merchants at Exeter founded landed families, as for example the Hursts, the Martins, the Periams, the Davys, and the Prestwoods. The real estate of old William Hurst, who died in 1568, was exceptionally large. It included six manors, farms in more than a score of parishes, and a certain amount of house-property. John Periam had probably inherited some lands from his father William, but of these we know nothing. By 1572, when he made his will, he was able to set up his elder son William (the future judge and baron of the exchequer) with the manor of Pancrasweek and lands in Pyworthy, Ottery St. Mary, and Pinhoe, while to his younger son he left houses in Exeter and lands in half a dozen other parishes. This was not a large accumulation by comparison with the Hurst estate, but that was quite untypical. The successful Exeter merchant could probably hope for the lordship of one or two manors, and to possess farms in perhaps half a dozen parishes. Many big merchants achieved less than this.

The majority of merchants in the Elizabethan period had begun their careers as apprentices to Exeter merchants, though there was, as we have seen, always a small but important influx of men who had been apprenticed elsewhere and who had come to the city as mature men. These are usually distinguishable in the city records by the fact that they obtain the freedom of the city, without which they could not trade within its bounds, by fine and not by apprenticeship. Those born in Exeter received their education at the High School, the only grammar school in the city. From this they passed on to a seven-year apprenticeship and then set up in business on their own account, unless, as in a few cases, they remained in the family business, like John Periam, or Thomas Prestwood, or Thomas Chappell.

Marriage was the next important step, and it was most likely to be to the daughter of a fellow-merchant. The close relationships by marriage among the leading Exeter merchant-families at least (perhaps there was a slightly wider choice of partner among the lesser men) have been worked out by Professor MacCaffrey, and could certainly be paralleled in other commercial cities. By his marriage, then, the Exeter merchant became related to a more or less numerous group of leading families, and his social standing was henceforth assured. Sometimes the merchant married into a small landed family. Thomas Prestwood the elder married the widow of another Exeter merchant who had been the daughter of a Kingswear gentleman; and his son married the daughter of William Strode of Newnham near Plymouth.

As time went by his family grew. Nothing could be farther from the truth than that sixteenth-century children died like flies, or that the average family of survivors was a small one. Certainly it is not true of the latter half of the sixteenth century and of the first generation of the seventeenth. At Exeter the court of orphans records give us a good picture of the typical family. Out of thirty-three merchant-households in the Elizabethan period, in which the father had died before his time, about one in seven (15 per cent) had seven, eight, or nine children. At the other end of the scale, one-third had only one, two or three children. The average number of children for the thirty-three households was 4·7; but against this we must set the fact that many men in the sample had died relatively young and before they could produce a 'normal' family. The largest single group (40 per cent of the total) had five or six children, and this must be regarded as the 'normal' family in this social class. Of all the children in the sample, 55 per cent were male, 45 per cent female.

A very small sample of merchant-wills from Totnes, the wills moreover of men who lived (as far as we can discover) their normal term of life, shows forty-one living children in five well-to-do families, an average of eight per family. A fuller sample, were it obtainable, would unquestionably lower this remarkable figure; but it serves to indicate that our 'normal' figure for Exeter of five or six children is a very credible one. To this typical family of seven or eight, including the parents, we have to add probably two apprentices at any given time and at least a couple of maid-servants, giving us a household of some dozen people.

With such a high figure in mind, we need not be surprised at the number of rooms in the Elizabethan merchant's house as we find it described in the Exeter inventories. A sample of twenty houses described between 1564 and 1609 shows that only six were smaller than ten rooms, eleven contained ten to fifteen rooms, and three more than fifteen rooms.[1] The largest houses were those of Henry James (22 rooms) in 1578, and Robert Parr (20 rooms) in 1608. Seven of the eighteen houses had fourteen or fifteen rooms and may be regarded as the typical dwelling of the wealthier merchant.

There is good evidence for saying that houses became larger and grander during the Elizabethan period, either by additions to an existing house or through a complete rebuilding. Thus the inventory of Richard Beavis in 1603 shows a 15-room house of which at least two rooms are described as 'new'. More often, however, a completely new house was built on the site at some date in the Elizabethan period or in the early seventeenth century. In particular there seems to have been some considerable rebuilding in the 1550s and 1560s. We have already seen that Thomas Prestwood the elder built some good houses before he died in 1558, and there are dated houses (1564, 1567) still surviving in the High Street as well as others of exactly the same design which no longer exist but which can be recovered in old drawings and photographs.

The fact that larger and more ostentatious houses were being built in increasing numbers is suggested by a civic by-law, made

[1] In counting rooms I have excluded the shop, cellar, warehouse, stables, and any 'domestic offices' such as a brewhouse.

in 1563. 'For avoidance of sundry inconveniences which daily do grow by the excessive buildings in sailing (sealinge) themselves further out than it appurtaineth or should be used: it is ordered that no manner of person or persons shall build nor attempt to build any house or houses within this city outwards towards any of the streets whereby the same shall have any sailing into the streets without the view and assent of the mayor, aldermen, and of the chamberlain be first had therein.' On the same day (21 August 1563), Robert Hunte was ordered to pull down forthwith a room and a projecting window in it which exceeded the limits of an earlier regulation. This regulation permitted a room to be built outwards to a depth of four feet beyond the principal of the house, and a window to project not more than sixteen inches farther, giving a maximum total projection of five feet four inches beyond the principal. The new regulation, made the same day, fixed no maximum measurements for over-sailing, but required each building to be inspected and approved by the mayor and others.

We learn a great deal from the inventories about the houses of Elizabethan merchants, though we cannot always be sure of their exact plan in default of surviving buildings. Several such buildings survive, but most have been altered internally to meet later needs and do not therefore help us as much as we could hope over the original Elizabethan plan. Indeed it is unrealistic to assume that there was a single type of house inhabited by merchants at this period. For one thing, the merchant class covered a wide range of worldly wealth. Table I shows that even in the limited period between 1590 and 1603 the richest merchant was worth ten times more than the smallest merchant and their houses would have been correspondingly different. And further, in any given generation (especially before the early seventeenth century), some merchants would have been living in houses that were survivors (slightly modernized perhaps) of the middle ages, while others were living in pure Elizabethan 'mansions'—for so they are repeatedly called in the records of the time—which were the result of a complete rebuilding on the old site.

To illustrate the variety of merchants' houses therefore we may take two or three examples in detail from the inventories. The house of Edmond Whetcombe, who died in 1565 worth just under £800, was one of only six rooms, or seven if we count the 'spence' separately. Apart from the shop, it had a hall, a parlour, kitchen and spence, and three bedrooms, called respectively, 'the Forechamber', the 'high chamber', and 'an other chamber'. It is difficult to be certain about the plan of this house and the disposition of the various rooms, but it may well have been a medieval hall-house of which a few (somewhat battered) still remain in the street where Edmond Whetcombe lived. The simple plan of shop, hall, parlour, and kitchen, with some chambers over, suggests a medieval house with a large open-roofed hall.

Nor was the six-roomed house of Richard Mawdytt very different at his death in 1592. He, too, was a small merchant worth only £356 gross. His house is described as consisting of a shop, a hall, parlour, and kitchen, and of three chambers (bedrooms) above—one over the kitchen, another over the parlour, and 'the maidens chamber'. Here there was pretty certainly no chamber over the hall, for the maidservants' chamber would have been a small one tucked away somewhere. It was still the open-roofed medieval hall, dating in all probability from the fifteenth century, like so many surviving examples in the city.

As against these smaller and older houses, occupied by the lesser merchants, we have the new-built grander houses of what may be called the civic merchants, that is those belonging or related to the governing oligarchy of the city and likely to fill the office of mayor, sheriff, or receiver. The house of Thomas Prestwood the younger (1576) is a fine example of this type, possibly one of the beautiful houses built by his father before 1558. Such houses, with fifteen or more rooms, are best described by means of conventional plans of each floor, which, while not accurate in every detail, give the essential disposition of the rooms beyond much doubt (see Fig. 1).

The Prestwood house, like all the larger town houses of the time, occupied a long narrow site, fronting on to the main street and running back to a smaller street which acted as what we should call a service-road. A side-passage, running the length of the house and generally known as 'the entry' or occasionally as 'tween doors', gave access to the ground-floor rooms and finally emerged at the back gate. The total depth of the house and all its appurtenances was considerable—in all probability about 140 feet. The frontage, on the other hand, was probably no more than 20 to 24 feet.[1]

[1] The Prestwood house, which stood in St. Stephen's parish, on the High Street and pretty certainly near St. Stephen's church, has long ago been destroyed. Since the site is known, however, it is possible to give these measurements.

On the ground floor the almost invariable plan of the larger house from the middle of the sixteenth century onwards was that of two blocks of building separated by a small courtyard. The front block contained the shop with a parlour behind, and possibly a spence or small buttery. The back block contained the kitchen,

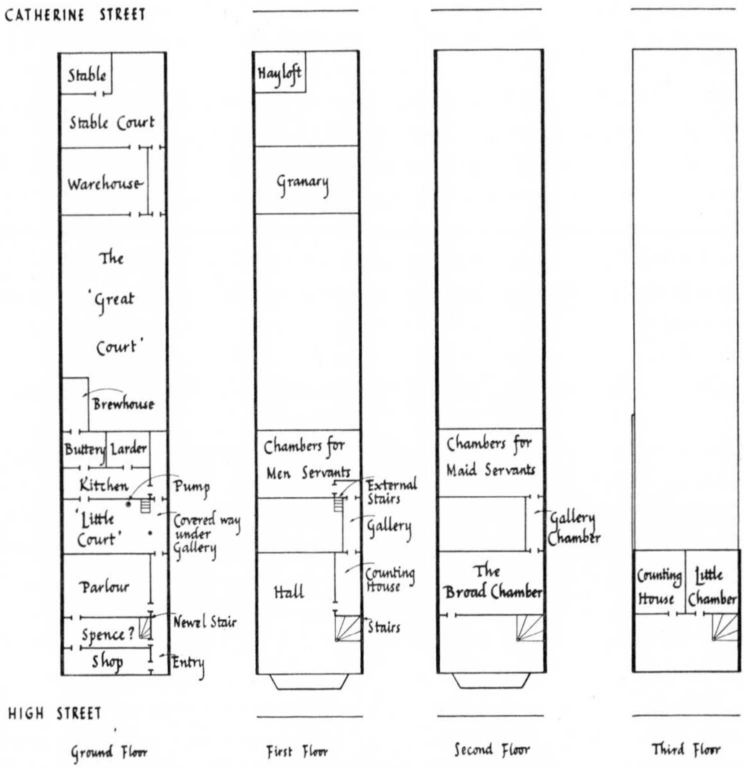

Fig. 1. Conjectural plan of the Prestwood house in 1576.
(Not drawn to scale)

larder, main buttery, and any other domestic offices such as the brewhouse. Access between front and back blocks in bad weather was provided by a covered way, formed by the first-floor gallery being carried on a short colonnade.

Behind the kitchen block of the Prestwood house lay a much larger court, called the Great Court in the inventory, on the other side of which was the warehouse. Behind that again was a little court containing the stable with hay-loft over, which abutted directly on to the back street and so completed the property. Above the warehouse in all probability was the granary. Stable and hay-loft, warehouse and granary, could be serviced (in or out) by way of the back street. The problem of handling heavy or bulky loads on such a narrow urban site was easily solved. It is an arrangement we find all along the main streets of Exeter. Back streets run parallel to the High Street and Fore Street on both sides, and all the largest properties extended right through from the main street to the back street. Many do so to this day.

Access to the first floor of the front block was by means of a newel stair which carried on indeed up to the top of the house. In the Prestwood house, the hall, which was of course the principal living room, overlooking the main street with a handsome oriel window, occupied the whole of this floor except for a small room where the stairs came up. This little room was used in the Prestwood house as 'the counting house by the hall'. A covered gallery connected the hall with the rooms over the kitchen block. These rooms probably comprised the men's bedroom and small service rooms. Food could be carried under cover from the kitchen along the gallery into the hall.

On the second floor we find the two principal bedrooms over the hall, called the forechamber and the broad (i.e. great) chamber. The stairs did not open directly into the great chamber but were shut off in some way. The forechamber overlooked the street by means of a handsome mullioned window (see plate opposite for a typical example) and the great chamber overlooked the inner courtyard. A higher gallery connected the great chamber with the back block, probably with 'the maidens chamber'. Finally, the front block rose to a gabled attic floor, which in the Prestwood house contained 'the higher chamber', the 'little chamber', and another little 'counting house'.

Thus the Prestwood house rose to a height of four floors (including the ground floor) on the street. It was not the largest house in Exeter. The plate facing p. 176 shows an even more elaborate house (or rather pair of identical houses, for they are divided vertically all the way down) rising to five floors. This pair would have contained up to twenty rooms each, the additional rooms being chiefly bedrooms for servants and apprentices.

A pair of Elizabethan Merchants' Houses in Exeter High Street, built in 1567

The inventories of the larger houses naturally show minor variations from the Prestwood house described above. Perhaps the most important variation was that on the first floor there were more usually two halls instead of one. That overlooking the street was called the fore-hall, while the hall proper overlooked the central courtyard by means of a mullioned window running the width of the room. The hall was generally the more important room, judging by its furnishings, but the fore-hall was nearly as comfortable. The fore-hall was probably more of a drawing-room (to use a later term), while the hall was the place where meals were taken by the family. Hall and fore-hall were separated by a small middle chamber where the stairs came up. The only other point worth noticing is that the Prestwood house was exceptional in not having a cellar. Most of the houses along the four main streets of Exeter had cellars, in order to make the greatest possible use of restricted sites. These cellars were frequently excavated during the fifteenth century, when urban sites were becoming increasingly valuable; but some may be older.

The richer merchants of Exeter lived in considerable state, as the inventories show. Their plate, 'napery', and apparel, as listed in the inventories, are all very considerable, indeed ostentatious. It is not unusual to find plate worth £100 or more in a merchant's house. The mayor of Exeter was an important man and was expected to entertain well, and to live well when not entertaining. Although he received a large allowance from the Chamber, his expenses were usually higher than this.[1] Only a rich merchant could afford the honour, and John Woolcot was passed over for many years because he was not considered rich enough to sustain the dignity of the office.

Woolcot in fact finally achieved the mayoralty in 1565. Of him Hooker says: 'this mayor had passed all the offices towards the mayoralty for about 22 years past and by reason of his age and his small wealth it was not thought nor meant that ever the office of the mayoralty should have fallen unto his lot. Nevertheless, when the matter so fell out, and no means found how the same might be avoided, order was taken both that his house should be prepared and also he to be furnished with money for his diet with liberality. The Chamber did consider he was in times past a great

[1] The mayor's allowance had been raised to £40 in 1551, to £66. 13*s*. 4*d*. in 1564, to £80 in 1579, and to £120 before the end of the century.

merchant and adventured very much, whereby he had great wealth, but in the end his losses were so great that he was very poor and lived in very mean a state'.

We know little that is personal of these merchants of Exeter beyond the brief glimpses Hooker gives us. John Woolcot was one of the old way of thinking. 'He was a zealous man in the Romish religion and too much addicted unto papistry, and in the commotion time'—the local description for several generations afterwards of the rebellion of 1549—'when the Commons of Devon and Cornwall were up in rebellion for the same, and he was in the city the time of the besieging of the same: yet his affection was such towards them that upon a day, when he was captain of the ward for the charge of the West Gate of this city, he went out at the West Gate to the rebels without any commission and had conference with them, which was not after forgiven but turned him to displeasure.'

Hooker was an old Protestant and doubtless remembered where others charitably forgot. Many of the leading merchants in that year had been Catholics—the city seems to have been pretty evenly divided at the top—but the older generation were dying one by one, and the younger men seem to have changed over easily enough. Indeed, it was not always a case of conforming to the established order of the new Settlement. John Periam had assisted Russell to crush the Catholics in 1549 while old William Periam, his father, kept his Catholic sympathies to the end. One would give much to know what passed between father and son in that bad year; but we do not even have William Periam's will to guide us. He was still a Catholic a year or two before his death, when he refused to give up a chalice and a pair of vestments to the Commissioners for Church Goods. He had given these to his parish church of St. Olave about 1547 and had taken them back again when the Commissioners appeared.

The Elizabethan merchants were probably Protestants to a man. Of Thomas Prestwood the younger we have a more certain glimpse. A man's character is revealed by what he reads (above all when he has to buy his own books) and Prestwood's books are very revealing. The inventory of 1576 speaks of 'two bibles, one of Geneva making, and Calvin's book [presumably the *Christian Institutes* published definitively in 1559], Turner's *Herbal*, two books of service, one book of *The Fall of Princes*, a bridgement of the Statutes, Hall's *Chronicles*, with divers other books of Latin, French and English'. Prestwood read at 'a desk for a book' in the hall, looking out on to the teeming High Street below, though it was quiet enough in the evenings. Everybody was indoors by nine o'clock, and most were asleep.

Most merchants, apart from their business, lived private lives. The opportunities for public service were very few. There were only twenty-four places on the Chamber and once admitted a man stayed on for life. Vacancies occurred only at long intervals on the death or disablement of a sitting member. The great majority even of the merchant class could not expect to reach the Chamber, least of all the mayoralty. Members of parliament for the city, sheriffs, and receivers, all were chosen from the Twenty-Four. Beyond that, there were no opportunities for a man to make a public mark.

In the prime of his life, usually, the Exeter merchant made his will. By this he generally settled such real estate as he possessed—houses and other small properties in the city, farms, tithes, and even manors in the country if he were a successful man. He also distributed considerable sums of money among his wife and children. John Periam (*c.* 1510–73) disposed of nearly £3000 in money by his will, chiefly to his two sons (William got £1400, John £800, and an unmarried daughter £300). Some of the sons' money may have been re-invested in the family business. But it is evident that in many families, especially where a merchant died young and the court of orphans administered his estate, the distribution of his personal wealth must have involved the end of the business, rather like the savagery of death duties today. Of Alexander Germyn's net estate of £550 11*s.* 5*d.* (1608), his widow got about £367 (two-thirds of the whole) and the five children got about £36 14*s.* 1*d.* each. Robert Parr's nine children (1608) got £82 6*s.* 10*d.* each, the widow just over £740. Harry Maunder apparently left £360 net estate in 1564, with no surviving widow but nine children, each of whom got £40. So the Maunder business dissolved at once. Thomas Chappell left a widow and ten children in 1590, and even his large business (worth over £3224 net) is heard of no more. Where the legacy was a large one, it may, as suggested above, have been reinvested in the business; or an elder son may have used his small inheritance to build up another business almost from scratch. But the general tendency was for a business to dissolve in every generation, mainly because its assets had to be realized and distributed among a considerable number of children. A large number of daughters was a particular misfortune from this point of view; the average merchant had to provide for the marriage of three or four daughters. Even here, a dowry might go to fertilize the son-in-law's own business. Only the really large businesses, however, could stand the effect of the merchant's death, and only these therefore survived into a second generation and, more rarely still, into a third.

In every generation, some merchants had left money for charities according to their means. Professor Jordan has recently traced the tremendous flow of charitable bequests in the sixteenth and seventeenth centuries, above all from the merchant class in the leading towns. How do the Exeter merchants stand up to this scrutiny?

A number of merchants took a special interest in the welfare of poor and friendless prisoners. Griffith Ameredith, who died in 1558, had been appalled in his lifetime by the way in which the bodies of those hanged were treated. They were brought back from the gallows, a mile or so outside the city, slung on a staff between two men, and having been brought to Exeter they were then flung into a grave in their clothes. Ameredith left a piece of property in east Devon, yielding 38 shillings a year, to provide a shroud and a coffin for each body. William Tryvett, mayor in 1573, bequeathed 'one great Brass Crock, to boil meat therein, for the Use of the Prisoners in the Southgate Prison'. The main flow of bequests was, however, for the relief of the poor, more especially those who were old, and for the encouragement by timely loans of young artificers. The largest single benefaction was that of William Hurst in 1567, when he founded an almshouse for twelve poor men and endowed it with lands to the value of £12 4*s*. 0*d*. per annum. Both Thomas Prestwood (1576) and John Davy (1599) left money also for the foundation of smaller almshouses.

In 1572 John Periam left £100, to be lent to two young merchants freely for four years in order to set them on their feet. And from 1599 onwards there was a steady flow of bequests designed to provide free loans for young artificers or tradesmen for a period of years. The main flow of benefactions at Exeter came, however, a generation or two later, well into the seventeenth century, and even then Exeter saw nothing to match the noble foundation of Peter Blundell, of a school at Tiverton (1599). But Blundell had accumulated a fortune as a cloth merchant at Tiverton, fourteen miles to the north, far beyond that of the richest merchant in Exeter at this time.

The rich merchant's funeral was usually a costly affair. For some of the lesser men a sum of £10 to £20 sufficed to cover all the charges; but Thomas Chappell's funeral in 1590 cost as much as £120, and Walter Horsey's £100 in 1597. The funeral charges of Thomas Prestwood in January 1577 amounted to a modest £12 7*s*. 2*d*. This included the cost of ten yards of black cloth 'for the children's gowns and coats' £4, 'to a tailor for making the boys' coats, 3*s*.', six shillings to a joiner 'for the chest', 'for a tombstone 13*s*. 4*d*.' and 'for engraving the Tombstone, 9*s*.'. At William Newcombe's funeral in 1609 the mourning clothes cost £42, the actual burial in the Cathedral £20, and finally—the closing scene in the life and death of the merchant—the funeral dinner, in the hall of his dwelling-house, costing £13 6*s*. 8*d*. But it is, perhaps, more fitting to say farewell to the Exeter merchant as he is lowered into the grave, in the nave of his own little red-sandstone parish church to the mournful singing of the Vicars Choral and amid the darkening light of a cold January afternoon.

VII

Touching The Writ of Latitat: An Act 'Of No Great Moment'

MARJORIE BLATCHER

ONE of the charms of the Elizabethan Commons Journal is the juxtaposition of high politics and measures to regulate the nation's mundane affairs, here the succession to the throne, there the paving of streets. In this legislative sea the whale is more spectacular than the sprat, but the sea is the natural element of both; and the existence of these less ambitious topics of parliamentary interest testifies that some at least of Elizabeth's faithful Commons were not devoting their whole energies to the Queen's business but were attending to these matters of commonwealth which were traditionally their own. Policy, although it deals with national issues, is of its nature ephemeral. Sectional interests live longer, and the bills which concern them may be landmarks on a very long by-path of the nation's history. Such a landmark is 'An Act for the avoiding of wrongful vexation touching the Writ of Latitat' which forms chapter two of the statute passed in the second session of Elizabeth's second parliament.[1] It is an innocuous-seeming measure, and one which D'Ewes was later to dismiss as 'of no great moment'. Initiated in the Lords on Thursday, 14 November, it was read for a second time on Wednesday, 20 November, ordered to be engrossed, and passed its third reading on the following Saturday.[2] Serjeant Carus and Sir Richard Rede delivered it to the Commons on the same day, and there it had its three readings on 27 November and 9 and 18 December. It received the royal assent with thirty-three other bills on 2 January 1567.[3] The resulting act consists of a preamble and four clauses. The preamble recites how

divers persons, of their malicious minds, and without any just cause, do many times cause and procure others of the Queen's Majesty's loving

[1] 8 Eliz. c. 2. [2] *Lords Journal*, i, 645*b*, 648*a*, 649*a*.
[3] *Commons Journal*, i, 78–81 *passim*.

Subjects to be very much molested and troubled by attachments and arrests made of their bodies, as well by Process of *Latitat*, *alias* and *pluries Capias*, sued out of the Court commonly called the King's Bench, as also by plaint, bill, or other Suit, in the Court commonly called the Marshalsey, and within the City of London, and other Cities, Towns corporate, and places where any liberty or privilege is to hold pleas of Debt, Trespass and other personal Actions and Suits: And when the parties that be arrested or attached are brought forth to answer such Actions and Suits . . . then many times there is no Declaration . . . whereunto they may make an answer: and so the party arrested is very maliciously put to great charges and expenses, without any just or reasonable cause; And yet nevertheless hitherto By order of the Law the party so grieved and vexed could never have any Costs or Damages to him to be judged or awarded for the said vexation and trouble.

The first clause provides that where the defendant has put in bail and the plaintiff has not declared against him within three days, or after declaration has not prosecuted his suit, the court may award the defendant his costs, damages and charges against the plaintiff. The second provides remedies for the victims of similar abuses by plaint, bill, action or suit in the marshalsea court and the courts of cities and towns. The third concerns those who maliciously feign bills and writs of *latitat* in the names of persons who have not been consulted or are non-existent, and awards against such malefactors a sentence of six months' imprisonment, treble costs, charges, damages and expenses to the defendants to such suits, and to the plaintiffs whose names they have used, where such persons exist, the sum of £10 for each offence. The last clause provides those vexed by such malicious suits their remedy by action of debt, bill or plaint in any court of record to recover the costs and damages awarded by the act.

The misdoings of suitors by bill or plaint in the marshalsea and other courts mentioned in the act will not concern us here. The victims of abuse by bill or plaint had been given their remedy in an earlier act,[1] and it is clear from the title of this act and from the entries concerning it in the Journals that the main interest for contemporaries was in that part of it which applied to process by *latitat* in the court of king's bench.

By 1566 the writ of *latitat* was no upstart process in that court. A manuscript book of precedents, bearing on its flyleaf the name

[1] 23 Hen. VIII c. 15.

of Sir William Huse, contains two entries under the heading 'Latitat' and the earlier comes from Trinity term 1373.[1] The purpose of the writ was to enable a plaintiff, who had sued out writs first of attachment and then of arrest in vain, to testify in court that he knew that the defendant *latitat et discurrit* (and sometimes even *vagatur*) in another county so that he might have a writ of arrest addressed to the sheriff there. If this writ of *latitat* failed, it could be followed by writs of *sicut alias* and *sicut pluries capias*. The *latitat*, therefore, was the third writ issued to get the defendant into court. Although it may have come as a shock to those defendants whose consciences were clear, or whose memories of past misdeeds were poor, to be thus summarily arrested, there were many who could be reached only in this way. The writ met a genuine need, and it had its counterpart in the court of common pleas.[2] It was regularly used throughout the fifteenth century and was applied both to suits begun by original writ and to those instituted by bill of trespass.

Actions for trespass committed in the county in which the king's bench sat were traditionally, although not exclusively, brought into that court by bill; and since from the beginning of the fifteenth century the court normally sat at Westminster that county was Middlesex.[3] Now Middlesex was peculiarly the county of the passing visitor, for Westminster and its environs were the centre of political and legal business and London a meeting-place for those engaged in commerce. Nowhere in England was it more natural to encounter an old enemy or to make a new one. Those aggrieved at such meetings, the victims of damage to person and property, usually sought redress by bill of Middlesex, and if the offenders had judiciously regained the shelter of their homes in other counties they had often to be pursued there by the appropriate writs of *latitat*. Because we know that the bill and writ were to combine to form the basis of one of the most notorious of legal fictions, it is easy to be over-suspicious of all fifteenth-century litigation by bill. Though the memorandum of the bill may complain merely that the trespass has taken place in Middlesex, the cited bill, declaration and pleadings are full of detail as to what

[1] B.M. Add MSS. 16168 f. 249*b*; Huse was L.C.J. from 1481 to 1495.

[2] Margaret Hastings, *The Court of Common Pleas in Fifteenth-Century England*, 183.

[3] G. Crompton, *Practice of the Courts of King's Bench and Common Pleas*, ed. B. J. Sellon, i, p. xxxviii; *Select Cases in the Court of King's Bench under Edward II*, ed. G. O. Sayles (Selden Soc.), iv, pp. lxxxiv–lxxxv.

took place in Edmonton, Isleworth or Kensington. The defendant denies that the entry is trespass and that the violence is on his side, but he does not deny the encounter with the plaintiff, or the place. It was this committal of the offence in Middlesex, not the residence of the parties there, which gave the plaintiff the right to sue by bill; and indeed a case of 1412 which has been treated as an example of the fictitious bill of Middlesex in its final shape is on the contrary an illustration of its legitimate use.[1] Since the documents in the case are easily accessible in print, it is unnecessary to epitomize them before adding significant details from other sources.[2]

Sir Edward Butler, who held the manor of Higham Gobion from 1360 until his death in 1412, was a cantankerous old man, notoriously addicted to taking the law into his own hands as well as to litigating.[3] His way to Westminster from his home in Bedfordshire lay through Islington, and it was there that he and his young cousin and heir, Philip Butler, encountered Alexander Head. They attempted to seize him as a villein belonging to Sir Edward's manor, an attempt accompanied perhaps by more force than they admitted but with less than Head claimed or the jury believed. Alexander Head, citizen and waxchandler of London, can have had no serious doubts about his free status by 1412;[4] but as there were Heads in the neighbourhood of Higham Gobion, his family and even he himself at one time may have lived there in villeinage.[5] He brought his action into the king's bench by bill because, the trespass having occurred in Middlesex, this remedy was open to him. Since the question of his status had been raised, he was doubtless glad to have it settled, and in view of his established position in the city he could be sure of a verdict in his favour from a Middlesex jury. (In this he was not disappointed, save in respect of the beating which he claimed Philip

[1] Professor Sayles believes that what constituted the fiction was 'the supposition that the defendant was resident within the county of Middlesex' (op. cit. p. lxxxvi), but writers from the sixteenth century onwards held that it was the trespass in Middlesex which was pretended.

[2] H. Hall, *Formula Book of Legal Records*, 214–17.

[3] *V. C. H. Bedford*, ii, 345; Margery Bassett, *Knights of the Shire for Bedfordshire* (Beds. Hist. Rec. Soc. xxix), 25–26, giving the date of Butler's death as 3 March 1412; it took place on 10 Nov.: C. 137/90/16.

[4] *Letter Book I*, 229; K, 69; *Cal. Plea and Memor. Rolls City of London*, 1413–37, 218.

[5] For Heads in Bedfordshire see *Beds. Hist. Rec. Soc.* iii, 37 (1227); xxxix, 60, 61, 82 (1297); *Two Beds. Subsidy Lists* (Suffolk Green Books, xviii), 162, 165 *bis* (1332); and in London, *Letter Book H*, 10, 37 (1375–6).

Butler had given him.) The Butlers, equally willing to fight the case, stayed in Middlesex long enough to be attached there and to appoint attorneys. Had Sir Edward been less pugnacious, they might well have returned to their respective homes. There, after the failure of writs of attachment and arrest, Head would have needed to sue out additional writs of *latitat* to the sheriffs of Bedfordshire and Hertfordshire; but these would not have made the case any less genuinely one of trespass in Middlesex. Nor did the Butlers' unsuccessful attempt to attaint the jury for a false oath: in legal matters Sir Edward was always a sticker.[1]

The plea rolls abound with examples of 'genuine' bills of Middlesex throughout the fifteenth century, and, indeed, many later examples may be found. But their liability to abuse must have lain from the beginning in the ease with which they could be abandoned. Although all the stages of procedure—bill, writs of attachment, arrest and, where necessary, *latitat*—were duly enrolled on the plea roll until late in Henry VIII's reign, and cannot surely have been enrolled without some payment, the plaintiff had nothing further to fear if he then failed to prosecute his suit. If the defendant appeared, the plaintiff's non-appearance was noted, but only his pledges were 'in the mercy' of the court: such amercements were not in fact estreated from the plea roll for collection by the exchequer, which was just as well, for although Messrs. Doe and Roe had not yet established a monopoly in the field of fictitious backers, the names of their rivals seldom inspire confidence. Admittedly, very many suits begun by original writ were abandoned likewise (and with equal impunity) before the full course of procedure to enforce the defendant's appearance had been run; and probably in litigation by either method plaintiffs were willing to spend a little in the hope of getting redress at law or a settlement out of court, but were not prepared to throw good money after bad. But while neither litigant had any further pecuniary loss to fear, he who sued by bill had had his initial fling for less expense and less anxiety, because the bill, unlike an original writ, did not need to conform in all particulars with the subsequent declaration. It is this point which has confused so many writers on the bill of Middlesex, who argue that because 'variance hurts not' a man arrested for trespass could be declared against for debt.

[1] C 47/2/21: *certiorari* and copy of enrolment of appeal, not printed in Hall, op. cit.

This was in effect what was to happen, but not because the declaration on the bill could depart so radically from the action cited in the bill: it was because the first bill having achieved its end, the appearance of the defendant, it could be dropped and another method of procedure could be embarked upon.

This other procedure was made possible by the fact that the king's bench could offer another form of litigation by bill which all plaintiffs must have coveted but which could only come their way honestly by a coincidence. It was the right to sue by bill prisoners in the custody of the marshal of the court in all personal actions.[1] To avoid confusion, this type of bill will be called (although it was not so called by the lawyers of the time) a bill of custody. The right to use it arose from a recognition of the injustice which would result if a man, arrested to answer one person's suit against him in the king's bench, should thereby become immune from all other claims against him: a creditor, for example, ought not to have to wait for his money until the court had tried the debtor for another offence. The question whether a prisoner who had been let out on bail, or later any person who had given bail, was technically in the marshal's custody was thrashed out in the reign of Henry VI, and the judges eventually decided that he was.[2] It was a momentous decision. Whether it was arrived at in the interest of justice, to pass on to other suitors the advantage which one plaintiff had won over that elusive creature the defendant, or whether the justices of the king's bench were loth to see good business go elsewhere, we may guess but cannot prove. Whichever it was, custody thereafter did not necessarily mean detention.

Many suitors availed themselves of the opportunity thus offered, but not nearly so many as would have liked to. For the happy coincidence whereby a new plaintiff found a defendant where he wanted him had only been brought about by someone's trouble and expense. A new plaintiff, or his attorney, ready to reap where another had sown, was quick to regard any appearance in court as tantamount to custody; he might even put in an additional bill against a man brought into the court by his own original writ on another charge.[3] The gods help those who help themselves, and

[1] Coke, *Second Institute*, 23. [2] Y.B. 31 Hen. VI, Mic. Pl. 10.

[3] Ashby *v.* Toft, K.B. 27/917/r. 22; cf. K.B. 27/913/r. cxiii*b*, 27/915/rr. 30–30*b*, 27/916/r. lxix*b*.

many forms of self-help must have been tried to add to this number of easily available defendants. Certainly the number of Londoners suing each other for debt, detinue and covenant by bill of custody suggests that, as the fifteenth century advanced, they must have fee-ed attorneys to exploit every such opportunity. Perhaps the suitability of the bill of trespass for the purpose of securing the defendant's appearance was discovered by a plaintiff who had, among other grievances, a genuine trespass to complain of and who made the cheaper method serve to summon the defendant to answer them all. It was the first step towards the discovery that even a feigned trespass would do as well.

The belief that the bill of trespass in Middlesex had become entirely fictitious by the end of the fifteenth century appears to be founded on Reeves's statement that procedure by feigned bill of Middlesex and *latitat* 'became the settled practice towards the latter end of the period of which we are now writing'.[1] As Reeves is concerned at that point of his narrative with the reigns of Henry VI and Edward IV, it is natural to infer that this is the period which he had in mind. But may he not have been thinking of the period of his survey, which ends with the reign of Philip and Mary? If by 'settled practice' he meant usual practice, the later time would be the more appropriate. Many cases of 1470 and 1490–91, when traced through the records of the court, reveal that the defendants technically in the custody of the marshal had arrived there through the orthodox process on original writ or in answer to another plaintiff's bill of trespass. Professor Neilson's 'some thirty' actions on Bills of Middlesex found on the plea roll for Easter 1470[2] resolve themselves on analysis into seven cases of trespass in Middlesex heard in court, ten composite entries of process on such bills of trespass, and nineteen custody cases, of which seven had begun in an earlier term. In Michaelmas 1490 there were four cases of trespass heard, only two entries of process (one of which is proved by a later hearing to concern a genuine trespass in Middlesex) and ten suits against defendants in the marshal's custody, of which four had joined issue in previous terms. Many more cases would have to be traced backwards and

[1] J. Reeves, *History of the English Law*, 2nd edn. iii, 388.

[2] *Year Books 10 Edward IV and 49 Henry VI A.D. 1470*, ed. N. Neilson (Selden Soc. xlvii), p. xxvi.

forwards on the plea rolls and other records of the court to prove that no bill of trespass was at that time fictitious, that is to say, that no plaintiff had sued out a bill of Middlesex, which he had then abandoned, against the same defendant as he subsequently sued in the custody of the marshal. It can only be said that, if the practice was common in those years, investigation of any sample of custody cases should have yielded some instances of it, and that so far none has been found. But by the end of Henry VII's reign the number of bills of Middlesex with writs of *latitat* into other counties somewhat exceeds the number of itinerant trespassers that could reasonably be expected in that county: there are, for example, twenty-seven of these, against only four Middlesex trespasses heard, in Hilary 1509. Some litigants are trying to stretch the long arm of coincidence for themselves, but as yet only some.

The evidence of the plea rolls that procedure by bill was still far from being general during the first years of the sixteenth century bears out the assertion of the anonymous writer who addressed a complaint 'Towchinge Latitats sued in the Kinges Benche upon untrew surmises' to Sir John Puckering while he was lord keeper, that is, between 1592 and 1596. This critic maintained that procedure by bill and *latitat* 'haith of late tyme crepte into be used' and that many men still living could remember when this became the most common way to proceed in that court.[1] If he was not relying mainly on the testimony of Old Parr, this Elizabethan was presumably referring to old men who could look back fifty years or so to the 'forties, when in fact both forms of procedure were sufficiently common for a biased or selective memory to regard one as normal and the other as exceptional. Those who were contemporary with the increase of bill procedure were certainly aware as early as 1532 that it was no longer exceptional. In the act of that year which awarded damages against plaintiffs who commenced personal actions by writ or bill and then failed to prosecute them, the bill was not included, we may be sure, through excess of legal caution.[2] We may perhaps detect a less direct attack on the bill in another act of the same session which by providing that process on writs of trespass (committed without violence)[3] and covenant should extend to the

[1] B.M. Lansd. 621 ff. 4*b*, 5.
[2] 23 Hen. VIII c. 15.
[3] As defined by 5 Ric. II c. 7.

arrest of the defendant, may have been designed to give these originals parity of advantage with common writs (and bills) of trespass and thus help them regain popularity.[1] These were actions which it was becoming customary to bring by bill against those in the custody of the marshal of the king's bench.

The acts of 1532 do not appear to have checked the growth of procedure by bill, nor was the resourcefulness of the court by any means exhausted. From 1539 the bills of Middlesex and writs of attachment and arrest begin to be enrolled intermittently, and by Michaelmas 1542 their enrolment ceases altogether.[2] Their composite entry is then replaced by one which records only the failure of the sheriff of Middlesex to arrest the defendant as a preface to a *latitat* into another county.[3] The *latitat* has clearly become in fact, although not in theory, the first process on the bill, and the bill itself has dropped into oblivion. It may be surmised that this innovation gave litigants immunity from the penalties against those who failed to prosecute their suits by bill, since no bill remained on record for them to prosecute.[4] Certainly the saving of clerical labour effected by the change made the procedure even more economical and vastly more expeditious for the plaintiff: he had indeed reached that enviable position so bitterly assailed by seventeenth- and eighteenth-century critics of the procedure.

This was the use of the *latitat* which the act of 1566 sought to penalize and eradicate. If all plaintiffs had had to pay damages on abandoned suits of trespass brought in by *latitat*, these would have become a very expensive way of getting defendants into the custody of the marshal and thus amenable to the plaintiffs' real purposes in going to law.

For these real purposes were not what any respectable lawyer (save the justices and other officers of the court itself) could look upon with equanimity. The majority of the actions brought into the king's bench by this combination of two fictions were for debt, detinue, covenant and account, matters which already

[1] 23 Hen. VIII c. 14. [2] K.B. 27/1125.

[3] This remained the form of the writ thereafter: G. Jacob, *Law Dictionary*, *s.v.* Latitat.

[4] Later writers claimed that the bill had to be enrolled when the defendant appeared, but this was not made obligatory until the statute of limitation of 1624, 21 Ja. I c. 16; cf. J. Palmer, *The Attorney and Agent's new Table of Costs* (1796), p. xv.

came within the jurisdiction of the court of common pleas. What had once been an exceptional remedy for an exceptional hardship was being offered to all comers at a price which undercut anything the rightful court could offer. The opportunity of suing a defendant in custody, which nearby Londoners had been so quick to seize on in the late fifteenth century, but so far as can be proved quite legitimately, plaintiffs all over the country could now make for themselves. By this means Richard Robinson, clerk, could call Wolsey's spendthrift 'nephew' Thomas Winter, archdeacon of York and provost of Beverley, to account for two at least of his debts, and although Winter imparled (that is, gained a term's respite for consultation) in both cases, his sureties gave some guarantee of his future appearance or settlement.[1] During the same term Winter was trying to have reversed in the king's bench an earlier judgment for debt awarded against him in the common pleas: his writ of error brought the whole proceedings before the justices for scrutiny, and the case, initiated by original writ, makes a striking contrast with litigation in the king's bench by bill.[2] Two terms had been consumed by the issue of unavailing writs of process to secure his appearance in the court of common pleas and a third in getting a judgment against him. This hard-won award he might have upset had he been able to point to a mere slip of the pen in the record. In this he was unsuccessful and the judgment was affirmed; but John Cooke, citizen and mercer of London, must have spent a large part of the £25 which was at stake by the time that the case had been settled in the lower court and reviewed by the upper, and he had still to collect his money. All judgments in the common pleas were vulnerable to writs of error, while those of the king's bench were very difficult to reverse until late in Elizabeth's reign. The moral could not have been more clearly pointed: it was less troublesome to sue by bill, by way of *latitat*.

This method of beginning was particularly useful in a field which was to see much extension under the Tudors. Even before the fifteenth century opened, the king's bench had made good its

[1] Trin. 32 Hen. VIII, K.B. 27/1116/rr. 36–36*b*. This case occurs during the period when the earlier processes are ceasing to be enrolled, and no process has been found to account for Winter's appearance; since both the clerks who enrolled process, and those who today search their records, have been proved fallible, too much importance must not be attached to this.

[2] Ibid. rr. 40–40*b*.

claim to share with the common pleas actions on trespass, since these, when committed with violence (*vi et armis*), were of a quasi-criminal nature. From this it went on to assert jurisdiction over those from which violence was absent, although most suitors clearly felt safer if they could represent the offence as containing some element of physical danger. But trespass, which in the fifteenth and sixteenth centuries embraced more as a term of art than it now conveys to the layman, was being stretched to include new wrongs, and an offshoot, trespass (or action) on the case, was offering a remedy to those whose cases were not covered by existing writs. Those who sued in either bench for action on the case had to specify in detail in the writ itself the nature of the trespass, an expensive and hazardous proceeding, since the subsequent declaration must agree with it in every particular. The king's bench was well equipped by its improved procedure to compete with both the common pleas and the conciliar courts in this new and growing branch of litigation. The common law had been slow, for instance, in evolving a remedy for actionable words. In 1535 we find the justices willing and eager to provide one, but baulked by the nature of the case before them since, if the defendant had sought to justify calling the plaintiff a heretic, 'nous ne pouvons discusser s'il soit heresie ou non'.[1] A simpler problem was set the judges of the king's bench in Hilary 1540, when Walter Herenden brought a 'trespass on the case' before them against Robert Fenton for declaring at Maidstone that he 'was a false knave and that he had made false writinges wherefore he was worthy to stand on the pyllory'. The expression of this unflattering opinion cost Fenton £3 3*s*. 4*d*., but as he had been actively employed in the court during the previous term gathering in debts by his own bills of custody, he could afford to pay for his fun.[2] A more damaging talker was brought into the court by a *latitat*[3] during the following term when Richard Westcott, wheelwright of Tamworth, was called upon to answer Richard Archer, esquire of the body to Henry VIII and a justice of the peace in Warwickshire.[4] Archer declared that on the previous 16 March at Coughton,

[1] W. Holdsworth, *History of English Law*, 3rd edn. iii, 411, citing Y.B. 27 Hen. VIII Mic. Pl. 4.

[2] K.B. 27/1114/r. 23; again no process has been found to account for Fenton's appearance in custody.

[3] Enrolled on K.B. 27/1115/r. 33.

[4] W. Dugdale, *Antiquities of Warwickshire*, ii, 781.

in the presence of Sir George Throgmorton and others, Westcott had uttered these *verba scandalorum*:

Mayster Richard Archour hathe donne greate and many wrongs and extorcyons here within the county of Warwyke to diverse powr people; that it is well knowen that he hath undone more poore men here in these partes then all the rest of the gentilmen of this whole shyre; And where he is verye hastye with me and other the kinges poor tenauntes here, he was slowe Inoughe when he shoulde have servyde the kynge, for he being the kinges sarvaunte satt at home when the insurrection was in the Northe, and wolde neyther goo hymself nor suffre others that would have gone.[1]

Since Archer estimated the damage done to his reputation at £200, we cannot wonder that Westcott imparled into the next term and then again and again: he had need of the delay. Nevertheless, Archer had aired his grievance. The court of star chamber, tender of official reputations, would have been glad to offer Archer the opportunity to vindicate his character, but it could scarcely have given him a speedier hearing than he had from the king's bench, where he enjoyed the prospect of damages as well.

The king's bench needed all the new business that it could attract. While everyone who has worked on the plea rolls agrees that they cannot be judged by weight alone, no-one who has read the king's bench rolls for the 1530s and early 1540s can doubt that they record a shrinking volume of business. Crops of cases varied, like the harvest, throughout the fifteenth and sixteenth centuries, but an exceptionally light term was usually followed by a heavier one. No sufficiently heavy terms have been discovered in the late 1530s to suggest that the falling-off in any of them was merely accidental. The criminal side of the court's business (that is, the determination of indictments of treason, murder, and acts of violence sent up to it by inferior courts, usually sessions of the peace and of gaol delivery) does not concern us here, save in so far as its condition affected the fortunes of the court as a whole. This Rex Roll usually covers between one-half and one-third of the space allotted to it during Henry VII's last terms, and although this allowance is not less than is to be found in light terms in the 1480s and 1490s the cases are less economically entered, so that they seem more numerous than they are. The falling-off of this side of the business gives some colour to the belief that here the

[1] K.B. 27/1116/r. 34.

common law was in danger of supersession by the more flexible conciliar courts or, in the case of treason, by special commissions.

The impression left by scrutiny of the plea side is similar. Fifteenth-century plea rolls were closely written and carefully kept, and if they did not often much exceed seventy rotulets they were seventy rotulets crammed with true judicial business. They bear the imprint of professional self-respect. It is quite otherwise with the later plea rolls of Henry VIII. Made up in the expectation of the same seventy rotulets of business, and sometimes exceeding that in mere number, they belie their appearance by the reality of what is entered on them. The first nineteen rotulets, traditionally allotted to the filacers, or filing-clerks, of the court to enter process on original, often contain only single items or are numbered but left blank, and the supplementary allotment of space for the same purpose is frequently omitted altogether, although counted in the total numbering of the roll. The filacers' work is careless and full of gaps. This shrinkage and deterioration, which could be explained by the growth, at their expense, of procedure by bill, is not in fact compensated by the chief clerk's rotulets which enrol this part of the business. His share of the plea roll, although relatively so much fuller, is padded with many blank but numbered parchments and contains much matter which cannot be regarded as in any way judicial. Rotulet after rotulet is covered by the enrolment of indentures and recognizances—seventeen such entries, some running over several sides of parchment, appear in Trinity 1539, eighteen in the following term. Fees for the enrolment of such writings, to place them on record, would not have been turned away in earlier times, and there are few plea rolls without one or two of them; but they form so significant a part of the later rolls as to suggest that some effort had been made to attract them there. Most, although still not all, of the cases recorded by the chief clerk as heard in court were prosecuted by bill, and the enrolment of writs of *latitat* (and the gradually fading earlier processes on the bill of Middlesex) indicates how the appearance of future defendants will be procured. The fashionable view that Maitland, in his *English Law and the Renaissance*, exaggerated the dangers facing the common law courts at this time may hold good for the court of common pleas, which had enjoyed so much business before that it could afford to live in reduced circumstances until better days returned. It does so for the more vulnerable criminal court only if we recognize that most of its small amount of business at this time was new business brought in by its own ingenuity.[1]

The court's accelerated bill procedure offered suitors a better chance of coming to grips with defendants than they could hope for elsewhere. It only remained to defend and exploit it. No-one knows better than a lawyer that men cannot be made virtuous by act of parliament; and just as the court had found a way round the acts of 1532, so it set out to mitigate the effects of later legislation against the *latitat*. The abuses described in the act of 1566 make it clear that by that time many writs of *latitat* were being doubly feigned: over and above the fictions of the process itself there was the practice of malicious or timid litigants of using other men's names. This may well have continued, in spite of the penalties for it, since it was an offence difficult to detect. Vexatious and malicious plaintiffs figure prominently in all later descriptions of bill procedure. For the more straightforward plaintiff by *latitat* the court itself was able to soften the consequences of the act. By judicial construction the costs which it allowed were awarded to the defendant only if he appeared in person[2] and were assessed at a mere 13*s.* 4*d.*[3] The act had left the award of damages to the court's discretion. The court used it.

The threat inherent in the act of 1566 was not, however, the most serious facing the court. Among the vested interests which it had been flouting none was so formidable as chancery. Much of the attraction of the bill and *latitat* lay in its economy: some of this the court had effected at its own expense by cutting down the enrolment of process and halving the clerks' fee on damages awarded,[4] but most at the expense of the clerks in chancery. When

[1] All methods of estimating the volume of work passing through the courts by counting plea-roll entries are open to some objections. A rough count of the cases which have reached issue, that is, a hearing in court, omitting the mere enrolment of writs to compel the attendance of parties or to enforce the payment of damages and also disregarding all cases brought into the king's bench by writs of error, gives the following results for four periods each of four consecutive terms: Mic.—Trin. 6 Hen. VII, 379; East.—Hil. 28 Hen. VIII, 225; Mic. 30—Trin. 31 Hen. VIII, 280; Mic. 31—Trin. 32 Hen. VIII, 339.

[2] M. Hale, 'Discourse concerning the Courts of King's Bench and Common-Pleas' (*Hargrave Law Tracts*, i), 366. [3] B.M. Lansd. 621 f. 6.

[4] 'Damages clear' were one shilling in the pound on cases brought in the king's bench by bill, two shillings on cases brought into the common pleas by original: T. Powell, *Attourneys Academy* (1623), 168.

a litigant sued out an original writ for the recovery of debt or damages he paid a fine ranging from 6*s*. 8*d*. on £40 to roughly one two-hundredth part of the sum claimed on larger amounts, nominally to the Crown but actually to the clerk who made out the writ. A critic of the *latitat* procedure, who tried to interest Lord Chancellor Hatton in the 'sondrie great wronges' which it gave rise to, estimated that the Queen lost through it at least £1,600 a year in profits on her seals.[1] Such fines were well worth collecting and well worth avoiding. No fine was payable on litigation by bill.

Chancery had its own weapons to defend its income. Our anonymous writer of the 1590s reminds Sir John Puckering that 'suyinge by Latitat . . . hath allwayes from the first common use of it ben ympugned by writtes out of the Chaunceryе as may appeare by severall process from tyme to tyme awarded'.[2] His assertion is borne out by a fragment which has survived from 'An Order in Chauncery touching Injunctions for staying of sutes in the Kinges Bench'.[3] This lists seven plaintiffs in chancery who are defendants in the king's bench to suits for debts or damages and stays proceedings on them under penalties far greater than the sums involved. Four belong to the years 1556 and 1557, three between the same parties to 1559, and one each to 1565 and 1595; since the first folio is numbered 6, there is reason to believe that similar injunctions had been issued earlier, while a note at the end that injunctions for staying suits in the king's bench had been much used in Lord Keeper Puckering's time and until 'this Lord Chancellor's time', shows that they continued. At first they must have appeared a most formidable obstacle to the use of the *latitat*, and if chancery had indeed been able to stay proceedings on every one that was fineable it might have brought the use of the process to an end. But a note on one of the cases that, since the fine (£5 on £1,000 claimed) has been paid, the injunction is dissolved, shows the limit of chancery's power: it could establish its claim to the fines but could not remove the cases out of the king's bench. Moreover, chancery could intervene only if moved to do so, and would be so moved only by a defendant who hoped to profit by delay. Obviously some defendants made use of these injunctions throughout this period, but others did not. Even when one was sued out, all that a determined plaintiff had to do was to

[1] S.P. 12/288/4. [2] B.M. Lansd. 621 f. 6. [3] S.P. 15/39/46.

pay the fine which he would have paid on an original and then proceed, no worse off, in this respect than if he had taken the case into the common pleas and, in others, still in pocket.

One other act passed during Elizabeth's reign may have seemed (and been intended) to act as a check on bill procedure. This was the act of 1585 which constituted the barons of the exchequer and the justices of the common pleas a court of appeal for errors in personal actions in the king's bench.[1] Hitherto the judgments of the court could only be reversed in parliament. By setting up a court of appeal in personal actions the act put these on a par with actions in the common pleas, which could be reversed in the king's bench. If it slightly diminished the attractiveness of bill procedure, the act also afforded that procedure statutory recognition, since personal actions were by that time predominantly actions by bill.

The fictitious bill of Middlesex survived and with it most of its abuses. Debtors visited London at their peril. Mr. Langton, burgess for Newton, Lancashire, falling sick on his way to the parliament called for October 1601, sent his solicitor ahead to pay a debt for him to one John Lacy of Cheapside. Langton's fellow-burgess informed the House on Thursday, 19 November, that

> this solicitor was arrested on Sunday Night last in Gray's-Inn-Lane, by a Bill of Middlesex, at the suit of William Muskett a Taylor, and carried prisoner to Newgate. And there, after a discharge gotten, because he said he was a Servant to a Parliament Man; he was no sooner discharged, but he was straight again Arrested, and carried to the Compter, and there laid all Night, until he sent to the Serjeant at Arms, who fetched him out.[2]

Fortunate the man who had parliamentary privilege to plead, where another defendant

> shall remayne in warde in the Marshalsey untill he have found suertie which a man of the Countrie not acquainted at Westminster cannot doe, and should pay fees and lose his business in the mean tyme.[3]

The summary arrest upon the writ of *latitat* appears to have been modified by the 1620s, when the defendant 'must eyther give the Sheriffe good Bond, of 40 *l.* at Least, with 2 good sureties, subsidy

[1] 27 Eliz. c. 8; amended by 31 Eliz. c. 1 §§ 2, 3.
[2] H. Townshend, *Historical Collections*, 225.
[3] B.M. Lansd. 621 f. 3.

Men dwelling in the same county, or must goe to prison'.[1] But either prospect made it a formidable first process, and the fact that the defendant must appear in person, 'where if he were empleded in the common place . . . as indeed it oughte to be he myghte appear by Attorney . . . and remayne at home himself aboute his busines',[2] was felt by many to be an unnecessary imposition.

Perhaps the defendant's greatest hardships were the uncertainty of the cause for which he was arrested and the anxiety about further bills that might be brought against him once he was actually or technically in custody. Unable to estimate how much bail he would need, he found it difficult to find sureties and so might have to go to prison, although neither destitute nor friendless. If he was arrested outside Middlesex, undersheriffs 'will sit two or three *Habeas corpus* before they will bring up the prisoner; and untill he hath drawn from the prisoner, considerable summes for the charge of his remove'. When he reached the bailiff's house he was charged exorbitantly for his keep, but if he was carried to Newgate for want of means to maintain himself he could not force the plaintiff to declare against him without suing out a *habeas corpus*, which cost 11*s.* 4*d.* at least. If he could not find bail he had to lie in prison for anything up to two terms, as this was the time allowed to the plaintiff to declare. As his expenses mounted his ability to pay debts or damages diminished.[3]

Coke, for all his disapproval, took the view that 'the proceedings in the court of King's Bench for so long time, and under so many honourable judges, and reverend sages of the law, have gotten such a foundation as cannot, without an act of parliament, be shaken'.[4] The act of parliament was tried in 1661,[5] but no sooner tried than evaded. It provided that no-one should have to find security above £40 on process 'not expressing any particular or cause of action'; the court, with a slickness that was almost impudent, tacked on to its writ of *latitat* the note *ac etiam* with an imaginary sum of money. The common pleas, disappointed that it had not 'nicked them' by the act, produced its own fictitious action in an endeavour to compete.[6] The bill of Middlesex and

[1] S.P. 14/203/41 p. 4. [2] B.M. Lansd. 621 f. 3.

[3] W. Gery, *Proposals for Reformation of Abuses and Subtilties in Practise against the Law and in Scandall of it* (1659), 2–3. Gery says that the defendant must wait three terms for the plaintiff's declaration, all other authorities two.

[4] *Fourth Institute*, 72. [5] 13 Cha. II St. 2 c. 2.

[6] R. North, *Lives of the Norths*, ed. A. Jessopp, i, 86, 128–31.

latitat developed further fictions so that by the time the procedure was abolished in 1832 some writs of *latitat* were merely a summons to appear and some meant business—arrest or heavy bail. Procedure by bill in the king's bench had come such a long way since the judges had made the fateful decision to treat bail as though it were actual custody, and so many of its modifications had been effected by the accretion of further fictions, as to make the many later treatises on it misleading guides to the practice of the fifteenth and sixteenth centuries.[1]

Through all the attacks on the procedure there runs a note of exasperated helplessness. It defrauds the Crown of the fines on originals (long since the perquisite of chancery clerks, but their only fees), it deprives the common pleas of its rightful jurisdiction, it has ousted the filacers of the king's bench from their offices and fees, it oppresses the subject and makes a mockery of justice: in short, it is a monstrous make-believe, and someone ought to do something about it. The problem was then, as it had been from the beginning: who? and what?

The court's affairs were its own concern. The lord chief justice and his three or four puisne justices heard its cases; the chief clerk was in charge of the administration which secured the appearance of parties and juries before term began and continued to function during the hours when the court was not sitting. The court controlled what it saw and heard, the chief clerk controlled what the court did not see and hear. He and his clerks were responsible for all procedure on both types of bill and for the enrolment of pleading, issue and judgment on them; he acted as attorney in the court, drew up pleadings for parties who had not the services of counsel, advised the court on matters of procedure. He was of all the court's officers the one best qualified to grasp the advantages that the fusion of the two bills could offer its clients and the one best placed to cover up the manoeuvre. His own office had most to gain from it. The risk of detection was small because there was little to connect the two self-sufficient and orthodox entries save his own knowledge that they were connected. Although he was subject to the court, he could take care of any difficulty created; a defendant arrested for trespass who found

[1] For the clearest account of the later procedure: *Statutes, Rules and Schedules governing the disposal of Public Records*, 31–40.

himself saddled with a bill of custody for debt was unlikely to ask why the action for trespass had not been prosecuted.

In the fifteenth century the office was held by men of modest origin who grew more substantial with it. The two Sondes (William and his son Reginald)[1] held it from Trinity 1434 to Michaelmas 1491, with an interval from Michaelmas 1458 to Trinity 1461 when it was in the hands of William Brome (Brown).[2] John Bray officiated from Hilary 1491 to Hilary 1498.[3] Thereafter, until 1616, it was occupied by the Roper dynasty (John, William, Thomas, and John),[4] working either singly or in association, with Richard Heywood[5] acting as William Roper's partner between Hilary 1549 and Michaelmas 1568. Whereas the Sondes, Brown and Bray had learned their trade as clerks in the court's offices and had been content to marry into other clerical families, they left an office important enough to attract John Roper, possessor of considerable property in Kent and product of a legal education at Lincoln's Inn. His four successors all brought to the office an academic training at the same Inn. The Ropers married into families of the legal Establishment, whose social background they shared, and the last of them was created Baron Teynham before he vacated the office in 1616. Thereafter it became a sinecure, with the secondary, or chief clerk's deputy, in charge of the work.

The secondary and his clerks (for soon it was they who were doing the work) came in for much of the blame for the bill and *latitat* in the seventeenth and eighteenth centuries. The secondary, whose office certainly went back to the beginning of the sixteenth century, and in a shadowy way still further, had succeeded to the criticism with the work. There is every indication that the chief clerk took responsibility for the office, as well as a principal's share of the fees, well into the sixteenth century and probably until the close of the Roper period: it was John and Thomas Roper who had to defend the enrolment of writs of *latitat* to

[1] Originally of Sondes Place, Dorking, William acquired Throwley, Kent, by marriage and rapidly established the family there: Manning and Bray, *History and Antiquities of Surrey*, i, 567; Hasted, *History of Kent*, 2nd edn. ii, 450–93 *passim*.

[2] Previously filacer for Yorkshire.

[3] Perhaps younger brother to Sir Reynold Bray: Manning and Bray, op. cit. i, 523.

[4] *D.N.B.*; R. W. Chambers, *Sir Thomas More*; *Black Books of Lincoln's Inn*, i.

[5] Probably son of John Heywood who married Joan Rastell, niece to Sir Thomas More: *D.N.B.*; P.C.C. 18 Lyon.

Queen Elizabeth, not their secondary.[1] If we look to the chief clerks as the promoters of bill procedure, we may confine ourselves to two families. The Sondes were chief clerks during the period when the justices were wavering between real and nominal custody; it is tempting to believe that they persevered with test cases until the decision suited them. The Ropers' long reign embraces the development of the second fiction; they were the 'ill-disposed Clerks of this Court' of Coke's account,[2] and perhaps religion was not the only subject on which they deemed it wise to keep their own counsel. William Roper bequeathed 'unto the prisoners of the highe Court of the Kinges benche Fourtie poundes'.[3] Was this a recognition of unwilling service rendered to his family?

How far the bench connived at the innovations remains a matter for speculation. The marriage which made lord chief justice Fineux father-in-law to the first John Roper during the early years of the practice may not be without significance. Although it might have begun in a small way under Sir William Huse (lord chief justice from 1481 to 1495), it could hardly have enjoyed the blessing of a man whose favourite manual was the *Registrum Brevium*. During Fineux's term of office the number of process enrolments so far exceeds the number of trespasses in Middlesex heard in court as to suggest that fiction is already creeping in. Although he bore an unblemished name, and was later credited, on somewhat tenuous evidence, with being an opponent of the 'abuse' of the Bill of Middlesex,[4] his training would have taught him that advantages were there to be used, and procedure by bill and *latitat* might have seemed to him just such an advantage; he had been promoted, moreover, from the common pleas, where he could have learned how much good business there was to be diverted to the rival court. After his death in 1526 there was no lord chief justice of high standing until 1559, when Catlin was appointed; for Fitzjames (1527–39) was both a moral and a legal featherweight, Montagu (1540–46) was timid, and five nonentities followed in quick succession. By the time of Catlin's appointment bill and *latitat* were well established. He is reputed to have had little judicial business to perform, although the plea rolls suggest that he had more than would have fallen to

[1] J. Trye, *Jus Filazarii* (1684), 108.
[2] *Fourth Institute*, 76.
[3] P.C.C. 27 Langley.
[4] B.M. Lansd. 621 f. 5.

him twenty years earlier; in any case he was unlikely to want to eliminate the mainstay of the work on the plea side. He was an honest judge who died poor; without this he would have died poorer still. For the lord chief justice's salary from the Crown was but a small part of an income derived from many sources, of which fees for the sealing of judicial processes issued by the court (as opposed to the first or original writ sued out of chancery) were the most lucrative. It was not for reasons of prestige alone that the lord chief justice wished to see business flourish within his jurisdiction.

The only authority with a clear right to interfere in the affairs of the king's bench, in more than limited instances, was the High Court of Parliament. We have seen that parliament's measures to curb the growth of bill procedure were ineffectual. The reason for this was that parliament was composed of those who understood too little of the working of the court to combat this procedure effectively or too much to wish to do so. It is easy to forget that landlords and merchants were not the only Members with interests to look after in that assembly. The law officers who sat in the Lords, and whose knowledge was so often called upon in the drafting of bills, had sometimes more than an academic interest in their contents; the fifty or more lawyers[1] in the Commons who allowed the bill 'touching the Writ of latitat' to pass had to consider their own as well as their countrymen's welfare. The lawyer's loyalties were further divided according to his sphere of activity. The bill against the abuse of *latitat* procedure must have had the lord keeper's backing and may have owed something to his influence, for it was begun in the Lords; it was sure of the support of all good common-pleas men. When Sir Richard Rede and Serjeant Carus brought it down to the Commons, Rede, a civilian and master of requests, may have hoped that it would do even more than it overtly stated, while Carus, puisne judge of the king's bench of a year's standing, may have been determined that it should not. Parliament could only have stemmed the development of bill procedure if informed of it before its trend was perceptible to laymen and if advised by lawyers united in condemning it. Neither requirement was fulfilled. What the lawyers as a body were prepared to support in the way of legal reform can probably be read upon the statute book, and it is neither extensive

[1] Norah Fuidge, 'The Personnel of the House of Commons, 1563–67' (London Univ. M.A. Thesis, 1950), table I.

nor drastic. Adjustments of procedure to secure jurors[1] and to reduce the pressure on Middlesex jurors caused by the increasing flow of business to Westminster,[2] safeguards to acquaint outlaws of their outlawry,[3] attempts to mitigate some of the effects of the common law's extreme formalism and retentive memory,[4] all these were in the true medieval spirit and admirable as far as they went: but it was not nearly far enough. For the legal reforms which individuals or sectional groups failed to make acceptable to the majority in parliament we have to turn to the Journals.

The Commons Journal opens in 1547 with a measure of law reform in the grand manner. The 'Bill for the Reformation of the Common Laws of the Realm' was twice read and argued in the first session of Edward VI's first parliament.[5] There is some reason to believe that a thirty-page document among State Papers Supplementary, at present unnumbered, may be a copy of this bill. If so, it was entirely concerned with procedure and recommended some drastic reforms within the framework of the existing system, among them the abolition of the writ of *latitat* grounded on the Bill of Middlesex. The author's confidence that 'there is no mischief in ministracion of Justice for whiche wytt of man being willing thereunto cannot provide remedye' was long to await exemplification.[6] This was the nearest that the common law came to a thorough overhaul by statute during the century, although a similar measure appeared in the second session of Mary's first parliament[7] and some vaguely-worded later entries in the Journal may record further efforts in the same direction. But the impetus towards large-scale reform slackened as the reforming spirit dwindled and as business in the common law courts revived. Members then began to bring in bills concerning certain symptoms of that revival and it is these which help us to put the act 'touching the Writ of Latitat' in perspective. The session which produced that act also included a reading of 'The Bill, that Jurors in Myddlesex shall have their Costs in divers trials'.[8] What is probably the same bill had one reading in 1571 and appeared again in 1572 and 1576 with a reading and a committal.[9] This last session also produced the first and second readings of 'The Bill for traversing of

[1] 4 Hen. VIII c.3; 5 Hen. VIII c.5; 4 & 5 Ph. & M. c.7; 27 Eliz. cc. 6, 7.
[2] 18 Eliz. c. 12. [3] 5 & 6 Edw. VI c. 26; 31 Eliz. c. 3.
[4] 32 Hen. VIII c. 30; 18 Eliz. c. 14; 31 Eliz. c. 5. [5] *C. J.* i, 2*b*.
[6] The writer hopes to deal with this document more fully elsewhere.
[7] *C. J.* 27*a*. [8] Ibid. 77*a*. [9] Ibid. 90*a*, 96*a*, 97*a*.

the County in Actions upon the Case of Words', while in the parliament of 1584–85 a 'Bill concerning Actions upon the Case to be tried in their proper Counties' was committed on its second reading, after a debate which had aroused feelings that could only be vented by coughing and spitting, and passed on its third.[1] These were straws which showed which way the wind was blowing, and it was not in the direction of thoroughgoing legal reform.

The concern with the expenses of Middlesex jurors and the traversing (that is, denying) of the county in actions on the case were by-products of a further fiction, which was to make most of its growth in the sixteenth century. This was based on the theory that such personal actions as were not of their nature bound to a specific place were 'transitory' and might be laid in any court to suit the plaintiff or to bring them within common law jurisdiction.[2] In this way actions on the case for words could be tried before a Middlesex jury rather than before one of the county in which the words were spoken. This was a departure from the medieval conception of the jury of neighbours who could bring to their task common local knowledge. The extension of the scope of transitory or foreign actions to mercantile affairs brought many actions (such as debts contracted beyond the seas) to the common law courts where they had not had jurisdiction before: thus by drawing the distinction between local and transitory actions the common law could compete with the court of admiralty in the expanding commercial field, and by ridding itself of the incubus of venue in many personal actions it could render less slow and uncertain that trial by jury which had previously handicapped its competition with chancery and star chamber. As early as 1539 some lawyers had sought to free contracts made abroad from the limitation of venue, but their bill failed in the Lords.[3] Others continued to oppose the fiction, for when the bill to grant the jurors of Middlesex 'xvj [d] apiece for their appearance in every action layd in their shire and not being there' was debated in 1572, Thomas Gent protested, 'A bill rather to be made forbidding any action to be served but where the fact was commytted'.[4] Thus while lawyers were divided, fictions grew.

[1] Ibid. 104*a*, 105*a*, *b*; D'Ewes, *Journal*, 335*a*, 365*a*.

[2] Holdsworth, *Hist. of Eng. Law*, v, 140–8. [3] Ibid. 142, citing *L. J.*, i, 112*b*.

[4] Thomas Cromwell's Journal, Trinity College Dublin MSS. N.2.12, 75–76: quoted by permission of the History of Parliament Trust. Cf. Hastings, op. cit. 160.

For although lawyers were not ready to overhaul their heritage in the light of changing circumstances, those circumstances made that heritage quite impossible to live with. Procedure on original writ might be extolled, but it was outmoded. The five processes to outlawry designed to ensure the defendant a hearing when communications were uncertain and travel laborious had been allowed to become a virtual denial of justice to the plaintiff. Whatever the theoretical disabilities suffered by the outlaw, they rarely forced him to appear in court to answer the complaint.[1] Sheriffs returned the glib answers *nichil habet* and *non inventus* with impunity, and we know of one who preferred to suffer the pains of that distress so aptly named 'infinite' for thirty-three years rather than comply with inconvenient orders from the court.[2] The writ of *latitat* was not an infallible weapon either, but in purchasing it the plaintiff was not settling down to a long drawn-out siege but sending out shock troops who could easily be withdrawn. For there is little evidence, in spite of Coke's testimony to the contrary, that litigants by writ of *latitat* proceeded to outlawry, or even that they often proceeded at all, if the first writ failed.[3] Above all, that writ, however erroneously founded on fiction, was beautifully simple, for

> the *Latitat* is like to Doctor Giffords water, which serves for all diseases, and so It holds one forme in all cases and actions whatsoever.[4]

We have seen that lawyers were not prepared for reform in the sixteenth century, and we know that, even in the revolutionary atmosphere of the Interregnum, although they could see what needed doing,[5] those who had the power could not bring themselves to press for it. Although he served conscientiously as chairman of the committee concerned with law reform, Sir Matthew Hale was not only loath to sacrifice his own court of exchequer, he was also too much obsessed with the notion of offices as property to envisage their abolition without a shudder. To him it was a serious objection to the reform of process in the king's bench that it would destroy some offices, 'notably

[1] An analysis of the actions pending in Michaelmas 1488 shows that two-thirds of those brought by original proceeded to outlawry and were heard of no more.

[2] Marjorie Blatcher, 'Distress Infinite and the Contumacious Sheriff' (*Bull. Inst. Hist. Res.* xiii), 146–50.

[3] *Fourth Institute*, 76.

[4] T. Powell, *Attourneys Academy*, 166.

[5] W. Gery, *Proposals for Reformation of Abuses*.

Henley's'.[1] Reformers should be made of sterner stuff. Within the court itself acceptance of what had so long been done blunted the critical faculty, so that the filacer and his deputies could answer the commissioners as late as 1829 that 'they were not aware of any inconveniences attending the practice of commencing actions by original writs' or that they were 'incompetent to judge'.[2]

Sir Henry Maine has said:

> It is not difficult to understand why fictions in all their forms are particularly congenial to the infancy of society. They satisfy the desire for improvement, which is not quite wanting, at the same time that they do not offend the superstitious derelish for change which is always present. At a particular stage of social progress they are invaluable expedients for overcoming the rigidity of law . . . To revile them as merely fraudulent is to betray ignorance of their peculiar office in the historical development of law.[3]

Pending the time when whole-hearted reformers could regard the common law courts as one and recommend integrated changes in them all, the king's bench had done what it could to free itself from medieval bonds. Although the motive was self-interested and the means a fiction, those who employed the writ of *latitat* to achieve that end were serving the cause of necessary change.

[1] 'Discourse', 372; cf. F. A. Inderwick, *The Interregnum*, 205–12.

[2] *First Report of Commissioners appointed to inquire into the Practice and Proceedings of the Superior Courts of Common Law*, H. of C. 46 (1829), 497.

[3] *Ancient Law*, 16th edn., 26–27.

VIII

The Elizabethan Exchequer: War in the Receipt

G. R. ELTON

In the government of Elizabeth, the exchequer, reformed in 1554, once again handled the bulk of the Crown's revenues; it was the dominant ministry of finance, though two lesser offices, the court of wards and the duchy of Lancaster, remained outside its control.[1] The exchequer was divided into two departments, a treasury and pay-office (exchequer of receipt) and a court of audit (exchequer of account), which had almost developed into separate institutions. The administration of the Queen's money was indeed shared by them, but each operated as a unit, contacts between them were interdepartmental rather than casual, and only one man (the chancellor of the exchequer who was also always undertreasurer of the Receipt) had a standing in both sections. The various early-Tudor experiments in financial administration, which had in the end produced the reformed exchequer, had left that office with an increased jealousy of irregular or novel procedure and a more specific interest in its own venerable methods; respect for their indisputable safety would admit no recognition of their devilish clumsiness and soon grew into an unthinking affection for any established practice. The feeling appeared in the number of notes and accounts of the exchequer's vast organization and esoteric ways scattered through the papers of the time; one of these, written by Thomas Fanshawe who was queen's remembrancer under Elizabeth, appeared in print in 1658.[2] Departmental devotion was further encouraged by the needs of the exchequer's staff. Next to the royal household, the exchequer was easily the largest department in existence; served by men who usually entered

[1] G. R. Elton, *The Tudor Revolution in Government*, 223 sqq.

[2] *The Practice of the Exchequer Court and its Several Officers*. The book enjoys a not altogether deserved reputation for correctness and completeness.

young and worked their way up by seniority, it constituted the most complete example of a civil service structure in the Queen's government. Like nearly all Tudor officers, those of the exchequer drew their income from three sources: they had official salaries, took fees from revenue officers and others for such requirements of the accounting process as the making out of documents of or certified copies from the record, and could hope for perquisites and bribes intended to dispose them favourably to those who got involved in the exchequer's machinery. On the whole it seems clear that this last source of income did not amount to much among the rank and file of officials, and salaries were certainly never adequate. In consequence the fees, levied on a fixed scale, provided the chief means of livelihood and attraction of office; conservatism in procedure was assisted by the fact that reforms, if efficient, would probably reduce the chances of earning them. Nothing so well illustrates the facts of life in the exchequer as the war over precedence, duties and fees waged throughout Elizabeth's reign between two officers in the Receipt, the writer of the tallies and the clerk of the pells, a war which left behind a mass of complex materials.[1]

The medieval Receipt was in the charge of the treasurer and the two chamberlains of the exchequer, and its organization was therefore determined by the existence of three head-officers designed to act as checks upon one another. The only public records in the Receipt consisted of rolls of receipts and issues, called pells, one of each being kept on behalf of each officer. There were thus six rolls, two treasurer's pells and four chamberlain's counter-pells. These were, in theory, made up on the spot, each item of money received and paid being entered as it came in or went out; they were really journal books from which it was both difficult to establish accurate totals and impossible to analyse either the items of revenue or the nature of government expenditure. Such money as there was in the exchequer was supposed to be in the custody of the treasurer and chamberlains whose representatives kept the keys

[1] The bulk of the papers is found in one bundle of Miscellanea of the Receipt, P.R.O. E 407/71; most documents in this are numbered individually but in no sort of order. The next five bundles (72–76) of unnumbered papers consist of the office correspondence of one writer of the tallies and contain some helpful details. In addition material is found in B.M. Lansdowne MSS. and in Hist. MSS. Com. *Salisbury MSS.* In the compass of this paper it will be necessary to omit many of the often fascinating details.

to the money-chests. In practice two things had happened to modify this theoretical picture. One was the emergence of the treasurer's clerk (or deputy) as the effective head of the Receipt with the title of undertreasurer, an event which Elizabethans liked to link with Henry VII's reforms[1] but which had taken place by the middle of the fifteenth century.[2] The other—which alone made the system workable—was the near-disappearance of cash from the exchequer, whose transactions came to consist predominantly in the issuing and auditing of tallies of assignment (anticipations of revenue), so that a detailed record of revenue and expenditure proved the less necessary.[3]

However, the reorganization of government begun in the late fifteenth century touched also the exchequer, and certain reforms had been carried out before the accession of Henry VIII. Sir Vincent Skinner, writer of the tallies, describing them in the course of his war with Chidiock Wardour, clerk of the pells, put them down to Henry VII, 'being, as he is right worthily styled in story, a prince of prudent and politic government'.[4] The king, we are told, found the pells a useless record which did not enable him to plan an increase in revenue and decrease in expenditure, or to 'understand thereby what remained due and answerable to him'; he regarded the cost of these various rolls as excessive; and he therefore instituted the 'formal and orderly course of account' since in use. He retained one pell of receipt 'as a ledger and coucher in court to serve as a double voucher for his more security', but abolished the issue roll altogether; this was done also because he did not wish too many people to know how his money was spent. Secondly he transferred the actual custody of money to the four tellers who were to pay it out only on a warrant from the lord treasurer and undertreasurer, an order which in turn must rest on a warrant under the great or privy seal. Allegedly the establishment of the undertreasurership was another part of the reforms. Lastly, he instituted the making and presenting of annual 'Declarations of

[1] e.g. B.M. Lansd. 151 ff. 103 sqq.

[2] J. L. Kirby, 'The rise of the under-treasurer of the Exchequer' (*E.H.R.* lxxii), 666 sqq.

[3] For the fifteenth-century Receipt cf. A. Steel, *The Receipt of the Exchequer 1377–1485*, pp. xxix sqq.; J. L. Kirby, 'The Issues of the Lancastrian Exchequer' (*Bull. Inst. Hist. Res.* xxiv), 121 sqq.

[4] There are several drafts of Skinner's discourse, written between 1601 and 1604: E 407/71/13; E 407/75 (unnumbered); B.M. Lansd. 151 ff. 103 sqq.

P

the State of the Treasury' in which all receipts and payments, in cash or by tally, were reduced into digested form, giving a clear view of the nature of both revenue and expenditure as well as making plain at a glance what the reserves were.

These reforms certainly took place: were they Henry VII's? The habit now is to see in him nothing but the heir of Yorkist practice, and it is certainly true that the office of undertreasurer was older. Moreover, the last medieval pell of issue now extant is that of 19 Edward IV (1479), and it is claimed that no later one was known even by the end of Elizabeth's reign.[1] Yet this cannot quite be: Wardour discovered a writ of 20 Edward IV ordering the entry of certain payments on the issue roll and transcribed it for his purposes.[2] He also thought that the custody of money was not transferred to the tellers until early in Henry VIII's reign,[3] but in this he postdated events. It certainly seems that the institution of the vital 'Declarations' only began about 1504: Skinner claimed to have the first of them in his office and that it belonged to 20 Henry VII.[4] In all probability the duplicated pells ceased to be kept in course of time and without any specific orders of reform; the surviving series are patchy enough throughout, and even in 1550 (and later), when no counterpells had been known for decades, officers were still paid a nominal fee for writing them.[5] The more precise reforms which put the tellers, controlled by the undertreasurer, in charge of the cash, and which relied on the annual statements to the king and lord treasurer—these may safely be left to Henry VII's credit.[6]

Though these reforms do not look big, they did in fact amount to an upheaval in the Receipt. The chamberlains' deputies ceased to have any controlling influence; everything fell on the treasurer's deputy, the undertreasurer. But he in turn had to depend on active

[1] *Third Report of the Deputy Keeper of the Public Records*, App. ii, 173.

[2] E 407/71/11. [3] B.M. Lansd. 106 f. 4.

[4] E 407/71/13. The earliest extant now is E 405/183, for 23–24 Henry VII (1507–8).

[5] Each chamberlain had a deputy in the Receipt, with a fee of £10, for the striking of tallies, and a clerk to write the counterpell who got £6: E 405/212 (1550).

[6] Sir Julius Caesar thought that 'a new establishment' in the Receipt dated from 20 Henry VII and that the pell of issue was discontinued in 21 Henry VII: B.M. Lansd. 168 f. 284. But it is possible that he relied on, and misinterpreted, Skinner's discourse which was certainly available to him since the fair copy is among his papers: B.M. Lansd. 151 ff. 103 sqq.

officers in the Receipt, especially from 1543 onwards when his office came to be held jointly with the chancellorship of the exchequer, a post in the upper or audit court.[1] And since the roots of the quarrel with which this paper is concerned lie precisely here, it will be necessary to say a few words about the working of the Receipt—its so-called 'course'.[2] When an officer accountant, or a debtor, paid money into the Receipt, he set in motion a complicated machinery designed to produce a tally which he could present in the exchequer of account to have his payment or debt discharged. He paid the money to a teller who (having entered the receipt in his own book) put a bill 'down a trunk' into the Receipt (later known as the tally court) on which he had entered the date, year and term, the payer's name and county, and the sum received. This was now in effect entered three times. It was transcribed for record into the pell of receipt; it was transferred onto a tally (the sum being cut in notches and the other matter written on the sides of the wooden stick); and it was also registered in a book kept by the officer called writer of the tallies. The tally was then struck (split), and the accountant could depart for his audit.[3] The teller's bill remained in the Receipt and came to be kept by the writer of the tallies. Payments out of the Receipt rested ultimately upon Crown warrants, either dormant (for recurring payments) under the great or privy seal, or special warrants under the privy seal only. The tellers, however, could not pay any money except on receiving letters grounded upon the royal warrants. In the case of recurring payments, the patent, registered in a book kept in the Receipt, was retained by the payee who obtained and deposited a dormant writ of *liberate*; each individual payment then required a debenture to the teller. Privy seals for special payments, addressed to the treasurer and chamberlains, resulted in letters from the lord treasurer and undertreasurer (usually made up into weekly

[1] Cf. Elton, op. cit. 254.

[2] This description, reduced to essentials, is in great part derived from two documents: E 407/71/82 ('an old report found in the Receipt of the service there used by the officers attendant') and ibid. no. 3 (based on this but with some variations in detail and annotated by Skinner). Other descriptions occur among the papers.

[3] In fact revenue officers usually came to their account much later, and there were careful rules about the transfer of the countertallies or foils to the custody of the deputy chamberlains in the upper exchequer, there to await the production of the tally and the joining which constituted the chief proof of payment accepted by the exchequer.

statements) to the Receipt where an order assigning the payment to a specified teller was then made out. The privy seals were filed in the department, which also kept an entry book of the lord treasurer's weekly orders.

The essential problem in the Receipt consisted in controlling the tellers who alone handled the money for which they rendered half-yearly account. There had to be one officer in the Receipt who kept the material for auditing their books. The old treasurer's clerk, out of whose office the exalted undertreasurer had grown, had kept the rolls and written the tallies himself;[1] by the late fifteenth century these duties had come into the charge of the clerk of the Receipt of whom there is no trace under the Tudors;[2] but from the middle of the fifteenth century anyway one can trace two sets of officers who were respectively responsible for keeping the pells of receipt and issue, and for writing the tallies.[3] On the face of it, the first was a much more weighty office, and Dr Steel considered the clerk of the pells to be the treasurer's true representative in the fifteenth century Receipt.[4] Yet it is curious to find that certain clerks of the pells appeared later as writers of the tallies, a point not missed by the embattled tally writers of Elizabeth's reign.[5] These men had evidently been promoted to a higher and more profitable office. The explanation lies almost certainly in a fact which appears at first to contradict it. The Tudor 'Declarations of the State of the Treasury' used somewhat surprising terms in describing these various officers.[6] The undertreasurer appeared as *clericus thesaurarii Anglie*, the writer of the tallies as *unus clericorum ex parte thesaurarii Anglie*, and the clerk of the pells as *alter clericus thesaurarii Anglie* (in that order). In other words, this official record, using, in the Exchequer manner, an old-fashioned terminology, equated as treasurer's clerks two officers whose salaries were £173 6*s*. 8*d*. and £17 10*s*. respectively; while the tally writer,

[1] R. L. Poole, *The Exchequer in the Twelfth Century*, 73 sqq.; J. Willard, 'The treasurer's issue roll and the clerk of the treasurer' (*Bull. Inst. Hist. Res.* viii), 129 sqq., esp. 133.

[2] Kirby, *E.H.R.* lxxii, 676. Does the absorption (re-absorption?) of this office into the undertreasurership explain the conviction that Henry VII had instituted this last office?

[3] I have easily compiled complete lists of them from the admissions registered in the Black Book of the Exchequer: E 36/266.

[4] Steel, op. cit. 3.

[5] e.g. John Leyton, clerk 1460 and writer 1464; Thomas Bulkley, clerk at an unknown date and writer 1471; John Lewes, clerk 1486 and writer 1489.

[6] e.g. E 405/183, Declaration of 23–24 Henry VII.

earning at that time £28 6*s*. 8*d*., seemed in title inferior to the lowest paid. All this suggests that the clerk of the pells had a longer independent history and that the tally writer had risen to prominence as a special agent of the undertreasurer, the titular head of the Receipt. Certainly he had come to be relied on for the keeping of the papers and records to audit the tellers' accounts and for the preparation of the material needed for treasury statements.

Two events in the first half of the sixteenth century assisted these developments, which reduced the clerk of the pells to inferiority in the Receipt. One was a purely personal matter. In July 1517 Thomas Danyell became writer of the tallies, while five months later, in November, John Uvedale obtained the clerkship of the pells. Danyell was succeeded by Thomas Felton in May 1550; Uvedale held his office till he died in 1549. During this long common tenure Danyell was nothing except an exchequer official, while Uvedale, a Yorkshireman, held a variety of other offices, culminating in the active secretaryship of the council of the north from 1536 onwards.[1] He can never have attended in person to the pells at all, and it is known that he exercised his office through his son-in-law.[2] At this very time the need for someone connected with the accounts to take charge grew urgent as the undertreasurership passed from such professional hands as those of Sir John Cutt (1506–21) to the hands of lawyers and courtiers like Sir Thomas More (1526–28), Sir Richard Weston (1528–42), and Sir John Baker (1543–58). The writer of the tallies, active in person and relied on by his superiors, necessarily took over. Secondly, there was the growing practice of introducing new sources of revenue into the exchequer, culminating in the reforms of 1554 which, while they restored exchequer supremacy in the finances, also meant that the bulk of exchequer revenue was new and no longer handled by the 'old course' of the exchequer.[3] That is to say, it stood outside the tally system proper, and since the old pells were designed for a register of tallies the clerk of the pells had ever greater difficulties in asserting supervisory powers. All this came to a head with Thomas Felton, tally writer from 1550 to 1556, who (according to Sir Julius Caesar)[4] was first called by the novel but descriptive title of auditor of the Receipt.

[1] *D.N.B.* Uvedale served in the north with short interruptions from 1528 to his death. [2] E 407/71/96. [3] Elton, *Tudor Revolution*, 254 sqq.

[4] B.M. Lansd. 168 f. 353*b*. Skinner thought that the title first appeared in 1566 when Humphrey Skelton took over from Felton: E 407/71/96.

From this time, however, the counterattack began. Behind it there lay complex and obscure relationships between these exchequer officials and the great officers of state. Both the writership of the tallies and the clerkship of the pells were in the gift of the lord treasurer, and it appears that while most treasurers relied more on the writer, one of them, the marquess of Winchester (1550–72) leaned towards the clerk. At any rate, trouble seems to have begun with Edmund Cockerell's appointment as clerk of the pells late in 1555,[1] and his successors Robert Hare (1560–70) and Chidiock Wardour (1570–1611) appear to have been clients of the 'old treasurer', as he was later called.[2] On the other hand, the important writers of the tallies were both Burghley's men. Robert Peter (1569–93), appointed nominally still by Winchester but in fact apparently a servant of that good Cecilian, Sir Walter Mildmay, chancellor of the exchequer since 1566,[3] had the closest ties with Burghley, who consistently relied on him for the running of the Receipt.[4] Peter's successor, Vincent Skinner, was a much more striking case. He had no previous professional experience of the exchequer but was a trusted servant of Burghley's, employed by him from at least 1578 onwards in many affairs: making peace at Cambridge, dealing with prisoners in the Fleet, devilling for him on the subject of prohibitions at common law (for which purpose he read the subject up in Fitzherbert and Brooke), investigating the history of negotiations over contraband.[5] From 1584 Skinner sat in the Cecil interest in parliament,[6] and his appointment as writer of the tallies was very much a personal reward to a favourite servant. A copy of the treasurer's patent appointing him survives among Burghley's papers;[7] and Skinner was admitted to the office, not (as was proper) at the Receipt but at court, on 11 November 1593, taking the oath of supremacy (the first holder of the office

[1] Below, 230.

[2] Letters from Winchester to Hare describe the clerk specifically as his servant and are signed 'your master': S.P. 12/8/62; 12/83/138. They required Hare to do the sort of thing for which Burghley relied on the auditor of the Receipt.

[3] Mildmay was later described as Peter's 'especial good master' who had assisted him in various usurpations 'without the consent of the old lord treasurer who then [1572] lay at Basing and never returned hither again': E 407/71/51.

[4] S.P. 12/105/90; 12/192/art. 9; cf. Hist. MSS. Com. *Salisbury*, ii, 106, 107, 187, 217, 264, 339; iii, 105.

[5] Hist. MSS. Com. *Salisbury*, xiii, 156 sqq., 158, 446; S.P. 12/233/art. 29; 12/238/142–3.

[6] J. E. Neale, *The Elizabethan House of Commons*, 207, 243.

[7] Hist. MSS. Com. *Salisbury*, iv, 377.

to do so) with Burghley signing the entry.[1] In office he continued a Cecil client, a fact to which Burghley's death and the lord treasurership of Lord Buckhurst made no difference.[2] In 1599 he acknowledged to Robert Cecil Burghley's 'honourable favour and goodness' by which 'I received the place, though with small desire and less affection unto it, being unknown to me then how painful and otherwise troublesome it was and hath proved since, saving that it was a continuation of my service under him'.[3] He no doubt regarded himself in great part recompensed when he was among the first knights dubbed, on 7 May 1603 at Belvoir castle, by James I.[4]

Thus out of these gradual but marked changes in administrative practice grew the war between the two most important officers in the Receipt, a war for control of affairs on the one hand and over the fees paid by the public on the other. The first shot, however, was fired, early in Elizabeth's reign, not by a clerk of the pells but by an anonymous deputy to the earl of Shrewsbury as chamberlain of the exchequer.[5] He demanded a full restoration of the ancient course so that the chamberlains' clerks should once again exercise some control over the lord treasurer's clerks. Things seem to have been bad in the Receipt under Mary. An usher who allegedly sold half a cart-load of treaties and other records in St. Paul's Churchyard was never punished till executed for a treason in which he had also got involved; the tellers had embezzled much money and died in debt to the Queen. The author of this memorandum relied heavily on Cockerell, who (according to Robert Peter) had begun the recovery of his office by improperly obtaining custody of the old pells records;[6] he also attacked Felton. Most interesting is the story with which he concludes. In the previous Michaelmas term, lord treasurer Winchester had declared in full court that the departures from the ancient course had resulted in nothing but abuse and had sworn that he would have it reintroduced 'or else he would give up his staff and leave his office'. However, he was

[1] Black Book, E 36/266/89*b*.

[2] This is shown by his correspondence with Robert Cecil: Hist. MSS. Com. *Salisbury*, ix, 131, 298; x, 83, 281, 292 sqq.; xii, 435.

[3] S.P. 12/271/177. It should be noted that despite all these personal attachments both officers, holding for life, were civil servants who stayed on regardless of changes at the top.

[4] W. A. Shaw, *Knights of England*, ii, 104.

[5] B.M. Lansd. 106 ff. 8–15.

[6] E 407/71 (unnumbered), Peter's memo. of January 1584.

blocked by his own chancellor of the exchequer, Sir John Baker, with whom he appears to have been on bad terms—Baker who (our writer says) calls himself by the new-fangled name of undertreasurer. Winchester, when 'at great contentation' with him, had been heard to assure his underofficer that before Henry VII there was no better title than treasurer's clerk. Anyway, Baker managed to persuade the Queen that Winchester was merely working off his resentment over certain land sales which he had opposed, and she would not permit the restoration of the discarded rolls.

This story throws some light on the history of the Receipt in the first ten years of Elizabeth, when there is otherwise little evidence. All we know is that in the three years 9–11 Elizabeth (1567–9) the issue roll suddenly reappeared.[1] It therefore looks as though, with Baker and Queen Mary gone (they both died in 1558), Winchester got his way in the end. That he was acting on behalf of his special servant, Robert Hare, is also clear enough. Peter later told how Hare 'revived' the issue roll: he borrowed from the writer of the tallies the fully audited tellers' accounts and copied them into a parchment roll which he then pretended was the true record of payments made.[2] 'This he did to make a show of some service in respect of the great allowances that he a little before had procured.' Hare, in fact, got his fee increased from the traditional £17 10*s.* to £67 13*s.* 4*d.*,[3] and the tally writers thereafter maintained that that increase was granted to pay for the labour and costs of an issue roll the making of which was again abandoned in 1572 without any surrender of fee. What they did not stress was that in the same year they too obtained an increase of £50, to raise their salary to £91 13*s.* 4*d.*[4] Having got his extra fee, Hare allegedly sold the office 'at the best' to Chidiock Wardour. The charge was therefore that Hare had artificially inflated its value in order to get a good price; it is very probably true and explains something about Wardour's immediate and never-ending endeavours to get the most for and out of his purchase.

The real war began with Wardour's appointment to the pells in April 1570, coming as it did on top of Peter's succession as auditor to the colourless Humphrey Skelton (July 1569): and its first stage lasted from 1570 to 1584, when Wardour secured a favourable verdict from a committee of exchequer officials. Many

[1] E 403/858–60.
[2] E 407/71 (unnumbered).
[3] B.M. Lansd. 28 f. 2.
[4] Ibid.

of the vast number of memoranda are hard to date, a difficulty aggravated by Skinner's habit of scribbling marginalia against his predecessor's papers when he was constructing minutes of his own out of them. But the arguments were nearly always the same, with minor variations, and it will be as well to summarize the main ones here. Until 1597 things turned in the main on Wardour's demand that the pell of issue be restored, though he kept a few lesser hares (custody of records, matters of fees, the making out of certificates of payments, etc.) running with his leading entry. A fair summary of his position is found in a document which belongs to shortly after 1584 but clearly adds nothing new to what he must have put forward in the previous dozen years.[1] This begins by stating that 'there ought to be two principal records kept daily in the Receipt of her majesty's exchequer', a 'pell of introitus' or receipt and one of 'exitus' or issue. The former records all money paid in, from whom and for what cause and on what day it was received, and the name of the teller who took it. The latter should record all payments of fees, annuities, pensions, rewards or other money, with details of day, cause and warrant, as well as all money paid on imprest. The officer responsible for keeping these records is the lord treasurer's clerk, otherwise now called clerk of the pells of receipt and issue, an office dating back to Henry II. Wardour thus claimed to be the true heir of the clerk mentioned in the *Dialogus de Scaccario*. Skinner's marginal note against this sums up the repeated arguments of Peter and himself: the old treasurer's clerk was 'superintendent over all the officers and under-ministers of the Receipt' and was in the sixteenth century really represented by the under-treasurer. That this is correct has already been shown. But we have also seen that conservative practice preserved a nomenclature in the early-Tudor records which gave some colour to Wardour's claim by seeming to equate his office with that of the under-treasurer.[2] Nevertheless, it can be said at once that Wardour's desire to inherit the office of lord treasurer's clerk *par excellence* was at best a piece of mistaken antiquarianism. Peter was fond of pointing out also that Wardour's office was properly clerk of the pell, only Wardour himself having invented the plural (a point I have been unable to establish); from this Peter argued that the writing of the issue roll had never been part of his duties. In the

[1] E 407/71/51. It has later marginal notes by Skinner. [2] Above, 218.

declaration of receipts and issues which Robert Hare rendered in 1568, the clerk called himself the treasurer's clerk, but another hand on the cover described him as *clericus pellis*.[1] It is in truth hard to discover who wrote the fifteenth-century issue rolls; there were then three underclerks on the treasurer's side in the Receipt who no doubt divided the actual work between themselves.[2]

Wardour went on to state that he kept the receipt roll, though Peter's jealousy prevented him from making it perfect: the tellers received money and tallies were cut that were never brought to his notice. Against this Skinner noted another standard reply of the tally writer's: the receipt roll, which had used to be written day by day in court and kept locked up when the court was not in session, was now being copied from rough notes and entirely open to falsification. As for the issue roll, Wardour complained that it had been totally discontinued 'without cause, warrant, or order', which left the payments in the sole control of one man—'so as her majesty for the state of her treasure is subject to the particular honesty of the said Mr Peter'. He then went on to claim the rights of his office which he rested on the title conferred by his patent which described him as *clericus thesaurarii ad scribendas pelles recepti et exitus*. Here he touched on a tricky point. That his patent ran this way was admitted, but Peter asserted that Hare's patent, the precedent for Wardour's, had been altered from standard form. He ascribed this to Hare's influence over Winchester in his declining years.[3] Cockerell's, certainly, said nothing of the issue roll.[4] In this connection the admissions registered in the Black Book of the Receipt are of some assistance. There is no mention of the issue roll after its cessation until Richard Browne came to be admitted on 11 February 1550 when a later hand inserted '& de exitu' above the line in a record which originally spoke only of the receipt roll.[5] Cockerell was admitted 'ad officium scriptoris pellis',[6] but in Hare's case the traditional formula was again amended by the later addition of '& de exitu', and for Wardour the full duties of keeping both rolls were carefully noted.[7] Of course, when he took office the issue roll had temporarily been revived. But there seems no doubt that Hare and Wardour deliberately saw to the inclusion of the issue roll in the latter's patent (and probably tampered with the Black Book as well), so

[1] E 405/379.
[2] Kirby, *E.H.R.* lxxii, 668.
[3] E 407/71/75.
[4] Ibid. no. 18.
[5] E 36/266/73.
[6] Ibid. f. 74*b*.
[7] Ibid. ff. 75*b*, 78.

that Wardour's reliance on his patent was at best the exploitation of a prepared line of attack. Peter once analysed his rival's patent for the lord treasurer's benefit: it entitled him to call himself treasurer's clerk, to write tallies and enter them in the receipt and issue roll, to put the seals to the bags of money, to oversee the Receipt and know all things there, to be responsible for supplying its financial needs. (That is to say, it granted the office of the thirteenth-century treasurer's clerk.) In this way, Peter went on, 'he seeketh to intrude' on the undertreasurer's title, on the writer of the tallies, on the ushers, on the undertreasurer's duties twice over, and even on the lord treasurer who would not do without a warrant what Wardour here arrogated to himself in his patent. He concluded that the patent was therefore void.[1] But there could be no question that, however they had got it out of Winchester, Hare and Wardour had staked a strong claim. Their office was in Winchester's gift, and Skinner had cause to note at the end of one of Wardour's plaints the dubious 'Quere whether an office being in the gift of a superior the grantor may alter the form from the ancient grants'.[2]

The question—to which the answer surely is, yes, he may—was the more serious because the writer of the tallies could not usefully rely on his patent which granted him nothing but the writing of tallies.[3] He was therefore inclined to fall back on his oath of office and on lists of duties performed in the past. But the latter—though they might be used to justify his taking more fees than Wardour[4] —could not constitute a title, and so everything turned on the oath.[5] By this he swore to write tallies; to help discharge accounts

[1] E 407/71/16. [2] Ibid. no. 51: dorse of last sheet.

[3] Ibid.: several examples cited by Wardour without comment from Skinner.

[4] This was the purpose of the list in E 407/71/79. Others (ibid. nos. 14 and 45) recorded Peter's office work. He made (1) a book of entry in which he personally entered all tellers' bills; (2) an entry book of payments in which he entered transcripts of the treasurer's warrants; (3) the equivalent of a year's entries in that he wrote all orders for payment himself; (4) a half-yearly audit of the tellers' accounts; (5) half-yearly books of views (views of tellers' accounts); (6) translations into Latin of all dormant privy seals, entered in a ledger in the office; (7) a book of annuities and fees on which debentures were based; (8) payments by assignment engrossed on parchment and added to the tellers' accounts yearly; (9) paper drafts, transcribed into a ledger by his clerks, of prests which were engrossed and delivered to the queen's remembrancer; (10) two entry books of patents and privy seals for payments; (11) a weekly certificate to the lord treasurer of receipts, payments, and remain, a matter so secret it could not be delegated to a clerk. [5] Transcribed in E 407/71/79.

'according to the ancient custom of this court'; to make declarations of all receipts and payments to the lord treasurer and under-treasurer; and to have a special care and charge of the treasury of the Receipt, the main record depository of the Crown where treaties and other important state documents were kept. On the second and third of these promises the writer rested his claim to audit the tellers' accounts and act as the general link between the head-officers and the Receipt. Wardour had much formal right on his side when he maintained that 'all men are officers by their patents and admittances and not by their oaths'.[1] Peter could only protest, unconvincingly, that his office 'by the grant of the lord treasurer is *ad scribenda tallia et contratallia, ac ad facienda et exercenda omnia alia que ad officium predictum pertinent*, the which by mine oath is explained': the oath justified the vast expansion of activities which the phrase *omnia alia* was perhaps intended to cover.[2] Since Wardour had cited patents of the tally writers (and a copy of Skinner's survives),[3] it seems mere subterfuge on Peter's part to pretend that his case was one of those where an office was granted by a superior officer for life and without patent; in such cases, he claimed, exchequer practice was to regard oath and admittance as perfect definitions.[4] In any case, Wardour had a larger argument against the oath: he charged Felton with having deliberately torn it out of the Black Book and replaced the missing sheet with a new one on which he had written an oath of his own devising.[5] This charge Peter evaded rather than refuted by showing evidence that earlier predecessors of his had done all the things which in his own oath he had sworn to do.[6] An inspection of the Black Book suggests that Wardour was right,[7] but the point is not material. At most Felton found it necessary, perhaps under instruction, to revise the oath in accordance with changing practice, and practice had changed because of far-reaching reforms in the Receipt which unfortunately had been carried through without regard to bureaucratic record and precision.

[1] This, he said, Peter was told by the chief baron: ibid. no. 51.
[2] Ibid., unnumbered. [3] Above, 220. [4] E 407/71 (unnumbered).
[5] Ibid. no. 51; B.M. Lansd. 106 f. 4. [6] E 407/71 (unnumbered).
[7] E 36/266/98, which contains the oaths of both the writer of the tallies and the clerk of the pells, looks to have been glued into the book. The two oaths, each at the head of the page (ff. 98 and 98*b*) are written in a fifteenth-century exchequer hand, which could of course be a deliberate copy. Underneath each there are entries in a mid-sixteenth-century hand. F. 97 is later in purport than 98; ff. 99 sqq. contain pre-Tudor entries.

In the document which has guided us so far, Wardour followed his exposition of the old course and his list of helpful precedents by what he himself called his demands. He wanted the custody of all warrants for payment, claiming that he could produce in his office his predecessors' warrants down to the first year of Henry VIII. This, of course, once again ignored more recent developments: in 1576, one of the tellers told Sir Walter Mildmay that privy seals and accounts 'ever remained with the auditor of the Receipt' who by an order of Sir Richard Sackville's (chancellor of the exchequer 1558–66) always got all warrants because he alone knew which teller had enough money to pay them.[1] Wardour wished to make the weekly reports of payments, revenue and reserves which, according to him, had been the clerk's duty till Peter filched it from him in 1572. He wanted to enrol patents and warrants, with allowance for so doing, to sign debentures to the tellers (with allowance), and to make constats for prest money and for 'tallies missing or not joined'.[2] In other words, he demanded that after the restoration of the issue roll he should be equipped with independent powers not only to share in controlling the transactions of the Receipt but also to supersede the writer of the tallies. He reminded the lord treasurer that his office was 'a clerk's office that maketh a special record for her majesty's service . . . and that Mr Peter's office is but a single office that maketh no record . . . And by this ground of truth your lordship may easily judge what right he hath to the fees he now taketh so far exceeding mine . . .' Wardour constantly claimed to be fighting for the proper functions of his office, for the Queen's service, and for safeguards against peculation; as constantly, his mind was really fixed on increasing the income of his office by either duplicating, or preferably by taking from the auditor, such duties as carried fees payable by the public.

This document was drawn up after 1584, but the same demands and arguments were clearly being pressed on Burghley between 1572 and 1584. In January of this latter year Peter produced a counterstatement in which he made no very good historical case for himself (since he was a necessary innovation, there could hardly be one) but convincingly disproved Wardour's claim to be the

[1] E 407/71/26.

[2] Constats were certificates from the lower to the upper exchequer, testifying to the receipt of a payment.

true treasurer's clerk.[1] In another paper he stated some of the fees he took, to show that Wardour was thirsting after a poorish brew.[2] At some time or other he put together the auditor's four standard arguments against reviving the pell of issue.[3] The pell had been replaced by better and more significant records in the form of the annual 'Declarations' and the half-yearly engrossed tellers' accounts, all produced or audited by the writer of the tallies; the revival of the pell, involving necessarily the revival of the chamberlains' counterpells, would acquaint too wide a range of officials with the state of her majesty's finances; the clerk of the pells having got an increment for keeping the issue roll, the chamberlains' deputies would also seek one, to the detriment of the Queen's service;[4] since the pell would be written (as Hare's antics had proved) from the audited tellers' accounts, it would serve no purpose whatsoever.

Although the writer was of course pleading a case, it should be admitted that it was a good one administratively. This, however, availed him little in the face of official conservatism. Sometime in the 1570s Burghley was told by an officer connected with the chamberlains' side in the exchequer that Peter was monopolizing the work of the Receipt and earning good money from it, while Wardour did little and got little; the informant, though satisfied that the system recorded receipts accurately enough, thought payments too much in Peter's sole control and therefore asked for a return to the old course.[5] About 1580–81, Burghley asked Mildmay, as chancellor of the exchequer, and Sir Roger Manwood, chief baron, to investigate Wardour's complaints; their report does not survive but, according to Peter, found for the tally writer.[6] Wardour was not deterred; his long memoranda continued, and on 21 January 1584 he secured a hearing by a committee of exchequer officials which reported greatly to his liking.[7] He

[1] E 407/71 (unnumbered).

[2] Ibid. no. 79. He claimed that his fees amounted to just over £40 a year, no doubt an underestimate. The subject of fees, too big for a footnote, deserves the separate treatment it shall have elsewhere.

[3] e.g. ibid. no 17 which seems to belong to the early part of the reign.

[4] At other times the increased charges to the public were also used against the whole notion.

[5] B.M. Lansd. 106 ff. 18–20.

[6] Hist. MSS. Com. *Salisbury*, iv, 455 sqq.

[7] A copy of the report exists: B.M. Lansd. 171 ff. 356–7*b*. The committee were: Manwood (chief baron), Robert Shute (baron), John Sotherton (foreign apposer; later baron), Thomas Fanshawe (queen's remembrancer), Peter Osborne (lord treasurer's remembrancer), Thomas Morison (auditor). They sat for several days and 'heard at length all that Mr Wardour and Mr Peter did speak or show'.

went well prepared, with a list of precedents and arguments,[1] and the officials were entirely overwhelmed by his historical learning. They informed the treasurer that Wardour was clerk of both pells and Peter only writer of the tallies. They wished the issue roll to be restored, no tally to pass until entered in the pell and counterpells of receipt, the money to be in the chamberlains' charge. In fact, they wished to go right back behind Henry VII's reforms, and their loving preference for the full security of the ancient course promised to clog the machinery of a modern state by devices of extreme complexity and slowness. On fees, they judiciously recommended an equal division between the contending clerks. With regard to two of Wardour's more outrageous complaints, however, they were less single-minded: the keys of the treasury belonged to neither officer by right and could be assigned by the lord treasurer as he pleased, and if the queen's remembrancer chose, at the end of each term, to confer with Peter rather than anyone else about outstanding debts, that was his business. The remaining seven points dealt with a variety of practices in the office—the checking of the tellers' accounts, the keeping of warrants, the making of certificates of payment, and the like—on all of which the committee on the whole took Wardour's view, though they leant towards giving both officers a half-share in the work so that one might control the other. All told, therefore, they recommended the revival of the pell of issue, a return to stricter and much more cumbersome procedure, and the strengthening of the pells office as against the auditor's.

Peter at once riposted with a statement addressed to the lord treasurer which once again recited the work of his office and produced the evidence which, he said, had been put before the committee but ignored by them.[2] This consisted of the testimony of certain old and experienced officers of the Receipt.[3] William Walter, a man of nearly eighty who had entered the department in 1533 and served as a deputy chamberlain under three undertreasurers,[4] deposed that all that time Mr Danyell was chief officer next to the undertreasurer, taking the tellers' accounts, making certificates and declarations, keeping tellers' bills and accounts,

[1] B.M. Lansd. 106 ff. 4–6. [2] Hist. MSS. Com. *Salisbury*, iv, 455 sqq.

[3] Peter briefly summarizes it; it was later used again by Skinner and survives in greater detail from that occasion: E 407/71/96.

[4] Alleged to be Wyatt, Weston and Baker, but Wyatt was never undertreasurer. If Walter's service began in 1533 he came in under Weston.

keeping the warrants and the keys to the treasury. Uvedale's 'substitute', his son-in-law Gilbert Claydon, did nothing but write the pell of receipt. Thomas Burrow, in the Receipt these forty years since he was fifteen, a deputy chamberlain from 1545 to the present day, said much the same. In Danyell's time the pell was at the day's end committed to Danyell and the chamberlains' deputies for safe keeping, 'which pell I very well also remember was by Mr Cockerell through the favour of the old lord treasurer in Queen Mary's time got to be kept by himself', since which time it was neither written in public nor kept in indifferent hands, as it used to be. As for fees, he only remembered that Danyell and Felton used to take the lot 'and pay the clerk of the pell a part', giving him much less than they kept for themselves. William Stanton, who had been first a teller's and later Cockerell's clerk, confirmed this and added that Cockerell had failed in an attempt to gain 'some addition to his place' out of Felton. Others who spoke to the same effect included Richard Stonley, a teller since 1553 and by 1580 senior of the four.

All this only goes to show that the reign of Henry VIII, in part because of Uvedale's absence, had witnessed a great expansion of the tally writer's activities and power; on the whole it is plain that this expansion did not so much rob the clerk of the pells as result from the changes initiated by Henry VII—the new position of the tellers and the new need to have an officer to supervise them. Wardour was trying to capture at least some of the new ground, and the exchequer committee took his side in part because they believed his precedents which identified the clerk of the pells with the old treasurer's clerk, and in part because the trained exchequer mind distrusted any official who seemed to have sole control of any important section of the work.

Burghley, however, was less impressed. Whether he agreed with Peter that to revive the issue roll now would be to brand the auditor as a bad and inefficient servant, we cannot tell,[1] but at any rate he did nothing further in the matter. That did not stop Wardour, but it made him turn to another court of appeal. He began to petition the Queen. Outflanking Burghley in exchequer matters can never have been an easy task, but the persistent clerk of the pells achieved it. The next stage of the business began on 5 August 1589, with a signet warrant signed by the Queen at

[1] Hist. MSS. Com. *Salisbury*, iv, 456.

Nonsuch.[1] Peter later asserted that Wardour had got it by false charges of mismanagement in the Receipt to which he, unaware of these machinations, was never allowed to reply; he hoped Burghley would enlighten the Queen about the true state of affairs.[2] After telling her treasurer that 'we are given to understand by our servant Chidiock Wardour, gentleman, that there is yet no final orders set down by you to authorize him to keep our record called the pell of exitus' as anciently kept by his predecessors, Elizabeth ordered immediate steps to restore the pell to its 'pristine state'. Wardour accompanied this deceptively peremptory command with another long bill, received by Burghley on 22 November 1589, to which Peter made an answer.[3] Matters dragged on. On 5 June 1590 Peter produced yet another set of replies.[4] He suggested that if the Queen wanted an issue roll, she should at least be spared the cost of parchment (which would come to £40 a year), a useful point to put before her and one which Wardour could never stomach; even the receipt roll was 'no use but an expense of parchment'. By Burghley's recent instructions (of which we are otherwise ignorant) Wardour was empowered to obtain a copy of the order and acquittance after payment, which was enough to secure a cross-check; his demand for enrolment of the order in the pells office before payment was made offended custom and had nothing in mind but gain and spite. All his ideas only tended 'to division and delays'. *Clericus pellium* was found in no record; he was appointed to write the one pell of receipt and should stop thinking of himself as the successor to the *clericus thesaurarii*. Wardour had apparently suggested that patentees and annuity holders should obtain a quarterly writ of *mandamus* for their instalments; Peter justly remarked on the burden this would be to them and defended the existing system with its dormant *liberate* kept by himself and its regular debentures made by himself for each payment.[5] As for debentures being a dangerous innovation, the only innovation would be to accede to Wardour's request that none should issue without his inspection and signature.

[1] E 407/71/53, a copy in Wardour's hand. There is no doubt that he submitted a warrant drawn by himself for the signet and sign manual.

[2] Ibid. no. 65. [3] Hist. MSS. Com. *Salisbury*, xiii, 417.

[4] E 407/71/77.

[5] Peter's papers are full of requests for debentures and orders from the holders of pensions and annuities: E 407/72–76.

Peter's comments on a draft set of articles prepared by Wardour for Burghley's signature and sent to his rival for his views were equally clear-cut.[1] The articles would have restored the issue roll; subjected payments out of the Receipt to the control of the clerk of the pells; arranged for the sharing of fees paid for debenture (Peter: 'that which is given in this respect is voluntary and is so small as is not fit to be apportioned'); authorized Wardour to audit the tellers' accounts; and ordered that all constats or certificates of money received at the Receipt (needed in audit) should rest on the pell and not on the documents retained by the writer of the tallies. A particularly devastating last paragraph reserved Wardour's right to renounce his compromise with Peter when a new writer of the tallies should succeed, a claim which Peter rightly described as prejudicial to the powers of the lord treasurer. But the tide would for the moment not be resisted. On 7 December 1590 the head-officers issued a tentative set of articles largely based on Wardour's, on which Peter again commented.[2] For clarity's sake, and so as for once to get the full flavour of this business, it will be best to follow the orders through by the numbers they bear in the document.

1. Wardour is to keep a pell of issue.—Peter: This will cost the Queen a lot, especially as the chamberlains will raise similar demands next.

2. No payment except of regular fees and annuities is to be made without special warrant signed by the lord treasurer and under-treasurer, which order (written by Peter but addressed to him and Wardour jointly) shall specify which teller shall pay; no teller shall make payment until the order is entered on the pell.—Peter: This will cause 'manifest delay . . . abridging wholly the power of the tellers', and all this just to satisfy Wardour's desire for superiority.

3. All patents, privy seals and warrants, though remaining with Peter, are to be registered with Wardour.—Peter: The delay will be much disliked by patentees.

4. Debentures are to be signed by both Peter and Wardour, provided that neither delay nor new fees are thereby incurred.—

[1] E 407/71/8. These purport to be articles made on a date left blank by Burghley and John Fortescue (who succeeded Mildmay in 1589) in response to the signet letter of August 1589. They were drawn up by Wardour and have marginal notes by Peter.

[2] E 407/71/52, a set of articles with marginal notes by Peter; ibid. no. 65, Peter's counter-suit of 14 Dec. 1590 in which he attacked the articles.

Peter: What value is there in Wardour's signature since he has no materials against which to check the debentures?

5. The tellers are to cast orders and acquittances[1] into the Receipt for entry with the clerk of the pells who shall afterwards redeliver these documents to them.—Peter: The effect of this is contained in Art. 2.

6. No teller is to make payments without Wardour's knowledge; if he does he shall be liable to the Queen for the money; provided no delay is caused by the pells office.—Peter: This must cause delay, as well as great danger to any tellers who act 'for the more speedy furtherance of her highness' said service'.

7. Wardour is to examine the tellers' books every half year against the pells, and also weekly for his weekly report.—Peter: He cannot do any good because he has neither the tellers' bills[2] by which 'they are and will be charged' nor the warrants by which they are discharged.[3]

8. Constats and certificates are to be made by either Peter or Wardour, as the officer requiring such documents shall choose.—Peter: This belongs to my office; I cannot submit to an article which 'toucheth my office both in credit and profit so near'. The 'simplicity of Mr Wardour is such ' that he cannot understand how well protected payments are by the system of warranty in operation.

9. These orders are at once to cease if it be proved that they cause any delay or new charge, or an imposition on the Queen's subjects. To this point was added a futher proviso, protesting that no fee was to be taken from any officer who had so far enjoyed it; this was drafted separately and annotated by Burghley himself—'It is not meet to make any change of these things so claimed by him'.[4]

Even without Peter's vigorous protests, Article 9 really disposed of these orders. It did not need Peter to prove to Burghley that

[1] i.e. the orders to pay received from Peter, and the acquittances signed by the parties paid.

[2] The parchment certificate recording receipt of money which the teller cast down through a trunk into the Receipt and with which the whole accounting process began.

[3] In the department's technical language, 'charging' meant only demanding an account of money received of which proof of payment-in existed, and 'discharging' only allowing payments-out for which proof was supplied. Peter's point was that the tellers would not admit the authority of any records which Wardour controlled.

[4] E 407/71/39.

another parchment roll could hardly be produced without some cost to the Queen, and even if one could believe that all this red tape would lead to no delays in the transaction of business, it is hard to see how Wardour could have his greater share of the fees if Peter lost nothing and the public paid no more. In fact, the orders of December 1590 were never signed, and Wardour's great assault of 1589–90 was beaten off. But since he had got so far with Elizabeth by persuading her that all was not well in the Receipt while its auditor had sole control, we ought, before turning to Peter's counterattack and the troubles of Vincent Skinner, to see what can be discovered of conditions in the office. The overriding question is whether the tellers, in charge of all the Queen's money, were really sufficiently supervised or liable to run off the rails. As one would expect, there are some indications that things were not always as they should have been. In 1555, for instance, Sir Robert Rochester, controller of the household, was engaged with one of the tellers in trying to alleviate the chronic financial difficulties of the household.[1] He hoped the teller would not be blamed for letting certain money go out of his hand and promised that 'for as much money as you deliver unto Mr Cofferer I shall save you harmless'. But though it is impossible to reconstruct the whole affair from one short letter, it looks as though the difficulties in question were caused by the needs of the royal service, not in defiance of them. More suspicious is a letter from Robert Tailor, teller, to Sir Walter Mildmay, of 9 April 1576.[2] Mildmay was angry with Tailor for not keeping his entry books properly and failing to record the terms of the warrants on which he had paid in the past; to this Tailor replied that he had not had any privy seals but only orders from the lord keeper and 'my lord treasurer that now is then being secretary[3] (the old lord treasurer and Sir Richard Sackville signing these orders)'. This was certainly irregular, but Tailor was sure that no harm had been done; he had 'made the less haste' to put the books straight (they had been locked up with Peter for five or six years) because he knew that no cheating had taken place. Now he would go at once and complete the entries 'according to our orders in the Receipt'. If no harm was done, it was still very unsatisfactory that the apparently foolproof rules could cover up some very irregular

[1] Rochester to Brigham, 9 Oct. 1555: E 407/72.
[2] E 407/71/23. [3] Burghley.

practice, though it should be noted that the trouble dated back before Peter's time to the ascendancy of Robert Hare and the dotage of lord treasurer Winchester. Still, it is not surprising to find that as soon as they got their hands on the controls, in the Easter term 1572, Burghley and Mildmay drew up some stringent orders for the tellers.[1]

Tailor was once more in trouble in 1588 when one of his clerks, one Raven, robbed a money chest.[2] He did this by only pretending to turn the key in Peter's presence, so that the chest remained open even when the auditor had the key. But it appears that Tailor himself had been in the habit of using the Queen's money for his own purposes, though he had always put it back in time; he begged Burghley to distinguish between Raven's 'horrible practice' and his own 'over-boldness', promised to make the loss good, and only hoped the Queen would not have to be told until at least part had been repaid. In the same year, the senior teller, Richard Stonley, got obscurely into Burghley's bad books; there appears to have been a deficiency in his office, and he was forbidden, through Peter, to make any payments till the matter was cleared up.[3] These are surely disquieting pointers, but if things had been seriously wrong in so long a period of time one would expect more and worse instances. Moreover it is quite clear that the lord treasurer was throughout content to rely on Peter to manage the Receipt for him, and that he had no cause to regret his trust. There survive quite a few of Burghley's and his undertreasurers' orders to the auditor which simply entrust him with finding the money for often important business of state;[4] one paper shows how an order signed by the head-officers would bear a signed note from Peter allocating the payment to a teller chosen by himself.[5] Though things were not altogether perfect in the Receipt, they were—especially by sixteenth-century standards—remarkably good, and the writer of the tallies carried out his heavy duties well.

Minor irregularities of course occurred. The lord privy seal's clerk once wrote in some agitation to demand back a privy seal for new assignments to Ireland, issued in error for a signet warrant

[1] E 36/266/80–80*b*.

[2] Tailor to Burghley, 23 Sept. 1588: S.P. 12/216/art. 35.

[3] Hist. MSS. Com. *Salisbury*, iii, 377; iv, 401. The business thus lasted at least from 1588 to 1593.

[4] e.g. S.P. 12/199/art. 27; 12/239/128; 12/244/art. 114; Fortescue to Peter, 27 July 1591: E 407/76.

[5] B.M. Egerton 895 f. 4.

which would permit the balance of a previous allocation to be spent.[1] Sir Henry Radcliffe, anxious to sail from Portsmouth and unable to get an order signed because Burghley and Mildmay were not together, asked Stonley for some money and gave him a letter authorizing him to set it against the next lot due.[2] A complicated situation arose when a teller refused to accept £25 from a collector of the 1589 privy seal loan on the grounds that the sum was too small; when the collector offered this excuse, Burghley growled that the teller 'would have taken it if it had been much less'.[3] But when pressed, the treasurer could himself break the rules: in the middle of the Armada preparations he asked Peter to pay out £1,435 on his letters only and he would get a council order later; a postscript reveals how much he depended on the civil servant for a knowledge of the detailed procedure: 'I pray you, certify me whether I am to have my warrant for payment hereof from the lords of the Council or from the officers of the Admiralty, that the same may be accordingly procured'.[4] Yet such anomalies really only confirm the general impression of an efficiently and honestly run department, of an administration firmly in control and enjoying the services of reliable officers.

This is supported by a lesser point which yet has some significance. Among the aspects of Elizabethan administration more obviously capable of being turned into a ramp, the widespread system of rewarding service or friendship by pensions and annuities out of the exchequer was clearly one. The recipients, who usually got their money quarterly, normally lived far away from Peter's office at St. Stephen's, Westminster, and in the conditions of the time one might expect to find money collected for dead men, and similar tricks. That this happened was hinted by Wardour and denied by Skinner.[5] No pension could be paid except on a debenture from the auditor who held the dormant writ authorizing it, and he soon refused to issue one without proof that the beneficiary

[1] Fr. Mylles to Peter, 19 Feb. 1578: E 407/74.

[2] Radcliffe to Peter, 27 Dec. 1575: E 407/73.

[3] John Brokettes to Peter, 11 Dec. 1589: E 407/72.

[4] Burghley to Peter, 2 June 1588: E 407/76. In another ticklish situation, when money was to be paid for antipapist measures of which nothing must be known, a later treasurer (Buckhurst) was more careful: 'I will keep the privy seal myself and . . . no man shall know it but myself and Mr Chancellor, Mr Skinner and Mr Wardour, as all these of necessity must; but to pay her majesty's money without warrant of privy seal never was nor can be done, without an act of Parliament': S.P. 12/283/art. 69.

[5] E 407/71/92, 94.

was alive. The masses of certificates—ranging from solemn documents to a few roughly scrawled words—which survive among Peter's files testify to the rigour with which this order was carried out. It was in force by October 1574, and by October 1575 at the latest Peter would accept no certificate unless it was signed by two justices of the peace, though he could make an exception for a man whose handwriting he knew well. Some of the pensioners, sending in a note so signed every quarter, clearly got pretty tired of the necessity, but they complied. Peter was a good bureaucrat, and in his position it was better so for the state.[1]

Thus Peter defended a sound position against Wardour, and if he was moved by some self-interest—less for the fees which were usually safeguarded even when reforms were contemplated than for his ascendancy in the Receipt—it is also true that he stood for an efficient and sensible system against a more blatant and vastly more pointless self-interest. In 1591 he had once more to spare time from his duties to draft long memoranda. First Wardour, waiting for the issue roll to be restored, initiated a comprehensive attack on Peter's fees, which angered Peter greatly; his restraint at last broke down in such phrases as 'this man careth not what he informeth', or that Wardour 'might have been satisfied in this his ignorance'. Peter asked 'that neither the tellers nor myself may be further troubled with him', which would benefit the Queen's service.[2] An idle hope: Wardour replied with all the old arguments about his descent from the medieval treasurer's clerk and the rest, and continued to appeal to the Queen's and Burghley's 'honourable justice' for a fairer division of the fees. Peter's comments referred the lord treasurer to his previous paper.[3] Wardour was especially hard on Peter's 'man', Edmund English ('who plays Friar Rush's part between us for fear of his downfall'). He maintained that quarterly debentures for pensions were an extortionate practice for English's benefit and that the tellers used to pay 'upon sight of the party'; yet, as we have seen, many pensioners could not come in person, and in such cases control by debentures was highly desirable. One wonders whether Burghley ever read these

[1] Evidence for the statements here made is scattered through the unnumbered documents in E 407/72–76. Some proofs were necessarily a little dubious: thus Walsingham testified on 16 March 1578 that one of his agents, Richard Cavendish, was alive on the previous 8 January when he had written from Heidelberg.

[2] Peter's reply to Wardour's charges, *c.* March 1591: E 407/71/103.

[3] Ibid. no. 71 (26 March 1591).

mountains of paper of which only an inkling can be given here. The business about fees was the last straw for Peter: in April 1591 he went over to the offensive with various charges against his tormentor.[1] Wardour had allegedly promised, in his suit to the Queen, that his proposals would cost nothing; but now he had increased his claims for stationery. He is enlarging his demands on fees. He says he is entitled to a penny of all fees taken by the tellers in excess of 4*d.*, yet claims that anything over 4*d.* is extortionate. On 29 June 1591, Peter sent Burghley a formal petition in which he asked that Wardour's patent be revoked and reissued in a form more consonant with precedent; thus his encroachments on the lord treasurer, the undertreasurer, and the writer of the tallies would be stopped.[2] Nothing, of course, came of this, but at least as far as the evidence goes Peter was not troubled further for the two remaining years of his life. Though he had had to spend much more time than can have been convenient in beating off these attacks, he had not given an inch.

The succession of Vincent Skinner altered the situation for Wardour. On the one hand he now faced a foe—for the thought of giving up never entered his head—who knew little about the Receipt; the fact that Skinner diligently studied, annotated and used Peter's papers as the war progressed is proof of that.[3] On the other, Skinner was Burghley's particular servant and a man of higher social standing than Peter had been. Perhaps for this reason, Wardour did not immediately revive his demand for the restoration of the issue roll but first tested the ground upon the lesser issue of constats, a point which he had often raised before but on which he now concentrated his formidable fighting qualities. Constats (certificates of payments made into the Receipt) were something of an innovation and had grown out of the financial reforms between 1534 and 1554.[4] The old course of the exchequer relied at the audit on the proof supplied by the joining of the tally brought by the accountant with the foil kept in the exchequer. But the newer revenue incorporated in the exchequer in 1554—the accounts taken by the auditors of the land revenue and the

[1] Ibid. no. 37. [2] Two copies: ibid. nos. 78 and 101.

[3] In June 1595 Skinner sent Burghley a constat made by himself in response to Wardour's challenge 'to pose me with, as some elementary scholar and not so deeply seen in parchment as he': E 407/71/90.

[4] Cf. Skinner's statement in one of the papers composing a bundle concerning this stage of the dispute: E 407/71/77.

auditors of the prests—did not proceed to this joining of tallies.[1] The accountant still brought the tally which he had obtained when paying the Queen's money into the Receipt, but the auditor did not seek out a foil from the chamberlains' custody; instead he required an independent note, a constat, from the writer of the tallies, certifying that the payment claimed had been made. Wardour now raised a double demand: constats should be made for all payments, even when tallies were joined, and the clerk of the pells should share in the business.[2] In order to defend what was a most obvious search for more money, Wardour seems to have argued that tallies—used without question for hundreds of years and always praised for their certainty—could be tampered with by enlarging of the notches; he told the story of one Lawson, a clerk in the pipe office, who had thus conspired with one Langworth, collector of a subsidy. What he omitted in this story was that the fraud was discovered by the secondary of the pipe who in joining the tallies found that the notches did not match. In fact, as Skinner rightly pointed out, since no man could hope to falsify both tally and foil the system was entirely safe and required no cross checks.

Skinner continued to produce reasoned statements confuting Wardour's ever more extravagant claims and explaining convincingly that in the Receipt original documents rather than rolls —not necessarily made up at the time and often amended later— must be the fundamental record. Since Wardour was trying to acquire a duty which had, by good proof, always been carried out by the writer of the tallies, he could only hope to succeed by showing that his rolls, on which he proposed to rest his constats, were a better record than the tellers' bills used for the purpose by the writer; and this, Skinner said, he could not do. Burghley once again committed matters for investigation: on 12 February 1594 the chancellor of the exchequer, the chief baron and others sat to hear the dispute. It was agreed that constats were not required when tallies were joined, this being only a cause of cost and delay; that constats were not 'of any long continuance' or 'antiquity'; and that the evidence pointed to Skinner as the proper officer to make them. But Skinner had still to learn about Wardour. This

[1] e.g. in July 1579, E. Fetiplace, auditor, about to declare the accounts of the treasurer of Berwick before the lord treasurer and chancellor of the exchequer, found that he had 'mislaid' Peter's constats which he required to prove his audit; he asked for new ones for which he would pay: E 407/73.

[2] For what follows cf. E 407/71/77, a collection of several papers by Skinner.

defeat in no way abashed him, and by October 1596 he had somehow obtained a letter from the Queen committing the making of constats to himself alone,[1] the result of which, according to Skinner, was delay and chaos in the passing of accounts. To illustrate the mess, and also the unreality of Wardour's position, he related what had happened on 18 October 1596 when the son and executor of the famous Mr Customer Smyth came to the exchequer to settle a debt of his father's alleged to be £3,000. He produced constats from Wardour to show that £2,400 of this had been paid as long ago as 1571. Thus he went to the upper exchequer, but since he no longer had those twenty-five-year old tallies he got an order for 'innovates' (new tallies struck to replace lost ones).[2] This necessitated the production of the old foils for destruction. Wardour's clerk entered the transaction in the innovate roll, but when the new tallies were examined with this roll and with the old foils it was found that the entry in the roll differed from all the rest: where the correct form read 'pretextu obligationis', the roll had 'pretextu recognitionis'.[3] The clerk explained that he had remembered making the constats from the receipt roll and that there it stood 'recognitionis'; he had merely intended to keep the rolls in agreement. Upon this the chamberlains' deputies refused to deliver the tallies until the roll was amended: to them the old foil, not the receipt roll, was the true record. The clerk then cheerfully altered both rolls and also the constats. This, as Skinner said, threw a pretty murky light on Wardour's assertion that only his rolls were a good record in the Receipt. Yet the old campaigner, however bad his case and however much he bedevilled the running of the Receipt, knew his way about too well; he had won over constats and was about to win over the pell of issue.

On 24 March 1597, a privy seal, addressed to Burghley and Fortescue (chancellor of the exchequer since 1589), expressed the Queen's desire that 'our ancient record, called the pell of exitus, be immediately restored'. It was to be written and kept by Wardour

[1] E 407/71/33.

[2] When an accountant had lost any tallies he could make an affidavit before a baron of the exchequer ('the ordinary use in such cases') and could obtain a writ from the exchequer of pleas authorizing the Receipt to issue 'innovate' tallies based on the foils in the upper exchequer. These foils were then destroyed and replaced by the innovate foils.

[3] Obligations—bonds given in respect of a future duty; recognizances—bonds recognizing an existing duty or debt.

who was to have the necessary 'fees and commodities for the same', and the Queen's command was to be published to all the exchequer.[1] This time there was to be no evasion and little delay, though on 28 May Skinner tried a last protest.[2] On 9 June Burghley presented the privy seal in the exchequer court and ordered Wardour to revive the pell. On the 13th the writ was read again in open court, and on the 17th Fortescue commanded Thomas Agarde, deputy chamberlain, to have it published in the Receipt and entered in the Black Book there. This was done next day.[3] Triumphantly Wardour made up his first issue roll at Michaelmas 1597, putting—an unprecedented step—his own name in the superscription.[4] In his book of annual declarations, where hitherto he had been able to return receipts only, he wrote with glee: 'This was the first declaration that I made both of the Introitus and the Exitus.'[5] The long struggle seemed over: Wardour had achieved the real core of his war aims. However, wars are said never to settle anything, and the restoration of the issue roll (kept thereafter until its final abolition exactly 200 years later),[6] proved to be only a stage in the conflict. On 23 June Skinner received Burghley's more detailed orders designed to take account of the new situation.[7] The clerk of the pells was to be given means of making his shared control felt: he was to enroll all warrants for payment, to have a direct hand in the issue of money by the tellers, to sign debentures together with the writer of the tallies, and to inspect the tellers' accounts. Skinner protested at once,[8] and things in a way returned to the embattled state.

As Wardour discovered soon enough, it was one thing to get the pell revived and another to wrest from the auditor a power of control established over eighty years of administration. Thus he resumed operations with yet another memorandum, once again sent to Skinner for comment, in which he demanded that no

[1] E 407/71/34, a copy in Skinner's hand. [2] Ibid. no. 86.

[3] Ibid. no. 36, copy by Fanshawe from the memoranda roll, with Fortescue's holograph note to Agarde; E 36/266, ff. 94–94*b*, entry in the Black Book.

[4] E 403/865; neither the medieval rolls nor those of 1569–71 mentioned the name of the clerk of the pells at the top: ibid. 850, 858. [5] E 405/243/138.

[6] The roll was never again a serious record, being made up at leisure from rough books kept in court. These books continued to the abolition of the exchequer in 1834: M. S. Giuseppi, *Guide to the Public Records*, i, 184 sqq.

[7] E 407/71/12.

[8] A badly mutilated letter from Skinner to Burghley's clerk Maynard, 26 June 1597: E 407/71/59.

payment be made to the tellers without entry on the receipt roll, that payments follow the course established by Burghley's orders, that he be given a chance of enrolling all warrants, that prest money be certified by constats out of the pell and not otherwise, and that he be permitted to see the tellers' accounts.[1] Skinner swept these plaints aside by referring to the by now established practice and charging that Wardour's demands were only meant 'to give colour to the reviving of such a pell'. Wardour, in some despair now that his ends were ostensibly won without a reality in the victory, asked the lord treasurer to assist him in getting co-operation from Skinner and the tellers.[2] Then Skinner found an opportunity to draw attention to the consequences of Wardour's victories. The needs of war were again forcing the Crown to sell lands, and Wardour wanted the money so obtained to be recorded on the receipt roll and accounted for by tallies. Skinner argued that a muddle had been made in the recent changes when insufficient thought had been given to 'the difference grown by change of times'; in other words he was, quite rightly, pleading for a sensible understanding of the realities in preference to Wardour's kind of antiquarian researches.[3] In his opinion, the sales money was in the same category as the surplus paid into the exchequer by the court of wards and the duchy of Lancaster which, it had been decided, should not pass by tally because those departments had nothing to do with the course of the exchequer and tallies were not recognized by their auditors.[4] Money from sales and loans appeared in the tellers' accounts and the tellers were charged by confession and acquittance, 'the two usual, ordinary and only means of charging any accountants in any courts her majesty hath besides the exchequer'. Since the tellers would not accept a charge based on the rolls and would recognize only their own bills, acquittances and accounts, there was no point in entering in the rolls any transactions not designed to lead to the joining of tallies.

Not content with restricting Wardour to the least important part of the exchequer's work, Skinner, deprived after 1598 of his

[1] E 407/71/63. [2] Ibid. no. 88. [3] Ibid. no. 20.

[4] Cf. Edmund English to Edward Latymer, 13 June 1598: S.P. 46/25/241–2. English could not remember that any tally ever passed for wards' or duchy money paid into the exchequer by the Queen's warrant, the only (and sufficient) record being the teller's bill which remained with Mr Peter. He advised Latymer that a tally was only necessary if expressly demanded in the warrant, but that he would now have to get the bill registered in the pell as well as with Skinner.

old master Burghley, tried to get the new treasurer, Buckhurst, to see how disastrous the 1597 reforms had been.[1] He renewed the old plea that the existence of the pell gave too many people a chance to know the state of the Queen's finances. Perhaps discouraged by the change of treasurer he offered to resign: 'wherein that I make thus bold to enlarge myself I humbly crave pardon and beseech you to consider that as I only served in one house so I never sought dependence elsewhere.' But the threat was not real; the next year, when Wardour suddenly renewed the war, found Skinner alert at his post.

Wardour had by this time clearly decided that his victory of 1597 was hollower than he had supposed; alternatively one may see him determined, after consolidating his bridgehead, to break out into Skinner-held territory beyond. At any rate he launched a fresh attack on 10 July 1600 which included matters both new and familiar. As usual, they were replied to, point for point, by Skinner.[2] Wardour first asked the head-officers fully to define the spheres of the two disputing officers. As to this, Skinner produced much history. Though Wardour seems to have agreed that events since Henry VII's reign favoured his rival, he rested his case on the earlier precedents. Skinner pointed out that even in the fifteenth century some men had been promoted from Wardour's office to his, which showed clearly whose was the more important; he drove the point home by citing respective salaries, the granting of rewards for special work, and payments by the Crown for assistant clerks in the writer's office while none were allowed to the clerks of the pells. An interesting addition to these recurring arguments gives some indication of the effect which the exchequer reforms of 1554 had had on the Receipt.[3] Wardour, of course, could not accept an exposition which rested the auditor's superiority on the developments of the last century. Yet while he may have had some ancient and dubious precedents on his side, he was in a real sense the innovator because he was trying to get control of business that at the time of his precedents had not existed.

[1] E 407/71/60, 7 July 1599.

[2] E 407/71/57, an abstract of the articles submitted by Wardour to Burghley and Fortescue; ibid. nos. 55, 75, 98, three papers embodying Skinner's answers.

[3] Ibid. no. 98: 'when the court of augmentations was dissolved and united to the exchequer, as the matters fell out most properly pertinent some were distributed into Mr Fanshawe's office [queen's remembrancer], some to the pipe office, some to other places. And the books of enrolments of letters patent for grants of fees and annuities were delivered over to mine office, and nothing to his.'

Others among Wardour's points are also only too familiar. Once again we hear that he has a claim to the custody of privy seals, certificates and other working papers of the Receipt; that constats for prests should be made out of the pell; that patents for pensions must be registered with him; that the tellers must certify him at once of their receipts and payments so that he can render the weekly certificate which now he wants to make side by side with the auditor's; that he wants to keep the entry book in which the weekly orders for payment from the head-officers were registered. Skinner's replies, to the effect that all this work is and ought to be his, are equally familiar. Two of Wardour's demands broke new ground. He wanted an authoritative ruling on the custody of all bonds and obligations taken in the Receipt, to which Skinner returned that such bonds for payments as were kept there had to be in the keeping of the tellers because from the accounting point of view the bonds were treated as cash and charged to the tellers at their account. Lastly, and very outrageously, Wardour suddenly claimed that debentures were more properly issued by his office than by Skinner's. Since debentures were in effect introduced by the writer of the tallies, Skinner was rightly contemptuous of the claim. It seems, however, that in the bad years in the middle of the century there had been some lapses when tellers had paid annuities without debentures, with the result that Mr Lichfield, under Burghley's instructions, recovered some lost money for the Queen;[1] then Peter revived debentures and all was well.

It does not appear that Buckhurst listened to Wardour on this occasion, for about a year later, on 27 June 1601, the indefatigable clerk was at it again.[2] His last bill repeated the points about the spheres of office, obligations, custody of privy seals, enrolling of patents, the weekly certificate, and debentures; on all this Skinner's replies, too, added nothing fresh. There is perhaps a little less disguising in Wardour's memorandum of his real desire—fees—and a little more exasperation in Skinner's. Wardour had also thought up one new complaint. Since, he says, he now has to attend at the Receipt as much as the other officers (itself a consequence

[1] Cf. B.M. Lansd. 28 ff. 2–3, for a fragment of evidence relating to Lichfield's investigations in 1579.

[2] E 407/71/56 and 92, Wardour's articles; ibid. 94 and 95, two drafts of Skinner's answers.

of his campaign), he wants a part of the house occupied by Skinner and the tellers. He argued that the building—St Stephen's[1] —must be big enough to hold them all because in Peter's time even Mildmay had had offices in it. Skinner was highly indignant: the house was 'little enough for his own use for the service of her majesty and the matters that concern his office, and but competent and necessary for receipt of his family [staff]'. It was true that Mildmay had used it, but he had had the 'help of some other rooms' and had never brought in the sort of numbers contemplated by Wardour. By this time Skinner must have been even fuller of the sort of despair he had described to Robert Cecil two years earlier: 'The distraction I have had about quarrels to my place have hindered me much and now so utterly discouraged me that the service I intended to have done I could not....'[2] Still, so far he had prevented Wardour from ruining the efficiency of the Receipt by making a reality of the revived pell of issue.

But the head-officers were still thinking things over. On 28 October 1601, the lord treasurer, chancellor, chief baron, and the other barons heard what Wardour, Skinner, and their learned counsel had to say, and on 1 February 1602 Buckhurst and Fortescue alone once more went over the ground with the two disputants. Then, on 26 February, they at last produced a large parchment of orders. The war had drifted into an exhaustion where arbitration could take over, and these orders endured.[3]

1. All bonds in the Receipt to be taken by Skinner and enrolled by Wardour, each of them taking 2*s.* per bond.

2. Privy seals to be enrolled in the pells office but to be kept by 'him who shall have the custody of the tellers' accounts' (that is, the auditor). No fees for copies, except 'where it tendeth to the private and particular benefit of the subject', when both may take 3*s.* 4*d.* for the copy and the enrolment respectively.

3. The tellers not to make payment on any order before it is entered in the issue roll, but orders as hitherto to be made by Skinner.

4. Both officers to render independent certificates of all imprest money every Trinity term.

[1] Described in a letter of W. Fitzwilliam to Peter, 2 Dec. 1577, as 'beside the Star Chamber stair': E 407/74.

[2] Skinner to Cecil, 7 July 1599: S.P. 12/271/177.

[3] E 407/75. The heading to this paper describes the history of meetings and hearings.

5. Constats for imprest money to be made by either, as the officer accountable shall choose; patents of fees and annuities to be endorsed in future by the lord treasurer himself with the name of the teller who is to pay.

6. All warrants dormant for recurring payments to be first enrolled by Skinner and then by Wardour, the first taking 6*s*. 8*d*. and the other 3*s*. 4*d*. The writs to remain with Skinner.

7. Debentures to be made by Skinner, with the usual fees, but the tellers to have no allowance for payments made on any debenture not first entered with Wardour.

The document ended with a promise to settle outstanding differences soon. On the face of it Wardour had won some further small victories; though he did not gain control of either the tellers' accounts or the papers used in auditing them, his office was now indispensable to those using the Receipt to pay in or take out money. In particular, the pells office now had a part in the profitable dealings with private persons—annuitants and holders of fees. Buckhurst seems to have intended to establish the clerk of the pells simply as a control on the auditor, but in effect he allowed him to settle parasitically upon the course of the Receipt: all the essential work and the real supervision remained with the auditor, while the clerk of the pells acquired the sort of income which made his office significant in the age of sinecures about to begin. Skinner, admittedly, was not satisfied and tried to reopen the whole business when the accession of James I, his knighthood, and the promotion of his patron, Cecil, to the treasurership seemed to make this worth while;[1] but there is no sign that any further changes were made by order, though no doubt the years brought adjustments in practice. The two officers now existed side by side, in theory overlapping and controlling each other in the best exchequer manner, delaying especially payments out of the exchequer now that no teller could pay until the order bore the *recordatur* of the pells office, and charging the public double for their often needless services.[2] That in practice the auditor remained the much more important official cannot be in doubt; though after the Restoration both of them

[1] Skinner's petition to Salisbury, Caesar (chancellor of the exchequer), Sir Laurence Tanfield (chief baron), and others, giving a brief and one-sided résumé of the whole war: E 407/71/33.

[2] The developed dual procedure was set out in the act 8 & 9 Will. III c. 28; its so-called 'old' course is that established after 1597.

were sinecurists, the auditor's office continued to do a great deal of vital work.[1]

The thirty years' war in the Receipt naturally tells us a great deal about the Elizabethan administration and bureaucracy, but also something about Elizabethan society. The great reforming era of Henry VII and Cromwell came to an end with the restoration of exchequer supremacy in 1554, and Burghley could do no more than fight a rearguard action on behalf of what to him were sensible innovations, an action which just before his death he had to acknowledge had failed. The notorious persistence of 'medievalism' in English government would seem to have been largely due to the power of certain interests and individuals and the respect paid to them in the reign of Elizabeth, though Winchester must bear his share of the blame; if Burghley had had a free hand he would probably have developed rather than arrested the tendencies of Henry VIII's reign. There was nothing in the running of the Receipt that demanded the restoration of the pell of issue, nor did that pell serve any useful function when it was restored. Corruption was to be feared not from the auditor's alleged independence, but, as the reign of James I proved, from the failings of kings and ministers. The means by which Wardour won his victory are also highly significant. His arguments depended on distant and selected precedents, amalgamated into bad history; yet against them the voice of sense and good history, which Skinner kept trying to use, availed nothing. What is more, Wardour managed to impose his errors on later generations. In the nineteenth century it was authoritatively held that 'the Auditor of the Receipt appears to have succeeded in keeping up the jealous policy of Henry VII, by procuring the suppression of the Pell of Issues until 1597',[2] though if 'reforming' be substituted for 'jealous' this statement makes sense. The view of the Public Record Office seems still to be that the auditor was at fault in resisting the clerk's demands.[3] More surprisingly, even R. L. Poole was deceived into believing that the clerk of the pells was the true continuator of the treasurer's clerk mentioned in the *Dialogus*.[4] Nor is it too fanciful to see a likeness between the precedent-hunting of Chidiock Wardour, intent only on increasing the profits of an office which he had

[1] S. Baxter, *The Development of the Treasury 1660–1702*, 124 sqq.
[2] *Deputy Keeper's Third Report*, App. ii, 173.
[3] Giuseppi, op. cit. i, 180.
[4] Poole, op. cit. 73 sqq.

bought somewhat dearly from his predecessor,[1] and the sort of historical arguments which were soon to beset the controversies over the nature of the constitution. Peter, of course, was no better: he, too, believed in this typical search for 'good title' in documents produced by quite different conditions. Vincent Skinner stands out as the one man capable of seeing and saying that arguments from the past can be only part of the story, that changes made in the course of history must affect the meaning of precedents, and that the efficiency of the service should in any case be studied first.

[1] His concern with fees bore noble fruit, for he built not for himself alone, the clerkship of the pells becoming virtually hereditary in his family for a century: Baxter, op. cit. 124.

IX

Mr. Myddelton the Merchant of Tower Street

A. H. DODD

'ENRICHISSEZ-VOUS' was the advice by which Guizot hoped to divert the French *petit-bourgeois* from his political discontents. The same advice was implicit in the policy of the Tudors towards their fellow-Welshmen; and it was widely followed. Welshmen flocked to court and law courts, to businesses and fat livings in and around the city, to the service of the great ones of the land; Elizabethan dramatists seldom had to search far for models when a stage Welshman was in demand.[1] The policy has been denounced as sordid and denationalizing—unworthy of a race of kings acclaimed by bards as the destined restorers of their race. On a long-term view there may be truth in the charge, but for Tudor Wales the advice involved more than mere personal enrichment. The newly rich Welsh—*parvenus* in England, but at home often scions of old and distinguished families—were not all lost to Wales: many returned after a successful career, not (as Miss Wedgwood would have it) to 'preside and judge', Victorian fashion, at local *eisteddfodau*,[2] but to provide a more effective leadership by settling themselves or their sons on the land, or at least securing a footing on it without transplanting themselves. By these means they promoted a much-needed inflow of capital, with all its quickening and stabilizing effects on the nation's economy and even on its culture.

An outstanding example of the process is Thomas Myddelton, already 'a great merchant in Tower Street'[3] before the end of Elizabeth's reign and destined for the lord mayoralty and a knighthood in the next. The Myddeltons, despite their English surname

[1] *Trans. Cymmrodorion Soc.* 1948, 9–15.
[2] C. V. Wedgwood, *The King's Peace*, 56.
[3] *Cal. S. P. Dom.* 1598–1602, 272.

(assumed in the fifteenth century as a result of the marriage of Rhirid ap David with the daughter of Sir Alexander Middleton of Middleton, Shropshire), sprang from the pre-conquest Welsh aristocracy, with roots in Merioneth. Rhirid's great-grandson became receiver general of North Wales under Edward IV and Richard III; from him descended three main families and a number of minor branches, all settled on Denbighshire estates and all retaining, in true Welsh fashion, a close connection with each other. The parent stem was at Gwaenynog, a mile or so south-west of Denbigh, and there were branches at Galch Hill, a little closer in, and at Llansannan, between Denbigh and Llanrwst. It was at Galch Hill that Richard Myddelton, governor of Denbigh under Elizabeth, brought up his nine sons and seven daughters: the modern visitor to Galch Hill—where a plaque commemorates the most famous of the sons, Thomas and Hugh—may well wonder where he stowed them! A memorial brass at Eglwys Wen, on the other flank of the town, shows them all kneeling, the sons on one side of the parents, the daughters the other. Thomas was the fourth.[1]

As fourth son of a junior branch, it is not surprising that he should have sought his fortunes in London. Members of other branches of the clan had long been established in trade there or in Chester or Beaumaris;[2] his own elder brother William was fighting under Norris in the Low Countries before 1580, and he may even have been among the London merchants recruited for the service by his countryman Thomas Morgan 'the warrior', when the revolt flared up in 1572. But he married a Catholic lady from Ghent, adopted her faith, and settled down there as a trader for the rest of his life.[3] Thomas was apprenticed to Ferdinando (or Fernando) Poyntz, a London grocer with extensive dealings in the

[1] J. E. Griffith, *Pedigrees of Anglesey and Carnarvonshire Families*; W. D. Pink, *Notes on the Middleton Family* (repr. from *Cheshire Sheaf*, 1891); W. M. Myddelton, *Pedigree of the Family of Myddelton*.

[2] Myddelton, op. cit. 59, 62*n*; *Y Cymmrodor*, xxiv, 172.

[3] This William Myddelton is often confused with his cousin and namesake of the Llansannan (and Chester) branch, the soldier and sea captain, bard and prosodist 'Gwilym Canoldref'. Pink and W. M. Myddelton both fall into this trap, and most later writers have followed them. The relationship is correctly given in *Dict. of Welsh Biog.*, 632–3. Thomas's ledger attests his cousin's relations with Norris and Morgan in Flanders, his marriage and change of faith, and his dealings in cloth; cf. *Cal. S. P. Dom. Add.* 1598–1601, 272, and references to Richard Myddelton's nine sons in bardic elegies: B. M. Add. MSS. 9817 ff. 128, 132; 14872 f. 219.

Netherlands, especially in refined sugar, and by 1578 he was factor to Poyntz at Flushing. Four years later he was out of his apprenticeship and a freeman of the company, trading in sugar at Antwerp as member of a London firm.[1]

It is here that entries begin (in May 1583) in a ledger inscribed by him 'A Jurnal of all owtlandishe accompts', covering the remainder of Elizabeth's reign. The words 'jurnal' and 'owtlandishe' soon ceased to be appropriate, the former because weeks sometimes went by without an entry, the latter because in the end the accounts become primarily domestic. It is a sort of monster memorandum book including indiscriminately both receipts and expenditure, sometimes even personal and household expenditure, but with marginal references to the more detailed records of his numerous transactions, and with each of the 1772 entries (or 'clausae') consecutively numbered. The detailed ledgers, with one exception, have perished; the survival of the 'jurnal' is due to the fact that blank pages at the end were used by his son for his Chirk castle accounts, among which it now reposes in the National Library of Wales. It is inevitably the principal source for this paper.[2]

Myddelton stayed at Antwerp until the following August, engaged almost exclusively in sugar transactions (amounting to a turnover of something like £6,000 to £7,000 during the three months), with a small deal in jewels on the side.[3] But Antwerp was rapidly ceasing to be a healthy place to trade in; its capture by Parma in 1585 sounded its death knell as a European *entrepôt*. In November 1585, entries in the 'jurnal' are resumed from London after a gap of nearly two and a half years. He had to pay another short visit to Antwerp that year, and dealings with the 'sugerbaekers' there continued till 1586; after that other sources of supply had to be sought, of which more will be said later.[4] It was probably during this period that he reconstructed his business, setting up his own 'sugerhowse' in Mincing Lane (one of seven in the country) in partnership with Nicolas Farrar and

[1] *D. N. B.*; *Dict. Welsh Biog.* 675–8; Pink, op. cit. 12; *Cal. S. P. Dom.* 1595–97, 91; K. R. Andrews, *English Privateering Voyages to the West Indies, 1588–95* (Hakluyt Soc. 2nd ser. cxi), 339*n*.

[2] N. L. W., Chirk castle MS. F. 12540, described in *N. L. W. Journ.* i. 85–86. References to the 'jurnal' ('Jnl.') are given in pages, but pp. 137 sqq. are inadvertently repeated in the MS.; the duplicate pages are indicated by '*bis*'.

[3] Jnl. 1–8. [4] Jnl. 20, 22, 28.

Erasmus Harby, skinner. The firm was again reconstructed on Harby's death in 1593, when Myddelton's brother-in-law Edmund Walden became a partner; some three years later Myddelton himself sold out to his younger brother Robert.[1]

In the meanwhile the partners were extending the range of their operations and experimenting in other depôts. Between 1585 and 1591, and occasionally later, Middelburg was found convenient, and from time to time resident agents were kept there, including Myddelton's brother Robert and his stepson John Ducket.[2] But a more lasting arrangement was the establishment in 1588 of a depôt at Stade on the Elbe, which opened up a wide range of trade in Germany and beyond. For this a 'flyboat', the *Hare*, was employed by the partners from 1590. At Stade his agent for seven years was Thomas Pettyt; although seemingly still in his apprenticeship and partly dependent on his father and brother, Pettyt was responsible for transactions amounting to thousands every year, and for making rapid and crucial decisions with no possibility of consultation, only once incurring a reprimand for exceeding instructions. When he was out of his apprenticeship (and after Harby's death) Myddelton took him and (for a time) his brother into partnership along with William Stone, the London agent. The partnership lasted till after another seven years Myddelton dissolved it, dissatisfied with the 'verie smale profitt considering what long time I have forborne my money, and the great hazardes of adventure of the sea'.[3]

Grocers' wares were not the only, nor even the principal, object of commerce at the Stade depôt; for a freeman of a city company was in effect free of all the other companies so far as actual trading was concerned.[4] The partners exported in bulk Hampshire and Surrey kerseys and Holmes fustians and traded them against Italian mercery wares. These in turn were sold to retailers not only in London but as far north as Edinburgh, as far west as Bristol, and to places as deep in the country as Ruthin and Denbigh, in Myddelton's home county.[5] There was a hungry market at both ends, and the scale of the transactions was impressive; but they involved little immediate transfer of cash, imports being balanced

[1] Ibid. 139, 214, 185; *Cal. S. P. Dom.* 1595–97, 91.

[2] Jnl. 18, 25, 27, 30, 55, 81, 87, 89, 195, 206, 217.

[3] Ibid. 35, 45, 58, 75, 76, 139, 189, 164 *bis*; cf. R. H. Tawney, *Business and Politics under James I*, 38–41.

[4] Tawney, op. cit. 9*n*.

[5] Jnl. 47, 50, 52, 69, 151, 184.

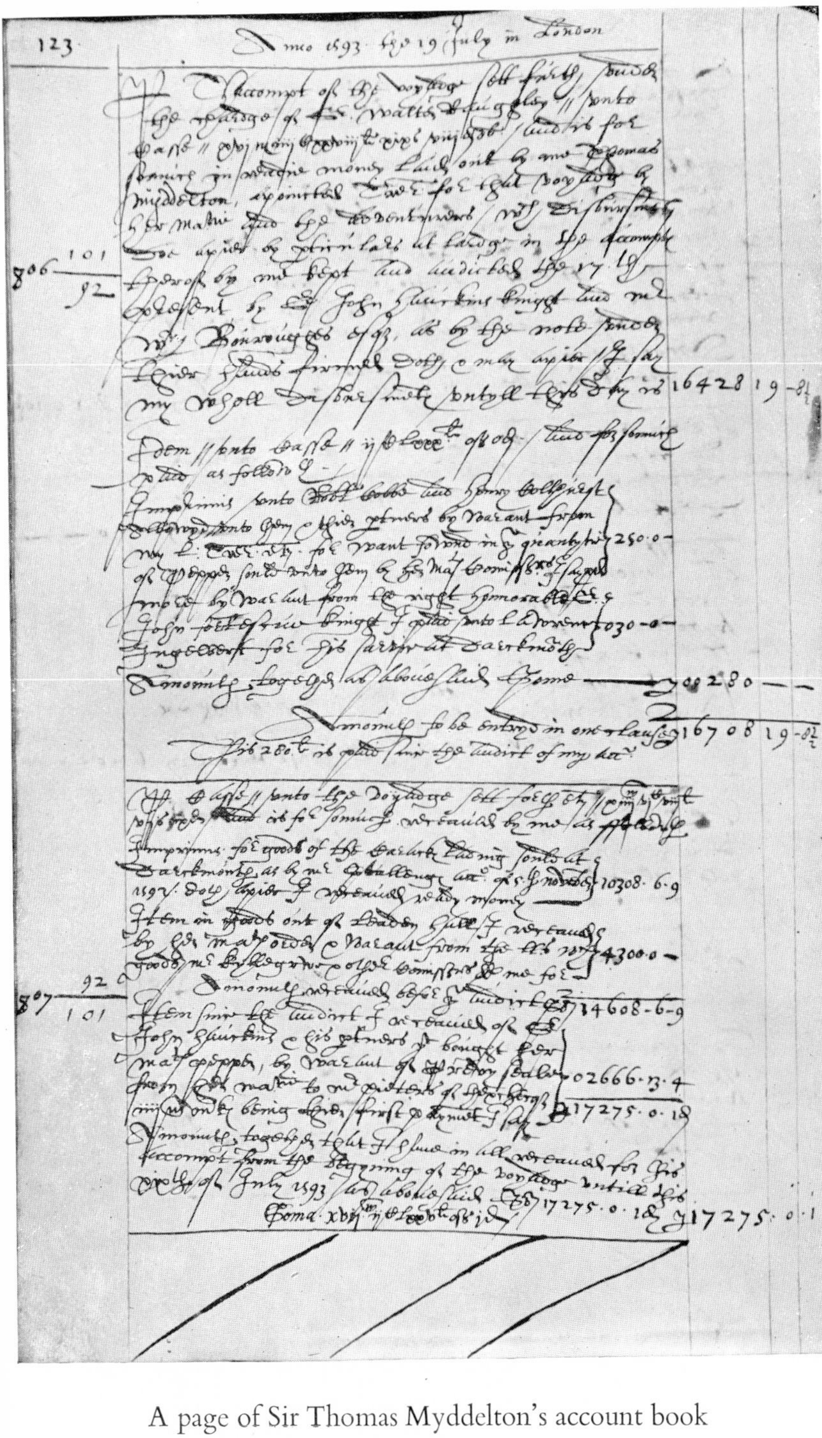

A page of Sir Thomas Myddelton's account book

against exports by direct barter or by an exchange of 'bills' or promissory notes; 'readie money' or 'casse' transactions are matters calling for special note in the 'jurnal'. They also traded in flax, dyestuffs (especially cochineal and brazil-wood), and now and then in rare and expensive drugs like 'benjamin' (benzoin).

Myddelton was by now a man of some standing in the city, on terms with most of the leading business houses. One of his earliest customers for sugar was Gerard de Malynes, a native of Antwerp but English by extraction and adoption, who became commissioner for trade with the Low Countries and a recognized expert on currency. In 1585 Myddelton and his partners presented Malynes (perhaps on his appointment as commissioner) with three gilt bowls—one of the earliest commissions put in the way of Thomas's younger brother Hugh, whom he had just been helping to set up as a goldsmith in Cheapside.[1] Each of Myddelton's four marriages helped to widen the range of his business contacts. His first wife was Hester, daughter of Richard Saltonstall, skinner, a connection by marriage of his old employer Poyntz. Saltonstall represented the city in parliament in 1586, became an alderman in 1587, master of his company in 1589 and later, and lord mayor in 1597,[2] and Thomas Myddelton was associated with him in many commercial ventures. His brother Robert married Hester's sister, widow of John Harby, who was doubtless related to Myddelton's partner in the 'sugerhowse'. His 'sweet Hester' died in the year of her father's election to parliament, leaving two infant sons; and in the next year he married a widow named Elizabeth Olmstead, stepdaughter of another alderman who was a frequent business associate—Robert Tailor, haberdasher and teller at the exchequer. Thomas's brother Hugh the goldsmith later married (as his second wife) a daughter of Elizabeth's first marriage.[3] His third wife, who had herself married twice before, was the daughter of a vintner, but the date of the marriage is unknown; it was in his old age and as lord mayor that he excited city ribaldry by marrying as his fourth wife the young Flemish widow of a London brewer.[4] Then again

[1] Ibid. 16, 17, 18, 21, 24, 25. [2] *D.N.B.*

[3] Jnl. 26, 33, 42, 149, 185; E 351/2504. Saltonstall's son and namesake, one of the founders of Massachusetts and Connecticut, became during the Protectorate a neighbour and associate of Myddelton's son, but adopted extreme puritan views which the latter repudiated: *Bull. of Bd. of Celtic Studies*, xvi, 31–2, 36.

[4] Pink, 8, 14–15, 41, 59; Jnl. 152 *bis*.

his sister Barbara married Edmund Walden, a London ironmonger with whom he had frequent and cordial dealings.[1] The circle in which he moved among his 'in-laws' was, as will appear later, strongly puritan in sentiment; it also introduced him to a widening range of business. Haberdashery figured in many of his deals, and one small but profitable transaction in squirrel skins is recorded in the 'jurnal'.[2] The fact that his father-in-law was by 1588 a governor of the Merchant Adventurers must also have been helpful.

Geography provided him with other useful contacts. The parish of St. Mary Aldermanbury in Cripplegate ward, where at one time he did business in the churchyard and worshipped in the parish church, had many 'fair houses . . . meet for merchants or men of worship'.[3] In one of them lived the Walsingham family; Sir Francis's father was buried in the church, and the son may well have been born in the parish. In May 1585, Sir Francis was granted a lease of certain customs; five months later we find Myddelton at court, and by 1587 he is collecting these customs—doubtless on behalf of the lessee, to whom we may reasonably attribute this further step towards fame and fortune. The patent appointing him one of the four surveyors of the outports followed naturally five years later.[4] This employment offered two very solid advantages. In the first place it gave him control over large sums of ready money (always an acute need in Elizabethan business dealings) from the time of collection until they had to be accounted for at the exchequer—and contemporary business ethics saw no objection to their use in the meantime for private speculation. In 1589, for example, he used £700 of customs money (with the full consent of Lady Walsingham) to finance his own share and those of his brothers Hugh and Foulk and other business associates in the 'Goldsmiths' voyage' of that year.[5] Unfortunately the Goldsmiths' records for 1580–91 are missing, but the nature of the 'voyage' may be conjectured from a similar one undertaken in 1592, when three wardens of the company and two others put up £1,200, payable in fixed proportions by monthly instalments, apparently

[1] Jnl. 65, 71, 144, 161 *bis*.
[2] Ibid. 12, 29; Conyers Read, *Burghley and Elizabeth*, 425.
[3] *D.N.B.*; Stow, *Survey of London* (Everyman edn.), 262.
[4] *D.N.B. s.v.* Myddelton, Walsingham; Jnl. 17, 30.
[5] Jnl. 56, 58, 62, 63, 73; for other examples of borrowed customs money, ibid. 77, 81, 110, 229, and cf. Tawney, *Business and Politics*, 90–93.

to provide shipping and crews for a buccaneering expedition against Spain.[1]

If this was indeed the character of the 'voyage', it was one of many which Myddelton helped in one way or another to finance between 1588 and 1596, and the investments brought him fabulous gains, lessened by occasional setbacks and losses. His business at the ports brought him into contact with both sea captains and shipbuilders, and the building of the Queen's ships was financed mainly from the customs. Sometimes he acted as treasurer to the enterprise, sometimes his investment took the form of victualling ships provided by others, sometimes he was a shareholder in the vessel itself. Whatever the arrangement, he had either a direct share in the prize cargo or the chance of buying what he wanted at the source, and his established business connections provided him with a ready-made market—primarily in the commodities he was used to handling, occasionally in experimental wares, but nearly always at a handsome profit.

In the Armada year Myddelton acted on behalf of the master of a vessel at Weymouth (where his brother Robert was established) to secure payment from Sir John Hawkins, the Queen's treasurer at Plymouth, for the services of his ship in action. His intervention in this case seems to have been purely charitable, and all he got out of it was £10 for his expenses; but it was the beginning of a long and lucrative association with Hawkins and his son.[2] Next year began the long series of 'reprisalls' against Spain. Myddelton and his partners Harby and Farrar promptly took out a share of one-third in the vessel *Elizabeth and Mary*, and in the commerce raiding of that year she took as prize a Spanish cargo including a hundred chests of sugar and over thirty bags of raw cotton; these were very profitably disposed of at Middelburg. Myddelton's brother Charles (governor of Denbigh) was admitted to a £20 'venture', and his sister Barbara to one of 50*s*. He was able to pay them off in gold at the rate of something like four or five hundred per cent on their outlay. Such figures help to explain how when James I made peace with Spain he seemed to the 'embarrassed gentry' (in Professor Trevor-Roper's words) to be closing their 'last safety-valve'.[3] No wonder Myddelton went on investing in

[1] W. S. Prideaux, *Memorials of the Goldsmiths' Company*, i, 85–86.

[2] Jnl. 44, 56; cf. W. T. MacCaffrey, *Exeter, 1540–1640*, 240.

[3] Jnl. 45, 53–55, 77; H. R. Trevor-Roper, *The Gentry, 1540–1640* (*Econ. Hist. Rev*. suppt. i), 37.

'reprisalls' year after year until at last he burnt his fingers. Nor was this his only contribution to the campaigns of 1589. It was a blend of family piety and religious and patriotic zeal rather than an eye to profit that prompted him to 'lend' £30 towards equipping a company of foot to serve under his cousin William ('Gwilym Canoldref') in the futile Portuguese campaign: 'I pray god blesse him', he ejaculates in recording the payment.[1]

Myddelton again seems to have acted as treasurer to the expedition to the Azores—best known for the epic of the *Revenge*—which was the major item in the campaigns of 1591. For his services he was paid £200 as a first charge and at least as much again on the distribution of spoils.[2] Cousin William was in command of the *Riall* and nephew John of the *Moonshine*, but there is no evidence that Thomas had at this stage any financial interest in these vessels.[3] He was, however, partner with Richard Hawkins to the tune of £200 in the *Dainty*, which sailed to the Indies, and with Thomas Thynne and Carew Raleigh (Sir Walter's son), in the *Galleon Raughley* in European waters.[4] Each of these brought in valuable prizes, which helped greatly to swell the volume of Myddelton's business, though sometimes the fruits were not reaped till after interminable delays caused by disputed rights: for example it took two years to settle his and his partners' claim on an Italian vessel carrying sugar, pepper and ivory, because her Florentine owners denied that she was engaged in the Spanish service.[5] Sugar and other groceries again figured largely, but a cargo of dried fish and train oil which fell to the *Raughley* added two new commodities to his wholesale dealings,[6] and a third—iron—came as a result of his purchase from Sir Walter Raleigh of the cargo of four Biscayans taken in European waters.[7] All these items recur constantly in his export dealings for years to come. There was a less happy issue to the small loan he advanced that year to Thomas

[1] Jnl. 40. [2] Ibid. 119–20.

[3] Andrews, *English Privateering Voyages*, 175*n*; *Acts of P. C.* 1591, 376. It seems that the Myddelton who brought to the Azores news of the approach of the Spanish fleet was not William (as commonly stated) but John, probably a son of Thomas's eldest brother Richard: Pink, 10.

[4] Jnl. 119, 148.

[5] *Cal. S. P. Dom.* 1591–94, 214, 294–6, 312–13, 332–3, 343, 397–8; *Acts of P. C.* 1590–91, 24, 40; 1591, 230–1, 383, 433–4; 1591–92, *passim*; 1592, 26, 92–93, 176–7; 1592–93, 356–7, 385–6; 1595–96, 117–18.

[6] *Cal. S. P. Dom.* 1591–94, 231, 249–51; Jnl. 148.

[7] Jnl. 114, 118, 120, 129, 143, 144, 148, 150, 157, 166, 168.

Cavendish the cirumnavigator on the eve of his last disastrous voyage to South America.[1]

He was treasurer once more to the West Indian expedition of 1592, financed mainly by Raleigh but commanded by Frobisher. His detailed accounts were kept in a separate ledger which has survived alongside the 'jurnal', and for the same reasons.[2] The most sensational episode in an otherwise colourless campaign was the capture of the East Indian carrack *Madre de Dios*—the richest prize of the war. The story of the 'wild orgy of pillage'[3] as she lay at Dartmouth shows the other side of the medal. Myddelton was sent to the scene to help Robert Cecil, the lord treasurer's son, to safeguard and assess what was left of the cargo until the Queen's commissioners should settle on an equitable division of the spoils. That the Queen's share should amount to one-half (consisting mainly of pepper and spices) naturally caused no dispute; and Myddelton negotiated for a syndicate of which he was one the purchase of £4,600 worth of these.[4] There were many provisional allocations of the remainder, in some of which the treasurer of the expedition shared, but it took a chancery suit to secure him his allotted £200. He showed particular regard for the interests of the lord admiral when there were signs of his being passed over, but he fell violently foul of Alderman Billingsley, who represented the interests of the city.[5] The final settlement of accounts, audited by a new lord treasurer, did not come about until early in the next reign—twelve years after the capture.[6] For the next four or five years 'carrack goods' are prominent in Myddelton's ledger; they include calicoes, lawns, silks, hides and wax as well as pepper and spices.

The year 1593 was much leaner, but desultory commerce-raiding continued. Myddelton again adventured £200 with Richard Hawkins in the *Dainty* and smaller sums in other vessels, including one commanded by his nephew John. In association with his brother Robert and with Farrar (who also took over part of his share in the *Dainty*) he laid out nearly £300 in 'vitualling of

[1] Ibid. 69, 100.

[2] N. L. W., Chirk castle MS. F. 12629, described in *N. L. W. Journ.* vii, 347–53; Jnl. 123, 139, 140.

[3] E. P. Cheyney, *History of England, 1588–1603*, i, 538.

[4] Jnl. 117, 187, 155 *bis*.

[5] Hist. MSS. Com. *Salisbury*, iv. 244, 301, 308–9, 358, 472, 279; *Acts of P. C.* 1592, 181, 204, 218, 234–5, 237, 269, 275; 1592–93, 51; Jnl. 117, 119, 159 *bis*.

[6] E 351/2504; cf. Hist. MSS. Com. *Salisbury*, xvi, 231.

Divers barkes' at Weymouth. But no rich prizes came in, and the operations did nothing to advance his fortunes.[1] In true Elizabethan fashion, he went on combining his private ventures with the treasurership of official operations. These were on a very small scale in 1593, and the fact that his accounts with Sir John Hawkins were not cleared by the treasury till six years later suggests that, as with the customs, he had no qualms about using idle public moneys to finance his freebooting.[2] Similarly in 1594–95 he was treasurer to the Azores expedition led by Drake and Hawkins, who guaranteed a third of the cost to the Queen's two-thirds. He was also partner with them in the *Help*, each of them contributing a third of the total cost of £850.[3] In addition he renewed once more his partnership with Richard Hawkins in the *Dainty* (bound this time for the south seas); he adventured smaller sums with Captain Lewis in the lord admiral's old galleon the *White Lyon*, in partnership with Thomas Lother, a business associate since his earliest days in the sugar trade.[4] Finally, in 1594 he spent £40 made by a deal in fustians to buy, with Farrar and six others, an eighth share in the *Roselyon*, which was used at first for normal trading to Stade and then turned to privateering.[5]

Myddelton's cousin William and his nephew John were both with Drake and Hawkins when the long-delayed fleet set sail in August 1595, William and a fellow-sailor from Flintshire speeded on their way by small loans from him at the port. But the campaign proved as ill-starred to Myddelton personally as to the country at large. Drake and Hawkins died at sea, and their fleet was with difficulty rescued and brought home. John Myddelton fell into enemy hands (for the second time), and the uncle was still pressing for his exchange three years later.[6] Richard Hawkins was captured in the *Dainty*, and Myddelton lost £150 on that venture, and nearly £100 on the *White Lyon*.[7] The one bright spot was *Roselyon*, which captured a Spanish vessel with a cargo of sugar and ginger.

[1] Jnl. 113, 128, 143, 167.

[2] Ibid. 139, 154 *bis*; cf. Corbett, *Drake and the Tudor Navy*, ii, 71–72. In spite of frequent payments on account his final settlement with Lady Hawkins in 1602 involved him in a disbursement of nearly £1,100: Jnl. 180 *bis*.

[3] Jnl. 171, 180, 190–1; Hist. MSS. Com. *Salisbury*, vi, 542; Corbett, ii, 432*n*.

[4] Jnl. 219; cf. ibid. 1, 13, 16, 22, 23; *D.N.B.*; Hist. MSS. Com. *Salisbury*, xvi, 145.

[5] Jnl. 156, 159, 165–6; Andrews, *English Privateering Voyages*, ch. xvii.

[6] Corbett, ii, 400–1, 405 sqq.; Andrews, 36, and cf. ibid. 32–33, 175–6, 212, 273, 299, 302–6; Hist. MSS. Com. *Salisbury*, viii, 306–7, 362; Jnl. 198, 215.

[7] Richard Hawkins, *Observations* (Hakluyt Soc. i), 11–12, 226; Jnl. 219.

Even this cost the partners a lawsuit; but their sales of sugar after the cargo was released amounted to some £1,200, enabling Myddelton to record as 'the gaynes which god hath sent' a profit of 25 per cent on his 'sugerhowse' stock.[1] In this same year 1595 he appears to have contracted to supply Bagnall's army in Ireland (which was starved by the government) with provisions raised in Denbighshire, advancing much of the cost from his own capital; for Ireland lay uncomfortably close to Wales, and Bagnall, with Welshmen in large numbers in his army, was related to Welsh families among whom Myddelton counted many friends.[2]

After this, apart from his treasurership to the land and sea expeditions of 1596,[3] he stuck firmly to the arts of peace until the final flare-up of the Spanish war in 1602.[4] In June of that year he invested nearly £150 in 'victualing divers shippes gone forth upon reprisall'; but no prizes were taken and the money had to be written off. A further sum of nearly £300 was 'cleerly lost' in an adventure of *Roselyon*, leading him 'Utterly to Renounce the ship' with maledictions on the 'badd Dealling' of the captain.[5] On the other hand, a much more ambitious venture in the same campaign brought him handsome returns. He paid well over £1,500 towards the cost of sending the *Vineyard* on two voyages to the West Indies, the remaining £900 being borne in equal shares by his brother-in-law Samuel Saltonstall and another city man and by his old partner Richard Hawkins, just released from his Spanish prison with the help of pressure from Myddelton;[6] and so successful was she that he was able to pay venturers in the second voyage at the rate of thirty per cent—partly in pearls and cloth and the balance in 'readie'.[7] Another carrack was brought in from this expedition, and Myddelton was one of the six commissioners for the allocation and valuation of the cargo.[8]

[1] Andrews, ch. xvii; Jnl. 191, 199, 210, 214, 244.

[2] Hist. MSS. Com. *Salisbury*, v, 369, 379; Griffith, *Pedigrees*, 57, 59; A. H. Dodd, *Studies in Stuart Wales*, 79–80.

[3] Hist. MSS. Com. *Salisbury*, vi, 213, 215, 390.

[4] Except for a prize taken by Sir John Gilbert in which he appears to have had some financial interest not reflected in the 'jurnal': *Acts of P. C.* 1599–1600, 424.

[5] Jnl. 165 *bis*, 182 *bis*; cf. Corbett, *Successors of Drake*, ch. xiv.

[6] Hist. MSS. Com. *Salisbury*, xii, 505. There is a slight puzzle about Hawkins, because on the date given by Myddelton he had not left Spain, and certainly had no £300 to invest (*Cal. S. P. Dom.* 1601–3, 212); but round this period the dating of the 'jurnal' is very erratic.

[7] Jnl. 172 *bis*, 178 *bis*, 182 *bis*.

[8] Hist. MSS. Com. *Salisbury*, xii, 47, 100, 273, 478.

Privateering, even at its height, by no means exhausted his energies; he was equally alert in seeking new avenues for peaceful trading; and his age knew no inhibitions against a deal with the enemy. Only two years after the Armada Myddelton was associated with Daniel Poyntz (doubtless a relative of his old employer) in shipping Netherlands says and linen to Spain from Hamburg against Andalusian olive oil; trade was resumed in 1595–97, this time in partnership with his brother-in-law Walden, and with Middelburg as depôt; but as the last voyage ended in loss, the trade was abandoned.[1] German copper was included in one of the cargoes to Spain, and in 1596 he tried out a new market for this by shipping ore (in association with three partners) to be smelted at Neath. This led to his acquisition of a fifth share in the copper works. In the two following years he embarked also on calamine production at Lambeth, and leased from the crown the Cadoxton copper mines (near Neath), at £200 a year rent. The Neath works turned out copper wire, bell metal and household goods such as kettles; but the mining venture failed and the partnership seems to have been dissolved in 1603.[2] A French depôt for continental sales, presumably of cloth, was opened at Caen for three years between 1591 and 1594; here his associates or agents were his young brothers Robert and Peter and again his brother-in-law Walden.[3] Another venture in which he came to grief was the export of fish, especially pilchards, from Plymouth. There were some eight partners in this concern, including his brother Peter, his brother-in-law Weych and the inevitable Farrar, and for a time they employed two ships in the trade; but it landed him in a loss of £500—not without suspicions of a lack of 'honest dealing', whether on the part of partners or of crews.[4]

Not content with commerce and industry, he also tried his hand at farming. In 1590 he took a lease of some 160 acres of pasture and meadow land at Long Sutton, Lincolnshire, installing one of the inexhaustible stock of 'in-laws', living in Boston, as bailiff. Apart from one bad winter when he lost 280 sheep (worth nearly £180) from foot rot, he seems to have done reasonably well.[5] But this

[1] Jnl. 84–85, 90, 204–5, 230.

[2] *Acts of P. C.* 1578–79, 113; Jnl. 215, 221, 231, 245, 172 *bis*, 187 *bis*, 259 *bis*.

[3] Ibid. 93, 97, 104, 130, 168.

[4] Jnl. 86, 95, 101, 132, 134. The destination of the fish is described vaguely as 'the straieghts'. There was a brief return to the traffic, with Weych and Poyntz, in 1597–98: ibid. 233, 251.

[5] Ibid. 78, 138, 182, 169 *bis*.

was a very minor activity, involving only small sums; and in the middle 'nineties, as he became more and more a sleeping partner in both the 'sugerhowse' and the Stade partnership (before selling out of both), even trade was taking a back seat. It was now that he slipped into the position of those who, in Tawney's words, 'while retaining the traditional designation, abandoned trade for finance or combined the two'.[1]

It began in the most natural way, soon after his return from Antwerp, with small accommodation loans such as were inevitable between business associates in pre-banking days,[2] and others to members of his widespread family in temporary difficulties. By 1587 he was in a position to lend £100 for four months to a Guildford clothier, and—more significantly—£50 for six months to a landlord on the security of his land.[3] Increasing contact with public figures kept widening the range of his money-lending business. In 1589 he lent £20 for nine months to Job Throckmorton, the 'explosive Puritan' whom Sir John Neale is inclined to identify with Martin Marprelate; the loan was repaid with commendable promptitude—in fact a week before it fell due.[4] Many of his other clients also came from the puritan *milieu* into which marriage had introduced him. William Charke, the Fellow of Peterhouse who was expelled for his opposition to episcopacy, was connected by marriage with Myddelton's second wife, and a number of clients came from among his acquaintances and on his introduction. The most interesting of these was that redoubtable protector of puritans Lady Bacon and her not-so-puritan son Francis, then a young barrister at the beginning of his career; a six-months' loan of £200 in 1589 was also repaid to the day—Lady Bacon no doubt saw to that![5] On the other hand there can have been no puritan taint about the loan of £6 in 1586 to redeem from prison (presumably for debt) the curate of South Ockendon, Alderman Saltonstall's parish in Essex; for the rector, who stood surety for him, was by no means *persona grata* to Essex puritans.[6]

He found it politic at times to lend small sums (on their masters' credit, and sometimes even free of interest) to dependents of the

[1] *Business and Politics*, 114. [2] Cf. MacCaffrey, *Exeter*, 266–7.
[3] Jnl. 16, 17, 25, 31.
[4] Ibid. 42, 49; Neale, *Elizabeth and Parliament, 1584–1601*, 105, 220.
[5] Jnl. 35, 42, 48, 63, 81, 99, 103, 168.
[6] Ibid. 26; T. W. Davids, *Annals of Evangelical Nonconformity in the County of Essex*, 88, 104; *D.N.B.*

great—who were so often fellow-Welshmen to boot;[1] but his biggest advances were to courtiers and officials. In 1593 he advanced £500 to Sir John Fortescue, chancellor of the exchequer, a further £120 to enable him to buy a jewel for the Queen from brother Hugh the goldsmith, and more the following year; the debt was not completely discharged in 1595, when not a penny of interest had yet been paid.[2] Lord Keeper Egerton, to whose son he sold the parsonage of Gresford for £1,000 on the father's bond in 1598, was so long overdue with his payments that when he paid the last instalment in 1602 Myddelton was 'glad to take my principall' and to forego the £150 interest due, although he himself had had to borrow the money at interest.[3] Lord Chief Justice Popham, who borrowed £1,100 to buy a manor in 1594, proved a more satisfactory client: the debt was cleared by the end of the next year. By 1596 Myddelton was well enough established to afford a loan of £500 for a year to Sir Thomas Gorges (uncle to Sir Ferdinando, the founder of Maine) completely free of interest; but with a courtier so near the Queen (for Sir Thomas's wife had previously married Catherine Parr's nephew) he felt safe in recouping himself out of customs money.[4] Generally loans of this order were hedged about with greater precautions. From 1591 the earl of Shrewsbury, then at odds with all his family and in the toils of the law, borrowed well over £1,000 on the security of his jewels, which were not redeemed till 1596.[5]

This was by no means either his first or his last experience as pawnbroker in the grand manner. As early as his Antwerp days he had advanced £50 on the security of a jewel to his remote kinsman Sir John Norris, commander of the English forces, then in desperate straits for money to pay his men.[6] He lent £40 on a gold chain to a fellow-townsman of Denbigh in 1590, and £50

[1] e.g. Thomas Bruyn, servant to Walsingham, 1588 (39, 32, 217), who went into business with Myddelton after his patron's death; Evan ap Howell, servant to Secretary Davison, 1589 (44); Walter Cope, in Burghley's service (later master of the wards), 1590 (83); Myddelton's Denbighshire kinsman Thomas Panton, servant to Attorney General Egerton and then to Lord Keeper Puckering, and related to the master of the revels, 1594 (27, 177, 204); William Brereton, attendant on Cecil, 1602 (180 *bis*, 182 *bis*).

[2] Jnl. 151, 156, 158, 203.

[3] Ibid. 234, 150–1 *bis*, 157 *bis*, 167 *bis*, 171 *bis*.

[4] Ibid. 185, 188, 196, 217, 229; *Letters of John Chamberlain* (ed. N. E. McClure, Amer. Phil. Soc. Mem. xii), ii. 233*n*; Hist. MSS. Com. *Salisbury*, xi, 456.

[5] Ibid. 153, 155, 169, 213, 217.

[6] Ibid. 16; cf. Froude, *History of England* (1872–5 edn.), ch. lxviii; W. M. Myddelton, *Pedigree*, 63*n*, 64.

to Cavendish the explorer (in association with his own partners) on a 'feather of gold', the following year. It was probably in the cause of exploration also that in 1591 Walsingham's stepson Christopher Carleill, the soldier and sea captain, pawned for some £400 a whole chestful of plate, which was only finally redeemed by his widow and executors after his death.[1] A single valuable jewel procured an eight-months' loan of £500 for a courtier in 1592, and another £1,000 was advanced the same year to Oliver Cromwell, uncle and godfather to the future Protector, with two associates—no doubt on the security of expectations from the immense fortune of his ageing father, the 'golden knight' (which Oliver dissipated in the next thirty-five years).[2]

With the exception of land (which will be dealt with later on) jewels and gold were Myddelton's favourite securities—partly, perhaps, because his brother Hugh could help him to appraise and if necessary to dispose of them; but he accepted almost anything negotiable. Sir John Norris's brother Henry raised £37 on his horses in 1585; a pair of broadcloths covered a loan of £13 in 1586, 'household stuff' one for £2 in 1590. Some 'green hangings' on which he lent £10 free of interest in 1598 were left on his hands because the man died and his widow could not pay up. Sixteen bags of nutmegs in 1594 were deposited against a loan of as much as £40; in the same year he lent £100 to a London merchant on his armour, which was stored in the warehouse in Mincing Lane (now Robert's).[3] A puzzling transaction was the loan of £80 (later made up to £100) to Sir Thomas Morgan 'the warrior' in 1594 on the security of 130 gold rose nobles; as the rose noble was worth fifteen shillings, it is hard to see how Morgan benefited by the loan, unless he was holding the coins for a rise in the Netherlands market, where their exchange value was going steadily up (and continued to do so despite proclamations to check the drain of gold); but Sir Thomas died the following year, and Myddelton does not seem to have been interested in speculations on the exchange.[4]

[1] *Jnl.* 62, 96, 102, 129, 140; Conyers Read, *Walsingham*, i, 26; E. P. Cheyney, *Hist. of Eng. 1588–1603*, i, 362.

[2] Jnl. 69, 153, 105, 182; M. Noble, *House of Cromwell*, i. 40–53; Hist. MSS. Com. *Salisbury*, xi. 260.

[3] Jnl. 13, 26, 78, 180, 204, 140 *bis*, 145 *bis*, 169 *bis*.

[4] Jnl. 174, 179; G. C. Brooke, *English Coins* (1950), 149, 155, 193–4, 197–8; W. A. Shaw, *History of Currency*, 113, 130–1.

His invariable rate of interest (except for some expressly stated reason) was ten per cent, and his debtors rarely defaulted. This meant a steady and handsome return on his capital without the ups and downs of foreign commerce or 'adventures in reprisall'. No wonder people with capital to invest began entrusting it to him as broker. An early example comes in 1587, when a Mrs Longston handed to him £20, 'being all the poore stock she hath left her', to be 'employed the best I cann for her proffytt', and he determined to pay her interest at the rate of twenty per cent per annum 'whatsoever is gotten thereby'. Two years later his partner Farrar similarly entrusted him with £20 on behalf of his daughter (who was Myddelton's godchild) 'to trade for her': he doubled it for her in five years.[1] At the other end of the scale was the £500 deposited with him in 1601 by Sir Thomas Gorges (who had only recently discharged his debts to Myddelton) for the depositor's 'use and profyt upon the exchange'. He fulfilled the obligation by lending the money out on bonds taken in Gorges' name until two years later Sir Thomas—now Myddelton's fellow-commissioner for the carrack recently brought in as a prize—recalled all but £100 of it for his daughter's marriage.[2] To the government he was sometimes debtor, sometimes creditor, frequently financial assessor.[3] Add to all this his investments in the East India Company when it was formed in 1600,[4] and we have the picture of a capitalist on a very considerable scale.

Increasing affluence is reflected in his mode of living. When he first set up in the city on his return from Antwerp he was glad to replenish his wardrobe by buying two second-hand doublets (for office use, no doubt) from 'Aunt Poynctz' for 16*s.* 8*d.*, with a further 5*s.* 3*d.* to the tailor for mending them; for city wear he had his gown furred at £1 5*s.* 4*d.*, and lace for his finery cost him as much as £20. When his first child was born, he took charge of the household, paid the wages of maids and nurse (partly in goods from the warehouse), bought feather beds and dress material

[1] Jnl. 30, 63, 179.

[2] Ibid. 159 *bis*, 161 *bis*, 179 *bis*; Hist. MSS. Com. *Salisbury*, xii, 173; *Letters of Chamberlain*, i, 152, 153.

[3] Hist. MSS. Com. *Salisbury*, ii, 426–7. The *Acts of the Privy Council* from 1596 onwards show many commissions of this type entrusted to him.

[4] Pink, 12. Thomas's nephew John sailed as captain of the *Hector* with the company's first fleet in 1601, and died on the voyage: *Purchas his Pilgrims*, 1905 edn. ii, 413.

for the household staff, and 'confetts' (for the christening party?) to the surprising amount of 43*s*., sending Pettyt from the office to do the marketing.[1] There was nothing of the merchant prince here; but the accounts give the impression of an increasing staff of employees both in business and at home. Several of the latter are Myddeltons of various branches; many are Welsh; some we have seen rising to partnerships. His journeys to the ports, to Lincolnshire and to Wales called for horses, for which the 'jurnal' records such items as £1 for an 'old nagg' in 1593, £8 10*s*. for a grey gelding and £10 for another nag in the following year—quite a good price in an age when the best horses seldom went as high as £15.[2]

In 1595 he moved to a new house—The Bear in Tower Street, newly vacated by the death of its owner, Lady Holcroft of Vale Royal, Cheshire; she was daughter of an alderman (whose home it had been) and mother-in-law to the third earl of Rutland.[3] This was the house that became linked with his name for the rest of his active life: he rarely left it for long except on business journeys to the country.[4] Mincing Lane remained his chief business address, but his visits there seem to grow rarer as he becomes more the financier and less the merchant; for personal supervision of wares was no longer required of him, and moneys due could be received at any place mutually agreed on—sometimes his own house, sometimes the debtor's, once at least at the new Royal Exchange. If a business visitor called at The Bear in his absence his wife, like so many business men's wives of the age, was quite capable of deputizing for him.[5] But the 'jurnal' he kept in his own hand (and his highly individual spelling) except during the latter half of 1602, when he fell ill and had to leave it to a clerk; entries in his characteristic hand are not resumed till the autumn of 1603, after six blank months.[6] Even when in 1593 he paid a brief visit with his second wife to the house at Shenfield in Essex which may have belonged to her first husband, he took his books with him and

[1] Jnl. 14, 18–19; interesting comparisons can be made with the personal expenditure of Exeter merchants recorded in MacCaffrey, *Exeter*, 270.

[2] Jnl. 124, 164, 176; Thorold Rogers, *Agriculture and Prices*, vi, 244–55.

[3] Jnl. 199; Ormerod, *Cheshire*, ii, 154.

[4] Where he lived before this is not known—probably at St. Mary Aldermanbury; his other London houses, St. Bartholomew's 1589, near St. Paul's 1595, Barnard's Castle 1602, seem to have been investments only: Jnl. 43, 201, 164 *bis*.

[5] Jnl. 201, 207.

[6] Ibid. 161–2 *bis*, 163–80 *bis*; Hist. MSS. Com. *Salisbury*, xii, 478.

went on writing them up. Only in 1615—two years after his mayoralty—did he copy the example of his father-in-law Saltonstall and buy his own estate in Essex, at Stansted Mountfichet.[1] This went to the eldest son of his second marriage. One of the staff he employed there was a remote kinsman from Merioneth—John Jones of Maes y garnedd, later a Roundhead colonel under his son the second Sir Thomas, and eventually one of the two Welsh regicides.[2]

Such a career suggests obvious comparisons with that of Lionel Cranfield in the next reign. Both had depôts at Stade, dealing in the same wares, by the same methods and often with the same customers.[3] Both contracted for the government and were called in for financial advice. Yet Cranfield became earl of Middlesex and chief minister of the crown, whereas Myddelton lived and died a merchant and financier. It does not appear that his ambitions ran to politics. He performed the local duties required of his station conscientiously, but never with any appearance of relish; he sat four times in parliament but no speech of his is recorded; even civic office in London was accepted with reluctance.[4] His dominant ambition was to emulate his twelfth-century ancestor Rhirid Flaidd, lord of Penllyn, by founding a family of 'worship' in his native land—and how amply he realized it!

Of Thomas Myddelton's elder brothers, Richard, the eldest, had married a Flintshire heiress and settled on her estate, and Simon graduated at Oxford; both were dead by 1586.[5] The third, William, may have already settled abroad when the father died—at any rate he seems to have been passed over in the settlement of the estate. So Thomas was, for practical purposes, the heir. Under his father's will he was made guardian of his youngest brother Peter until he attained the age of twenty-five (in 1589), when Thomas duly handed him over his inheritance of £100;[6] he also assumed, as will appear later, a general responsibility for all his younger brothers and even many of his more distant cousins—probably

[1] Jnl. 128–32; Pink, 14; Trevor-Roper, *The Gentry*, 14, 17.

[2] N. L. W. Chirk castle MS. E. 5602; Dodd, *Stuart Wales*, 47.

[3] e.g. Pieter van Lore, Jnl. 142, 145, 153, 166, 175, 181, 193 (1593–94); cf. Tawney, *Business and Politics*, 82, 170; Trevor-Roper, op. cit. 14.

[4] *D.N.B.*

[5] Pink, 10; Simwnt Vychan, 'Marwnad am Risiart Miltwn', B. M. Add. MSS. 14872/219 vss. 75–84 (written between 1586 and 1594); Foster, *Alumni Oxon.* i (2), 1011.

[6] Jnl. 43.

because he was the man of means of the family. What is to the immediate point is that he inherited the paternal estate of Galch Hill, subject to certain limitations. In the first place Richard, the eldest brother, had a certain undefined interest which had to be bought back from his family before Thomas could obtain clear possession. Another obstacle was that Richard senior, whose means must have been stretched to the utmost by the needs of his quiver-ful of children, had alienated portions of the estate: something had passed to the earl of Leicester during his rule as lord of Denbigh, and outlying sheep-runs in Llansannan had been sold to a Denbigh neighbour. Thomas Myddelton's first efforts, as soon as his position in business was secure, were directed towards establishing himself as a Denbighshire landowner. He began in 1589 (in a small way, as ever) by acquiring from a local carrier a stable where he could put his horse up when he visited the town; in the following year he employed a local man as bailiff; four years after that he bought out Leicester's surviving heir, Lady Warwick, and his own brother Richard's family; the Llansannan lands were retrieved in 1597.[1] Galch Hill was let out to rent, and other properties in and around Denbigh were added, until by 1594 Myddelton's Welsh rent-roll amounted to £156.[2]

He could now consider himself as having stepped into his father's position, but he was aiming at far higher game than this. In 1588 the earl of Leicester died, and his brother and heir the earl of Warwick outlived him by only a couple of years, when the lordship of Denbigh reverted to the crown. Myddelton promptly withdrew £700 from his 'sugerhowse' stock with a view to making a bid, and he even struck an inferior bargain by selling sugar 'out of season' because he might need the ready money quickly.[3] But the Queen had other views. Leicester's lordship had carried the title of baron, and Elizabeth was loth to grant it out again; instead she kept it in her own hands and made a new composition with the tenants, who had been much aggrieved at Leicester's extortions. In these negotiations Myddelton was again called in as adviser, and he advanced £250 in arranging 'searches', surveys and in other necessary expenses.[4] In all the Queen's Welsh lordships an important feature of her land settlement was the

[1] Ibid. 32, 72, 97, 109, 166, 230. [2] Ibid. 103–4, 131, 137, 158, 171, 196.
[3] G. E. C., *Complete Peerage*, vii, 550–1; Jnl. 83, 84.
[4] J. Williams, *Records of Denbigh and its Lordship*, chs. x and xi; Jnl. 87.

treatment of holders of former 'bond' land, to whom she offered, on surrender of their copyholds, the security of long leases. But the transaction involved the customary fine—usually two to four years' rent[1]—and many of the tenants could not raise the money in time. Here Myddelton's capital was a crucial factor in the settlement. He had already extended his money-lending operations to North Wales by small loans to Denbighshire neighbours and to tradesmen in the town, and in 1591 he went as far as lending £300 for a year to the bishop of St Asaph (William Hughes); even the family of the wealthy Sir Richard Clough were not above raising £40 on their plate.[2] During the next five or six years he disbursed over £500 (in sums ranging from £10 to £200) in advancing the fines of crown tenants in Denbighshire—sometimes with the express condition that in case of failure to repay, the lease should be transferred to him.[3] The settlement also included the town, which had likewise suffered under Leicester; it culminated here in the new charter of 1597. In this too Myddelton was concerned, and his dealings provoked a breach with the neighbouring Salusburys of Llewenny (henchmen of Leicester) which was not fully healed in the next century, despite the olive branch of a marriage between the families.[4]

Disappointed in his hopes of becoming lord of Denbigh, Myddelton turned his attention to Leicester's other lordship of Chirk, which the Queen had allowed Lord St. John of Bletsoe to buy. He in turn was willing to sell, and in 1595 Myddelton bought it for £4,800. This was how he invested the fruits of his privateering ventures, at a time when Spain's new naval tactics made it unlikely that the good times would last. From now on transactions in Wales, whether loans or purchases, occupy most of the space in his ledger. He achieved a second-best in Denbighshire by buying the 'barony' of Henllan for £500 in 1599;[5] but apart from manorial rights, he was in the market for the land itself, and between the purchase of Chirkland and the end of the reign he spent well over £3,000 on buying estates and plots within the lordship, and

[1] Rhys and Brynmor Jones, *The Welsh People* (1909 edn.), 407–23.
[2] Jnl. 34, 43, 97, 108, 151.
[3] Ibid. 101, 107, 109, 137, 160, 171, 174, 182, 223–4.
[4] *Cal. Salusbury Correspondence*, ed. W. J. Smith (Univ. of Wales Bd. of Celtic Studies, Hist. and Law Ser. xiv), 38 no. 52; cf. Hist. MSS. Com. *Salisbury*, iv, 375–6; xiv, 173; *Trans. Denbighshire Hist. Soc.* iii, 42–48; *E.H.R.* lix, 353.
[5] Jnl. 152 *bis*.

rather more in the rest of Denbighshire and the neighbouring parts of Flint. In 1596 he paid £360 for some 'good land' in Montgomeryshire, and between 1598 and 1603 nearly £1,000 on small properties in his ancestral Merioneth, together with a lease of the herbage of a royal forest there. Some of these lands were acquired by straightforward purchase, some as a result of foreclosure on mortgages. For the small moneylending operations begun among Denbighshire neighbours in 1588 grew like a snowball until his clientèle embraced a substantial part of the landowners of North Wales, struggling on inadequate incomes (often further reduced by litigation) to rebuild their houses and generally to step up their scale of living to match what they were meeting, since the Act of Union, across the border; and their land was the only security most of them could offer.[1] All this meant a growing army of bailiffs, stewards and other agents not only at Denbigh (where from 1595 his brother Foulk, after working for both Thomas and Hugh in London, became his agent for the recovery of 'Welsh debts'), but in Chirkland from at least 1597 and in Mongomeryshire by 1601.[2]

There was even some infiltration into South Wales—chiefly through Haverfordwest, which of all Welsh towns had the closest ties with London. Robert Bateman, his agent and partner in many deals, who kept the accounts of the carrack for him in 1592 and managed the 'sugerhowse' from the following year, came of a Haverfordwest family into which his brother Charles married; and Charles's son William, a London merchant with whom Thomas and his partners sometimes did business, retained a strong connection with Haverfordwest, which benefited under his will.[3] Thomas's sister Alice married two successive husbands from the same town; one was William Walter, brother to the mayor of 1587 (who incidentally was great-grandfather to Charles II's Lucy Walters, the duke of Monmouth's mother). It was through Walter that Myddelton was put in touch with his most important South Wales client, John Philipps of Picton, who borrowed £110 for a year in 1593 and kept it for eight.[4]

[1] Dodd, *Stuart Wales*, 1–5.

[2] Jnl. 202 sqq. ; cf. ibid. 38, 52, 54, 78 sqq., 224, 177 *bis*.

[3] Pink, 8; W. M. Myddelton, 14: Jnl. 52, 55 sqq., 117, 122, 210, 214; T. J. Warren, *History of St. Mary's Haverfordwest*, 37.

[4] Pink, 9; *Arch. Camb.* 1904, 273–4; Jnl. 152–3, 187, 161 *bis*. Another of the clan with whom he had some dealings had settled at St. David's: ibid. 159, 217, 156 *bis*.

Naturally, however, the northern counties were his main field of operations. Between 1593 and 1602 he invested nearly £10,000[1] in mortgages on land there, ranging from £50 on a house and lands in Denbigh in 1594 (which was repaid in four years) to £1,000 advanced in 1599 to Sir Henry Bromley, the lord chancellor's son, on his lordship of Deythur in Mongomeryshire; this also was redeemed within a few years.[2] Many of the loans started with trivial sums borrowed on personal security, which often doubled themselves in five or six years[3] because the borrower failed to meet his interest (which was then added to the principal), or borrowed further sums on the prospect of a 'good thing' which failed to materialize, until he had to put in his lands as security and eventually to part with them. The 'jurnal' is too fragmentary to enable us to follow up these transactions in detail, especially as they were so often complicated by transfers and re-transfers; but it provides enough material for a few examples of Myddelton's methods and their effects on Welsh society.

The Salusburys of Bachymbyd (Denbighshire) and Rûg (Merioneth) were kinsmen with whom—in contrast to the Llewenny branch—Myddelton was always on good terms. Robert, who succeeded to the estates in 1580, was hampered at the start by debts his father had incurred to the court of wards during his minority, and tried to recover his fortunes by service in Ireland. For this purpose he began in 1590 borrowing from his wealthy kinsman; but it gained him little beyond a barren knighthood.[4] By 1596 most of the loans had been repaid, but he had to borrow afresh just before his death in 1599, leaving his brother and heir Captain John Salusbury to take over responsibility for his debts.[5] John in turn tried to retrieve the family fortunes by serving the earl of Essex not only at Cadiz and in Ireland, but in his reckless

[1] This is not a net addition to the sums given above for land purchase, for many of these advances were included in the final purchase price of the property.

[2] Jnl. 156, 218, 158 *bis*, 169 *bis*; Powys-land Club, *Montgomeryshire Coll.* xlix, 15–17, 20, 30–33.

[3] e.g. £40 borrowed on bond by John Wyn ap Hugh of Chirkland in 1596 had become £148, secured on his lands, by 1603; £430 borrowed by John Puleston of Bersham in the same year had become a mortgage of £500 a year later and nearly £1,000 by 1602; Edward Thelwall's mortgage of £200 in 1598 amounted to £410 in 1602. Detailed references to the 'jurnal' are given only for the more important transactions.

[4] *Cal. Salusbury Corr.* intro. 13–14 and table IIA; J. Hurstfield, *The Queen's Wards*, 179.

[5] Jnl. 86, 206, 217, 153 *bis*, 157 *bis*.

bid for power in 1601, and landed himself in costly Star Chamber suits in the process. All this involved further borrowings from Myddelton (on expectations, from an uncle, of lands at Segrwyd in Denbighshire) to pay for his armour and to provide him with ready money; but so far from getting anything out of them he was lucky, on the last occasion, to escape imprisonment or even the gallows. In the following year Myddelton bought the Segrwyd lands, but these did not wipe out the debt; the *débâcle*, however, was postponed till the next reign, and Myddelton (who had in this case shown exemplary patience) was not responsible: the captain had to mortgage the ancestral estate of Bachymbyd for £3,000 to another London Welshman, John Williams the King's goldsmith, and finally to surrender it to him for a further £3,300.[1]

Another relative by marriage who gave him a lot of trouble was Richard Rogers, a London saddler of Flintshire origin who owned lands there and apparently also at Killowen, near the English base of Newry in Ulster. Dealings with him started innocently enough with a £10 loan in 1590; three years later this had become a £100 mortgage, and in 1598 Myddelton very reluctantly settled the debt by taking over the lands at Killowen, which did not repay his outlay. It may be that one purpose for which Rogers needed money is indicated by the Star Chamber suit he instituted in 1598 against Wrexham neighbours for maypole-dancing on Sunday and other practices offensive to his puritan conscience.[2] Thomas Williams of Bodfari, a Flintshire neighbour of Rogers, allowed an original debt of £30 in 1589 to run up to over £800 in the next eight years, and Myddelton took over his lands by paying another £300.[3] There can be no doubt that the £100 borrowed in 1598 by the registrar of St. Asaph was for his new house Vaenol Fawr—then newly built and still standing almost unaltered. One of his Merioneth clients was Robert Evans, a yeoman of the guard, who mortgaged his lands in Trawsfynydd to Myddelton for £60; Myddelton leased them to the owner of a neighbouring estate, leaving open to Evans's son the option of redeeming them at the same figure.[4]

[1] Ibid. 212, 232, 137 *bis*, 139 *bis*, 146 *bis*, 168 *bis*; *E.H.R.* lix, 353, 359, 361, 363–4, 367–8; *Cal. Salusbury Corr.*, loc. cit.; *Acts of P. C.* 1599–1600, 216.

[2] W. M. Myddelton, 33; Jnl. 81, 116, 193, 144 *bis*; I. ab O. Edwards, *Star Chamber Proceedings relating to Wales*, 67.

[3] Jnl. 49, 51, 98, 134, 226.

[4] Ibid. 205, 143 *bis*, 148 *bis*, 166 *bis*.

In Chirkland he seems to have deliberately pursued a policy of gathering into his hands as many of the small freeholds as he could —especially in the immediate neighbourhood of the castle; certainly a number of them, large and small, fell to him as a result of loans on mortgage. The largest was Gartheryr, for which in 1602 he paid Roger Kyffin £650, including £230 previously borrowed on it.[1] Another of the Kyffin family—Richard of Glascoed (Llansilin)—inherited, about 1597, lands in Chirkland already burdened with an old debt of £150, of which £100 was secured on them; he further depleted his fortune by four Star Chamber suits. In the end Myddelton took him (and his nephew and heir Watkin after him) into his service as steward, and in 1603 he bought from him three tenements worth £140 towards wiping off a debt which had now reached £300.[2] Another considerable Chirkland property acquired through mortgage was Yr Orsedd Wen (bought in 1597 for £500), of which the owner, John Launcelot, J.P., already owed £400 in consequence of a costly Star Chamber suit. The transaction was in this case sweetened by the gift of £10 to Launcelot's wife for a gown.[3] Smaller estates raked in in the same way were those of William ap Robert and David ap Thomas ap Llewelyn, bought in 1602 for £386 and £102 respectively, both prices including a four-year old mortgage covering part of the value.[4] On the other hand at least two Chirkland tenants—Thomas Tanat of Carreghova and Ieuan ap David of Geyfron—succeeded in paying off mortgages (one of £200, the other of £20) and keeping their Naboth's vineyards.[5] So too did a far more important landowner, Owen Vaughan of Llwydiarth, whose main lands lay in Montgomeryshire, but who in 1597 mortgaged an outlying estate in Chirkland for £200 to pay off the accumulated debts with which his father's incessant lawsuits had burdened the estate for over twenty years. Within six years Owen had paid it all off without (so far as can be seen) anything to draw on but his lands—which suggests that even the 'mere gentry' if they eschewed the wilder forms of extravagance, were not doing so badly from their lands after all; the Vaughans

[1] Ibid. 241 *bis*, 269 *bis*.

[2] Ibid. 163 *bis*, 167 *bis*, 185, 189, 220, 224; J. E. Griffith, *Pedigrees* 198; *Trans. Denbighshire Hist. Soc.* iii, 44–45; Edwards, *Star Chamber Proceedings*, 57–58.

[3] Jnl. 202, 207, 223, 232; Edwards, *Star Chamber Proceedings*, 58.

[4] Jnl. 235, 137–8 *bis*, 167 *bis*.

[5] Ibid. 202, 164 *bis*, 138 *bis*, 168 *bis*.

were still important and wealthy landlords through the next century.[1]

Some of his mortgagees died before they could redeem their lands. A Chirkland widow in 1602 agreed to the purchase of her husband's lands for £50 on top of the £450 debt he had already accumulated. A Denbigh neighbour, who started in 1593 with a debt of £12, mortgaged his house and lands the following year for £28, then incurred further debts to other creditors which Myddelton took over so as to rescue him from the debtors' prison in London (not his only intervention to save a Denbighshire man from this fate); he died in 1597 with his debts still unpaid. His widow made further borrowings till the total was nearing £100, and in 1602 Myddelton was considering the outright purchase of her estate by way of final settlement.[2]

The motives for Myddelton's acquisition of Welsh lands are clear enough. It was in the first place an investment: not so profitable as his money-lending, on which he had his regular ten per cent, whereas the rents of his lands (so far as can be judged from samples in the ledger) seem to have amounted on the average to about seven per cent on his outlay, and might sink below five; certainly not so profitable as his more successful privateering ventures; but probably safer than either—and recent experiences, when his large-scale investments in Wales began, had enhanced the attractions of a 'safety first' policy. 'Around the 1580s', says Professor Hexter, 'the land market began to boom, and . . . the annual rental on some estates climbed to a third of what those estates had sold for a decade earlier.' Myddelton was all set to take advantage of the boom. The yield of the five manors of Chirkland, estimated when he bought them at £150 a year, might easily be 'advaunced or Raysed . . . by the opinion of moste men' (he noted in the 'jurnal') 'unto £250'. A more thorough exploitation of manorial rights, indeed, was a general aim of those who implemented the Tudor land settlement of Wales—as it was of the Crown itself.[3] How soon the new lord put this policy into

[1] Ibid. 215, 223, 225, 181 *bis*; Edwards, *Star Chamber Proceedings*, 119–20, 122, 128–9; Dodd, *Stuart Wales*, 116, 212–13; *Montgomeryshire Records* (suppt. to *Montgomeryshire Collections*, 1896–1928), 120, 123 (exchequer suits), 450–501 *passim* (feet of fines); *Dict. Welsh Biog.*, 997; cf. J. H. Hexter in *Encounter*, x, 28.

[2] Jnl. 109, 153, 162 *bis*, 172, 211, 219, 142–3 *bis*, 173 *bis*.

[3] Ibid. 192; *Montgomeryshire Coll.* li, 23–24; Hurstfield, *The Queen's Wards*, ch. 1.

action is seen in the institution of Star Chamber proceedings against him for enclosures in the lordship within two years of the purchase; and friction with tenants and neighbours flared up afresh when his son settled there in 1612. The opposition was led, characteristically enough, by the neighbouring family of Edwards of Plas Newydd, dyed-in-the-wool conservatives in religion, in culture and in agrarian practice who resented the intrusion of a city 'usurer'.[1] Yet an economic explanation is far from telling the full story; the clue is given in a comment made by Myddelton on special precautions he adopted over the purchase of Yr Orsedd Wen, 'least I hurte my lytle Son'. The son (whose elder brother Richard had died in infancy) was the future Sir Thomas, the Roundhead general. He came to live at Chirk castle in 1612, and his family continued to dominate the politics and society of east Denbighshire till the eighteenth century; his descendants occupy Chirk castle today.[2]

The effects of his transactions on Welsh society are more complex. His loans certainly helped many Welsh landlords to tide over the difficult period of the Tudor land settlement, even if in some cases (especially in Chirkland) they promoted the eclipse of the small freeholder and the consolidation of large estates. They also helped some landlords to discharge the new public obligations thrust upon them, by advancing what was needed to equip them for military service or for maintaining the dignity of civil office.[3] Young Welsh lawyers were often given a start, especially in the purchase of their chambers, by loans—occasionally without interest, but with one of them Myddelton found a very paying substitute: that was when in 1598 he lent £40 free of interest to Peter Mutton—a Flintshireman (and an old client) destined to become a Welsh judge—on condition that 'for the interest he giveth Councell freely in all my causes'.[4] Many of these loans were

[1] Edwards, *Star Chamber Proceedings*, 61; N.L.W. Edward Owen deeds, 31, 38; *Cal. S. P. Dom.* 1611–18, 220; Dodd, *Stuart Wales*, 29.

[2] Jnl. 207; A. H. Dodd ed., *History of Wrexham*, 53–83.

[3] e.g. Thomas Prys of Plas Iolyn, who like 'Gwilym Canoldref' was at once poet, critic and buccaneer, borrowed over £200 (including the cost of silver plate) for his year as sheriff in 1598–99; the debt had not been discharged when the ledger closes: Jnl. 155 *bis*, 178 *bis*; *Arch Camb.* 1869, 27–28; N. L. W. MSS. Llanstephan 156/146, Mostyn 112/343. A loan of £30 to Myddelton's cousin, the head of the Gwaenynog house, was also made in preparation for his shrievalty: Jnl. 154 *bis*.

[4] Jnl. 146 *bis*; cf. ibid. 189, 195, 209, 228, 164 *bis*; and for other Welsh lawyers, ibid. 127, 147, 177, 181, 204, 218, 142 *bis*, 155 *bis*, 173–5 *bis*.

negotiated in the hope of using them to meet the expenses of procuring a government job such as would amply cover them, but the hopes were not always justified. Thomas Tanat borrowed £10 in 1595 (with the backing of John Edwards of Plas Newydd) 'towards the bwying A clarcks place', but he did not repay it for seven years. Still worse was the case of William Penrhyn, whose loan of £15 in 1592, for the purchase of a butt of sack to the chancellor of the exchequer and spices for his lady 'to further his suite', grew in four years to a mortgage of over £700 on lands the title to some of which Myddelton disputed. It must have been soon after this that he was given a minor legal office in the counties where his estates lay (Denbigh and Montgomery), enabling him to pay off some of his debts and perhaps to avoid the threatened sale of his land at Carreghova; but he is still nearly £400 to the bad when the ledger closes.[1]

The part played by litigation in swelling the debts of the Welsh gentry has appeared more than once; sometimes Myddelton lent money specifically for the purpose of meeting these legal costs. Peculiarly addicted to law was the family of Lloyd (alias Rossindale) of Denbigh, one of whom had married the sister of William Myddelton of Gwaenynog, Thomas's cousin. Myddelton not only advanced money to meet his suits, but even had on one occasion to lend him pocket-money to take him home from the Star Chamber; Thomas Lloyd, of the same family, was rescued by him in 1594 from the debtors' prison after a Star Chamber action, and even a further loan two years later 'to end all sutes in the Star-chamber against him and his freinds' did not prevent him from reappearing there in 1599.[2] In this and other ways Thomas Myddelton may be said to have helped many of his neighbours, however inadvertently, on the road to ruin; but for most of them collapse did not come until the next century.[3]

In other respects his capital certainly had a stimulating effect. If there was only one Welsh industrial enterprise (the copper works at Neath) which he directly promoted, his dealings with the craftsmen and retail traders of both Denbighshire and Pembrokeshire, and the wide participation of his ramified family—even

[1] Ibid. 102, 193, 204, 221, 154 *bis*; *Cal. S. P. Dom.* 1597–1601, 388; *Montgomeryshire Records*, 455.

[2] Jnl. 110, 118, 154, 176, 200, 208; cf. ibid. 110, 178; Griffith, *Pedigrees*, 287; Edwards, *Star Chamber Proceedings*, 57, 59, 60, 67.

[3] Dodd, *Stuart Wales*, 3–4; cf. *Hist. of Wrexham*, 67–68.

those who stayed at home—in his trading, especially his privateering ventures, infused new blood into the Welsh countryside. A similar effect on agriculture must have been produced by his purchases of grain and other foodstuffs in the virtual capacity of government contractor for the Indies expedition of 1593 or for Sir Henry Bagnall's Irish campaign in 1595, as well as by the interchange of Welsh cattle between his Welsh properties and his Lincolnshire farm.[1] On a different plane, and certainly bringing no profit, were his investments in the publication of religious works in Welsh. In 1593 he advanced £10 to Thomas Salusbury, of the Stationers' Company, and his nephew Rev. Henry Salusbury, for printing in Welsh a tract entitled *The Sickman's Salve* by the militant Protestant Thomas Becon. These Salusburys were of another branch of the Rûg and Bachymbyd family. Thomas (a friend of Peter Wentworth) published several books in Welsh—probably at a loss—and Henry was responsible for an early Welsh dictionary; but there is no sign that *The Sickman's Salve* ever appeared, or that Myddelton attempted to recover his loan. Better luck attended a commission to print the Welsh metrical version of the Psalms by 'Gwilym Canoldref' nine years later; this time Myddelton lent his cousin £30 'to be repaid without intereste so sone as convenientlie he can sell those psalme books'. Publication took place next year—too late for the 'jurnal' to tell us whether he got his £30 back.[2]

His official career in Wales was of less importance. He was elected (not without opposition)[3] M.P. for Merioneth in 1597, five years or so after he first became a landowner there, and was *custos rotulorum* for the county two years later. To follow in office men like Baron Owen and Elis Price—considerable figures in the Tudor government of Wales—and to be consulted in the choice of sheriffs, meant at least a recognition of status, and it is not without unction that he refers to the clerk of the peace for the county as 'my servant in livery'.[4] In his native Denbighshire he was on

[1] Jnl. 124, 160, 186, 188, 193; Hist. MSS. Com. *Salisbury*, v, 369, 379.

[2] Jnl. 138, 178 *bis*; *S.T.C.* 21611; W. A. Jackson, *Records of Stationers' Co.* 145; Hist. MSS. Com. *Salisbury*, vi, 288–9; *D. N. B.*; *Dict. Welsh Biog.* 899–900; T. Parry, *Hanes Llenyddiaeth Gymraeg*, 146.

[3] But the opposition came from two corrupt deputy lieutenants who were soon afterwards relieved of their posts: *Acts of P. C.* 1597–98, 448, 457, 463, 557; 1599–1600, 180–1; Edwards, *Star Chamber Proceedings*, 90.

[4] Breese, *Kalendars of Gwynedd*, 28; Hist. MSS. Com. *Salisbury*, xii, 482–3; Jnl. 177 *bis*.

the commission of the peace by 1594, and became constable of Denbigh castle by 1597.[1] The panegyric of the Denbighshire bard who hailed the new constable as gallant warrior, true pillar of his shire and keeper of the gateway to three nations, contrasts oddly with the comment in his hero's ledger when he had to advance over £300 on arming the county levies for Ireland: 'wishing I hadd once my money back and it should never come to armour again' (actually he had it back within a year).[2] It was two years after this that he was called in to supervise the clothing by London drapers of another batch of Welsh levies for Ireland.[3]

Business, religion, family: these were Myddelton's three dominant interests, and it would perhaps be over-bold to guess in what order he placed them. A keen business man he certainly was, but that does not necessarily imply a harsh or unscrupulous one. So far as can be judged from his ledger his dealings were all above board;[4] and he does not seem to have pressed his debtors unduly. It is true that when Sir Matthew Morgan, nephew of 'the warrior' and an old debtor of Myddelton's, went bankrupt in 1602 he charged the debt (together with 'Charge in Lawe and forbearaunce') on the lands of his fellow-surety Sir George Leicester, brother-in-law though he was to cousin William the bard; true also that in the same year he resorted to the rigorous procedure of outlawry against another debtor;[5] its use against Edward Brereton of Marchwiel (who also owed him money) a few years earlier was however on the initiative of a different creditor, and the sheriff accused of suppressing the writ was his friend Sir Robert Salusbury.[6] More often he avoided extremities by a reasonable composition, by extending the time limit or even by writing off the debt. Every now and then he reviewed his 'desperate debts' and ceased to count them among his assets: if anything came in after that he reckoned it as a windfall; and when

[1] Simwnt Vychan in B. M. Add. MSS. 14872/219 vs. 112; Hist. MSS. Com. *Salisbury*, vii, 185; *Acts of P. C.* 1597, 165–6.

[2] Edward ap Raff in N. L. W. Llanstephan MS. 36/37 vss. 5, 8, 27, 35; Jnl. 139 *bis*, 252 *bis*, 271 *bis*.

[3] *Acts of P. C.* 1598–99, 469.

[4] A possible exception is the 25 bags of pepper taken from a prize cargo in 1591 and alleged to have been 'falsely' marked in behalf of Myddelton, Harby and Co. while the case was still sub judice; but the blame was officially placed on Myddelton's brother Robert and his partner Harby: *Acts of P. C.* 1591–92, 386, 588–9.

[5] Jnl. 164 *bis*; cf. ibid. 122, 163, 165, 185, 192–3, 233; G. T. Clark, *Limbus Patrum Morganniae*, 327; W. M. Myddelton, 59.

[6] Edwards, *Star Chamber Proceedings*, 61; Jnl. 151, 158, 148 *bis*.

he entered on the lands of a mortgagee he was often ready to leave a loophole for their recovery, and to let the former owner remain in possession as tenant in the meanwhile.[1] His very charities, down to his £6 to a 'blynd pooer man' (of which half was repaid in nine months), were entered as interest-free loans, whether he expected repayment or not; for he liked to have everything on a business footing. He even adventured £50 for a year, free of interest, in the vessel of a London shipper on the ground of his 'present need and great Losses'.[2]

In many ways he is the typical puritan business man, believing, as Baxter did a century later, that 'if God show you a way in which you may lawfully get more than in another way (without wrong to your soul, or to any other) if you refuse this and choose the less gainful way, you . . . refuse to be God's steward and accept his gifts'.[3] When, as happens from time to time, he makes a loss or brings off a poor deal, he must account for it in the 'jurnal' kept for his private eye. Murrain among the stock, debtors who died with no provision for their debts,[4] even an unwise or dishonest agent—these may be written off as Acts of God, but a bad bargain calls for explanation. It may be the need for realizing capital quickly, as in the purchase of Chirkland; or friendship, as when he overpaid a much-liked brother-in-law, 'but upon Walden all is well bestowed'; or just 'a Foolyshe Agreement' over tare; or again money 'fondly by me lent from tyme to tyme . . . so much as I have no delight to sett it particularly in my book hier'—which ended by saddling him with a Shropshire property he did not want and exchanged as soon as he could for Merioneth land. One Chirkland transaction in which he pays Roger Kyffin £650 for land on which the immediate return is under five per cent is characteristically explained in the gloss that 'it is verie well wodded which Is the Cause I paid so deere as allsoe the povertie of the man'.[5] Contrariwise, thanks are given to God for any uncovenanted gains 'to the glorie of god and my comfort', and pages of the ledger recording such transactions (as well as in the special ledger for the expedition of 1593) are sometimes headed 'Laus deo'.[6]

[1] Jnl. 56, 220, 149 *bis*, 166 *bis*, 171 *bis*. [2] Ibid. 31, 37, 145 *bis*.

[3] Baxter, *Spiritual Directory* (1678), i, 378*b*.

[4] e.g. a Southwark innkeeper, 1594, a Welsh soldier killed on service in Ireland, 1602: Jnl. 182, 171 *bis*. [5] Jnl. 83, 144, 201, 221, 164 *bis*, 169 *bis*, 180 *bis*.

[6] Ibid. 29, 31, 96, 172 *bis*.

Another facet of his puritan piety is seen in payments like ten shillings to the 'Dutch precher' or 18*s*. 10*d*. towards the 'parsons wadgs' for a quarter. The latter suggests something of the nature of that characteristic puritan device, a 'lectureship' in which the preacher is chosen and paid by private individuals of the congregation who approve his views. On the other hand the purchase of advowsons, also popular with puritans both as an investment and as a means of controlling the church, does not seem to have appealed to Myddelton. The parsonage of Gresford was the only one he acquired; this came to him in settlement of the accumulated debts of Elis Wyn, who farmed the tithes for the dean and chapter of Winchester, and he unloaded it as soon as he could on the lord keeper's son.[1]

Staunch Protestant as he was, Myddelton had no more scruples about trading with the ecclesiastical enemy at home than with the political enemy abroad. The religious allegiance of the Salusburys of Rûg was highly dubious; Captain John, as we have seen, got himself mixed up in the Essex affair, and so did several of Myddelton's other clients—most of them men suspected of leanings towards Rome. The most notorious was another offshoot of Llewenny stock, Captain Owen Salusbury of Holt, destined to perish in the Essex House scuffle in 1601. It was only in 1589 that Owen returned to England from the Low Countries and sued for pardon for his part in betraying Deventer to the Spaniards; within a few years he had become a debtor of Myddelton's and perhaps an agent on his Lincolnshire property, until in 1596 he attached himself to Essex and joined him in his Cadiz and Azores expeditions. His kinsman Captain John Salusbury was a comrade-in-arms both in the Netherlands and under Essex, and so was John's brother-in-law John Lloyd of Bodidris, another debtor and vendor of lands to Myddelton. John Trevor of Trevalyn, who was in the same group of swordsmen though probably a safe Protestant, eventually paid off Lloyd's debts; Owen Salusbury seems to have wiped his off before he died.[2] Most striking of all, however, are Myddelton's relations with his own brother William, whom he continued to befriend after he had changed his faith and settled

[1] Ibid. 131, 155, 171–3, 197, 211, 234; D. R. Thomas, *History of the Diocese of St. Asaph*, iii, 247.

[2] Jnl. 101, 104, 155, 167, 182, 216, 234, 161 *bis*; *E.H.R.* lix, 357–68; *Cal. Salusbury Corr.* 28 no. 16.

down in Ghent, caught up in the toils of civil war and religious strife; he was a guest at the Tower Street house even after he had become a pensioner of Spain and an associate of Hugh Owen, the notorious Caernarvonshire exile and conspirator.[1]

Blood was after all thicker than water, and the wide diffusion of the Myddelton blood seemed to do nothing to thin it out. Like any good Welshman, Thomas of Galch Hill and Tower Street was in touch with the whole *cenedl*, paying marked deference to the *pencenedl*, his Oxford-educated cousin William of Gwaenynog—poor relation though he was to the wealthy capitalist of the clan. His business dealings with his younger brothers—Charles, Hugh, Robert, Foulk and Peter—have cropped up again and again in these pages; nor was it all business. The bard Thomas Prys singled out Thomas's love of his kin as his outstanding trait—and that was in a poem written years before Prys became his debtor![2] While Hugh was away in the Netherlands, Thomas arranged the purchase of material for his first wife's wedding gown in London, as well as advancing the fee for his freedom of the Goldsmiths' Company. When his youngest brother Peter fell ill in 1593 he twice sent him on a horse litter to Bath, with £40 for his expenses there; and when he died the following year it was Thomas who arranged and paid for the funeral at Denbigh—a bill of nearly £70, including as much as £13 10*s*. for three visits of the doctor and surgeon.[3] Other more distant members of the clan—and of the family of Poyntz, his first employer—are from time to time found in his service, or in receipt of loans, or provided for by payment of what he called 'agyst' of £10 to one of his business associates to take him on as apprentice.[4]

Great things lay ahead of Thomas Myddelton when the Queen died: his knighthood; his lord mayoralty, inaugurated by the dramatist Thomas Middleton with a pageant making great play of the name they shared; eight years later 'a very religious speach and exhortation' made by the ex-lord mayor to 'the whole assemblie of the Misterie of the Grocerie of London'.[5] More significant for Wales were his further purchases of Welsh lordships—Ruthin in Denbighshire and (for a time) Arwystli and

[1] Jnl. 13, 25; *Cal. S. P. Dom.* 1581–90, 532; 1598–1602, 272; *E. H. R.* liii, 629.
[2] B. M. Add. MSS. 14782/219 vs. 113. [3] Jnl. 25, 128, 134.
[4] e.g. another nephew named John Myddelton: Jnl. 93.
[5] Pink, 12; Heath, *The Worshipful Company of Grocers*, 443–59.

Cyfeiliog in Montgomeryshire; above all his share in financing the publication, just before his death, of the first portable Welsh Bible in 1630.[1] But no ledger survives to light up this period, nor even the text of his 'religious speach'. The knight of Stansted Mountfichet remains a more shadowy figure than the merchant of Tower Street.

[1] *Dict. Welsh Biog.* 675–8; *Mongomeryshire Coll.* xlviii, 73, 75.

X

Foundations of Anglo-Scottish Union

GORDON DONALDSON

The treaty in which it was finally agreed that 'the two kingdoms of England and Scotland' should on 1 May 1707 'and for ever after, be united into one kingdom by the name of Great Britain' had been preceded, a century earlier, by the union of the two monarchies. But constitutional instrument and dynastic accident, while they could unite two states, could not in themselves unite two peoples. Nor was it inevitable that a union of those two kingdoms which had for so long existed in one small island would be enduring, for continental history presents us with plenty of examples of the disruption of similar unions—the Scandinavian kingdoms, Holland and Belgium, Spain and Portugal; in each of those instances, although union was for a time achieved, the ultimate solution was separation. The path to a lasting union of England and Scotland was neither straight nor smooth, and it would not have come about without the assistance of non-political factors.

A sixteenth-century Scot was not far wrong when he observed that since the Norman Conquest 'there had not been an English king who had not seriously aimed to unite the two kingdoms'. Nor were all the attempts at union by way of conquest: while there were phases of attempts at conquest, by 'the more warlike and ambitious' English kings, 'the wiser . . . sought to unite the two dynasties by marriage, with the view and intent that an heir should be born to succeed naturally to both realms'.[1] But if there were thus phases when statesmen strove for union by peaceful means—not excluding guile—there were also long periods when there was only the persistent, but often unobtrusive, penetration into Scotland of English culture and English institutions, quietly

[1] Thomas Craig, *De unione regnorum Britanniae* (Scot. Hist. Soc.), 242.

working to bring about the assimilation of the two peoples. And a good deal of Scottish history has been nothing else than the story of a conflict, or at least a tension, between two opposing tendencies —the tension between native and external influences, between independence and domination from the south.

When anglicization was first seriously attempted in Scotland, in the eleventh century, it had produced a sharp enough reaction: on the death of Malcolm III and his English queen, Margaret, in 1093, the Scots 'drove out all the English who were with King Malcolm before', and accepted Duncan II as king only on condition that he dismissed his English and French followers.[1] But the reaction was neither lasting nor effective. Anglicization progressed so far in the twelfth and thirteenth centuries that Edward I's marriage scheme was welcomed by the Scots, and there can be little doubt that had it matured there would long ago have been a union closer than that achieved in 1707 and closer than that existing today. Scottish institutions would not have been differentiated from those of England, Scottish nationality would never have developed. But the three centuries of war (1296–1560) which followed the two centuries of peaceful penetration conditioned the two peoples to enmity. A traveller in Scotland in 1435 had remarked that 'nothing pleases the Scots more than abuse of the English';[2] an act forbidding any Englishman to 'have benefice, secular or religious' in Scotland was passed by the Scottish parliament in 1466,[3] in the early years of a king who was ultimately overthrown by subjects who accused him of 'inbringing of Englishmen';[4] the records of seaport burghs contain frequent entries about guarding the secrets of the town from English sailors;[5] and so late as 1566, when men were still unaware that Anglo-Scottish relations had been permanently altered by the Reformation, the Scottish government, on the ground that Englishmen were 'searching out of secrets and taking of inspection of sundry strengths and other sure places', appointed a 'searcher of all Englishmen resorting and repairing within the realm of Scotland'.[6] In England, so late as the first year of Elizabeth,

[1] A. O. Anderson, *Scottish Annals from English Chroniclers*, 118.

[2] P. Hume Brown, *Early travellers in Scotland*, 27.

[3] *Acts parl. Scot.* ii, 86 c. 9. [4] Ibid. ii, 210.

[5] I owe this information to Professor W. Croft Dickinson, who read a draft of this paper and made many valuable suggestions.

[6] *Registrum secreti sigilli*, v, 2921.

parliament revived an act of Henry VIII making it a felony to sell, exchange or deliver a horse to a Scotsman;[1] a statute of Richard II forbidding the sending of arms or victual into Scotland without licence had never been repealed;[2] and when the English taught their children archery they encouraged them to take good aim—so at least a Scot believed—by saying, 'There's a Scot! Shoot him!'[3]

Thus, when Henry VIII brought forward a marriage scheme identical with that of Edward I, the task confronting him was far more difficult. Even in the promising early months of 1543, when there seemed to be no obstacle in the way of the betrothal of the infant Queen Mary to Prince Edward, the English envoy in Edinburgh reported that if the Scots were threatened with subjection to England 'there is not so little a boy but he will hurl stones against it, and the wives will handle their distaffs, and the commons universally will rather die';[4] and by September, when the situation had taken a turn for the worse, he was complaining that 'never was so noble a prince's servant so evil entreated as he is among those rude unreasonable people, and never had to do with so inconstant and beastly a nation'.[5] Henry handled a delicate situation with singular ineptitude, and in succeeding years Hertford's devastating invasions, the battle of Pinkie and the English occupation of south-eastern Scotland further alienated the Scots, who had to appeal for French help to drive out the English and who sent their queen to France to be betrothed to the heir to the French throne. The campaigns of the 1540s represented the last active phase of the three hundred years of war, which thus ended in failure for England.

But England, which had lost the war, was to win the peace. Ever since Flodden thoughtful Scots had been reflecting that continued hostility to England and the continued use of their country as a tool of France were likely to lead to further disasters and that there might be a better future in collaboration than in antagonism. When the Regent Albany proposed to invade England in 1523 he met with opposition from those who said:

For the love of France the realm of Scotland suffers great pain as daily appears, for our nobles are slain or taken, our commonalty murdered,

[1] 23 Hen. VIII c. 16; 1 Eliz. c. 7.
[2] 7 Ric. II c. 16. [3] Craig, op. cit. 393.
[4] Sadler, *State Papers*, i, 70; cf. *L. & P. Hen. VIII*, xviii (1), 184–5.
[5] *L. & P. Hen. VIII*, xviii (2), 90; cf. 81.

our lands overrun, our houses and fortresses burned and razed; we lose the profits of our lands; which mischief we need not have had, but for the love of France and what helps France . . . If we would keep amity with the realm of England we were out of all these dangers.[1]

Other Scottish rulers were to find, like Albany, that while the Scottish nobles would defend their own soil they would no longer cross the Border in the interests of France. Such opinions were reinforced in the 1550s by the fear of French domination. It proved to be altogether too much for the Scots to have their country ruled in the French interest by a Frenchwoman, Mary of Guise, French troops garrisoning Scottish fortresses and Frenchmen thrust into offices in Scotland, and there soon had to be a statute against those speaking evil of the queen and the French.[2] The fear grew that Scotland was going to share the fate of Brittany and, through marriage, be absorbed as a province into France. The earl of Argyll was heard to remark in 1559 that 'the France ar cumin in and sutin down in this realm to occupy it and to put furtht the inhabitantis tharoff, and siclik to occupy all uther menis rowmes pece and pece, and to put away the blud of the nobilitie'; and, it was added, he 'makis the exampill of Brytanny'.[3]

But another cause was operating in favour of Anglo-Scottish amity, and that was the progress of the Reformation. Already in the 1530s England was at once an example and a refuge for Scots who had adopted reforming opinions; then, in 1543, the policy of an Anglo-Scottish alliance accompanied by the authorization of the vernacular Bible in Scotland had been adopted for a brief space; and in the years following, when English military policy did so much to alienate Scotland, sympathy with the Reformation was sufficiently strong to ensure that England still retained allies among the Scots. Only the existence of some motive stronger than patriotism can account for the very considerable countenance which the English received from Scotsmen between about 1545 and 1548, and neither the compulsion which armies could exert on the inhabitants of occupied territory nor the existence of financial inducements can explain the number of collaborators whom the English found in Scotland.[4] The attraction exerted on the Scots by

[1] Hall, *Chronicle* (1809 edn.), 665. [2] *Acts parl. Scot.* ii, 499–500.

[3] *Scottish correspondence of Mary of Lorraine* (Scot. Hist. Soc.), 427.

[4] For observations on the record evidence in *Registrum secreti sigilli*, iv, see *Scot. Hist. Rev.* xxxiii, 42–43.

a country which had broken with Rome was not seriously interrupted by changes in the political and military situation: it was in February 1543, when the prospects of an Anglo-Scottish treaty were most promising, that Sadler reported that if a cartload of Bibles, Primers and Psalters were sent to Scotland 'they wolde be bought every one';[1] but on 1 November 1547, less than two months after Pinkie, the governor of the English garrison in Broughty Castle reported that there was much desire in Angus and Fife to have Bibles and Testaments and 'other good English books of Tyndale's and Frith's translations'.[2] In June 1548 Lord Methven, puzzled to find an explanation of 'the caus that Inglis men is fawvorit and the authorite nocht obeyit nor servit', found four 'prynsipall thingis quhilkis is the caussis': three of the four were material considerations—the desire for security, profit and stable government—but first, before those other three, he put the fact that 'part of the legis has tayn new apoynzionis [opinions] of the scriptour and has don agan the law and ordinance of haly kirk'.[3] When John Knox remarked to Cecil in June 1559 that the perpetual concord between the two realms, for which he had long looked, would be effected by the preaching of Jesus Christ crucified,[4] he was proposing to build on a well-laid foundation.

In the whole period down to 1603, religion probably did more than anything else to foster the consciousness of common aims and a common destiny. The later picture of Anglo-Scottish ecclesiastical relations, one of antagonism or at least diversity, has done much to obscure the unity which was uppermost in men's minds in the early years of Elizabeth's reign. This is not the place to recount the substantial approximation of the two Churches in that period, in respect of doctrine, polity and worship,[5] but some illustrations may be given of the cordial friendship and complete understanding between the Church defined by the Elizabethan settlement of 1559 and the Church which emerged from the Scottish revolution of the following year. The Scottish reformers thought of England as 'of the same religion' as themselves, and as having 'enterprised like reformation of religion' with them, while English churchmen noted with satisfaction that English intervention contributed to the success of the Scottish revolt in 1560 and

[1] *Hamilton papers*, i, 445. [2] *Cal. S.P. Scot.* i, 35.

[3] *Scottish correspondence of Mary of Lorraine*, 241. [4] *Cal. S.P. Scot.* i, 218.

[5] See G. Donaldson, *The making of the Scottish prayer book of 1637*, 7–22, and *The Scottish Reformation*, chs. iv–vii.

regarded that achievement as the culmination of their own triumph a few months earlier.[1] Archbishop Parker's apprehension about 'such a visitation as Knox hath attempted in Scotland, the people to be orderers of things',[2] belonged to a phase when the Scottish reformers were only rebels, with neither English countenance nor a constitutional position in their own country, and his oft-quoted comment, far from being typical, is an isolated jarring note.

In that early stage, a common Protestantism was no doubt the primary consideration, and in later years the political situation was sometimes such as to make men ready to emphasize the harmony between the two Churches, as in 1571, when the king's party in Scotland besought Elizabeth to 'take upon her the maintenance and protection of the true religion preached and established by law in both the realms';[3] and again in 1585, when the articles for a treaty between England and Scotland began with a reference to 'the better maintenance of the true, ancient, Christian religion which they now profess'.[4] But it is also true that the insular and unique character imposed upon the Church of England by the state was not much reflected in the thought and writings of the earlier Elizabethan churchmen, and was no obstacle to the recognition of other reformed churches, including that of Scotland, while the Scots on their side acknowledged the archbishops of Canterbury and York to be 'those whom God, of his providence and mercy, hath erected as principals in ecclesiastical jurisdiction in England'.[5]

Next to religion, it was language that was uppermost in men's minds as a link between the two peoples. In a letter which the English privy council proposed to send to the Lords of the Congregation in July, 1559, the hope was expressed that 'this famous isle may be conjoined in heart as in continent, with uniformity of language, manners and conditions'.[6] John Maitland of Thirlstane, who, as chancellor of Scotland from 1587 to 1595, 'held the king on two grounds sure, neither to cast out with the kirk nor

[1] Knox, *Works* ed. Laing, i, 382; vi, 44; *Zurich letters* (Parker Soc.), i, 88, 109, 113, 116, 124, 140.

[2] S.P. 12/7/32; *Parker Correspondence* (Parker Soc.), 105.

[3] *Warrender papers* (Scot. Hist. Soc.), i, 105. [4] Ibid. i, 192.

[5] See 'Inter-diocesan and inter-provincial communication before and after the reformation' (*Rec. Scot. Church Hist. Soc.*, xii), 77–80.

[6] *Cal. S.P. Scot.* i, 234–5.

with England',[1] thought of 'this isle' as 'naturally joined by situation, language and most happily by religion'.[2] And the king whom he advised likewise thought of the two countries as 'joined in unity of religion and language'.[3]

The history of an English dialect in Scotland goes back to the sixth and seventh centuries, when Anglian penetration made parts of southern Scotland racially and linguistically little else than an extension of northern England; and from the eleventh century, when those areas were incorporated in the Scottish kingdom, south-eastern Scotland, the most English part of Scotland, played a steadily increasing part in the development of the country.[4] Almost the entire eastern seaboard of Scotland and all the more fertile, productive parts of the country were by the sixteenth century Anglo-Saxon, in language if not in race, and the Gaelic-speaking Celts were confined to the barren mountains of the centre and west. The Scottish state—the Scotland which counted politically and economically—was consciously Anglo-Saxon, and would have indignantly repudiated the suggestion that it was anything else.[5] The linguistic triumph of the Anglian element in Scotland meant in itself that Scotland, viewed from the standpoint of English policy, presented a picture quite different from either Wales or Ireland.

The Gaelic-speaking area was all the time shrinking. Of course in the central and west highlands the old tongue was still an important element. When a new parish clerk was elected in the parish of Duthil, on upper Speyside, in 1537, he addressed the parishioners *in eorum ydiomate*,[6] and John Carswell, superintendent of Argyll and bishop of the Isles in the 1560s, found it advisable to provide a Gaelic translation of the Book of Common Order for congregations where the humbler folk, at any rate, knew no English. Sir Thomas Craig was probably going too far when he remarked at the opening of the seventeenth century that 'there is not a single chieftain in the highlands and islands who does not

[1] James Melville, *Autobiography and diary* (Wodrow Soc.), 271.

[2] *Cal. S. P. Scot.* x, 377–8; *Warrender papers*, i, 196; cf. ii, 82, 141.

[3] *Basilikon doron* (Scot. Text. Soc.), ii, 302.

[4] Already by 1200, it seems, the people of Perthshire, unlike those of Argyll, were acquainted with English: *Scotichronicon*, vi, 40.

[5] The Lowlander's contempt for the Highlander and his 'Irish' tongue appears in William Dunbar, *Works* (Scot. Text Soc.), ii, 121.

[6] William Fraser, *Chiefs of Grant*, iii, 269. I am indebted to Mr. D. A. McKay for this reference.

either speak, or at least understand, English',[1] for one of the provisions of the statutes of Iona in 1609 was that men possessed of goods worth 60 cows should send at least their eldest son or daughter to be educated in the lowlands until they could speak, read and write English,[2] and one of the reasons advanced for an education act in 1616 was the desirability of the suppression of 'the Irish language'.[3] At the same time, most men of substance in the highlands were probably already bilingual, and the paucity of deeds and records in Gaelic is so striking[4] as to suggest that there was no difficulty about the use of English for legal purposes. Apart from the central and west highlands, Lowland Scots had hardly a rival. In the reign of James IV an Ayrshire man who believed that Gaelic 'suld be all trew Scottis mennis lede [speech]' had yet to refer to that tongue as a thing of the past—'It was the gud langage of this land'.[5] And in Galloway, where in the later fifteenth century a priest had been considered disqualified for the service of a parish because he did not understand and could not speak intelligibly the language (*ydioma*) of the place,[6] there is no indication of any language difficulty at the Reformation.[7] In the three most northerly Scottish counties, again, the Norn tongue was extinct in Caithness and on the way to extinction in Orkney, and even in Shetland, where the latest deed in the old language belongs to 1607, there is a good deal of evidence that the majority of the inhabitants were now at least bilingual.[8]

Lowland Scots itself, a branch of northern English, had by the sixteenth century no doubt diverged widely from the English of England,[9] but those who used it were all but unanimous that the language which they wrote and spoke was 'English'. John Barbour

[1] Craig, op. cit. 288. [2] *Reg. P.C. Scot.* ix, 28–29. [3] Ibid., x, 671–2.

[4] Donald Mackinnon, *Catalogue of Gaelic MSS.*, 295–6. There are no Gaelic documents among the very ample muniments at Dunvegan Castle: I. F. Grant, *The MacLeods*, 242*n*.

[5] William Dunbar, *Works* (Scot. Text. Soc.), ii, 22.

[6] *Cal. Papal Regs.* xiv, 192–3. I am indebted to Mr. I. B. Cowan for this reference.

[7] W. L. Lorimer, 'The persistence of Gaelic in Galloway and Carrick', *Scottish Gaelic Studies*, vi, vii, shows how little credence is to be attached to statements that Gaelic survived in the south-west through the seventeenth century.

[8] Per Thorsen, 'The third Norn dialect—that of Caithness', *The Viking Congress*, 232–4; Hugh Marwick, *The Orkney Norn*, xxiv; G. Donaldson, *Shetland life under Earl Patrick*, 78–80.

[9] A Spanish visitor said that James IV's speech differed as much from English as Aragonese from Castilian: Hume Brown, *Early Travellers in Scotland*, 39.

(d. 1396), recounting a Scottish struggle for independence, in *The Bruce*, claimed to write 'Ynglis',[1] and the chronicler Wyntoun (d. *c.* 1420) professed to be translating from Latin into 'Inglis'.[2] Even Blind Harry, who in the late fifteenth century narrated the deeds of William Wallace in a work marked by bitter hatred of the English, had no doubt that the Scots shared the language of their enemies, for in describing a Frenchman he wrote:

> Lykly he was, manlik of contenance,
> Lik to the Scottis be mekill governance,
> Saiff of his tong, for Inglis had he nane.[3]

William Dunbar, who flourished at the beginning of the sixteenth century, wrote many of his poems at a time when the marriage of James IV to Margaret Tudor and the accompanying 'treaty of perpetual peace' promised to transform Anglo-Scottish relations, but he was not merely expressing his Anglophile leanings when he spoke of his language as 'oure Inglisch' or when he crudely expressed the superiority of the English spoken in Lothian over that which prevailed in Ayrshire:

> I tak on me ane pair of Lowthiane hippis,
> Sall fairar Inglis mak, and mair governance,
> Than thow can blabber with thy Carrik lippis.[4]

There were, indeed, one or two dissentient voices, but their claims that Scotland had a distinctive language lacked confidence. Thus, the Anglophobe who wrote *The complaynt of Scotlande* (1549), protested that he wrote in 'domestic Scottis langage' but elsewhere spoke of English and Scots as 'of ane langage';[5] and although the provincial council of the Scottish Church decreed in 1552 that a catechism should be set forth 'in our vulgar Scottish tongue',[6] when the Catechism appeared it contained a translation of the Lord's Prayer into 'Inglis'.[7] A little earlier, Gavin Douglas, who translated the Aeneid 'furth of Latyn in our Scottis Langage' or 'in the langage of Scottis natioun', had endeavoured to purge his

[1] *The Bruce* (Scot. Text Soc.), i, 91.
[2] *Original Chronicle* (S.T.S.), ii, 4–5.
[3] *Schir William Wallace* (S.T.S.), 245.
[4] Dunbar, *Poems* (S.T.S.), ii, 10, 15.
[5] *Complaynt* (E.E.T.S.), 16, 106.
[6] Patrick, *Statutes of the Scottish church* (Scot. Hist. Soc.), 144.
[7] *Catechism of John Hamilton*, ed. T. G. Law, 249. A similar uncertainty is reflected in an act and proclamation relating to the vernacular scriptures in 1543, for the act reads 'Inglis or Scots', while in the proclamation 'Inglis' is deleted and 'vulgare' substituted: *Acts parl. Scot.* ii, 415, 425.

forgetting 'our auld plane Scottis', and added: 'I am nocht acquyntit with your Southroun'.[1] But whatever the reason for the predominance of English in the Scottish Church, that predominance was so marked that Scottish ministers must have turned more readily to English than to Scots when they put pen to paper. The compilers of the Negative Confession, in 1581, again, like Knox, drew on themselves the derision of their theological opponents because they 'knapped suddrone' or affected English speech.[2] The Negative Confession was of course a formal document, for which Scots may have been considered unsuitable, and in the more intimate *Autobiography and diary* of the Rev. James Melville we find a language still Scots, though already modified by English influences. Within half a century, however, the anglicizing work of the Reformation had completed its effects on Scottish divines, and Robert Baillie, who was born in 1599, grew up to write pure English.

Already before 1603 the Scottish vernacular was in a fair way to being displaced as a literary language. English seems to have been favoured for verse before it was generally adopted for prose: James VI wrote his *Essays of a prentise* in almost pure English, his *Reulis and cautelis*, in the same volume, in pure Scots, and William Fowler likewise wrote Scots prose and English verse. The prevalence of English was complete in the poets William Alexander and William Drummond. The preference of poets for English was not the result simply of slavish imitation of English models, for Scottish poets used the 'Spenserian' form of sonnet years before Spenser, and it is the more striking that English was so readily adopted for verse, in that there was a long tradition of Scottish vernacular poetry. With prose there was no such tradition; it may be said that Scots prose was extinguished before it had a chance fully to develop and, while official records like the acts of parliament and privy council show how effective and vigorous it was, it was never adapted for use in the loftier subjects like theology and philosophy. In prose works generally there was a change direct from Latin to English, without an intermediate phase of Scots. King James VI's most important prose work, his *Basilikon doron*, has been pronounced to be 'practically the last serious piece of prose writing of which we can certainly say that it was

[1] Ninian Winzet, *Certane Tractatis* (Maitland Club), 118.
[2] *Catholic tractates of the sixteenth century*, 105.

conceived and written down in Scots while that was still a national literary language'; but, while the MS. was in Scots, the printed versions, even that produced for very private circulation in 1599, were in English.[1] One later work, Habakkuk Bisset's *Rolment of courtes*, written in the reign of Charles I, was said by the author to be in 'my awin maternal Scottish langaige', and has been claimed as 'perhaps the latest specimen of literary Middle Scotch existing',[2] but it has little of Scots about it save the spelling. It is plain that about the period of the union of the crowns Scots, as a literary language, passes into a tunnel from which it was to emerge—and then merely for restricted use in verse—only in the eighteenth century; and this could not have happened had the domination of English not been assured by developments before 1603.

The lowering, and finally the disappearance, of the language barrier between the countries would of itself, even had there never been political union, have resulted in the dissemination of English literature in Scotland. Already, in and before the reign of Elizabeth Tudor, the two nations had come to share a common literary heritage. Chaucer of course inspired many Scottish poets and was hailed by William Dunbar as 'reverend Chaucere, rose of rethoris all' and as 'all the lycht' of 'oure Inglisch'.[3] To Scottish poets he was 'our Chaucer'. But it was not only poets to whom he was known. Among the 'tales' mentioned in *The complaynt of Scotlande* 'the taylis of Cantirberrye' have first place,[4] and among the proverbs recorded by a Scottish minister in the early seventeenth century is this: 'Ye are lyk Chaucers cuke, ye seime busier nor ye are'[5]—though the allusion should have been to the serjeant of law. Sir David Lindsay refers to 'Chawceir, Goweir and Lidgate laureate', whose 'sweit sentence through Albione bene song', and mentions that 'Chauceir wrait of Troilus, how that he luiffit Cressida'.[6] Robert Maxwell, bishop of Orkney from 1526 to 1541, had 'ane Inglis buke of Goweir' and David Panter, bishop of Ross from 1547 to 1558, had copies of the works of both Gower and Chaucer.[7]

[1] *Basilikon doron* (S.T.S.), ii, 105, 117. The same practice had been followed in the composition and printing of William Fowler's account of the baptism of Prince Henry in 1594: Fowler's *Works* (S.T.S.), iii, pp. xxvii–xxviii.

[2] *Complaynt of Scotlande* (E.E.T.S.), p. xxvii.

[3] Dunbar, *Poems* (S.T.S.), ii, 10.

[4] *Complaynt*, 63.

[5] M. Anderson, *Proverbs in Scots*, no. 1731.

[6] Lindsay, *Works*, i, 56, 147.

[7] *Innes Review*, ix, 7.

The existence of a common language, or at least the ability of educated Scots to read English, may well have militated against the development of a Scottish printing press. The first experiment in printing in Scotland belongs to the earliest years of the sixteenth century, but until the middle of the century activity was intermittent and, so far as can be judged from the books which have survived, the total production down to 1600 was still very small. Copies survive of no more than thirty books which were printed in Scotland before 1560, and only some 380 items are known to have appeared by 1600.[1] (Besides, two printers who were temporary migrants from south of the Border—Vautrollier and Waldegrave—were responsible for 120 or so out of this small total.) There was necessarily a large import trade, and, while Latin works for scholars seem to have come mainly from the continent,[2] books from England were in a tongue readily enough understood by Scottish readers with less pretension to scholarship. Some imported volumes were not welcome to the authorities: in October 1555 it cost the burgh of Edinburgh 18*d.* 'for hadder [heather] to burn Inglische buiks on the mercat croce';[3] but as the entry is the first in a series dealing with church expenditure no doubt these volumes were heretical. It is hardly likely that John Norton, an English bookseller, would have set up a business in Edinburgh, as he did about 1588, had there not been a market in Scotland for English books, though he proceeded to import directly from Germany so that continental books might be as cheap in Scotland as in England.[4] Whether Scottish works were sometimes printed in England because of the lack of presses at home may perhaps be doubted: it is true that three editions of the Negative Confession were printed in London[5] and that the first edition of Knox's *History of the Reformation* came from Vautrollier's press there, but these issues may have been designed for the English puritan market.

At a time when the vehicle of advanced instruction was so often still Latin, linguistic approximation did nothing of itself to make

[1] Aldis, *Books printed in Scotland before 1700* (annotated copy in Nat. Lib. Scot.).

[2] *Innes Review*, ix, 15. The library of Clement Little, preserved in Edinburgh University, shows an overwhelming preponderance of books of continental origin, and the items published at London were mainly theological—the works of Calvin, Peter Martyr and Bishop Jewel.

[3] *Extracts from records of burgh of Edinburgh*, ii, 363.

[4] *Reg. P.C. Scot.* iv, 459; Calderwood, *History of the Church of Scotland* (Wodrow Soc.), v, 77.

[5] *S.T.C.* 22020–2.

England an educational centre for Scots. Yet, in the eyes of the discerning, English universities already offered certain advantages. It may have been indoctrination with protestant theology rather than the dissemination of southern culture that was in the mind of the duke of Norfolk in April 1560, when he suggested to Cecil that the Scottish hostages for the treaty of Berwick should be placed at Cambridge or Oxford,[1] but the suggestion was in any event consonant with the wishes of some Scots, for Lord Ruthven, father of one of the hostages, asked specifically that his son should be sent to Cambridge 'to be brought up in fear of his Lord God'.[2] It appears further that native education, whatever standards it may have achieved later, was not at that time highly thought of by the more cosmopolitan or far-seeing among the Scots. It is true that as early as 1496 there had been an act of the Scottish parliament ordaining that barons and freeholders of substance should send their eldest sons not only to grammar schools but also for three years to 'the sculis of art and jure',[3] whereas it was not until 1559 that a comparable measure was even proposed in England;[4] but Scottish performance lagged far behind legislative intention. John Major remarked, early in the sixteenth century, that it was a reproach to the gentry of Scotland that they educated their children neither in letters nor in morals,[5] and while Major's views were coloured by his own affectionate memories of his studies at Cambridge it is only right so say that he was so fair-minded as to admit that Cambridge was 'somewhat inferior to Oxford'[6]—a proposition which became more doubtful at and after the Reformation, when most of the intellectual activity was at Cambridge.

In the appreciation of the merits of an English education, as in so much else that contributed to Anglo-Scottish amity, one of the pioneers was John Knox, who insisted that both his sons should have a sound Anglican upbringing, and sent them to school in England; subsequently they both graduated at Cambridge and the elder was beneficed in the Church of England.[7] Adam Bothwell, who, as bishop of Orkney, introduced the Reformation to that diocese and was himself a student of theology, Hebrew and science, recommended that his nephew, John Napier—later famed as the

[1] *Cal. S.P. Scot.* i, 344. [2] Ibid. 325. [3] *Acts. parl. Scot.* ii, 238.
[4] Hist. MSS. Com. *Salisbury*, i, 163; this document is discussed above, 80 sqq.
[5] *Greater Britain*, 48. [6] Ibid. 25–26.
[7] Knox, *Works*, ed. Laing, vi, pp. lxiii–lxv; McCrie, *Knox* (1874), 416; *D.N.B.* *s.v.* Knox, John.

Apologia Ecclesiæ Anglicanæ.
ROMA. I.
Non enim me pudet Euangelii CHRISTI. Potentenia siquidem est Dei, ad salutem omni credenti, &c.
LONDINI
Anno Domini
M. D. LXII.
IAM GEVIN TO EDINBVRGH & KIRK OF GOD BE MAISTER CLEMENT LITIL THAIR TO REMAN. 1580
Virtus pro diuitijs
M L

Flyleaf and title-page of Bishop Jewel's *Apologia*, 1562

nscription on the flyleaf shows that this copy was presented by Thomas Randolph to Lord James ewart, later earl of Moray and regent. The title-page bears a stamp (*inset*) showing that it was subsequently in the possession of Clement Little, an Edinburgh lawyer, and that it passed, with many other volumes from his collection, to the library of Edinburgh University

inventor of logarithms—should be sent 'to the schools' abroad, 'for he can learn no good at home'.[1] Another of Scotland's reforming bishops, Alexander Gordon of Galloway, seems to have agreed with his brother of Orkney about the poor quality of Scottish education: at any rate, he followed John Knox's example of sending his sons abroad, for John Gordon, after studying at Paris and Orleans and spending many years in France, ultimately settled in England as dean of Salisbury,[2] and his brother, Laurence, spent some time at Cambridge.[3] While some Scots clung to the tradition of completing their education on the continent, the Reformation had created difficulties which explain a petition of the general assembly in 1579 that the sending of children to continental universities should be prohibited, because through foreign education 'the youth of this realme is corrupted by pestilent popery'.[4] Some may have thought that Scottish education was sound intellectually as well as safe theologically: it was said of Glasgow under the principalship of Andrew Melville that 'ther was na place in Europe comparable for guid letters, for a plentifull and guid chepe mercat of all kynd of langages, arts and sciences',[5] but this was merely the opinion of the principal's admiring nephew, and Melville's own successor, Thomas Smeton, took a different view. Smeton, who had been a schoolmaster at Colchester before becoming principal at Glasgow in 1580, began to send students to England for advanced studies—Hugh Fullerton, who had graduated at Glasgow in 1578 and who later became minister at Dumfries and Kilmarnock; William Lynne, who had graduated at Glasgow in 1583 and was later admitted to Emmanuel College, Cambridge;[6] John Gibson, who graduated at Glasgow in 1583, then matriculated at St. John's, Cambridge, and was ordained in England;[7] and possibly Archibald Anderson, who matriculated at Cambridge in 1585.[8] But Glasgow students were not alone in pursuing this course: Alexander Hume, after graduating at St. Andrews, proceeded to Oxford in 1580;[9] Thomas Maxwell studied

[1] Mark Napier, *Memoir of John Napier of Merchiston*, 67. [2] *D.N.B.*

[3] *Cal. S.P. Scot.* iii, 530; iv, 504. [4] Calderwood, iii, 446.

[5] James Melville, *Diary* (Wodrow Soc.), 50.

[6] *Cal. S.P. Scot.* vi, 635–6; *Munim. Univ. Glasguen.* iii, 3, 4; Venn, *Alumni Cantab.* iii, 122; Hist. MSS. Com. *Salisbury*, viii, 192.

[7] Register of Presentations (H.M. General Register House), ii, 113, 115; Venn, ii, 211; Hist. MSS. Com. loc. cit. [8] Venn, i, 28.

[9] McCrie, *Melville*, note FFF.

at Trinity College, Cambridge, before being ordained in London in 1578;[1] Thomas Richardson, a native of Leith, graduated B.A. at Oxford in 1575;[2] Patrick Simpson, after graduating at St. Andrews in 1574, completed his education in England and then returned to the ministry of the Church of Scotland;[3] Thomas Davidson, from St. Andrews, was a 'bursar' at Cambridge in 1587;[4] and Richard Murray, who graduated at Edinburgh in 1597, went on to Cambridge for a B.D.[5] When, in 1595, the twelve-year-old earl of Moray proposed to go to 'the schools' in England, he had no difficulty in obtaining his tutor's approval.[6]

There was not as yet a two-way traffic in education in the sense that Englishmen attended Scottish universities. When Andrew Boorde wrote in 1536 from Glasgow 'wher I study and practyce physyk',[7] he did not mean that he was a medical student, and even an internationally famed Scottish scholar like George Buchanan obtained an English pupil only because the English ambassador in Edinburgh sent his son to him.[8] Nor were Scots yet receiving teaching appointments in English universities, though many of them attained distinction as professors on the continent. But Scots were already taking part in the education of Englishmen by teaching in schools in England: David Black was a schoolmaster in England for about seventeen years before he became minister at St. Andrews in 1590;[9] a Scot called Guthrie had an 'academy' at Hoddesdon, Hertfordshire, in 1584,[10] and between 1584 and 1586 one of his masters was William Cowper, afterwards bishop of Galloway;[11] Alexander Hume taught in an English school for some time before becoming rector of the High School of Edinburgh in 1596;[12] Andrew Oliphant had to be 'inhibited to meddle with the teaching of a school at Bridlington without licence' in 1564;[13] Thomas Smeton, as already mentioned, was a schoolmaster at Colchester for some years before he joined the staff of Glasgow university;[14] and in 1563 the town council of Edinburgh was very

[1] Venn, iii, 166.
[2] *Alumni Oxon.; Brasenose Coll. Reg.;* Hist. MSS. Com. *Salisbury*, v, 207.
[3] *Fasti ecclesiae Scoticanae*, iv, 318.
[4] Register of presentations, ii, 4, 33, 72, 75, 167, 169.
[5] *Scots peerage*, i, 226–7; Venn, iii, 229.
[6] *Cal. S.P. Scot.* xi, 530.
[7] *D.N.B.*
[8] *Cal. S.P. Scot.* v, 565.
[9] *Cal. S.P. Scot.* xii, 352; *Fasti eccl. Scot.* v, 420.
[10] James Melville, op. cit. p. xxxvii.
[11] *Fasti eccl. Scot.* vii, 345; *D.N.B.*
[12] McCrie, *Andrew Melville*, note FFF.
[13] Purvis, *Tudor parish documents*, 108.
[14] *Fasti eccl. Scot.* iii, 410; *D.N.B.*

diffident about inviting James White, 'Scottisman in Londone', to become master of their High School, because they understood that he 'hes greit proffit be his scole in Londone, and that he is ane man of excellent lernyng bayth in Lating and Greik tongue'.[1]

When we turn from academic education to other kinds of culture, there is less detailed evidence of Anglo-Scottish contacts. There is some reason to believe that there was a good deal of English influence on Scottish music, perhaps dating from the reign of James III, who patronized an English musician. According to John Major, the English were in their musical accomplishment 'first in all Europe. For though in France or in Scotland you may meet with some musicians of such absolute accomplishments as in England, yet 'tis not in such numbers.'[2] Allowance must, however, be made for Major's habit of upholding the superiority of England over Scotland—he professed even to love the peals of English bells,[3] which so many Scots have been temperamentally incapable of appreciating—and his testimony would not in itself prove that Scotsmen regarded England as a model. It is more significant that Robert Richardson, a Scottish commentator on the rule of St. Augustine, twice brackets England and Scotland together as the only countries where there prevailed certain forms of music which he detested, and from this it may be fairly inferred that the two countries shared a tradition in church music.[4] It seems that Scottish organists had learned from English masters,[5] and there is other evidence that English and Scottish music had the same characteristics.[6] The Scots did not look exclusively to England as a model, for in 1553 a prebendary of Edinburgh was permitted to leave for France as well as England, 'thair to remane for the space of ane yeir . . . to the effect that he may have and get better eruditioun in musik and playing nor he hes';[7] besides, James V patronized Italian musicians[8] and Queen Mary no doubt introduced French musicians. But the music of the court and chapel of King James VI was very largely provided by the Hudson family, five Englishmen

[1] *Extracts from records of burgh of Edinburgh*, iii, 157.
[2] *Greater Britain*, 27. [3] Ibid. 110.
[4] Robert Richardson, *Commentary on the rule of St. Augustine* (Scot. Hist. Soc.), 80, 142.
[5] John McQuaid, 'Musicians of the Scottish reformation' (Edinburgh Univ. Ph.D. thesis, 1949), 9–10.
[6] H. G. Farmer, *History of music in Scotland*, 86–87, 112–13.
[7] *Extracts from records of burgh of Edinburgh*, ii, 176.
[8] *Letters of James V* (H.M.S.O.), 169–70.

who enjoyed continuous royal patronage until the end of the century.[1] They represented a link between English and Scottish music even before they came to Scotland, for one of them had been acquainted with the Scottish priest-composer, Robert Johnson, after he had been exiled to England for heresy.[2] Two of the Hudsons contributed also to the poetry, as well as the music, of the Scottish court.[3] The family appears to have been introduced to Scotland by James's father, Lord Darnley, along with his other English servants,[4] and recalls the important link between England and Scotland which was provided by the family of Lennox, which, owing at first to its place in the royal succession after the Hamiltons and later to the marriage of Darnley to Mary and the accession to the throne of a king who was the heir of Lennox, played a part in affairs out of all proportion to its members' ability and gifts of leadership. Matthew, the fourth earl, Darnley's father, had taken Henry VIII's side against the French interest (and the rival family of Hamilton) in 1544 and, on his forfeiture, was an exile in England for twenty years. His wife, the daughter of Margaret Tudor by the earl of Angus, seems to have been essentially an Englishwoman in outlook and preferences; his brother, Robert, bishop of Caithness, shared in the family's exile and was appointed to a prebend of Canterbury, but returned to Scotland to work for the reformed church in his diocese. English musicians were only one part of the Lennox heritage—an English heritage—on which James VI entered as the heir of his father and his paternal grandfather.

In drama there is less evidence at our disposal than there is in music, though it is well known that English players were finding their way to Scotland, for they appeared in Edinburgh more than once in the 1590s and reached Dundee and Aberdeen in 1601.[5] But much more revealing is the evidence of English influence on what may be called folk drama, shown by the introduction to Scotland of the cult of Robin Hood. As a supposedly historical figure he was already well known in Scotland in the fifteenth century,[6] but his association with popular festivities seems to have been a development of the early sixteenth century. John Major said 'the feats of this Robert are told in song all over Britain';[7]

[1] McQuaid, op. cit. 29, 32 sqq. [2] Farmer, op. cit. 110.
[3] *Works of William Fowler* (Scot. Text Soc.), iii, pp. xix, xx.
[4] R. H. Mahon, *Tragedy of Kirk o' Field*, 117, 137–8 and *n.*; cf. *Cal. S.P. Scot.* ii, 215. [5] A. J. Mill, *Medieval plays in Scotland*, 299–306.
[6] Ibid. 23 and *n*, 25. [7] *Greater Britain*, 156.

Robene Hude and Litil Jhone is one of the very first works known to have been printed in Scotland, and it was one of the 'tales' mentioned in the *Complaynt of Scotlande*; and Robin's archery was proverbial—'Manie speiks of Robein Hude that never schot in his bow'.[1] It is certainly somewhat remarkable that in Edinburgh the festivities traditionally associated with 'the abbot of unreason' or 'the abbot of narent' were transferred to Robin Hood sometime between 1493 and 1518[2] and that in Aberdeen a similar change was made, because by 1508 Robin Hood and Little John had for the time being superseded the 'abbot and prior of Bonaccord'.[3] The celebrations were sometimes so boisterous that there was an act of parliament against them in 1555, but it was not successful in suppressing them.[4] One of the most curious illustrations of the increasing anglicization of Scotland in our own day has been the addition to the Scottish Kalendar of the alien figure of Guy Fawkes, the anniversary of whose attempt to blow up the English parliament (even though with a Scottish king) passed unnoticed in Scotland until less than a generation ago. It may be that the popularity of Robin Hood indicates a similar stage in anglicization in the early sixteenth century.

The Scottish educational system may, even then, have tended to produce more men with professional qualifications than could hope to find lucrative employment in their own poor country. It was not literally true, as was said, that Scottish universities were turning out more divines than could be absorbed at home,[5] for right down to the end of the century there were many Scottish parishes without ministers, but it was true that the level of stipends was at that time so low that the ambitious may well have felt that their noblest prospect was the highroad to England. A contemporary remarked that if richer livings were available in Scotland many 'clerks' would return from abroad:

> Our countrie clerkis beyond the seyis
> Wald draw thame hame from all countries,
> Of Ingland, France and uther partis,
> Quhair thay ar scatterit in all airtis,

[1] M. Anderson, op. cit. no 1128.
[2] *Extracts from records of burgh of Edinburgh*, i, 66, 176.
[3] *Aberdeen burgh records* (Spalding Club), i, 439–40.
[4] *Acts parl. Scot.* ii, 500; *Extracts from records of burgh of Edinburgh*, iii, 107–8; *Diurnal of occurrents* (Maitland Club), 263.
[5] *Cal. S.P. Scot.* vi, 635–6.

Becaus at hame thay will not give
Sufficient quhairon thay may live:
Quhais number as I understand
Is greiter nor is in this land
Of ministeris.[1]

Sir Thomas Craig, writing at the very beginning of the seventeenth century, made some pertinent observations. 'In England', he said, 'there are many wealthy benefices, and the Church has ample revenues; whereas in Scotland the Church is so lean and impoverished that its dignitaries can barely subsist on their stipends'. Craig does, indeed, qualify this statement elsewhere, but he also mentions, in more general terms, that all professional men were apt to feel straitened in Scotland: 'Nowadays in Scotland rewards for learning are few and far between, and they alone keep learning alive (for learning thrives ill on an empty stomach).'[2]

The material attractions of life in the south were considerable, and already in the sixteenth century Scottish clerics had learned—a thing they have never since forgotten—that there were good livings to be had south of the Border. To determine how many Scots were pushing their fortunes in the English Church would require prolonged searches in diverse sources, many of them unprinted, and all that can be done here is to mention the results of some sample investigations and to give a few illustrations. Naturalization in England was technically a requirement before a Scot could be appointed to a benefice, and many Scottish clerks appear in records of naturalization,[3] but it is by no means always possible to show that they subsequently obtained the preferment they sought. Nor is it always easy to trace the further careers of men whom Scottish records show to have emigrated, like John Hoggart, a prebendary of the collegiate church of Restalrig, who went to England in the 1560s.[4] But English diocesan records readily yield the names of Scots who held benefices, and state papers refer to others. In the diocese of Durham ten or more Scots were serving parishes in the 1570s;[5] in the diocese of Lincoln there

[1] John Davidson, *Dialog betwix a clerk and ane courteour* (1573–4), sig. A. vi. *b*.

[2] Craig, op. cit. 329, 332–3, 381, 455.

[3] *Letters of denization and acts of naturalisation* (Hug. Soc.), i; cf. *Scottish Antiquary*, viii, 9–14, 58–61.

[4] Books of assumption (Register House), i, 151*v*.

[5] *Injunctions and other ecclesiastical proceedings of Richard Barnes* (Surtees Soc.), 29, 31, 35–38, 55, 74, 76–77. The inhabitants of Durham and Northumberland

were at least four;[1] there were a few in London;[2] and others are to be found in York, Chester and Devon.[3] Already in the sixteenth century, therefore, we can discern the beginnings of that traffic which was to reach its full fruition in the late nineteenth and early twentieth centuries, when, out of five successive archbishops of Canterbury, three were Scots. The English house of commons really showed remarkable prescience when it recommended in 1607 that Scotsmen should not hold in England an ecclesiastical office entitling them to a seat in the house of lords, the headship of a university college or more than one tenth of the inferior church benefices.[4]

In so far as the motive of the migrants was nothing more than pecuniary advantage, the most appropriate comment on the traffic was made by Bishop John Skinner more than a century ago: the Scottish Church, he said, 'ought to have none for its ministers but those who expect their reward in a better country than England, and from a Master whose kingdom is not of this world'.[5] But it would be less than fair to believe that finance has been the only motive. Major, early in the sixteenth century, had been in no doubt that the standards of church life in England were far superior to those in Scotland—the parish churches were more numerous, they were more richly adorned, the churchmen were of 'an honest walk and conversation' and in general 'the ecclesiastical polity of Scotland is not worthy of comparison with that of England'.[6] As the century proceeded, a comparison between one 'ecclesiastical polity' and another came to have meanings which Major had never dreamed of, but at every stage there were those

complained in 1565 that many churches 'have no priests unless they be vagabond Scots, who dare not abide in their country': G. Baskerville, *English Monks and the Suppression of the Monasteries*, 284–5.

[1] *Lincoln Episcopal records in the time of Thomas Cooper* (Linc. Rec. Soc.), 6, 196, 203, 210, 212, 229. They were John Davidson (Saperton), George Frude (Braceborough), Thomas Maxwell (Scrafield) and John Menzies (Swayfield).

[2] Duncan Anderson, 'minister at Aldersgait' (*Cal. S.P. Scot.* ix, 280); James Coldwell (*Scottish Antiquary*, viii, 11; *Returns of aliens* (Hug. Soc.), ii, 50; *Cal. S.P. Scot.* iii, 541; iv, 38); John Douglas (Newcourt, *Repertorium*, ii, 542, 544); David Inglis (ibid. i, 741, 918–19; Hist. MSS. Com. *Salisbury*, vii, 353–4).

[3] Purvis, *Tudor parish documents*, 140; *Cal. S.P. Scot.* x, 20; Hist. MSS. Com. *Salisbury*, ix, 287.

[4] John Bruce, *Report on the . . . union . . . of England and Scotland* (1799), ii, pp. cxxxiv–cxxxv, cxxxix–cxl.

[5] F. Goldie, *Short history of the episcopal church in Scotland*, 72.

[6] *Greater Britain*, 27–28, 129.

in Scotland who would have subscribed his statement. In the later years of Henry VIII, and in Edward VI's reign, England received as refugees Scots of reforming views who were as yet obtaining no countenance at home. Many of them returned to Scotland after a Reformed Church was set up there in 1560,[1] but others remained, to serve in the Elizabethan establishment—John Mackbrair, for example, a Cistercian monk of Glenluce, who was imprisoned for 'heresy' in 1550 but escaped to England, where he became vicar of St. Leonard's, Shoreditch (1552–53), vicar of Billingham (1565) and vicar of Newcastle (1568);[2] and Robert Richardson, naturalized in 1540, who was presented in 1559 to the living of St. Matthew's, Friday Street, which he held until his death.[3] Such traffic was not entirely one-way, for the successive changes in the ecclesiastical polity of England had more than once sent refugees from England to Scotland, and Christopher Goodman, after associating with Knox at Geneva, became minister first of Ayr and then of St. Andrews.

The 'commodities' which 'might ensue' from 'a uniformity in religion in both these realms' had been perceived as early as 1560,[4] and such 'commodities' were increasingly appreciated as the years passed and a growing number of men in the two countries looked forward to the union of the two crowns, for contemporaries found it hard to conceive of unity without uniformity. The Scottish Reformed Church turned out to be essentially imitative, alike in its theology, its polity and its liturgy. The spark of originality which can be detected at the outset in the Confession of Faith of 1560 and the first Book of Discipline was soon extinguished, and when the initial agreement among Scottish reformed churchmen was disrupted Scottish ecclesiastical affairs were dominated by two factions, each of which was in agreement with a corresponding party in England. Scottish presbyterians maintained the closest relations with the English movement led by Thomas Cartwright and Walter Travers (who were invited to chairs at St. Andrews university in 1580), and the vision of a British presbyterian church, which was to inspire the Westminster Assembly in the 1640s, was present in many minds as early as the 1570s. The

[1] G. Donaldson, *The making of the Scottish prayer book of 1637*, 4.

[2] *Dumfries and Galloway Nat. Hist. and Antiq. Soc. Trans.*, 3rd ser. ix, 158 sqq; Newcourt, i, 687; *Injunctions of Richard Barnes*, 42, 55, 57, 75, 85.

[3] *Naturalisations*, i, 206; *Returns of aliens* (Hug. Soc.), ii, 11; *Sede vacante institutions*, 76; Hennessy, 435.

[4] *Cal. S.P. Scot.* i, 471.

Scottish presbyterians received a great deal of encouragement from ultra-protestant diplomats like Walsingham and William Davison, in whose hands the conduct of Anglo-Scottish political relations lay for so many years. In 1590 Queen Elizabeth, in her capacity as self-appointed governess to the Scottish king, wrote to him: 'Let me warne you that ther is risen, bothe in your realme and myne, a secte of perilous consequence, such as wold have no kings but a presbitrye';[1] but a more superfluous and impudent piece of advice has seldom been given: the peril was one of which James had been aware from almost his earliest awakening to political consciousness, it was a peril against which he had legislated six years earlier, and it was a peril which would never have reached the proportions it did but for the policy of Elizabeth's own servants. Scottish episcopalians, on their side, looked with no less fidelity to Anglo-Scottish uniformity, but they received no encouragement from Queen Elizabeth, who evidently did not regard Anglicanism as a commodity for export, and until the 1590s they received no appreciable encouragement even from English bishops.[2] Yet they could not but regard England with friendly eyes, and when reaction against presbyterianism went so far that it produced views on church order attaching to the 'apostolic succession' an importance which the first reformers had not done, Scots had the additional reason for seeking office in the Church of England that it was now thought to confer orders superior in validity to those conferred in Scotland. It was not until 1610 that Scottish bishops received consecration at the hands of English bishops, but David Lindsay, who was to be one of the bishops consecrated after the succession was thus restored to Scotland, had already in January 1604 sent one of his sons to be ordained by the bishop of London.[3]

It is only right to add that while some Scottish clerks passed into the English ministry because they were reformers, others crossed the Border because they were themselves in need of reform. The most conspicuous example is Paul Methven, who had been educated in England under Bishop Coverdale and had married an

[1] *Cal. S.P. Scot.* x, 350; *Letters of Elizabeth and James VI* (Camd. Soc. xlvi), 63–64.

[2] 'The attitude of Whitgift and Bancroft to the Scottish Church' (*Trans. R.H.S.* 4th ser. xxiv), 95–115.

[3] Ordinations register, Bishop of London, 1578–1628 (London Guildhall Lib. MS. 9535/2) f. 112*a*.

Englishwoman, before becoming minister of Jedburgh in 1560. In 1562 he was deposed for adultery, and took refuge in England, where he seems to have been commended by Coverdale and Grindal to Parkhurst, bishop of Norwich, who welcomed him as 'an excellent preacher' and 'a good and learned man'. The Scottish general assembly was indignant that such a man should intrude himself into 'the ministry of England', but in 1570 Methven obtained naturalization and was subsequently instituted to four benefices in the south-west of England. The peerage writers, ignoring his earlier career, know him only as the respectable prebendary of Wells who was the ancestor of the noble family of Methuen.[1] Another Scottish delinquent was David Wood, minister of Kinghorn, who was deprived at the beginning of 1563 because he had defamed a reader, and disappeared from Scotland. At the end of 1571, 'Davie Woode, Scotte, denyzen and preacher', was said to have been in England for ten years. He seems to have retained the hot temper which had occasioned his expulsion from Scotland, for in 1567 Bishop Grindal described 'Wood the Scotsman' as 'a factious fellow', and his connection with two benefices which he held in the diocese of Lincoln seems to have been none too happy, ending in deprivation in one case and resignation in the other. Apparently, too, Wood's Scottish orders were called in question, but not until 1581, when 'David Wood, a Scottishman pretending himself a minister in the church' was 'by some vehemently suspected to have no calling in that function'.[2] More fortunate was John Morrison. Minister of Whitekirk, he was deprived 'for certain offences' in 1580; but in 1582, in a document which has attained some fame among those interested in the English attitude to non-episcopalian orders, he was licensed by Archbishop Grindal, and became curate of St. Botolph's, Aldersgate.[3]

The attraction of a more opulent country lay, in one way or another, behind many of the intellectual and ecclesiastical

[1] *Cal. S.P. Scot.* i, 680; *Fasti eccl. Scot.* ii, 124; *Zurich letters* (Parker Soc.), i, 131, 167; *Naturalisations*, i, 169; *Register of Matthew Parker*, i, 320; F. W. Weaver, *Somerset incumbents*, 115, 128, 474; Hist. MSS. Com. *Salisbury*, ii, 514; Burke, *Peerage*.

[2] *Reg. kirk session of St. Andrews* (Scot. Hist. Soc.), i, 176–7; Grindal, *Remains* (Parker Soc.), 291; *Lincs. Episc. Records*, 15, 20, 140, 203, 293, 314*n*; *Returns of aliens*, ii, 65; *Acts of P.C.* 1581–82, 71.

[3] Register of presentations (Register House), ii, 46; *Returns of aliens*, ii, 284; Newcourt, i, 916; Strype, *Grindal*, 596.

connections between England and Scotland, and some Scots were candid enough in their admissions of the impression made on them by the wealth of the south. What they thought of London, for instance, is clear enough from the verses, with the refrain 'London, thou art the flower of cities all', in which the English capital was praised by William Dunbar, a poet who was satirical enough about the dirt and untidiness of Edinburgh.[1] Dunbar's admiration for London was shared by Major, though Major, with his wider experience of cities, was less extravagant with his superlatives, and said only that London was 'the largest and fairest in its situation' of all the cities of Britain.[2] Such remarks show plainly enough that the Scottish inferiority complex was not the product of political union, and Dunbar and Major point forward to those denationalized Scots who are the greatest detractors of their own country. But to what extent the wealth of England affected the Scottish economy it is not so easy to determine. According to an observer in 1598, England came fourth in importance among the countries with which the Scots traded—after the Low Countries, France and the Baltic[3]—and, while there are no contemporary statistics to support his estimate, the impression one forms is that trade with the Low Countries and the Baltic, at least, played a greater part in the Scottish economy than did the English trade.

Yet trade with England was not negligible, and often prospered in spite of political hostility. It was so tenacious that in 1550, 1551 and 1552, after Scotland had been drawn completely into the sphere of French political influence, there was a stream of requests for safe-conducts permitting Scots to trade with England.[4] It may well be, too, that the proximity of England would always have nullified Scottish attempts, by legislation,[5] to keep their raw materials at home and encourage native manufactures; certainly Scottish wool was always welcome in England and English cloth welcome in Scotland, whatever the political situation might be and whatever acts of parliament and council might say—and an act of parliament condemned English cloth not only because its import drained coin from the realm but also because it had 'onlie for the maist parte ane outward shaw, wantand the substance and

[1] Dunbar, *Poems* (S.T.S.), ii, 261–3, 276–8. [2] *Greater Britain*, 21.
[3] Hume Brown, *Early travellers in Scotland*, 87.
[4] *Cal. S.P. Scot.* i, 183–90. [5] e.g. *Acts parl. Scot.* ii, 290, 347, 495.

strenth quhilk oftymes it appeiris to have'.[1] In 1546, when the two countries were at war, a correspondent of Cardinal Betoun wrote from Edinburgh: 'as to my lorde Borthuik, he hes sauld his woll to men that hes put it in Ingland, like as all the merchandices and vittales on this syde of the watter [i.e., south of Forth] passis thair'.[2] And in 1555 William Mudy, whose interests were in Orkney and Caithness and who dealt in the produce of the seas, complained to the queen regent, Mary of Guise, that although he had received nearly 1,000 marks for his 'schipe and fysche', he would have received £1,000 from 'the Inglis men' had he been licensed to contravene the statute forbidding the export of victual, fish or salt.[3] Not only was it recognized that England was an attractive market, but the complaints sometimes heard in our own day that the best Scottish produce is diverted to England were anticipated in the sixteenth century. In 1542, in spite of acts of parliament, Englishmen were buying white fish and herring on 'the north cost in Anstruthir, Crail, Sanct Monanys and in all utheris the townis of the cost side . . . and thairby makis exhorbitant derth of the fysche, sua that na freman of burgh can get ane pennyworth tharof'.[4] And in 1551 the Scottish privy council considered that the reason for 'the greit and exhorbitant derth . . . of all kynd of victuallis and viveris' was 'throw the having of the samyn furth of this realme to the partis of Ingland and uthairis', but perhaps overstated its case by going on to protest that English cattle were devouring the good Scots grass: 'the Inglis gudis of Ingland, sik as nolt, scheip and horse and uthairis, ar sufferit to gang and pasture within the boundis of Scotland'.[5] In 1566 there was again a complaint that 'Inglischemen dailie resoirtis and repairis within this . . . realme . . . and . . . frequentis marcattis, fairis and uthiris commoun places, and thair byis in grete quantitie sindrie marchandice guidis, coirnis, bestiall, armoure, wappinis and all uthir geir quhilk thai think necessare for thame',[6] and in 1576 and 1580 we find prosecutions for transporting horses, cattle, sheep, wool and other goods to England.[7]

[1] *Acts parl. Scot.* iv, 119.
[2] *Scottish correspondence of Mary of Lorraine* (Scot. Hist. Soc.), 162.
[3] Ibid. 398.
[4] *Acts of the lords of council in public affairs*, 513.
[5] *Reg. P.C. Scot.* i, 114–15. For similar complaints, see *Acts of the lords of council in public affairs*, 69, 361, 367, 369.
[6] *Registrum secreti sigilli*, v, 2921.
[7] Reg. sec. sig., xliv, 58; xlvi, 115.

It hardly modifies the general picture of England as a market for Scottish goods that Burghley was told in 1590 that horse dealers in the north of England could get higher prices in Scotland than in their own country, especially as his informant was concerned to emphasize the fellowship among the Borderers and 'their accordance of manners'—not, he added, 'that the Skottes take of us, but we of them, as the evill is ever more infectyve than the good'.[1] Concern over the fraternizing of Borderers was nothing new: the *Complaynt of Scotlande* lamented 'the grit familiarite that Inglis men and Scottis hes had on baitht the boirdours, . . . in marchandeis, in selling and bying hors and nolt and scheip, . . . the quhilk familiarite is expres contrar the lawis and consuetudis baytht of Ingland and Scotland',[2] and a Scottish statute of 1587, alluding to 'the mariage of the kingis majesties subjectis upoun the dochteris of the brokin men and thevis of Ingland', forbade Scots to marry 'ony Englishe woman dwelling in the opposite marchis' without express permission.[3] It was more important that no one could fail to see how adventurous Englishmen were to be found in every part of Scotland where commercial profit was to be reaped: they turn up on the farthest fringes of the land—in Shetland, in Mull and in Loch Carron.[4] Some proposals made in 1548, to the effect that England should provide ships to exploit the Scottish fisheries, and that under English auspices harbours should be built and craftsmen imported to give instruction in mining, the working of wool, skins and hides and other trades,[5] anticipate some of the eighteenth-century developments, when, after political union, English capital and English technical skill were applied to the exploitation of Scotland's natural resources. In the sixteenth century, however, little was achieved along such lines, though Bevis Bulmer, an English mining engineer, is heard of in Scotland in 1566,[6] in 1585 Englishmen were in partnership in working Scottish mines,[7] and in 1598 an Englishman called Gavin Smith was associated with James Aitchison, James VI's goldsmith, in the invention of an 'artificial

[1] *Cal. S.P. Scot.* x, 388.
[2] *Complaynt*, 106.
[3] *Acts parl. Scot.* iii, 464–5.
[4] *Reg. P.C. Scot.* ii, 654–5; xiv, 332 sqq.; *Cal. S.P. Scot.* v, 668; x, 503; G. Donaldson, *Shetland life under Earl Patrick*, 53, 70–71. *Reg. sec. sig.* ii, 1665.
[5] *Cal. S.P. Scot.* i, 144–5.
[6] A. L. Rowse, *The England of Elizabeth*, 131, and reference there.
[7] *Reg. P.C. Scot.* iv, 22–23.

pomp' for raising water out of mines.[1] All such activities, however contrary some of them were to the economic thought of the time, brought Englishmen and Scotsmen into contact with each other. There is nothing to suggest that their relations were as a rule other than amicable, and they must have fitted quite well into the pattern of an association between two races conscious of their common religion, common language and common political destiny.

The Franco-Scottish alliance had at one stage been so close that it anticipated Winston Churchill's famous offer of 1940, because French and Scots enjoyed common nationality, in virtue of a concession made by Louis XII and confirmed by later sovereigns down to Louis XIV and in virtue of a reciprocal concession by the Scottish parliament in 1558.[2] The Anglo-Scottish amity never went so far. The articles discussed in July and September 1585 included one to the effect that Englishmen and Scotsmen should be naturalized in each others' country,[3] but this was not incorporated in the treaty as finally agreed. It is, however, something of a curiosity that Elizabethan lawyers sometimes seriously contended that Scots were not aliens in England. The evidence is reviewed in part by Sir Thomas Craig in his *De unione regnorum Britanniae* (1605). He observed that, negatively, there was no English statute depriving Scotsmen of the power to enjoy the same rights and privileges as the English or debarring them from possession of property in England,[4] and went on to cite evidence positively favourable to his claim, beginning with a spurious law of pre-Conquest times whereby Scotsmen, in reward for their services against the Danes, were granted co-citizenship with the English,[5] but proceeding with opinions given in the courts during the sixteenth century. He relates that a Scotsman on trial in the court of king's bench on a charge of rape 'demanded as a foreigner the customary privilege of *dimidietas linguae* . . . that half of the jury should be of his own tongue[6] . . . After consultation the judges of both courts [i.e. both benches] disallowed the Scotsman's claim, and on the ground that a Scotsman had always been held an Englishman and not an alien or foreigner in England, and that the Scottish tongue was not a foreign language'.[7] The same

[1] *Acts parl. Scot.* iv, 176. [2] *Acts parl. Scot.* ii, 507, 515.
[3] *Warrender papers*, i, 194, 201. [4] *De unione*, 335, 339.
[5] Ibid. 341. [6] In terms of 28 Edw. III c. 12 and 8 Hen. VI c. 29.
[7] *De unione*, 347; Sir James Dyer, *Reports* (1714), iii, 303–4.

judgment is alluded to by Peter Wentworth in his *A pithie exhortation to her majestie for establishing her successor* (1598): 'There was a judgment in the King's Bench in Michaelmas term, 13/14 Elizabeth, that a Scot was not to be accounted in England for a stranger, but rather a subject, and also that the language of the Scots is not a strange language, but mere English'.[1] Craig also recounts that 'the question whether Scotland is within the realm of England, or, as the expression is, within the four seas, was keenly argued by John Stowell against George Lord Zouch in the Michaelmas term of the 4–5th year of Queen Elizabeth, as Plowden reports in his *Commentaries*'.[2] The argument in this case was founded on the supposed dependence of Scotland on the Crown of England, but it might have been relevant to cite the phraseology of 25 Edward III stat. 1, which was concerned with the rights of inheritance of children born 'beyond the sea, out of the ligeance of England', and which was possibly ambiguous in its relevance to Scotland.

Whether this evidence supports Craig's conclusion that 'Scotsmen are indisputably English citizens in the eye of the law'[3] is more than doubtful, especially in view of the abundant evidence that Scots did apply for naturalization—not to mention the statute 7 Henry VII c. 6, whereby all Scots not made denizens were to depart the realm. Yet the possession of a common language, which so impressed the judges of the English courts, must have made it hard for Englishmen to regard Scots as foreigners, just as it is hard for us today to regard Americans as foreigners. If Englishmen were prepared to acknowledge the dialect of the Scots to be 'English', strangers from the continent must have seen even less to differentiate one people from the other, and the similarity was such that it enabled Queen Elizabeth to expect the Spanish ambassador to believe her when she laid on the Scots the responsibility for unfortunate incidents: many of the pirates of whom he complained in 1565 were, so she said, Scotsmen (though she added, a little oddly, that they spoke English to avoid being known);[4] and when he complained about the extent of puritan nonconformity in 1566, 'she said that those who disobeyed were certain ministers, not natives of the country, but Scotsmen'.[5] Any

[1] *A pithie exhortation*, part ii, 11.
[2] *De unione*, 348; Edmund Plowden, *Commentaries* (1816), i, 368, 376.
[3] *De unione*, 347. [4] *Cal. S.P. Spanish*, 1558–67, 440. [5] Ibid. 553.

tendency there was to accept the Scots as in practice English citizens would be encouraged by the adaptability of the Scots who settled in England. The author of *The complaynt of Scotlande* looked with a jaundiced eye on the capacity of the Scots for merging their identity in that of the English: 'quhoubeit that there be abufe thre thousand Scottis men, and there wyfis and childir, that hes duellit in Ingland thir fyftye yeir by past, and hes conquest be there industre batht heretage and guidis, yit nocht ane of them dar grant that thai ar Scottis men, bot rather thai man deny and refuse there cuntre'.[1] But Peter Wentworth puts it more objectively: 'The meanest Scottishmen that are setled in England are content to forget their countrie, kindred and parents, and to frame and apply themselves unto us, that they may freelie enjoy their poor condition or calling.'[2] Two examples may be given of Scots of humble rank who settled in England: Isobel Barton, sister of James Barton, of Leith, was married in Newcastle about 1564 to Peter Richardson, 'ex genere nautarum quos *killmen* vocant', and had two sons, one of whom had to obtain naturalization in Scotland in order to inherit the property of his maternal kinsmen; and John Kene, of Alnwick, had similarly to obtain a licence to succeed his uncle, also called John Kene, in property in Selkirk.[3] The history of such self-effacing and adaptable Scots is not easy to trace; but the kind of contribution they could make to the life of England is shown by the careers of Edmund Anderson, one of Queen Elizabeth's chief justices, and William Davison, one of her secretaries, who were both of Scottish descent.

From the marriage of Margaret Tudor to James IV in 1503 a union of the crowns was never a remote contingency, for through the whole century, except during the twenty years between the birth of Elizabeth and the death of Edward VI, there was never more than one life between the Scottish line and the English throne, and more often than not the heir presumptive was north of the Border. And in the course of the twenty years when the Scottish succession did seem more remote there was the proposal for another marriage—of Prince Edward to Mary, queen of Scots—which was meant to hasten union. That project was accompanied in its later stages by an attempt at propaganda on the part

[1] *Complaynt*, 104. [2] *A pithie exhortation*, part ii, 76–77.

[3] *Reg. sec. sig.*, xliii, 30, 40. Thomas Short, of Holy Island, was heir of Thomas Short, armourer in Edinburgh, in 1546: *Reg. sec. sig.* iii, 1438, 1461.

of the English government and by discussion of the material advantages which would accrue from union,[1] and there were serious plans for the amalgamation of the two kingdoms into one kingdom of 'Great Britain'. That term already had a long pedigree, and this was not the first time that the negotiators of a marriage had used it, for in 1474, when a marriage between Cecilia, daughter of Edward IV, and James, son of James III, was proposed, the commissioners had declared their purpose to be the advancement of the peace and prosperity of 'this Nobill Isle, callit Gret Britanee'.[2] Besides, John Major had written his *Historia Majoris Britanniae* (1521) and his use was only one of many instances in the humanistic Latin of the period.[3] The name was in such general currency in the second half of the century that it was the obvious choice when James VI sought a name to designate the united realm after 1603.[4]

The currency of a single name for the island may itself have fostered the concept of a united Britain as a political unit. And it is also significant that there developed a new fashion in historiography which thought in terms of Britain. Major, on the Scottish side, dealt with English and Scottish history in alternate chapters of his *History of Greater Britain*. Polydore Vergil, though professing to write only an *Anglica Historia*, made a serious effort to trace Scottish material and did incorporate a good deal of information about Scottish affairs, not exclusively in so far as they impinged on English history.[5] Hall has a certain amount of Scottish material, though only in connection with Anglo-Scottish relations, but Holinshed, probably stimulated by the great likelihood of the accession of a Scottish king, produced a complete history of Scotland, detached from his English chronicles. Meantime Matthew Parker's church history had been *De antiquitate Britannicae ecclesiae*. By the time Camden wrote a description of Scotland for his *Britannia* it was not difficult to be prophetic, but he derived much satisfaction in his later editions from the 'divine

[1] *An exhortacion to the Scottes to conforme themselfes to the . . . union betweene the two realmes*, by 'James Harryson, Scottisheman' (1547); *An epistle or exhortacion . . . from the Lorde Protectour . . . to the . . . inhabitantes of the realme of Scotlande* (1548); *Cal. S.P. Scot.* i, 140–1, 180–1.

[2] Denys Hay, 'The term "Great Britain" in the Middle Ages' (*Proc. Soc. Antiq. Scot.* lxxxix), 61.

[3] Ibid. 62.

[4] S. T. Bindoff, 'The Stuarts and their style' (*E.H.R.* lx), 199, 201.

[5] Ed. Denys Hay (Camd. Soc. 3rd ser. lxxiv), pp. xix, 40, 238–42.

and heavenly opportunity now fallen into our laps . . . that Britain . . . should . . . by a blessed union be conjoyned.'[1]

The union of the two peoples who formed that united Britain had been in the making for generations, indeed for centuries, before political union was achieved, and the events of 1603 and of 1707 were only two incidents in the long process of creating a united nation. That process is one of which we have not yet seen the end: it is one of which it would not be easy to determine the beginning; but the process was carried a long way forward in the sixteenth century by many factors which contributed to the anglicization of Scotland, and the beginnings of most of the developments which have brought the two nations closer together during their political partnership can be discerned in the period before the union of the crowns.

[1] Camden, *Britain* (trans. Holland, 1610), 'Scotland', p. 3.

XI

Ireland, Elizabeth I and the Counter-Reformation

R. DUDLEY EDWARDS

IN THE preface to the new edition of his Tudor Bibliography, published in 1959, Dr Conyers Read remarked that in the quarter-century since the first edition appeared the significant contributions to Irish history had been relatively more numerous than those to English and that additions have been notable in the history of Roman Catholicism.[1] While this may be due in part to the more recent development of academic history studies in Ireland, it may also owe something to the growing realization that the source material for the history of the Counter-Reformation in Ireland reveals more fully than elsewhere in these islands the conflicts of the traditional cultures with the new forces of Reformation and Counter-Reformation.[2] The impact of that struggle in Ireland in its Elizabethan phase is here briefly surveyed both as it appeared to contemporaries and as it is treated in the literature of the succeeding half-century.[3]

At the end of the fifteenth century Ireland was emerging from an age of isolation. With the exception of brief occasional interventions, Lancastrian and Yorkist kings had left matters in the hands of the aristocratic inhabitants of Anglo-Norman origin, among whom the families of Burke, Butler and FitzGerald were the most prominent. More isolated still were leading Gaelic-Irish families like the O'Neills, O'Briens, O'Donnells, MacCarthys, MacMurroughs, O'Connors, and O'Mores, with whom most of

[1] *Bibliography of British History: Tudor Period, 1485–1603*, 2nd edn., p. xi.

[2] Cf. G. V. Jourdan in W. Alison Phillips ed. *History of the church of Ireland*, ii, 468–9.

[3] Thanks are due to Radio Eireann for permission to include material contributed in a Thomas Davis lecture entitled 'Ireland and Renaissance Europe' on 31 October 1954.

the great English families in Ireland had become allied matrimonially and otherwise. Despite appearances to the contrary, the real conflicts at this time were struggles for the viceroyalty rather than struggles of Irish versus English (or Gael and Gall, as writers in the Irish language describe them). And although the Butlers had supported the Lancastrians, and the FitzGeralds the Yorkists, Henry VII was not able to displace Gerald FitzGerald, eighth earl of Kildare, for more than brief periods.[1] But the anxieties in England over a possible intervention by the Emperor after Henry VIII's marriage with Anne Boleyn led to a decision to re-establish control over Dublin, which in turn caused the rebellion of the FitzGeralds in 1534 after Gerald, the ninth earl of Kildare, who had been summoned to London, was believed to have been executed there.[2] After a slow start an English army defeated the rebels, but mopping-up operations took more than two years.

From 1534 onwards, the new control over Dublin became permanent and a policy of expanding the area obedient to the king's writ began to break up the isolated lordships. Before 1534, fear of the Gaelic-Irish was endemic in the English sphere in Ireland, both in the English Pale proper and in the towns and lordships beyond it; and where this fear was diminished by the great ruling lords like Butler and FitzGerald, who virtually controlled the southern towns, Waterford, Youghal, Cork and Limerick, and considerable hinterlands of Gaelic-Irish and old English, it was because these had to some extent 'gone native', ruled the neighbouring Gaelic chiefs like their kings of an earlier time, and accepted Gaelic Irishmen as minor officials and freeholders in their quasi-palatinates despite legislation to the contrary.[3]

After 1534, it gradually became clear that another conflict of medieval Ireland, between the English by descent and the English by birth, was being revived. The old English, who are so described to distinguish them from the latest arrivals, the English by birth, began to experience the loss of offices which they had come to regard as their exclusive perquisites; and when they also ceased to be employed as a spearhead of resistance to the Gaelic-Irish, they began to adopt a new attitude in which a tendency to

[1] E. Curtis, *History of medieval Ireland from 1086 to 1513*, 2nd edn., ch. xvi.

[2] P. Wilson, *The beginnings of modern Ireland*, ch. ii.

[3] On the relations of the earls of Ormond with Irish lords see D. B. Quinn, *Irish Historical Studies*, i, 83.

oppose the government gradually became endemic. Their conservative outlook made for a divergence between the old English and the Tudor government with its advanced ideas concerning the prerogatives of a prince. During the sixteenth century some of them were to take arms against the new monarch. But until 1534 they were still too inherently loyal to the king of England to do this in alliance with Gaelic Ireland. The revolution in their attitude was only achieved when with the Reformation there arose a new force which could work against other loyalties.

A word may here be said about terminology. There can be considerable confusion about 'English' and 'Irish', terms which often suffer a sea-change in transition from England to Ireland. It is natural to an inhabitant of Great Britain to apply the term 'Irish' indiscriminately to the inhabitants of the neighbouring island. But in the middle ages, 'hibernicus' in Ireland was often understood as equivalent to 'villein' or 'serf',[1] and those of foreign origin domiciled there avoided 'hibernicus' as a description of themselves, insisting that they were English. The term 'Anglo-Irish' is not a satisfactory compromise, since it obscures some of the elements of the situation before the seventeenth century. When Richard II visited Ireland in the thirteen-nineties, he had reported that there was a threefold distinction between 'irrois savages, nos enemis; irrois rebelz; et les Englois obeissantz'.[2] Now 'les Englois' in the late fourteenth century, in Ireland as in England, were beginning to forget their Norman origin, although their upper classes still corresponded in French. Richard II had accepted the distinction ready-made for him by the professional loyalists of Dublin; by them there would be no mention of the ghost of the Angevin empire. Equally there could be no such concept as 'Englois rebelz', although in fact 'irrois rebelz' denoted 'degenerate English' who had gone 'native' while 'les irrois', as outside the law, were *ipso facto* 'savages'. But those loyal to England were themselves divided between the English by birth and the English by descent, who were prohibited by statute from referring to one another as 'English hobbe' and 'Irish dog'.[3] There were then at least these four elements, although as English rebels were from

[1] Curtis, op. cit. app. iv; J. Otway-Ruthven, 'The native Irish and English law in medieval Ireland' (*Ir. Hist. St.* vii), 7.

[2] Curtis, op. cit. 267 and *n*.

[3] Statutes of Kilkenny, 1366: E. Curtis and R. B. McDowell ed., *Irish historical documents, 1172–1922*, 53.

time to time being reconciled, and English by birth becoming English by descent, the elements were far from stable or easily distinguishable. It is often more satisfactory to distinguish zones of allegiance rather than settlement groups. In terms of landed areas, for over a century until the Henrician intervention in 1534, the English in Ireland, who at one time occupied two-thirds of the country, had steadily diminished while their traditional enemies had expanded. Territorially, it has been usual to see a threefold distinction: the English Pale and the towns, the border areas, and the autonomous lordships whether Gaelic or Anglo-Norman. It is customarily accepted that the area directly subject to the control of the Dublin administration in the early Tudor period hardly exceeded a radius of thirty miles from the capital, while beyond this lay an area in which some obedience was rendered fitfully.[1] To say that two-thirds of the country had ceased to be obedient because it had again come under the Gaelic Irish is perhaps an over-statement. But when allowance is made for the substantial elements of Anglo-Norman stock who were regarded as having 'gone native', the fraction which did not usually obey the orders of Dublin is much closer to nine-tenths.

Who then were the natives? Their speech was a branch of Celtic known as Gaelic, and within historic times they had colonized north-west Scotland, re-named after them when their language had displaced Pictish. They had also succeeded in eradicating all but a trace of pre-Gaelic inhabitants. Their historic tradition (*seanchas*) was antecedent in its inaugural date to the Scandinavian and Anglo-Norman invasions (ninth-twelfth centuries); they were the 'Gael', the newer arrivals the 'Gall'. The latter could be divided linguistically in the twelth century into Norse, French and English.

The term 'Irish' in English documents is ambiguous; it is also usually a term of opprobrium, just as the term 'English' is ambiguous and is also a term of essential qualification for full citizenship. In the seventeenth century the terms achieved new denominational significance under the Commonwealth, when the greater part of the land in Ireland was confiscated, and a twofold classification thus became sufficient from the legal standpoint. Under Cromwell all landowning papists were condemned to lose at least one-third of their property; while protestants were normally

[1] D. B. Quinn, 'Anglo-Irish local government, 1485–1534' (*Ir. Hist. St.* i.), 354.

presumed to be loyal, papists were presumed disloyal. In the record of the Cromwellian confiscation the population is classed as 'English protestants' (loyalists) and 'Irish papists' (rebels).[1] Cromwell's law had cut a Gordian knot.

Between the Reformation and the Civil War, however, three elements are often distinguished. These can best be described as the Gaelic Irish (Gael), the old English (sean-Ghall) and the new English (nua-Ghall). The last of these (often also called the planters) included, we must not forget, the official settlers from the time of Henry VIII's expedition against the FitzGeralds. Most of these immigrants had been rewarded with confiscated land, although the plantations proper did not begin until the legislation initiated under Mary, by which lands were confiscated, including those of the O'Mores of Leix and the O'Connors of Offaly, to form, in honour of Philip and Mary, the King's county and the Queen's county.[2]

Although Protestantism did not enter Ireland until the reign of Edward VI, with the extension piecemeal of the changes brought about in England under Somerset and Northumberland successively, religion as a vital distinction took its origin under Henry VIII once it was clear that his opponents among the old English were prepared, like the Gael, to appeal to the pope. Nor were suspicious or self-seeking officials slow to attribute to opponents an addiction to popery, thereby attaching to opposition a semi-religious aura which may not have been an inconsiderable reinforcement to it, even if one sometimes over-emphasized by historians.

With the advent of religious disunity there entered the factor which was in the long run to resolve the old latent conflict of Gael versus Gall; and by the early seventeenth century some of the old English were leading a country-wide, constitutional movement to preserve Ireland from a planter class which threatened themselves quite as much as it did the Gael. The first sign of a changed attitude among the old English had been given when the FitzGeralds of Kildare revolted against Henry VIII. Their leader Lord Thomas, heir to the earldom—known to romantic history as Silken Thomas—appealed for aid to European powers against the Tudor government. To the pope and to the Emperor Charles V

[1] Irish MSS. Com., *The Civil Survey, 1654–6.*
[2] An act for the disposition of Leixe and Offaile, 3 & 4 Ph. & M. c.1.

he represented the struggle as being a crusade against the heretical Henry VIII,[1] thus establishing its claim to be the first revolt within his dominions against Henry's ecclesiastical changes. It was stamped out after a spectacular siege of Maynooth castle, the chief stronghold of the Kildare lordship, in which gunpowder destroyed the sixty-year old hegemony of the FitzGeralds. The fall of the house of Kildare made it clear to Ireland that the English monarchy, for the first time in a century-and-a-half, dominated the political scene.

Immediately afterwards, at a parliament held in Dublin in 1536–37, the authority of that monarchy was proclaimed in church and state. In order to secure the passage of the laws concerned, members had to be threatened with the penalties of treason for alleged complicity with the rebels. The emphasis upon the rebellion is also apparent from the recitals of some of the statutes enacted.[2] When some of the old English resisted proposals to suppress monasteries, this was attributed to belief in a rumour that the defeated FitzGeralds were to be forgiven and restored. The reply was the execution of Silken Thomas (now the tenth earl, his father having died in the Tower) and his five uncles.[3] There was no further opposition to the parliamentary bills; indeed, when the suppressed monasteries were leased by the government, those who profited included Patrick Barnewall, who in the house of commons had questioned the King's power in this matter.[4]

For nearly thirty years thereafter politics moved more smoothly. The government took care to associate some of the old English with the new policy, although the major offices were steadily and increasingly reserved for new arrivals of English birth. The first scheme for planting Ireland was devised by some of the old English interest. If it is mainly from traditionally English spheres that there comes, under Edward VI, evidence of objection to the introduction of Protestantism, yet the old antipathy towards the Gaelic Irish was as strong as the enthusiasm for the Marian restoration of Catholicism and of the pope.[5] In the parliament of 1560, from which Elizabeth I expected resistance to the uniformity legislation, the evidence for opposition is vague; whereas in the

[1] *L. & P. Hen. VIII*, viii, 746; *Cal. S. P. Spanish*, 1534–35, 463; cf. G. V. Jourdan in Phillips, *Hist. of Church of Ireland*, ii, 202.

[2] See especially Irish Statutes. 28 Hen. VIII cc. 3, 8, 14.

[3] R. Dudley Edwards, *Church and state in Tudor Ireland*, 8.

[4] Ibid. 45.

[5] D. B. Quinn, 'Ireland and sixteenth century European expansion', *Historical Studies* ed. T. Desmond Williams, 26.

parliament of 1569 the hostility to the Gaelic Irish is apparent both in the act confiscating most of Ulster after the death of Shan O'Neill and in the resentment displayed towards John Hooker for his implied description of the opposition as 'kerns'.[1]

Archbishop Mathew has argued that by the time of Shan O'Neill the conflict in Ireland had become one between a decaying Celtic society and a vigorous Tudor state of the new Renaissance type.[2] Whether or not the Renaissance was merely a humanistic movement, it cannot be doubted that the Ireland of the Elizabethan age exhibits not one but two elements dominated by a revival of classical attitudes to life. It is not even necessary to bring in the controversy, revived by Dr Mathew, whether Gaelic Irish society, despite its ancient Christian tradition, was no more than nominally dominated by Christian ideas.[3] For while it is an undoubted fact that in the fifteenth century the Gaelic Irish had shown little awareness of Renaissance ideas it is equally clear that in the sixteenth some Gaelic lords were not unaware of the real dangers of Tudor imperialism. For one thing, they had ample opportunities, through their marriage contacts with the old English families of Kildare, Ormond, Desmond and Clanrickard, to learn of the new menace to Irish isolationism. For another, they were ready to imitate the new monarchical pretensions and they employed the new titles and grants of land from Henry VIII to demand from the inhabitants of their own lordships an authority comparable with that of any autocrat in Western Europe.[4] A convenient example of this can be found in the behaviour of the O'Neill of mid-Ulster.

Although Con O'Neill, when created earl of Tyrone, had been obliged by Henry VIII to renounce the pope, his son Shan exploited the English law of primogeniture against Con's successor-designate, Matthew baron of Dungannon, whom Shan insisted was but a suppositious child of Tyrone's.[5] It is even stated by Sir

[1] 11 Eliz. St. 3 c.1; Hooker's diary, Jan-Feb. 1569, in C. Litton Falkiner, *Essays relating to Ireland*, 239. Hooker's dates require checking.

[2] D. Mathew, *The Celtic Peoples and Renaissance Europe: a study of the Celtic and Spanish influences on Elizabethan history*, p. viii.

[3] Ibid. 118, 123; cf. A. L. Rowse, *The expansion of Elizabethan England*, 117. Both these remarkable works should be handled with caution where they deal with Ireland.

[4] The best evidence for the demands of Gaelic lords from their supporters is in the claims put forward to James I, the acceptance of which made possible the confiscation of six counties in 1609. Cf. *Cal. S. P. Ire.* 1606–08, 364, 374; T. W. Moody, *The Londonderry Plantation*, 29.

[5] R. Bagwell, *Ireland under the Tudors*, ii, 2–3.

Henry Sydney that Shan so departed from the custom which reserved the military profession to those of recognized pedigree that he 'armyth . . . the peasantes . . . the fyrst that ever so dyd of an Irishman';[1] Certainly Shan O'Neill became the greatest force in the north. He is said to have boasted that no one dare exercise political authority in Ulster without his approval.[2] Although his success bred an attitude which secured for him the sobriquet 'the Proud', Shan's decision to challenge all who would not accept his rule over Ulster led to his disastrous defeat both by the Gaelic-Irish O'Donnells of Donegal and by the Scottish-Gaelic MacDonnells, who, as much to Elizabeth's dissatisfaction as to O'Neill's, had recently infiltrated the Glens of Antrim.[3] But if Shan's fall implies that his outlook was a provincial one, inevitably involving him in conflict with other local powers (in marked contrast to that of his second successor Hugh, who has been acclaimed as the greatest Gaelic-Irish figure of Renaissance calibre), it is unnecessary with Dr Mathew to write off Shan as a moral and intellectual savage.[4] O'Neill's efforts to secure support from Philip II and Charles IX to maintain him in his independence led him to express himself very much as a man of the new age.[5] By his claim, however specious, to be a crusader for Catholicism against the heretic Elizabeth, he showed his awareness of the necessity, in that new age, of accepting the patronage of one of those rulers if the yoke of the other was to be avoided. And the fact that he has been dismissed as one possessed by a malignant spirit from another world need not blind us to the value of a brief consideration of his career, if only to demonstrate how positively his appeal to ancient rights could stamp him in the eyes of such different figures of the new age as the earl of Sussex, who was employed in Ireland to make parliament Catholic for Mary and Protestant for Elizabeth,[6] and David Wolf the Jesuit Nuncio.[7] Perhaps O'Neill's appeal to

[1] W. F. T. Butler, *Gleanings from Irish history*, 301; cf. G. A. Hayes-McCoy, *Scots Mercenary Forces in Ireland, 1565–1603*, p. ix.

[2] Ibid. 79; Sydney to Leicester, 1 Mar. 1566: S. P. 63/16/35 (*Cal. S. P. Ire.* i, 289).

[3] Bagwell, *Tudors*, ii, 117–18. [4] *Celtic peoples*, 123.

[5] Quadra to Granvelle, 3 Apr. 1562: *Cal. S. P. Spanish*, 1558–67, 235; O'Neill to the cardinal of Lorraine, 25 Apr. 1566: *Cal. S. P. Ire.* i, 299; M. V. Ronan, *The Reformation in Ireland under Elizabeth*, 658–9; Shan is described to France as 'princeps hybernicorum Ultoniae et defensor fidei in partibus Hiberniae': *Cal. S. P. Rome, Eliz.* i, 168–9. [6] Bagwell, *Tudors*, ii, 34–37.

[7] Ronan, *Reformation*, 220; cf. G. V. Jourdan in Phillips, *Hist. of Church of Ireland*, ii, 344*n*.

Elizabeth was neither intellectual nor moral, but Gloriana was rarely averse from using any art to preserve her throne or extend her empire save when her trustiest English subjects insisted upon a more mundane approach to charming foreigners. O'Neill, promised the earldom of Clogher to console him for being denied that of Tyrone (which in the end was to be allowed, at Sydney's instance, to lapse), was not even granted Clogher;[1] and, after his death in Antrim at the hands of the MacDonnells, the parliament at Dublin gracefully conceded the military laurels to Sydney, the viceroy, perhaps in the hope that he would be ready to support the proposal to endow an Irish university.

The need for an Irish university was apparent to upholders of both great sixteenth-century religious movements. As early as 1547 an unsuccessful proposal was elaborated by George Browne, whom Henry VIII had appointed to the Dublin archbishopric in 1536.[2] In 1564 David Wolf was empowered by Pope Pius IV, who seems to have been little in touch with Irish politics, to establish such an institution.[3] The project was evidently one which appealed to town dwellers in Dublin and elsewhere in Ireland, who regarded Oxford or Cambridge as too remote or too expensive. It was in these circumstances that Dublin students at Oxford in 1569 became concerned in a project which attracted an outstanding exponent of the new learning.

One of the more obscure episodes in Irish history is the coming of Edmund Campion, who later became a Jesuit and was martyred in England, executed on a technical charge of treason in 1581. After a short stay in Dublin, in 1570, Campion wrote a history of Ireland which, on 27 May 1571, he dedicated to Leicester.[4] Campion had been a guest in the house of James Stanyhurst, who had been the speaker of the Irish house of commons in the parliaments

[1] The title is not referred to in the printed calendar nor by Bagwell. After Sydney persuaded the Queen to drop the negotiations and authorize him to fight O'Neill, the latter appealed both to France and to the Fitzgeralds of Desmond: Ronan, op. cit. 220; Bagwell, *Tudors*, ii, 102–7.

[2] For Browne's university plan see G. V. Jourdan in Phillips, *Hist. of Church of Ireland*, ii, 247, 448.

[3] J. P. Mahaffy, *An epoch in Irish history: Trinity College, Dublin, its foundation and early fortunes, 1591–1660*, 26, quoting E. I. Hogan, *Ibernia Ignatiana*, 14–15.

[4] 'A historie of Ireland, written in the year 1571 by Edmund Campion sometime fellow of St. John's colledge, in Oxford' in (James Ware), *The historie of Ireland, collected by . . . M. Hanmer, E. Campion, and E. Spencer*. This work is more accessible in the second edition entitled *Ancient Irish histories*, 2 vols, 1809, from which quotations are here reproduced.

of 1557, 1560 and 1569.[1] The work of James's son Richard betrays the traditional hostility of the old English towards the Gaelic Irish. It suggests an almost pathetic anxiety to impress the traveller. The old English must not be regarded as natives. The Irish are barbarous and disorderly, as is clear from the description of their social system. Their literature is undeserving of study. It is almost implied that the only good Irishman is a dead one. And this though the Stanyhurst family had a particular interest in Renaissance culture which should have made such an attitude towards the Gaelic-Irish irrational, if not irrelevant. Of course, everywhere throughout Europe humanism was associated with a tendency to look down upon the vulgar tongues, and this could have appeared to justify a similar attitude towards Irish. Both James Stanyhurst and his son Richard were the authors of works written in Latin. They had almost the same attitude to English as had Sir Francis Bacon when the latter chose Latin as an instrument for his scientific work lest this most important of his studies should be overlooked by scholarly Europe. Whatever the reason Campion was aware of this limitation. While Richard Stanyhurst could complain that the English Pale was 'never in worse plight' than when 'the Irish language was free denisened' within it,[2] Campion's mind was more open and less concerned to point a moral. He admits that he has given the old English viewpoint on the Irish before the Norman Conquest: 'Irish chronicles, although they be reported to be full fraught of lewd examples, idle tales, genealogies . . . yet concerning the state of that wilde people . . . I am persuaded that with choice and judgment I might have sucked thence some better store of matter, and gladly would have sought them, had I found an interpreter . . .' Realizing then that there is a view other than that upheld in Dublin, he decided 'to gather so much as . . . the civil subjects could be content to read, and withall to give a light to the learned Antiquarians of this country birth, who may hereafter . . . supply the want'.[3]

In Campion's history, then, there is one of the first clear links between the new English antiquarianism and Ireland. Reference has already been made to the statute attainting the dead Shan

[1] For the relations of the Stanyhurst family with Campion see St. John D. Seymour, *Anglo-Irish literature, 1200–1582*, ch. x.

[2] Seymour, op. cit. 152.

[3] In his preface 'to the loving reader' concluding 'from Droghedah the 9 of June, 1571'.

O'Neill and confiscating Ulster. This deserves further mention here by reason of its recital from Geoffrey of Monmouth and Giraldus Cambrensis of mythological English stories about Ireland's subjugation in antediluvian days. Similar myths, perhaps from the same sources, emerge in Campion's history, but in its contemporary section it does endeavour to emulate such chroniclers as Polydore Vergil, particularly in its description of the war between Henry VIII and the FitzGeralds. The future martyr is discreet enough to omit all but the most perfunctory references to FitzGerald's appeal to the pope. There is little indication in this history that the question of religion is an issue of importance between the government and the old English. As Campion had been brought to Ireland for employment in the proposed Irish university it may well have been that he hoped in Ireland to find a place within an institution more Catholic than would be tolerated at Oxford.[1] Elizabeth might have turned a blind eye upon a recusant university in Dublin in 1568 while the possibility of her marrying the Archduke Charles was not yet completely abandoned. After the publication in London of her excommunication in May 1570 such a thing was out of the question. It was probably at this stage that Campion went into hiding in Ireland and wrote his history. That work ends with verbatim reports of the prorogation speeches on 12 December 1570 of the speaker and of the viceroy on the university question, in which Sydney explained that poverty alone prevented the government from approving this eminently desirable step. Thereafter Campion, who had been present, appears to have withdrawn into private life before proceeding to a Catholic college on the continent. When a successful scheme for an Irish university emerges in 1592 it is connected with the puritan school at Cambridge. The government may have thought it desirable to allow some of the more extreme members of that university to grapple with the dangers of popery in Ireland in the newly-established Protestant university of Dublin. In the

[1] That Campion hoped his patrons Leicester and Sydney would be permitted to revive the university of Dublin established by Pope John XXII is probable but not conclusive. The evidence is collected in Richard Simpson's biography and summarized in the *D.N.B.* Certainty is probably not now attainable, but it should be noted that Campion's supporters may have included Norfolk, from whose family a MS. copy of the 'Historie of Ireland' has been transmitted. Norfolk and Leicester were involved in 1569 in a move to get rid of Cecil, immediately before the rising of the north, and the consequent papal excommunication of the queen by St. Pius V: Conyers Read, *Cecil and Elizabeth*, ch. xxii.

meantime the other events in this parliament of 1569–71 provoked yet another difference with the English of Ireland.

About the time that Campion wrote his history of Ireland, a number of members of the families of Butler and Fitzgerald are found in arms against the government. These old rivals had been brought together when Sir Peter Carew and other land speculators were permitted by the Dublin government to claim rights over lands against old English and Gaelic possessors, on the plea of ancient titles. For generations it had been contended that the absentee English must give way to the claims of those who stayed on in Ireland and fought against the resurgent Gael.[1] The admission of the claims of Carew and others broke with this old policy. The alliance of Butler and Fitzgerald did not last very long; but it created sympathy within the Pale and a common policy against the government, which made the Irish parliament difficult to deal with except on such questions as the confiscation of the lands of Shan O'Neill and of other Ulster Irish lords. The excommunication of Elizabeth also presented the old English with a dilemma. Hitherto they had rarely been forced to choose between the pope and their English monarch. Now it was being made clear to them that these allegiances were incompatible, and although from time to time the government in Dublin was careful not to press anti-Catholic laws too severely on them, it was evident enough that most of them were no longer trusted; and the sense of indignation against the government grew white-hot when offices were given to the new settlers and old English estates were threatened.

In the parliament of 1569–71 there was, among the members of the house of commons, a figure of interest for the history of parliament in both countries: John Hooker.[2] Professor Butterfield has observed in sixteenth-century writers of English history the two characteristics of an interest in antiquarianism, particularly in legal affairs, and a strong anti-popish attitude in politics.[3] Hooker undoubtedly exhibits the first of these. When Sir Peter Carew sought to establish a title to lands in Ireland which went back for several centuries, he was advised to secure the services of Hooker

[1] H. G. Richardson and G. O. Sayles, *The Irish parliament in the middle ages*, 82, 93, 244, noting laws against absentees in 1297, 1342, 1368, 1380; 28 Hen. VIII c. 3.

[2] For Hooker and the English house of commons see J. E. Neale, *Elizabeth I and her Parliaments, 1559–1581*, 184, 189–90.

[3] H. Butterfield, *The Englishman and his history*, ch. ii.

as the best-known antiquary in Exeter. Hooker came to Ireland, was given free access to the government archives, and established to the satisfaction of the royal council the title of Carew to lands in co. Meath.[1] In the parliament of 1569 Hooker sat for the borough of Athenry and provoked great annoyance by his insistence on teaching the members procedure. His own account of this[2] reads entertainingly to anyone who has suffered similarly from a pedantic bore. But Hooker was more dangerous than academic pedants in that he set himself to teach the Irish parliament the doctrine of absolute obedience to the monarchy: thus he declared, with regard to customs duties, that the Queen was not obliged to proceed by statute but could 'establish the same without any of your consents'.[3] Hooker himself claimed, in recounting this, that he had to be escorted home by valiant friends to escape physical assault by members of the opposition. If Hooker may have impelled the Butlers into rebellion against the crown, it is only fair to add that his interest in antiquities was genuine and that in the next decade he was to edit for Holinshed the chronicles of Ireland incorporating much of the history of Campion,[4] a work on parliamentary procedure,[5] and the twelfth-century works of Giraldus Cambrensis, hitherto only available in manuscript. It seems unlikely that Hooker had much in common with Campion. While Hooker prints Gerald entire, Campion prefers to comment upon him. Hooker's was the new English Protestant world into which he wished to adjust the Irish. Campion, while revealing little of the spirit of the martyr of ten years later, clearly regarded Ireland as somewhat different from England. Unlike Hooker, he can be

[1] Hooker, 'Life of Sir P. Carew' in *Cal. Carew Papers*, 1515–74, pp. lxvii–cxviii. [2] Printed in Falkiner, *Essays*, 237.

[3] J. Hooker, 'The supplie of the Irish Chronicles extended to this present year of our Lord 1586': Holinshed, *Chronicles of England, Scotland and Ireland*, 1808 edn. vi, 344.

[4] The manner in which Hooker secured a copy of Campion's MS. is not clear, but as he had access to the government archives, and as he was licensed to print the statutes, he may have been able to acquire a copy from official sources. For his connection with the statutes see D. B. Quinn, 'Government printing and the publication of the Irish statutes in the sixteenth century' (*Proc. Roy. Ir. Acad.* xlix), (c), 45.

[5] 'The order and usage how to keepe a parlement in England in these daies, collected by John Vowell alias Hooker gentleman, one of the citizens for the citie of Excester at the parlement holden at Westminster, Anno Domini 1571, and Elizabethae Reg. decimo tertio; and the like, used in hir maiesties realme of Ireland': Holinshed, *Chronicles*, 1808 edn. vi, 345–62.

critical of his own imperfections, but then the Exeter antiquary, like Stanyhurst, seemed obsessed with the need to point morals for others.

In 1580 the revolt of Lord Baltinglass created much sympathy in the Pale on the religious issue. In government eyes this rising was of much less interest than the crusade which James Fitzmaurice Fitzgerald had begun the previous year to raise Munster for the pope against the Queen. Baltinglass, who had protested against the unscriptural primacy in religion accorded to a woman, got little direct support and soon fled the country. But many old English families, Nugents, Birminghams, Eustaces, Plunketts, Barnewalls, Wogans and Nettervilles, as well as the Gaelic O'Neills, O'Donnells, O'Rourkes, O'Connors, were suspected of complicity in the movement:[1] and it began to emerge that the Tudor state in Ireland was being opposed in conspiracies of Gaelic Irish led by the old English.

It is from about 1580 that we can date the second stage of the Counter-Reformation's impact upon Ireland. The first had begun with the brief visit of three Jesuits in 1542 and ended with the missionary work of David Wolf. When James Fitzmaurice Fitzgerald arrived he brought with him Nicholas Sanders, one of the few scholarly antiquarians in England on the Catholic side. But Sanders, although he wrote an account of the Reformation in England under Henry VIII,[2] seems to have had little time for anything literary in Ireland except in support of Fitzgerald's war effort, in which he engaged as papal commissary. He perished, probably of exhaustion, in the war in Munster in 1581. It is of interest that this figure of the Counter-Reformation should have had so little literary effect upon Ireland while his opposite number, Edmund Spenser, should have had so much.[3]

Spenser arrived in Munster as secretary to Lord Grey de Wilton, the viceroy who suppressed the rebellion of Fitzmaurice. Spenser's description of those events is well known, and he has put on record his admiration for the missionaries of the Counter-Reformation.[4] He has little to say, however, about their attitude except on such obvious matters as their attack upon Protestantism. But it is clear

[1] *Cal. S.P. Ire.* 1574–85, 238; *Cal. Carew Papers*, 1575–88, ii, 289–90.

[2] Above, 6.

[3] For Sanders' proclamation to his followers see J. H. Pollen, *E. H. R.* vi, 40; *Annals of the kingdom of Ireland by the Four Masters*, ed. J. O'Donovan, v, 1761*n*.

[4] *View of the present state of Ireland*, ed. W. L. Renwick, 209.

enough that at this time some of the missionaries, like Edmund Tanner, were extremely critical of their country because it fell so far below the moral standards taught in the schools of the continent:[1] and this was something which won the respect of Spenser. They were also quite as hostile as he was to certain aspects of medieval Irish tradition.

After the Munster rebellion was crushed the cold war was resumed. In the parliament of 1585 a government programme to increase the penalties on recusant Catholics had to be abandoned for the sake of the subsidy. The lord deputy, Sir John Perrot, was so indignant with the opposition that he wanted its leaders punished.[2] This attitude naturally strengthened the feeling of resentment towards the government, which heightened during the succeeding years. Alarmist reports of the activities of Catholic priests might suggest some complicity on the part of some of the old English in the Spanish Armada. But there is no reliable evidence that the old English in general were prepared to revolt in England's hour of danger. It is in smaller things that their attitude emerges. They listened to the advice that their children's religion could only be safeguarded by sending them to the Catholic schools founded for the Irish in the Iberian peninsula (Alcalá, 1590; Salamanca, 1592; Lisbon, 1593), in the Low Countries (Douai, 1594; Antwerp, 1600), and in France (Bordeaux, 1602).[3] Some, like William Bath, withdrew from the English universities to continental centres where they became notable figures in the world of scholarship.[4] But the old English antipathy to Gaelic life died hard both in Ireland and in exile on the continent. At Trinity College, Dublin—although here the responsibility rests with the members of the new official class who seem to have taken the first steps in its establishment—the anti-Gaelic prejudice existed. It showed itself in reluctance to encourage Irish studies;[5] and the first steps to secure the establishment of a lectureship in the

[1] *Cal. S. P. Rome, Eliz.* i, 467.

[2] Perrot's indignation was all the greater as his regime had been more lenient than that of his predecessor: *Cal. S. P. Ire.* 1574–85, 568; *E.H.R.* xxix, 108.

[3] For a list of these continental Catholic colleges attended by Irishmen see J. F. Kenney, *Sources for early history of Ireland*, i, 29; cf. J. Brady, 'The Irish colleges in Europe and the Counter-Reformation' (*Proc. Ir. Catholic Hist. Comm.* 1957), 1–8.

[4] T. Corcoran, *Studies in the history of classical teaching, Irish and continental, 1500–1700.*

[5] For old English antipathy to Gaelic studies in Trinity, Dublin: J. P. Mahaffy, *An epoch of Irish history*, 204.

Irish language were taken under direction from London. Admittedly some of the new English, like Spenser, regarded Gaelic law and Gaelic poets as hostile to their own interests, but from time to time there is evidence that the government in London was trying to force upon Dublin a more enlightened policy, if only to assist the Church mission to the Gaelic Irish.[1] Queen Elizabeth herself evinced some interest in Gaelic Irish and a catechism was printed under government direction in the early fifteen-seventies.[2] From time to time, efforts were made to secure the translation of the Bible into Irish. In 1602 or 1603 the New Testament was completed and printed.[3] The second generation of Trinity College students produced many religious controversalists, but it also included scholars like James Ussher, William Bedell and James Ware, who did much to encourage the preservation of Irish literary treasures and contributed to the re-interpretation of Irish culture in the atmosphere of Renaissance Europe.

Elizabeth also took a personal interest in Irish affairs because of her mother's connection with the Butlers of Ormond. Her great-grandfather, Thomas, earl of Ormond, had died without heirs male in 1515, and the title of earl of Ormond was for some years conceded to her grandfather, Sir Thomas Boleyn. After Anne Boleyn's disgrace the Ormond title was transferred to the Polestown branch of the family in Ireland in the person of Sir Piers Butler,[4] whose grandson, Black Tom, was brought up at court with Edward VI. Later, Elizabeth showed a marked partiality to him, particularly in his controversies with the earl of Desmond. But the connection of the Tudors with Ireland failed to produce the same emotional attachment to the Crown as that which manifested itself in Elizabethan Wales.[5]

The policy of educating the sons of nobles at court or in the great English houses certainly contributed to the anglicization of Ireland. The process, however, was not always successful, notably in the case of Hugh O'Neill, for whom the grant of the earldom

[1] For Spenser's antipathy to Irish studies see J. F. Kenney, *Sources*, i, 30; cf. his quotations from R. Cowley and T. Smyth, ibid. 30–31.

[2] E. R. McC. Dix, *Printing in Dublin prior to 1601*, 2nd edn. p. 8 and plate VI.

[3] J. T. Gilbert, 'Irish bibliography', ed. E. R. McC. Dix (*Proc. Royl. Ir. Acad.* xxv) (c), 136.

[4] D. B. Quinn, *Ir. Hist. Studies*, i, 373–5.

[5] Antipathy to Elizabeth showed itself, perhaps inevitably, in the rebellions where religion was a main factor; thus O'Rourke was executed at Tyburn for high treason, including insulting the Queen's portrait: Bagwell, *Tudors*, iii, 213–17.

of Tyrone was so long postponed that he had become re-hibernicized before it was finally granted. But when this first effective unifier of the Gaelic Irish commenced his struggle for local liberties against the Queen's government he got few supporters among the townsmen or in the Pale. The religious issues undoubtedly did win for him valuable helpers. Peter Lombard of Waterford, for example, made a spirited defence of O'Neill's Catholic crusade against forces in Ireland which, Lombard argued, had been destructive both of religion and of culture.[1]

On the other hand, distrust of O'Neill in the Pale was almost inevitable once a war situation arose, because many of the Gaelic element among the rebels were prepared to change the English allegiance for a Spanish one. There was a double justification for this; the first was the claim of Philip II to be, by the will of Mary queen of Scots, heir to the throne of England; and the second, the favour shown to Spain by the pope, whose right as overlord had been asserted in the middle ages as resting on the alleged donation of Adrian IV, known as 'Laudabilitur'. Philip II had wisely resigned his claims in favour of his daughter, the Infanta Isabella, who, with her husband the Archduke Albert, governed the Spanish Netherlands, and a group of English exiles, including the Jesuit Robert Parsons, favoured her claim.[2]

Pope Clement VIII was not so pliable. He had not been prepared to accept the Spanish claim to the French throne against Henry IV. And in the case of Ireland, while he agreed to appoint Matthew de Oviedo, a Spanish Franciscan, to the archbishopric of Dublin, he refused, despite strong pressure from Philip III and from Hugh O'Neill, to make Oviedo his papal legate or to excommunicate those who fought for Elizabeth against the Irish Catholic leaders. Philip retaliated by stopping Clement's legate, the Jesuit Mansoni, from leaving his dominions.[3] O'Neill's ally, the papal bishop of Cork, Owen MacEgan, issued a pronouncement which endeavoured to remedy the defect in the pope's brief giving crusader graces to the Irish rebels.[4] But though O'Neill had a following in some of the southern towns, Catholic lords like Barrymore stood

[1] Lombard's support for O'Neill was published posthumously at Louvain in 1632, as *De regno Hiberniae sanctorum insula commentarius*; ed. P. F. Moran, Dublin, 1868; the salient chapters trans. in M. J. Byrne, *The Irish war of defence, 1598–1600*.

[2] L. Hicks, 'Sir Robert Cecil, Father Persons, and the Succession, 1600–1' (*Arch. Hist. Soc. Iesu*, xxiv), 95–139.

[3] F. Jones, *Archiv. Hibern.* xvii, 1–68.

[4] R. Dudley Edwards, *Church and State*, 289.

out against him and insisted that the Queen had never refused liberty of conscience to them, an attitude in which the Queen's military officers encouraged those who deserted O'Neill.[1]

By the time Essex was appointed lord lieutenant in 1599 the conflict over the succession to Queen Elizabeth was under way and was even involving the viceroy. After the death of Burghley in the preceding year, the rivalry between his son Sir Robert Cecil and the royal favourite, Essex, had enabled exiles to speculate upon the chances of an English successor to Elizabeth in preference to either of the foreigners, Isabella or James VI of Scotland. James VI certainly played a masterly hand in the years just before the old Queen's death, and, while Essex had turned to him as the more likely candidate, James had not hesitated to maintain some contact with Hugh O'Neill unofficially in the latter's struggle against the Queen.[2] While some exiled Catholics even hoped that Cecil could be won to an English candidate if not to the Spanish, Hugh O'Neill in negotiating with Essex is reported to have temporarily won over the latter to the Spanish side.[3] As the friend of Essex, his successor Mountjoy was almost inevitably involved in the Cecil-Essex rivalry; though he was able to disengage himself from the Essex conspiracy, Carew's appointment to Munster was made partly because he was Cecil's friend. The defeat of the Spaniards at Kinsale won Mountjoy great renown in England in 1602. He was probably in the confidence of Cecil by the early weeks of 1603, but it was imperative to keep from O'Neill, when he was expected to make his surrender, the news that Elizabeth was dead, since the Irishman's relations with James VI were sufficiently close for him to claim the status of an ally if he had been able to stand out against the victorious Mountjoy for only a few weeks more.[4]

[1] Barrymore's statement (*Cal. S. P. Ire.* 1599–1600, 494–5) as to the position in Munster must be taken in conjunction with evidence on the north of Ulster as indicative of a change in policy in 1600–1 approved at London for the duration of the war. Cf. Docwra's encouragement to northern chiefs: *Cal. S. P. Ire.* 1600–1, 193. There is, of course, plenty of evidence for this. Cf. the direction by the privy council to Carew to distinguish religion and treason, 30 Sept. 1600, and the reply; *Cal. Carew Papers*, 1589–1600, 457, 469.

[2] L. Hicks, 'Cecil, Persons and the Succession' (*Arch. Hist. Soc. Iesu*, xxiv), 95; cf. Hayes-McCoy, *Scots Mercenary Forces*, 314–16.

[3] Archbishop Matthew de Oviedo to Philip III, 24 Apr. 1600: *Cal. S. P. Spanish*, 1587–1603, 655–6.

[4] Mountjoy's secretary, Fynes Moryson, describes O'Neill's emotion on hearing that he had surrendered to a dead Queen: *History of Ireland, 1599–1603*, 1735 edn., ii, 307–8.

Mountjoy was statesmanlike enough to see what was really involved, and worked for a peaceful uniting of the three kingdoms, although he had first to face a new crisis immediately after the Queen's death became known. If the provincial towns of Ireland had not been prepared to ally with O'Neill, many of them had not escaped suspicion of harbouring persons sympathetic with him. Government restrictions upon trade with Spain and France were much resented, and, when the war was over, hostility to the government's policy broke out in these places and Mountjoy was obliged to take swift decisions.[1]

With the Stuart dynasty on the English throne, it is possible to see the end of one phase of European impact upon Ireland. For more than a generation, until after the parliamentarians had dethroned Charles I, the question of a dynastic challenge was not seriously raised in Ireland; but in the first weeks after the death of Elizabeth the situation was far from clear. It is now evident that the seventeenth century was to see a new alignment of forces. At first the succession itself appeared in doubt and the Dublin government feared a revolt of the towns where many municipal authorities had permitted the public restoration of Catholic worship upon news of the Queen's death.[2] The pretext was that the laws against Catholicism had lapsed with the death of the sovereign. From Dundalk to Cork and Limerick, masses were publicly celebrated with the approval of the town magistrates; in some instances in the south there was reluctance to proclaim James VI's accession, despite Mountjoy's timely proclamation at Dublin, which he had taken the precaution to have countersigned, as witness, by O'Neill as earl of Tyrone, among others of the more prominent Irish nobility.[3]

Fearing that the Spanish enemy was about to return, Mountjoy went south with an army prepared to fight to the last man. But rumours of Spaniards were soon dissipated and the opposition of the towns easily overawed, the lord deputy making it plain that Catholic services would not be permitted in public. In the case of Cork city, where an attempt had been made to proclaim the

[1] Mountjoy to Cecil, 19 Apr. 1603: *Cal. S. P. Ire.* 1603–6, 20; cf. the Protestant archbishop of Dublin and the bishop of Meath to James I, 4 June 1603: ibid. 58; A. K. Longfield, *Anglo-Irish trade in the sixteenth century*.

[2] *Archivium Hibernicum*, iv, 232; Mountjoy to Cecil, 25 Apr. 1603: *Cal. S. P. Ire.* 1603–6, 25.

[3] Mountjoy to Cecil, 26 Apr. 1603: *Cal. S. P. Ire.* 1603–6, 27; lord deputy and council to privy council, 4 May 1603, ibid. 32.

Infanta Isabella, a show of force was first necessary.[1] From this time on it became increasingly clear that, since the Gaelic Irish had now submitted, the real strength of Catholic opposition would be found in the passive resistance of the towns.

The Anglo-Scottish rapprochement, which had culminated in the succession of James I, appeared to have conflicting consequences for the political and cultural future of Ireland. To the Dublin administration, as is clear from the public pronouncements of the attorney general, Sir John Davies, it presaged a closer intimacy with the greater island if not the inauguration of a golden reign of peace and wisdom. To the missionaries of the Counter-Reformation, some of whom had great hopes from the son of Mary Stuart, it was quickly followed by the menace of puritanism. Though the open conflict was to be postponed till the Civil War of the sixteen-forties, the infiltration of a Scots calvinistic ministry, particularly into the north-east of Ireland, created a new rivalry between the forces of Reformation and Counter-Reformation which appeared to be developing, though never exclusively, along the racial lines of Gaelic Irish against the English and Scottish combined.[2] The exceptions were mainly due to the survival of a Catholic element among the immigrant Scots as well as to the occasional survivals of old English in such areas as Lecale and Carrickfergus.[3]

If the emergence of the towns as the centres of Catholic strength in Ireland is the first sign of the new phase, the condemnation of Gaelic law is the second. This action of the Dublin government logically followed from the extension of the English legal system throughout the country as a whole. When the Tudor expansion took place it had not been essential to extend the Dublin administrative system so that the Gaelic as well as the old English lordships would be subjected to it. The creation in Munster and Connaught of the presidency system under a local lord president

[1] Mountjoy to Cecil, 4 May 1603: ibid. 36; on events in Cork, J. Walley to Carew, 6 May 1603, and Sir G. Fenton to Cecil, 7 May 1603: ibid. 46; brief relation of the rebellion of the city of Cork: *Cal. Carew. Papers*, 1603–24, 7; declaration of treasons in Cork, and mayor of Cork to Cecil, 26 May 1603: *Cal. S. P. Ire.* 1603–6, 50, 55.

[2] 'A discovery of the true causes why Ireland was never entirely subdued nor brought under obedience of the crown of England, until the beginning of his majesty's happy reign' (1612): H. Morley, *Ireland under Elizabeth and James I*, 213–342.

[3] *Description of Ireland . . . in anno 1598*, ed. E. Hogan.

and council had provided an opportunity, which was not taken, to experiment with a more elastic system. When Hugh O'Neill took arms it had been immediately because of the decision to impose English sheriffs upon the Gaelic lordships in Ulster. In the peace negotiations in 1597 he demanded that his lordship should be made a palatinate.[1]

The condemnation of Gaelic law which is described by Sir John Davies in his very revealing law reports was the judicial confirmation under James of the administrative decision which had precipitated Tyrone's revolt under Elizabeth. Its political complement was the 'flight of the earls'—the disappearance to the European mainland of Tyrone, Tyrconnell, Maguire and other northern chiefs. Had the earls not fled, they might have remained, at home, as loyal to the Stuart cause as were those Gaelic Irish who defended the successors of James I against Cromwell and against William III; but once deprived of their jurisdiction over their own people, the northern lords and chiefs appeared to have come to the conclusion that there could be no understanding with the English government. Admittedly, during the preceding war years, the Gaelic-Irish social system had been breaking down, as many traditional systems had broken down, in the absolutist atmosphere of Renaissance Europe. And with the absolutist authority to which they had become habituated from the days of their military might, they could have become a threat to the suspicious inhabitants of the shired lands. But their flight may have solved the question of the future allegiance of the old English; their disappearance created a new constitutional situation in Ireland. If the new King had attempted to carry out a policy in Ireland similar to that in the Huguenot parts of France under the edict of Nantes, history might have been different. James, however, maintained the Elizabethan attitude towards Ireland.[2] While some of the southern Gaelic

[1] Constantia Maxwell, *Irish history from contemporary sources*, 58–59; *A report of cases and matters in law resolved and adjudged in the king's court in Ireland*, collected by Sir John Davies (trans. Dublin, 1762); cf. Davies to Cecil, Morley, op. cit. 343–80; another version, Kenney, i, 33–34; for O'Neill's appeal for palatine powers see *Cal. S. P. Ire.*, 1597, 476, quoted G. Murphy, *D. O'Connell: nine centenary essays*, ed. M. Tierney, 1.

[2] There are many signs of a readiness to consider applying in Ireland the solution of Henry IV: cf. *Cal. S. P. Ven.* 1592–1603, 551; Bacon's views are well known: 'a toleration of religion (for a time not definite), except it be in some principal towns and precincts, after the manner of some French edicts, seemeth to me to be a matter warrantable by religion, and in policy of absolute necessity': quoted Bagwell, *Tudors*, iii, 475.

lords like the O'Briens of Thomond, habitually more adaptable than the intransigent northerners, accepted the end of Gaelic isolationism, many of the old English in the towns, together with the gentry of the Pale, resented the rise of the planters and the autocracy of Chichester and Strafford. Their opposition became more positive in Ireland where the ideas of the Counter-Reformation were spread generally and they learned to fear the intolerance and the growing strength of puritanism in Britain. James I, for all his attachment to England, failed to realize that, in consenting to the plantation policy, he was handing his Irish kingdom to a new political element who would side with his parliamentary enemies in the civil war of the sixteen-forties.

The parliament of 1613 witnessed a state of affairs in which the old English led a constitutional opposition. Upon such questions as anti-Catholic legislation, the activities of grasping officials and the pressure of arbitrary taxation, an attitude was maintained that was clearly representative of the pre-planter population of the country as a whole.[1] Viewed in retrospect it might appear to be due to a combination of Catholicism and nationalism, but it would be safer to regard it as a reaction of conservative traditionalism to that Leviathan, the new English state, and its exploiting adventurers. Rivalry showed itself among the new English interests, strong in the Ulster counties planted after the flight of the earls, but also in other confiscated areas in the Gaelic fringes of Leinster. The decision of the Stuart government to repress this constitutional opposition, first under Chichester, and later under Strafford, was ultimately to give the chance to some northern Gaelic hotheads to revert to rebellion. Faced with the threat from the puritans in the English parliament to extirpate Catholicism, the old English in 1642 allied with their former Gaelic enemies in the quasi-parliament known as the Confederation of Kilkenny. It was an attempt to draw the rebellious Gaelic element back again to a constitutional position. The Catholic Confederates at Kilkenny took as their motto in the struggle against the Scots and the parliamentarians, *pro Deo, pro rege, pro patria.*[2]

The early-seventeenth century constitutional struggle of the

[1] T. W. Moody, 'The Irish parliament under Elizabeth and James I: a general survey' (*Proc. Roy. Ir. Acad.* xlv) (c), 41.

[2] R. Dudley Edwards, 'Irish catholics and the Puritan revolution', *Father Luke Wadding commemorative volume*, 93–118.

old English in Ireland left its mark upon the interpretation of Elizabethan history. After 1603, Peter Lombard began to work out a scheme by which the Catholic subjects of James I could give their allegiance to the king in temporal matters while maintaining their spiritual loyalty to the pope.[1] From then on an increasing body of Catholic missionaries preached a loyalty to the Stuarts in matters temporal in an endeavour to secure immunity from religious persecution. Lombard's work leads to the beginning of a new writing of Irish history designed to combine the old Irish and the old English in terms of faith and fatherland. David Rothe takes up the same refrain and in his history of Catholic persecution in Ireland gives special attention to the parliamentary struggle against the implementation of Protestantism in the reign of Elizabeth.[2] Their emphasis is thus upon the constitutional tradition, and they have turned away from schemes for foreign invasions or efforts to bring back the northern earls. To a large extent this attitude was due to the continued loyalty to England of many of the old English in the catholic colleges abroad,[3] who convinced themselves that the preservation of Catholicism in Ireland necessitated an abandonment of any ecclesiastical approval of armed resistance to the Stuart government. Some, of course, did not take this view; many, especially of the Gaelic Irish, who went into the armies of Spain and of other foreign powers, continued to favour armed resistance to England. This is notable in the works of Don Philip O'Sullivan Beare, whose history of the Elizabethan wars in Ireland[4] is an attempt to prove that the compromisers had defeated the efforts of the Catholic church to secure Ireland by driving out the Protestant English.

The organization of the Capuchin mission to Ireland, led by Francis Lavallin Nugent,[5] and built in the first instance of personnel from the old English sphere in Ireland, witnesses the strength of the constitutional viewpoint in 1615. Nugent took up much the same attitude as did Lombard after 1609; and in the organization

[1] J. J. Silke, 'Peter Lombard and James I' (*Irish Theol. Quart.* xxii), 124–49.

[2] D. Rothe, *Analecta sacra nova et mira de rebus Catholicorum in Hibernia . . . gestis* (1616–17), ed. P. F. Moran, 1884.

[3] This loyalty is resented as early as 1600 in Spain by O'Neill's son Henry: Hist. MSS. Com. *Salisbury*, xiv, 146.

[4] P. O'Sullivan Beare, *Historiae catholicae Iberniae compendium* (1621), ed. M. Kelly, 1850; trans. in part, M. J. Byrne, *Ireland under Elizabeth*.

[5] My information on Nugent is derived from an unpublished study by the Rev. F. X. Martin, O.S.A., of University College, Dublin.

of this and other new Catholic missions in Ireland, a brake was put upon the claims of the exiled Gaelic lords to exercise quasi-sovereign patronage over the bishoprics in their quondam lordships. But the old English were too weak numerically to stand upon their own, and Nugent, for example, was obliged to qualify his first plan for the Irish province of his order and accept postulants of Gaelic Irish origin. The consequence showed itself after the failure of Strafford's attempt to balance the planters and the papists in the rebellion of 1641 and in the disastrous quarrels between the old English and the Gael at Kilkenny in 1645. Within the Catholic confederation the latter sided with the papal nuncio, Rinuccini, against the royalist plans of the former. The case for the Gael against the Gall was most powerfully stated by the two Capuchins, Richard O'Ferrall and Robert O'Connell, who in their defence of Rinuccini again made the case against the old English as the compromisers who defeated all chance of a united armed resistance in Ireland to the English parliamentarians, and to Cromwell.[1] And when in the long run the constitutional interpretation was re-stated, by men like John Lynch, it is clear that the Renaissance outlook was at work through the Irish seminaries abroad.[2]

Not all the historians were influenced by the new trends. Michael O'Clery and his colleagues, who compiled the 'Annals of the Four Masters' under Franciscan auspices, were concerned to identify Catholicism with the Gaelic tradition, though they avoid any condemnation of the old English.[3] On the other hand, John Colgan and his Franciscan colleagues, in their famous *Acta Sanctorum Hiberniae*, utilized the scholarship of the Renaissance to preserve the traditions of the early Irish saints.[4] And Geoffrey Keating, in writing his history of Ireland, seeks to identify the Gall and the Gael in a common Catholic tradition, with sharp denunciation of men like Spenser, Campion, Stanyhurst, Fynes Moryson and Sir

[1] R. B. O'Ferrall and R. D. O'Connell, *Commentarius Rinuccinianus de Sedis Apostolicae legatione ad foederatos Hiberniae catholicos, 1645–49*, ed. S. J. Kavanagh (Irish MSS. Com.), intro: 'De haeresis anglicanae in Iberniam intrusione.'

[2] Cf. P. J. Corish, 'Two contemporary historians of the confederation of Kilkenny: John Lynch and Richard O'Ferrall' (*Ir. Hist. St.* viii), 217–36.

[3] On the Four Masters cf. Kenney, i, 44*n*, 161.

[4] With Colgan in much of his research was associated Michael O'Clery; it is necessary to consider the annalist separately as regards his more famous achievement. Cf. B. Jennings, intro. to *The 'Acta Sanctorum Hiberniae' of John Colgan* (1948).

John Davies, as critics of the Gaelic Irish.[1] But Keating does not condemn the interpretation by David Rothe of the struggle in Ireland, though he does not continue his history down to the events of his own day, and so avoids more than a general reference to the controversies. Among the Irish warriors who fought abroad, the interest in the pre-Renaissance Gaelic tradition lived still with men like Colonel Somhairle MacDomhnaill of the family of Shan O'Neill's rivals the Scottish MacDonnells of Antrim, for whom Aodh O'Doherty copied the Fianna stories at Ostend.[2]

After the death of Hugh O'Neill at Rome in 1616, the 'Contention of the Bards' suggests that the poets were more alive to the old rivalries of pre-Norse Ireland than to the grim realities of the seventeenth century. Considering it more closely, perhaps Taig Mac Bruaidedha (Bruodin) is also asserting the need to follow the O'Briens of Thomond into a realistic acceptance of the English conquest. If the descendants of Eremhón—the O'Donnells and O'Neills—have gone into exile, their very title to rule Ireland has always been in doubt. The prime English families of Ormond and Desmond are related to the Gael through intermarriage.[3] Thus some of the Irish poets sought to adjust their old patrons to the new Ireland. In the process of adjustment, however, these patrons often abandoned the old traditions, in the desire to establish their credentials with the new allegiance, while few of the planters were prepared to substitute as patrons; and so the old traditions went underground.[4] It was a clash of forces begun under Henry VIII, locked in permanent conflict by the time of Cromwell, which had not become inescapably involved before the end of the first phase —the reign of Elizabeth. In that way, it was left to the conflicting champions of Calvin and of the Counter-Reformation to adjust the ideas of the new Ireland to a Europe re-born in the white heat of the Renaissance.

[1] G. Keating (Seathrún Ceitinn), *Foras feasa ar Éirinn* (*A history of Ireland*), ed. D. O'Connor, 1723; ed. D. Comyn and P. S. Dineen, 1902–14.

[2] *Duanaire Finn*, iii (1954), ed. G. Murphy.

[3] *Iomarbhagh na bhfileadh* (*The contention of the bards*), ed. L. McKenna, 1918. Cf. R. Flower, *Cat. Ir. MSS. in B.M.*, ii. 12.

[4] See the introduction to *Dánta Aodhagáin Ui Rathaille* (*The poems of Egan O'Rahilly*) ed. 1911 by P. S. Dineen and T. O'Donoghue, pp. xv–xxvi.

XII

Elizabethan War Aims and Strategy

R. B. WERNHAM

If the late Queen would have believed her men of war as she did her scribes, we had in her time beaten that great empire in pieces and made their kings kings of figs and oranges as in old times. But her Majesty did all by halves and by petty invasions taught the Spaniard how to defend himself, and to see his own weakness which, till our attempts taught him, was hardly known to himself.[1]

So DID Sir Walter Raleigh, looking back from James I's reign, reflect upon Elizabeth I's conduct of her war against Spain. His criticism won a wide acceptance from later historians and the picture of the war presented in most modern histories is still recognizably of his school.[2] Nevertheless, the criticism was never accepted without some modification and recently the modifications have begun to affect the main lines of the picture. To-day we realize more clearly that the men of war did not all speak with one voice and we are less sure (or less agreed) which of them the Queen should have believed. We also know much more about

[1] E. Edwards, *Life and Letters of Sir Walter Raleigh*, i, 245.

[2] The most complete accounts for the period before the Armada are in J. A. Froude, *History of England* (1910 edn.), xii and Conyers Read, *Mr. Secretary Walsingham and the Policy of Queen Elizabeth*, iii; for the period after the Armada in E. P. Cheyney, *History of England from the Defeat of the Armada to the Death of Elizabeth*; for the naval side in Sir Julian Corbett, *Drake and the Tudor Navy*, ii and *Successors of Drake*, M. Oppenheim's introductions to *Monson's Tracts* (Navy Record Soc.), i and ii, J. A. Williamson, *Hawkins*, *The Age of Drake*, and *The Tudor Age*, and A. L. Rowse, *Expansion of Elizabethan England*; for the continental side, in addition to Cheyney, the prefaces to *Calendars of State Papers, Foreign Series* for 1585–89, J. B. Black, *Elizabeth and Henry IV*, and Sir Clements Markham, *The Fighting Veres*. Professor Mattingly's *Defeat of the Spanish Armada* (1959), a brilliant account, which places this phase of the war firmly in its European setting, appeared just as this essay was finished.

the nature of the Queen's general policy and the limitations of her resources, as well as about the continental, military side of the war; and knowing more, we are inclined to forgive more. How far, then, does Raleigh's verdict still stand?

That verdict contains both an assumption about Elizabeth's war aims and a criticism of her methods. Let us begin by examining the assumption, for until we are sure about the Queen's aims we cannot safely criticize her methods, and it does seem certain that her aims, rightly or wrongly, were not those that Raleigh would have had her pursue. It was never her aim to destroy Spain and 'break that great empire in pieces'. England, she believed, needed a powerful Spain to countervail the power of France. For Elizabeth, and the older generation of her scribes, had grown up in a Europe dominated by the French monarchy and the house of Habsburg. Each of those two great powers far overtopped Tudor England in size, population, resources, and military strength. But, of the two, it was France that until recently had appeared the more dangerous.

In part this was because France was England's traditional rival, the ancient enemy of the Hundred Years' War. But the centre of French power also lay much closer to England than the centre of Spanish power; indeed, during the century before Elizabeth's accession it had come uncomfortably close. The French had conquered Normandy and Picardy from the English and their Burgundian allies. They had absorbed Brittany, another of England's old allies, in 1492. They had captured Calais from Mary Tudor in 1558. They had thus won control of the entire southern coast of the Channel and removed the land-buffer of cross-Channel possessions and satellites that had long cushioned England itself against direct attack. The Tudors had answered by building up English naval power. But in these waters, where the prevailing winds blew from between south and west, nature all too often gave the weather-gauge to the French, all the more since their main bases lay at the far western end in Brittany, while those of England must be at the far eastern end around the Thames estuary, close to the great supply centre of London and the all-important trade route to Antwerp. For sixteenth-century sailing ships, so subject to the weather and so limited in their ability to sail to windward, these were grave handicaps. The same wind that brought the French (or Spaniards) up the Channel might prevent the main

English fleet from the Thames and Medway joining its Channel advanced guard, as in 1545. If the two had already joined, it might pen them in their own harbours, as almost happened in 1588. Or, when they had eaten the west country bare, it might delay their supply ships, as did happen in 1588.

Sea power, therefore, though obviously England's first and principal defence, could not be regarded as an infallible shield. Henry VIII had felt obliged to build a string of coastal castles, from Sandwich and Walmer in the east to Falmouth and Scilly in the far west. Mary and, rather more effectively, Elizabeth herself were constrained to take in hand the reorganization and re-equipment of the antiquated shire levies. More and more those of the southern counties became tied to the defence of England's long southern coastline against invasion from the continent, as the northern levies had long been tied to defence against Scottish incursions. This reduced accordingly the forces available for cross-Channel offensives and further widened the military disparity between England and her great continental neighbour.

When Elizabeth came to the throne the situation had looked even more threatening, for the French were taking station on her northern as well as opposite her southern front. The Scottish queen, Mary Stuart, was married to the French dauphin, who in July 1559 became King Francis II of France. Her mother, Mary of Guise, had reduced Scotland almost to the status of a French province. Her Guise uncles, now all-powerful at the French court and fresh from the capture of Calais, were eager to exploit this situation further. For Mary Stuart, great-grand-daughter of Henry VII, had the strongest genealogical claim to be regarded as heir-presumptive to Elizabeth's throne and, in Roman Catholic eyes, a fair claim to its present possession. Thanks to the national and Protestant resistance to French rule that exploded in Scotland in 1559, to the opposition to the Guises that developed in France, and to the premature death of Francis II, Elizabeth was able to repel these dangers. Even so, at least until Mary Stuart's downfall in 1567 English policy was dominated by the fear that she would seduce the Protestant faction in Scotland, the Guises triumph over their enemies in France, and the two join forces in a Catholic crusade against heretical England. So, for at least the first decade of Elizabeth's reign, France remained the enemy most to be feared, while it was Spanish power and Spanish goodwill (or Spanish self-interest) that restrained the Pope from excommunicating Elizabeth and deterred the French from executing his unspoken censures.

However, within a month of Mary's enforced abdication, the duke of Alva marched into Brussels (August 1567) with a Spanish army that soon grew to 25,000 men. This was a move in Spanish domestic policy rather than in Spanish foreign policy; an expression of Philip II's purpose to be absolute and Catholic master in all the many mansions that were his share of the vast and rambling Habsburg house. He had sent Alva to crush finally the strong opposition that this policy had provoked in his Netherlands territories and to exact vengeance for the late excesses of the Calvinist minority there. However, so drastic a change in the character of Spanish rule in the Netherlands, so marked a shift in the centre of gravity of Spanish military power, could not remain of purely domestic import. The French were alarmed. Elizabeth, who had already manifested anxiety at the absolutist trend of Spanish government in the hitherto harmless and largely self-governing Low Countries, could no more allow those countries to be turned into the main base of Spanish military power than she had been able to let Scotland become a French citadel. To be prepared to defend the Channel against France was burden enough, without having Spanish armies controlling the shipping of Holland and Zeeland, and the resources of Flanders and Brabant, with only the Narrow Seas between them and the nerve centres of English government, sea power, and trade.

Yet this new alarm from Spain did not end anxiety about France. For, as the schemes of Coligny and Louis of Nassau soon manifested and as Anjou's enterprises demonstrated again in the later 1570s and earlier 1580s, the Netherlands rebels were only too ready to call in the French to save them from the Spaniards. And French armies, extending French control of the coast from Calais to Flushing, perhaps to the Ems, would be even more dangerous there than Spanish armies. As Sussex put it: 'the case will be hard with the Queen and with England if ever the French possess or the Spaniards tyrannize in the Low Countries.'[1]

Elizabeth's answer to this double problem was to try to persuade or force Philip II to recall his armies and restore the Netherlands to their status under his father Charles V, with some more tolerable

[1] *Cal. S. P. For.* 1578–9, 120.

settlement of their religious differences.[1] Her pressure took many forms—diplomatic expostulation, the seizure of Alva's pay ships (1568), unofficial aid to the rebels, raids by Drake and his fellows upon Spanish America, a defensive alliance with France (1572), even a wary encouragement of the projects of Coligny and Anjou. The forms varied, but the purpose never changed and it was this that eventually brought England and Spain to war. There were, of course, other causes of quarrel. Disputes over English merchants' privileges in their great Netherlands market; Philip's determination not to let Hawkins and his associates trade to Spanish America; the activities of the Inquisition in Spanish ports and of English privateers and pirates on the high seas; the difference of religion, which among other things made English ambassadors intolerable in Spain and turned Spanish ambassadors into Catholic plotters in England; all these played some part. Yet they would hardly in themselves have brought the two governments to war. Even before Alva's arrival English traders were beginning to escape from their difficulties at Antwerp by moving first to Emden and then to Hamburg; what happened on the Spanish Main or in the ports of the Peninsula was hardly yet of supreme concern to dominant English interests; piracy, long endemic in west European waters, was as much Huguenot and Dutch as English; and Philip II was a far more reluctant crusader than his ambassadors. It was Elizabeth's determination to frustrate his policy in his Netherlands provinces that eventually provoked him to the enterprise of England.

Even so, as long as France seemed capable of independent action and the Netherlands of prolonged resistance, Philip felt compelled to avoid a war with England and to yield somewhat to English pressure. He repeatedly assured Elizabeth that he desired no more power in the Netherlands than Charles V had possessed. In 1573, despite the collapse of France after the St. Bartholomew Massacre, he recalled Alva and opened negotiations with the rebels. The negotiations broke down on the point of religion; the rebellion went on; and the Spanish army remained. But in 1576 the Spanish Fury drove Catholic and Protestant Netherlanders to join to expel it and the Pacification of Ghent, confirmed in the Perpetual Edict (1577) by the new Spanish viceroy, Don John of Austria, gave

[1] This is more fully discussed in my 'English Policy and the Revolt of the Netherlands' in the forthcoming *Anglo-Dutch Studies*.

virtually all that Elizabeth had required. If the Netherlands could have maintained their new-found unity, England and Spain might have kept the peace.

As things fell out, the growing divisions in the United Netherlands from 1578 onwards opened the way for Parma to reconquer the southern and eastern provinces. By the summer of 1585, with William the Silent assassinated and Antwerp fallen, the returned Spanish army looked within striking distance of final victory over the rebels. Just then, Philip II was also able to eliminate all danger of French intervention. Anjou's death and the childlessness of Henry III left the Huguenot Henry of Navarre heir presumptive to the French throne. This drove the Catholic League and the Guises to take arms and place their cause under the protection of Spain. Their victory would make France the client of Spain. It would unite Catholic Europe under Spanish leadership just when Spain was building up the naval forces acquired by the conquest of Portugal (1580) into an Atlantic fleet that its admiral Santa Cruz believed could be made capable of challenging the sea power of Protestant England. If the League succeeded only in establishing itself in those northern and eastern provinces where its hold was strongest, most of the French shore of the Channel would be at the disposal of this gathering Armada. Thus, even if Philip had not decided to send his Armada against England without waiting for Parma to complete his conquest, Elizabeth could not have stood by and allowed the Dutch to be annihilated, the Huguenots crushed, and the French monarchy made a puppet of the Guises. She could no longer avoid open action against Spain.

Yet this brought no radical change in Elizabeth's aims. She could not allow Spain to destroy England's old enemy, France. Yet, equally, she could not afford to destroy her new enemy, Spain. For England could live, had been living, in a world of two Leviathans; she could not live where there was but one. Besides, a restored France that was not matched by a powerful Spain would be, if possible, a worse danger to England than a triumphant Spain that was not matched by a strong France. For the same reasons, Elizabeth must defend Dutch liberties, but would not fight for their independence. An independent Netherlands would be too weak to withstand a restored France and, if they became French, that would give France too dangerous a preponderance. So, while the whole Netherlands must be freed from Spanish armies, restored to their ancient liberties, and given some measure of religious toleration, they must remain under the nominal sovereignty of the king of Spain, who alone had the power to defend them against their mighty neighbour. This was no policy to please Dutch patriots or English puritans, but what happened a century later, when Spanish power did collapse and the Netherlands had to be saved from Louis XIV, suggests that Elizabeth's purpose was not wholly devoid of prescience.

The Queen had, of course, other war aims too. She wanted to secure English merchants and sailors against persecution by the Inquisition in Spanish ports and to obtain recognition of their right to visit the New World and the East 'for lawful trade of merchandise'. Yet while she insisted upon their right to trade freely to places where neither Spaniards nor Portuguese had 'any habitation, residence, or resort', she was prepared to accept in Spanish- or Portuguese-occupied territories any orders that had been in force under the Emperor Charles V or King Sebastian —and incidentally to recognize Philip's conquest of Portugal and deny aid to the defeated claimant, Don Antonio. Moreover, at the Bourbourg negotiations in 1588 her commissioners were instructed to deal with 'the great matter' of the Netherlands 'before any treaty for our own causes'. There seems therefore no real doubt that her principal war aim, the principal cause of the conflict with Spain, was her determination to restore all the Netherlands provinces to their ancient liberties and privileges 'wherein they lived before the persecutions and oppressions begun by the Duke of Alva'; and to secure the Netherlands Protestants 'their liberty of their profession and exercise of the Christian religion'. But nominally Spanish they must remain.[1]

To this policy she clung with extraordinary tenacity. It explains her refusal of the Dutch offer of their sovereignty in 1585, though there were financial and military reasons too. It accounts for her fury in 1586 when Leicester allowed, or inspired, the Dutch to thrust upon him the office of governor-general, with its implication that his mistress was their sovereign and he her viceroy. It was, as we saw, 'the great matter' at the Bourbourg negotiations two years later. It lay at the root of her extraordinary anxiety in 1590 over reports of the Dutch offering their sovereignty to Henry IV

[1] *Cal. S.P. For.* 1587, 475–9.

of France.[1] It explains her lack of enthusiasm in 1596 for Henry IV's dream of a great triple attack upon the Spanish Netherlands and her reluctance to admit the Dutch as equal and sovereign partners with herself and Henry in the Triple Alliance. It gathered new hope from the Archduke Albert's appointment as governor of the Spanish Netherlands and from rumours of his coming marriage to the Infanta, with the Netherlands as her dowry and the hope of a return to the ways of Charles V. It still formed the basis of English policy during the Vervins negotiations of 1598. The absolute refusal of the Dutch at that time and again in 1599 to contemplate even the most nominal return of Spanish overlordship marked its final frustration. In 1585 they might in their weakness have submitted to the Queen's policy if she could have forced it upon the Spaniards. Now, Maurice's victories had made Elizabeth's solution as intolerable to her ally as it was unwelcome to her enemy.

When peace was eventually patched up by James I, the French monarchy had been restored; the Spanish empire, though somewhat reduced, had certainly not been broken in pieces; the Flemish coast had been denied to the French and the Dutch coast to the Spaniard. But the Netherlands had been split in two, into a Spanish south and an independent north. The Spanish army remained in the south and the inclination of the new Dutch Republic towards France looked likely to open the way for new French designs upon Flanders. The Indies, East and West, remained closed by Spanish law to English traders. Altogether, the outcome of almost nineteen years of open hostilities would have disappointed the late Queen as well as her men of war.

How far were these disappointing results due, as Raleigh asserted, to Elizabeth's own faulty methods and half-hearted strategy? We may, I think, agree with that experienced man of war, Sir Roger Williams, that there were three possible ways of bringing the Spaniard to terms. One was to defeat 'his disciplined army', now based in the Netherlands; a second was to attack him 'on the main of Spain or Portugal'; a third was to intercept or interrupt the flow of silver from America, upon which he now

[1] R. B. Wernham, 'The Mission of Thomas Wilkes to the United Provinces in 1590' (*Studies presented to Sir Hilary Jenkinson*), 428 sqq.

largely depended to fit out his armadas, pay his armies, and subsidize the League.[1]

The first course, as almost all the critics agree, was by far the least promising. Willoughby did advocate something of the sort in 1589 and Williams thought it could be done in 1591 by aiding Henry IV. Of them we can only say, with a twentieth-century admiral, 'gallant fellows, these soldiers; they always go for the thickest place in the fence'.[2] If England had had even such continental allies as she was to have in Marlborough's time, it might have been possible to defeat a commander such as Parma at the head of the finest and most experienced army in Europe. Yet it was to take Marlborough six years to drive the French from the Netherlands and Elizabeth's allies were very different from his. Even in the early 1590s the Dutch could rarely extract more than two or three thousand men from their garrisons for offensive operations; and the French kings, though they could periodically get 15,000 or 20,000 into the field, could never keep them there long enough to achieve decisive results. The large armies must have been English; and they must have been large, at least comparable in numbers to the Spanish and so of the order of 20,000 or 25,000 men. Moreover, even if we allow them only half Marlborough's time to clear the Netherlands, this might still have meant sending 50,000 men or more from England in three years. For in sixteenth-century field operations the wastage rate was enormous. The 4,000 men taken to France by Willoughby at the end of September 1589 were down to a bare 1,000 by mid-December;[3] in 1591 Essex's forces dwindled from 4,000 to 380 effectives between early August and early December;[4] and the great Parma himself saw the force that he led so carefully into France in 1592 shrink by a half in five months.[5] Nevertheless, England might possibly have found the troops. More than 50,000 were in fact sent to the Netherlands, France, and the Peninsula between 1585 and 1597,[6] although sending 50,000 spread over twelve years was not quite the same thing as finding 50,000 in three years.

[1] Sir Roger Williams to the privy council, 24 April 1591: S.P. 78/24/79.

[2] J. North, *Gallipoli, The Fading Vision*, 135.

[3] Willoughby to the privy council, 23 Dec. 1589: S.P. 78/20/281.

[4] R. B. Wernham, 'Queen Elizabeth and the Siege of Rouen, 1591' (*Trans. R. H. S.* 4th ser. xv), 172.

[5] L. van der Essen, *Alexandre Farnèse, Prince de Parme*, v, 336–7, 351, 355.

[6] C. G. Cruickshank, *Elizabeth's Army*, 136, where the levies for Portugal in 1589 are put at only 6,000.

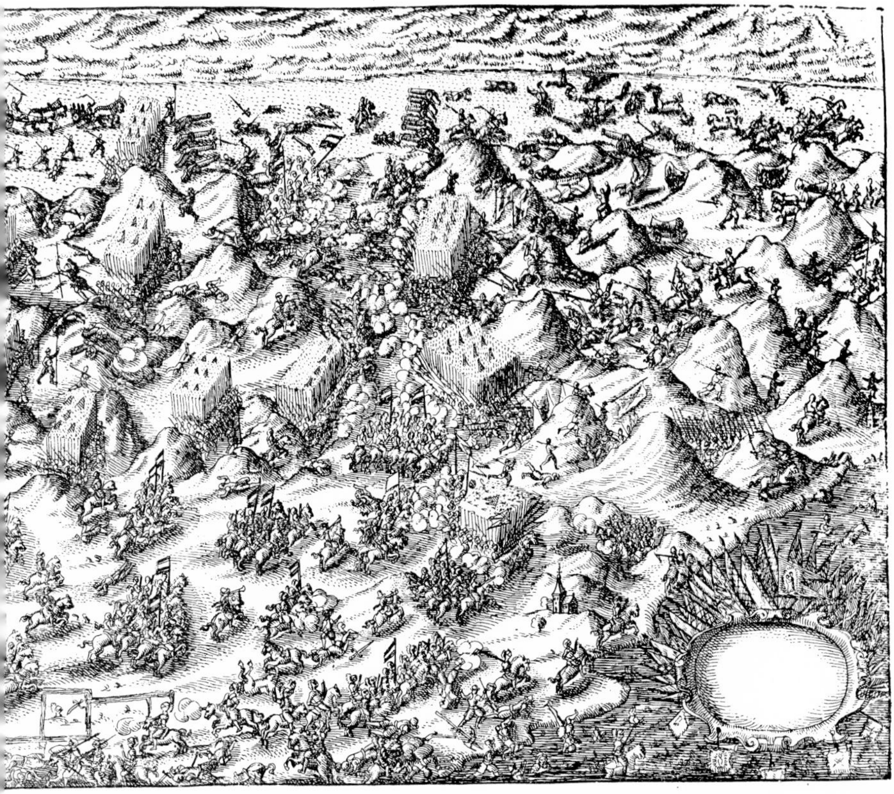

The battle of Nieuwpoort, 2 July 1600

But what about the money? The 6,000 auxiliary troops sent to the Netherlands in 1585 were expected to cost the Queen £126,000 a year, half as much as her whole ordinary revenue apart from parliamentary grants. Yet four-fifths of those troops served in garrisons, where the wastage rate was much lower than in the field. When we remember the shifts used to finance the Portugal expedition of 1589 and the long debates over taxation in the parliament of 1593, we may well wonder how the money could have been raised to keep in the field an army three or four times as big as the forces in the Netherlands.[1] Something approaching it was indeed done in Ireland during the last years of the reign.[2] But by then both French and Dutch were able to look after themselves. Besides, Ireland was virtually a matter of home defence; and in war all things, even national solvency, yield precedence to home defence.

Finally, large-scale land operations were not only militarily unpromising and financially intolerable, they were also, given the Queen's war aims, politically undesirable. She was hardly going to make such efforts to conquer the Netherlands from Spain merely in order to hand them back to Spain. Nor would she bankrupt herself to share her conquests with the French king. Clearly she had reasons not to do more by land in France and the Netherlands.

On the other hand, it is not easy to see how she could well have done less in either country. Imagine the position after the battle off Gravelines in 1588 if the Armada, with many of its 130 ships battered but only seven lost, had been able to find secure refuge and to refit at leisure in Flushing and the Scheldt. In 1585 the Dutch were in such political and military disarray that they could not be relied on to keep Parma out of these vital areas. That was why Elizabeth took them into her protection and sent Leicester over with 6,000 men, and another 1,100 to hold Flushing and Brielle as pledges for the eventual repayment of her expenses. It is true that Leicester's first, and only, campaign was around Zutphen and Deventer, well inland on the Ijsel (1586). But, if the Dutch were to maintain their resistance and preserve their coasts, such a move was very necessary. For Parma already controlled Groningen and a large part of Overijsel and Gelderland. To leave him master

[1] 'These hundred years and more never any king of this land was able to continue wars beyond sea above one year': Dr. Bartholomew Clerk's opinion, 30 Nov. 1586, *Cal. S.P. For.*, 1586–87, 248.

[2] C. Falls, *Elizabeth's Irish Wars*.

of the Ijsel crossings would have left him free to turn the Dutch eastern flank, roll up their main southern defence line along the Maas and Waal, and reduce them to a position more desperate than that of Holland and Zeeland had been in 1575–76.[1] Indeed, Stanley and Yorke's betrayal of the Zutphen and Deventer crossings in 1587 might well have led to just this, had Parma not then been preoccupied and his main forces detained in Flanders by the preparations for the enterprise of England.

It is also true that Elizabeth did several times send extra forces—to Sluys in 1587, Bergen-op-Zoom in 1588, Ostend in 1589. Possibly these would have been less necessary if the original body had been kept at full strength by more regular pay. But, as Sir John Neale has so lucidly shown,[2] the blame for this must rest upon the malpractices of Leicester and his captains rather than upon the Queen's parsimony. Anyway, the need for these extra troops was created far less by deficiences in the English auxiliary forces than by weakness in the Dutch. And that weakness grew largely from the disastrous quarrel between Leicester and the States, with the mutinies in the States' garrisons and the virtual civil war that developed out of it. Elizabeth's fury at Leicester's acceptance of the governor-generalship in 1586 helped a little to launch this quarrel and her peace negotiations with Spain in 1587–88, coming on top of Stanley and Yorke's treasons, helped a good deal to fan it. Yet the ultimate blame for it must lie squarely upon Leicester's flagrant disobedience to her instructions in 1586 and his utter inability either to check waste and corruption in his own forces or to co-operate amicably with the prickly Dutch. It was not the Queen's policy that was at fault. It was her inability to control its instruments. That being so, the extra forces had to be sent and even then Sluys was lost, although Bergen and Ostend were saved and the English garrisons secured Flushing and Brielle.

After 1589 the position was somewhat different. Philip II now turned from the enterprise of England to the enterprise of France. The Spanish army, preoccupied with bolstering up the League, had to stand on the defensive against the Dutch. So, during the next six years Maurice of Nassau was able practically to clear the north-eastern provinces of Spaniards. By thus extending the Dutch

[1] P. Geyl, *Revolt of the Netherlands*, chapter iv.

[2] 'Elizabeth and the Netherlands, 1586–87' (*Essays in Elizabethan History*), 170–201.

eastern flank to the neutral German frontier, he made their main southern defence line along the great rivers almost impregnable. In these operations Sir Francis Vere and part of the English forces had an important share, often in the earlier years providing a half or a third of Maurice's little army. Elizabeth herself had occasional qualms about her troops moving so far from the coast and would have preferred sometimes to see them launched against Brabant or Flanders to relieve Spanish pressure on the king of France. Yet 1585–89 had shown that such operations beyond the Ijsel were essential if the Dutch were to be able to hold their own; and it was largely because of their success that the Queen was occasionally able to draw upon her seasoned troops in the Netherlands for campaigns elsewhere, as for Portugal in 1589, Rouen in 1591, and Cadiz in 1596. Nor was it for want of trying that before 1598 she was unable, in her various negotiations with the States, to find some safe and mutually acceptable way of making such reductions permanent. Moreover, Vere seldom had with him many more than 1,500 English troops. At least two-thirds of the Queen's forces remained all the time in garrison at Bergen, Ostend, Flushing and Brielle, guarding the vital area where Spanish armadas might have refuged and refitted in safety. Antwerp might still point like a pistol at the heart of England, but the pistol could not be loaded.

In France it was much the same story. Here, again, we have only to imagine a Spanish armada with a secure advanced base at Brest and with the French Channel ports at its disposal, to see that Elizabeth could not stand indifferent to the fate of northern France. Admittedly, until Henry III's death in 1589 she did avoid any serious commitment. The outcome of the subsidy that she gave to Navarre's German levy in 1586–87 did not encourage active support of the Huguenots. She therefore fell back upon a waiting policy, trusting that the Huguenots would be able still to defend themselves and that Henry III and the Guises would prove incompatible bedfellows. Meanwhile, by diplomacy she smoothed the way for a Royalist-Huguenot understanding when King and League should eventually fall out. Her reward was that royalist influence kept a footing in Brittany, while most of the Channel ports remained in the hands of governors unfriendly to the Guises —Gourdain at Calais, Bernet at Boulogne, de Chatte at Dieppe. Now we may well doubt how far these flimsy barriers would have sufficed in 1588 if the Armada had adhered less rigidly to Philip II's orders that it must not stop or turn aside until it had made its junction with Parma in the Narrow Seas. But it is hard to see what else Elizabeth could have done without making matters worse. Until Henry III's assassination of the Guises (December 1588) and alliance with Navarre (April 1589), open English intervention could only have been in alliance with the Huguenots and against the French king as well as against the League. It could only, therefore, have plunged the Catholic Henry III more completely under the power of the League and rallied monarchist and patriotic sentiment to the League's cause. Nevertheless, in her French policy between 1585 and 1589 Elizabeth had certainly cut things very fine indeed.

After Henry III's assassination in July 1589, she could no longer afford such risks. For the accession of the Huguenot Henry IV inclined the League to desperate courses and soon brought Spanish armies into France. The parts of France that they were most likely to enter in force were just those that were nearest and most dangerous to England. For the main Spanish army was in the Netherlands and the main strength of the League was in northern France, stretching from Lorraine and the Netherlands frontier in the east, through the great central bastions of Paris and Rouen, to Brittany in the west. This long belt of territory, sympathetic to the League even if not everywhere fully under its control, also isolated the Breton harbours and the Channel ports from the main armies of a Huguenot king who drew much of his strength from beyond the Loire. Already Le Havre had gone over; St. Malo looked as if it might soon follow; and if the Spaniards entered in force, the position of the rest would be perilous in the extreme. Nor were Spanish designs upon them doubtful. The terms on which Philip accepted the formal protectorate over the League in January 1590 showed that he hoped to kill two birds with one stone, to secure a dominating position in France and also advanced bases for an invasion of England.

Here, again, as in the Netherlands, Elizabeth could not depend on her ally to avert the threatened calamity. Henry IV was not likely, except perhaps in defeat, to shut himself off in the Breton peninsula and leave to their fate other provinces of equal or greater importance to his cause. To him the Channel ports were no more vital, except for receiving English aid, than many other towns. He could not therefore be trusted to concentrate his whole attention upon these northern coastal areas, so vital to Elizabeth, so peripheral to him. Nor could he be relied upon, in periods of setback, to resist the temptation to withdraw southwards to the more friendly lands beyond the Loire. If the Channel ports and Brittany were to be kept out of Spanish hands, Elizabeth must herself accept a considerable share in the responsibility for their defence.

She accepted the responsibility and, however reluctantly, during the next five years gave the French king considerable military and financial help. Again, it is true that she usually ended by sending almost twice as much as she had promised. Four thousand men under Willoughby were sent over for a month in September 1589, only to rescue Henry when the League were besieging him in Dieppe. They arrived just after his victory at Arques and stayed with him until early January 1590, their extra pay (so far as they received any) being provided by an additional loan from the Queen. Another 4,000 under Essex, sent for two months in 1591 for the siege of Rouen, were twice replenished, by reinforcements amounting to a further 3,000 men in all, before Parma forced the king to call off his siege in April 1592. Even then the remnant of five or six hundred stayed on under Sir Roger Williams and received another reinforcement of 1,000 men in February 1593, before Henry's conversion to Catholicism brought their final withdrawal in November. The 4,000 sent under Sir John Norris to northern Brittany in May 1591, to counter the Spanish landing in the south, likewise had at least another 7,000 sent over to make good their losses and wastage during the four years that they served in the duchy.

This continual exceeding of estimates was made necessary (as with the Dutch) by the inadequacies of her ally. Whether from genuine weakness or from a feeling that Elizabeth could be safely left to look after parts of France that so deeply concerned her, Henry IV repeatedly failed to do his share and keep his promises. After Arques he and his supporters were indeed so poverty-stricken that he could not have kept the field without Willoughby's troops, and Elizabeth's loans to pay his very mercenary Swiss. With them, he was able to continue operations through the winter in the country between Brittany and the Seine. He was able to straiten Paris and Rouen so severely that in the spring the League was forced to challenge him to battle at Ivry.

His great victory there placed Paris within his grasp and, if he had pressed his siege with speed and vigour, he might perhaps have reduced this main citadel of the League before Parma could move to its rescue. He may have been wise to prefer the slower method of blockade, but it was dubious wisdom then to allow several thousand non-combatants to leave the starving city. Such lenience did more credit to his humanity than to his generalship and gave Elizabeth some excuse for annoyance. For, if Parma had come too late to save Paris in 1590, she would hardly have needed to send Essex and his expedition in 1591 against Rouen. There once more Henry failed to keep his promises, arriving before Rouen in November instead of in August. Thereby he wasted three months of the English troops' service and allowed the enemy ample time to victual and fortify the city. A siege that might have prospered in August grew increasingly hopeless as the winter months dragged past, until in the spring Parma's fresh intervention brought it to an ignominious end. Even Elizabeth must have felt that Henry's conversion a year later was almost worth while if it would end this exasperating game of snakes and ladders. In Brittany it was a similar story. Norris's troops seldom received the support that the French had promised and several times suffered sharply for their ally's default.

It is, therefore, difficult to see how Elizabeth could have done substantially less in France during these years. Without her loans and Willoughby's troops, Henry IV could hardly have campaigned through the winter of 1589; he could assuredly not have kept the field north of the Loire; and it is obvious enough what dangers his withdrawal must have brought to the Breton and Channel ports. To have done less in 1589 could only have made far greater help essential in 1590, when in fact Elizabeth had no troops at all in France. In 1591, without her further financial aid towards the levy of forces in Germany, Henry would again have been hard put to it to face the League and its Spanish allies north of the Loire. Without the additional reinforcement of Essex's expedition, it might well have proved impossible to bring him to centre his operations so near to the coast as Rouen. Elizabeth might perhaps have cut her losses somewhat more sharply on this occasion. She might have recalled the expedition, as indeed she threatened, when winter set in and the prospects of quick success faded. Yet with Parma gathering his *tercios* on the frontier and another Spanish force entrenching itself in south Brittany, it is hardly surprising that she let herself be over-persuaded. And in Brittany Norris's troops did not expel the Spaniards; they merely achieved the minimum requirement of keeping them out of Brest and away from the northern coast.

Now, all of this was surely a most necessary work. As Williams wrote in November 1590: 'without (the Spaniards) possessing either those ports or them of the Low Countries, our dangers cannot be very great.'[1] The converse was equally true. Whatever might be the best way of winning the war, one of the easiest and most obvious steps towards losing it would have been to let the Spaniards occupy the French Channel coast or the Netherlands coast or—worst of all—both coasts together. To prevent such a peril had to be one of the very foremost concerns of English strategy, a concern to which all else had to take second place except the defence of the Queen's own realms against direct invasion. We can hardly blame Elizabeth for giving it that priority. Nor can we fairly accuse her of employing upon these defensive tasks greater force than the tasks required.

Nevertheless, the effort absorbed in necessary home defence and in defending the French and Netherlands coasts was so substantial that it seldom left much to spare for offensive operations. The Queen's sources of revenue were limited and inelastic. Even in peace-time there was little margin between ordinary income and ordinary expenditure—in the last ten years of economical peace before 1585 no more than £300,000 could be put by, including the sizeable windfall from Drake's 1577–80 voyage.[2] Besides this, parliament's grants in 1585 and 1587 brought in, on average, about £72,000 a year in the three years 1586–88. In 1589 it voted twice the usual sum, but spread its collection over four years, so that the annual yield was still about £72,000 until 1593. In 1593 it granted half as much again, again spread over four years (though unevenly) and yielding between £150,000 and £160,000 in 1594 and 1595 and £104,000 in 1596, if we may trust lord treasurer Burghley's figures. It is, of course, true that by twentieth-century standards this taxation was not crushing. What counted, however, was the

[1] S.P. 78/22/121.

[2] For this and the following paragraphs see R. B. Wernham, 'Queen Elizabeth and the Portugal Expedition of 1589' (*E. H. R.* lxvi), 2–5, and references there; Cheyney, op. cit. ii, 244; F. C. Dietz, *Exchequer in Elizabeth's Reign*, 100–1.

steepness of the rise above the average £26,000 a year in the last seven years of peace. Nor must we forget the additional burdens that fell upon the maritime places in ship money and upon all counties in mustering and equipping their trained bands, levying and arming men for foreign service, and watching the beacons. Burghley believed, apparently with reason, that for some places these burdens amounted in 1587–88 to the equivalent of four parliamentary subsidies, twice the number voted by parliament in 1589. And the attitude of the house of commons in 1593, even in 1589, showed that the government must think carefully before stepping up taxation much more drastically.[1]

Yet for long periods the Queen's expenditure on home defence, the Netherlands, and France largely exceeded what parliament voted her. By the time the Armada came, she had already spent £378,000 in three years in the Netherlands and at least £220,000 in two years on preparations at home. Exchequer issues, a mere £149,000 in 1583, rose to £420,000 in 1588. The £300,000 of peace-time savings was almost gone by then, quite gone by 1590. Then from 1589 to 1595, though the Netherlands expenses were brought to or below £100,000 a year, new burdens were shouldered in France. At one point in the autumn of 1591 fully 15,000 English troops were—or were being paid for—on the continent: the 6,000 auxiliaries and 1,000 garrisoning the cautionary towns in the Netherlands, 4,000 in Normandy, and 4,000 in Brittany. During the next twelve months another 6,000 at least were sent to make good the wastage in France. Indeed, between September 1589 and February 1595 the Queen spent approximately £370,000 in aid to Henry IV,[2] substantially more than the entire parliamentary grant of 1589. Finally, from 1598 until the end of the reign greater sums still were swallowed up in Ireland in crushing Tyrone's rebellion.[3]

The Queen could, of course, borrow. Yet privy seal loans usually yielded only around £50,000 and they had to be—or at least, with one exception, were—repaid after one year. Moreover, English lenders, like English taxpayers, grew more reluctant as the war dragged on, while the failure of an attempt to borrow £100,000 in Germany in 1589 showed that foreign loans were hardly to be

[1] J. E. Neale, *Elizabeth I and her Parliaments, 1584–1601*, 298–312.
[2] S.P. 78/24/317; R. Winwood, *Memorials of State*, ii, 29.
[3] £1,924,000 from 1593, according to Hist. MSS. Com. *Salisbury*, xv, 2.

relied upon at all. The drastic expedient of selling crown lands—for example, £126,000 worth between November 1589 and November 1590—added something and there were occasional windfalls from naval expeditions. Yet it is no marvel that Elizabeth normally let those expeditions be financed by a kind of joint-stock partnership with private venturers or that she was always anxious that the war at sea should at least pay for itself. Even by such devices she could not mount offensive operations, costing perhaps £100,000 to fit out (like that of 1589), except in years when her home defence and continental commitments were relatively light.

Indeed, it looks as if finance, almost by itself, can explain much, not only of the character but also of the course of the offensive war, the war at sea. Certainly it emphasizes the attractiveness of a 'silver blockade'. For this idea had the same seductive appearance of simplicity and economy that the theory of 'independent' air power, of long-range strategic bombing, had before it was tested by experience in the war of 1939–45. Spain's power to wage war was coming to depend more and more upon the steady flow of silver from the American mines. That silver had to be shipped across the Atlantic. The Atlantic was, of course, a big ocean, but the silver had to pass certain fixed points within fairly well defined intervals. That from Peru came up the Pacific coast to the isthmus of Panama for transhipment to Havana. At Havana the silver from Mexico was added to it and the whole sent to Spain in ships that could hardly avoid touching at the Azores, the nodal point of the Atlantic sailing routes. Here were the hunting grounds where English sea-dogs might hope to deal Spain crippling wounds and to wage war, not just economically, but at a fabulous profit.

These ideas were already familiar before the war began. They had inspired Drake's raid of 1572; they were probably in his mind five years later; and if the Queen was aware of his intentions, then she herself was presumably ready in 1577 to use this method to put pressure on Philip II and to hamstring Don John in the Low Countries, a long-range version of the seizure of Alva's pay ships nine years earlier. Similar ideas were behind Drake's 1581 plans, to operate under Don Antonio's flag from the Azores. Elizabeth forbade that, but she did allow Hawkins during these years to rebuild and reinforce her navy with ships that had the range and endurance, as well as the fire power, for independent and long-range oceanic operations. The government, as well as the sailors, were obviously thinking along these lines well before the war began.

The question was, just how could this 'silver blockade' be made effective? Hawkins believed that it could be done by naval forces alone, by stationing the Queen's ships, in relays of half a dozen, off the Azores. This might perhaps have worked before the Armada's concentration at Lisbon in the later part of 1587 or again in 1589–90 before Spain had recovered from the 1588 disaster. But in 1585 Elizabeth preferred to loose Drake against Spanish America. In 1586 she did send Hawkins to sea with five of her ships, but the Babington plot and the uncertainty about French and Scottish reactions to the impending proceedings against Mary Stuart caused her to divert him to patrolling the Channel, unluckily just when the silver ships were coming home to Spain. In 1587 it was Drake who went out and by then his first task had to be to delay and disrupt the Armada's concentration. In 1589 the Queen again put her money on Drake. In 1590, however, Hawkins and Frobisher did cruise off Spain and off the Azores with half the royal ships (not the six which he had asked for, but thirteen) and did force Philip to order the year's silver shipment to be held in America. But in 1591 the Spaniards, with twenty good fighting ships and thirty or more other vessels, swept down upon the Azores, captured the *Revenge*, and forced Lord Thomas Howard and his five remaining Queen's ships off their station. 1590 had shown that Philip could manage without his silver for a year; 1591, that he could again provide an escort for it too powerful to be faced by such squadrons as Hawkins envisaged. In 1592 the lesson of 1591 was repeated, though this time a smaller English squadron got away without loss and was lucky enough to capture the rich carrack *Madre de Dios* before the enemy came down. After this, in 1593 and 1594, the Queen virtually gave up the attempt. And in 1595–96 Drake's and Hawkins's last expedition learned that what was true at the Azores was true also in the Indies. For on its journey homeward, after the deaths of the two commanders, it had to claw its way out of the Caribbean past a force sent from Spain against it and it owed its escape as much to its ships' superior sailing qualities as to their fire power. So long as Spain had a powerful fleet in being, an effective silver blockade was not possible unless forces comparable to Spain's could be sent to maintain it.

Such forces could hardly be spared. For the Spanish fleet, based on Lisbon, Cadiz, or Ferrol, could at its own time just as well strike northwards to the Channel to cover an invasion of England as westwards to the Azores to cover the silver ships. Elizabeth therefore felt compelled to keep comparable forces in home waters, ready to go quickly to stations where they could intercept such a northward move; and as Spain's naval power grew, 'comparable forces' came to mean the bulk of her navy. Her insistence upon keeping the Channel adequately guarded has often been ridiculed as feminine timidity. Yet even Hawkins's plan would have made half the royal navy, the essential fighting force of the nation, unavailable for home defence.[1] Could any responsible English statesman before 1588 have staked his country's security upon the assumption that one English warship could deal decisively with two Spaniards? Or, indeed, after 1588? For, after all, the Armada of 1588, by its strict adherence to Philip's orders, considerably eased the English navy's task of shepherding it past the danger points. It did not attempt to land in the far west. It averted its eyes from the chance to fall upon Howard's ships as they edged painfully out of Plymouth against the wind. It made no move towards Torbay or Le Havre. Nevertheless, though harried by the full might of English sea power and 'shuffled' past the Isle of Wight, it plodded stolidly up the Channel in unbroken formation until the fireships off Calais threw it into panic and allowed the English to get under its guard off Gravelines. Even after that, it had still lost only seven fighting ships and the English had used such unprecedented quantities of powder and shot that they were unable to finish it off, there upon their own doorstep. The victory was notable, but the manner of it[2] must have confirmed Elizabeth's reluctance to despatch large naval forces to the distant Azores or Caribbean so long as Spain had a fighting navy comparable in size to her own.

One later incident further justified her caution. In October 1597, when Essex had taken two-thirds of her ships to the Azores, the

[1] In the 1588 Armada campaign the number of genuine fighting ships on either side was about the same. On the English side nearly all these were the Queen's ships. Williamson, *Tudor Age*, 380; *Age of Drake*, 377.

[2] 'So much powder and shot spent and so long time in fight and, in comparison thereof, so little harm': William Thomas, master-gunner of Flushing, *State Papers relating to the Defeat of the Spanish Armada* (Navy Rec. Soc.), ii, 259.

Spanish fleet did sail north, intending to seize Falmouth, station its ships to windward off the Scilly Isles, and intercept the expedition as it straggled home. The Spaniards sailed from Ferrol just as the English were coming back singly or in small groups, some with their cannon stowed away in their holds. Neither fleet sighted the other and an autumn gale scattered the Spaniards back to their bases, so the attempt proved a fiasco. Yet it can hardly be said to prove that the Queen's caution was groundless. It was better to have her ships lying even at care and maintenance in the Medway, where they could quickly be prepared and brought round in good shape to the Channel,[1] than to have to recall them, foul and in need of overhaul, from the remote Azores.

Nor was it much less risky or more practicable to station the fleet off the Spanish coast to blockade the Spanish ports. Drake did this for nearly three months and with a comparatively small squadron in 1587, but the Armada was then in the midst of its preparations for the enterprise of England and too dispersed to challenge him. When it was both concentrated and ready, as later in 1587 and in the 1590s, the bulk of England's naval forces would have been required to deal with it. At some point they, or a considerable portion of them, must have gone home to revictual and refit. The Spaniards could then have caught England at a serious disadvantage, like a 1939–45 aircraft carrier with her fighters down refuelling. Indeed, the Armada of 1588 could thus have caught Howard's ships in Plymouth, replenishing their stores after being blown back from the Spanish coast by the winds that brought the Spaniards on. Again, in 1596 another armada did sail for England when most of the Queen's ships had recently returned from the Cadiz expedition and were in poor shape for immediate action. In 1588 the Spaniards, bent upon joining Parma in the Narrow Seas, ignored their opportunity. In 1596 autumnal gales scattered them before they could reach the English coast. Elizabeth, however, could hardly base her strategy upon an assumption of unvarying Spanish inefficiency.

Moreover, such a blockade of the Spanish ports or of the Azores would probably be ineffective as well as risky. For, to be effective, it must be continuous, lasting all the year round, perhaps for several years. It must stop the flow of silver from the New World,

[1] As they were against the 'Invisible Armada' of 1599: Corbett, *Successors of Drake*, 261 sqq.

and the hardly less important flow of masts, naval stores, and corn from the Baltic, for long enough to force the Spaniards in desperation to come out and fight. Now, it is very doubtful indeed if Elizabeth's navy was capable of this. Drake in 1587 only kept it up for three months in summer and the latest that any of the Queen's ships ever stayed on the Spanish coast was October 21,[1] whereas the silver ships several times stole home during the winter. A century later William III faced a rather similar problem in his French war. 'The difficulty of forcing the French to general actions in the open sea, the impossibility of blocking up their fleets for any considerable time at Brest in the stormy sea of the Bay of Biscay or at Toulon in the swelling sea of the Gulf of Lions, satisfied the King that the only way to conquer the fleets of France was in their own harbours.'[2] Elizabeth and some of her men of war were forced to the same conclusion.

This meant attacking 'in the main of Spain or Portugal'. It required not only a fleet strong enough to deal with the Spanish ships but also, as Drake soon realized, land forces strong enough to storm the Spanish ports and to hold a base from which the fleet could operate continuously and effectively. But where was the money to be found for this, while home defence, the Netherlands, France, and finally Ireland, swallowed up so much? Most of the time it clearly could not be found. From 1586 to 1588 home defence and the Netherlands claimed too much; from the autumn of 1589 until the end of 1594 France and the Netherlands left little to spare; from 1598 Ireland took all. During these periods the Queen had perforce to be content with operations at sea on a more or less limited scale, operations that might harry the enemy but could not hope to cripple him.

We are left with three brief periods of opportunity—right at the start of the war, before Spain's navy was fully developed or the Queen's funds exhausted; in 1588–89, between the Armada's defeat and Henry III's assassination; and from 1595 to 1597, when the heavy expenses in France had ceased and those in Ireland barely begun. Therefore, if the foregoing arguments are accepted, it is upon these three periods of opportunity that we must chiefly focus our criticism of Elizabeth's conduct of the war at sea.

[1] This was Monson in 1602: Corbett, op. cit. 383.

[2] Sir J. Dalrymple, *Memoirs of Great Britain* (1790 edn.), iii (3), 59, quoted in W. S. Churchill, *Marlborough*, i, 420.

In 1585 she did allow Drake's attempt to strike at the root of the problem. His expedition cost her only £10,000 and two of her ships, but all told it cost its backers £60,000. With the Netherlands commitment just beginning and the possibility still remaining that Spain might again yield to pressure as she had done in 1573, it is understandable if the Queen regarded this as enough for the time. Moreover, Drake apparently believed that, with his two Queen's ships and 27 others of various sizes and his 2,300 men, he could sack San Domingo and Cartagena, take Panama, and occupy Havana as a base for intercepting the treasure from both Mexico and Peru. And, in fact, it was not the smallness of the force that he set out with, but the unexpected wastage that it suffered during the campaign, which frustrated his design. In that graveyard of so many later expeditions, disease reduced his numbers so swiftly that he had strength only to sack San Domingo and Cartagena before he had to turn homewards. To blame the Queen for not foreseeing this would be even more unjust than to blame Drake, who knew the Spanish Main so well. After his return in 1586 the Queen, with the Netherlands and Mary Stuart on her hands, was back again upon the defensive.

In 1589 England was offered what was beyond all doubt the greatest opportunity presented to either side during the entire war.[1] Half the Armada had perished on the long voyage home. The fifty or sixty ships that had struggled back lay for months in Santander and San Sebastian unrigged, ungunned, unmanned, despite the efforts of the Spanish dockyards and recruiting officers. For a year the remnant of Spain's naval power lay there, not merely immobilized but helplessly inviting final destruction. Elizabeth was quick to see and seize her opportunity. While the Armada was still straggling home, she called together her men of war and her scribes to advise upon 'the intercepting of the King of Spain's treasure from the Indies'. Out of these conferences there came a counterstroke fully comparable to the Armada of 1588. The difficulties of finding money, and ships serviceable after the recent campaign, were overcome by the formation of something rather like a joint-stock company with the Queen as a partner. There were, of course, the deficiencies, disputes, and delays inseparable from a sixteenth-century enterprise. Nevertheless in April 1589

[1] This is more fully discussed in R. B. Wernham, 'Queen Elizabeth and the Portugal Expedition of 1589' (*E. H. R.* lxvi), 1–26, 194–218.

Drake and Norris sailed with six of the Queen's ships, 77 armed merchantmen of various shapes and sizes, 60 Dutch flyboats as transports, and 19,000 soldiers on their muster rolls.

The first, essential, task of this expedition obviously should have been to complete the work of 1588. One stroke would do it, for all but a dozen of the Armada survivors were huddled in the single port of Santander. Their destruction would ruin Spanish naval power past hope of recovery. If the English did that, then Hawkins's silver blockade, Drake's Lisbon dreams, all these things might soon be added unto them. The Queen saw this clearly and enjoined it emphatically in her instructions, but unfortunately Drake and Norris were so bent on taking the second step that they were reluctant to take the first. To Drake Lisbon was the key to the situation—as indeed it was when Spain had an effective fleet in being and not tucked away unrigged in Santander. Impressed in 1587 by Lisbon's strength, and perhaps growing more doubtful of Don Antonio's promised Portuguese revolt, he and Norris collected so large an army that the expedition became very unwieldy for operations against Santander, so far to leeward along the rough Biscayan coast. Elizabeth continued to insist upon that; but, being only a partner in the enterprise, her control was limited and the commanders compromised by going first to Coruña. It is just possible, though not very likely, that they planned to hold the place as a convenient base for operations eastward as well as southwards. But without the small siege train that Elizabeth had promised and not provided, they failed to take the upper town and after a fortnight's siege sailed off to Lisbon. They had given the Spaniards time to make their task there much more difficult. They now themselves made it impossible by dividing their land and sea forces for separate and unco-ordinated advances upon the city. There was no Portuguese rising and, with their forces wasting away from disease and desertion, they had to abandon the attempt. Contrary gales frustrated a move towards the Azores and, after sacking Vigo, the expedition straggled home at the end of June. By the end of July Henry III of France was dead; the Santander galleons, though by no means battleworthy, were able to work their way round to Coruña; and during the winter the year's silver shipment came safely in from America. The great opportunity had been missed. Some of the blame was clearly the Queen's; but it was not she alone, or most signally, who had done all by halves, and she had seen the essential objective more clearly than her men of war.

In 1595 the Queen was slower to seize her opportunity. Her anxiety about France and Ireland helped to delay Drake and Hawkins until most of the year's silver shipment was in Spain. Their expedition, too, though it started with 2,500 soldiers and aimed to seize Panama, was in scale more akin to the purely naval forces of 1590–91 than to the great expedition of 1589. A force of this size, the ravages of disease apart, was no longer enough to overcome the greatly strengthened and better forewarned defences of Spanish America; and so far as the Queen was responsible for the limitation of its strength, she was guilty here of doing things by halves. The next year it was not so. The treaty of Greenwich (May 1596) assured her that Henry IV would not immediately back out of the war, and its secret articles relieved her of any serious obligation to assist him on land or to conquests on his Netherlands frontier. Thereupon she loosed the Lord Admiral and Essex with 18 of her ships, 18 Dutchmen, 11 fighting Londoners, 60 or 70 transports, and rather less than 10,000 troops. The military contingent again looks over-large, as in 1589, but the expedition began well. It sacked Cadiz and destroyed there six galleons, three of the new *fregatas*, and 30 or 40 merchantmen. Then, however, sated with booty, and pleading (not altogether convincingly) a shortage of victuals, its enthusiasm died. Despite Essex's entreaties, 'every man cried to set sail homewards', apparently without a thought for the main Spanish forces still unscathed in the Tagus. The damage done to Spanish commerce and to Philip's credit was considerable, but very far from fatal. Indeed, as we saw, if the Lord had not blown with his winds more promptly in 1596 than in 1588, England that autumn might have paid almost as dearly as Spain for this 'summer's bravery'.

Essex at least had learned the lesson. He had begun to see before he sailed to Cadiz, and on his return he recorded in a paper recently discovered,[1] that what was needed was not a large army of invasion but an efficient landing force of, say, four or five thousand good soldiers, enough to seize and hold a base for the fleet and not too many to be kept supplied. The 1596 invasion alarm gave him the chance to start preparing such a force and in 1597 Elizabeth gave

[1] L. W. Henry, 'Essex as a Strategist and Military Organiser, 1596–97' (*E. H. R.* lxviii), 363–93.

him a heartier and more ungrudging support than she had given to any of her men of war—probably because she saw eye to eye with him rather than because Henry IV taunted her with keeping her favourite tied to her petticoats. After all, Essex's plan put the destruction of Spanish naval power first and foremost. It envisaged powerful and sustained operations to accomplish that purpose. It would station her forces where their pressure must compel the Spaniards to risk either wholesale destruction in battle or piecemeal destruction in port. In addition, it would station them in the one place where they could simultaneously blockade both the American silver route and the Baltic trade in corn and naval stores—at the receiving end.

Possibly the plan might have worked. Its small land force might have held Cadiz or some other base (as another force was soon to hold Ostend) long enough for the fleet to do its part. The fleet, if its powder held out, might have improved upon the performance of 1588. On the other hand, we must remember how susceptible Elizabethan soldiers were to disease, especially in warm, wine-growing climates; how subject Elizabethan fleets were to the weather; and how much more easily Elizabethan expeditions were swayed by considerations of profit than by considerations of power. Above all, we must remember that Essex's plan was never tried. Discouraged by administrative deficiencies, adverse weather, and disease among his troops, he dismissed his land forces. Then, assuming too easily that the Spanish fleet was immobilized at Ferrol for the season, he sailed off to the Azores. He was unlucky to miss the silver ships there, but lucky on his way home to miss the Ferrol fleet in the Bay of Biscay. By his rashness he had left England open to attack and by his lack of perseverance he had thrown away the last chance of dealing Spain a truly crippling blow. Henceforward Ireland claimed all attention.

All three opportunities were thus missed and for this the Queen must bear some of the blame. In 1589 she had allowed Drake and Norris to make their expedition too unwieldy for the essential operations against Santander and had left them without their promised siege train. In 1595 she had been slow to seize her chance. In 1596, if Essex is to be believed, it was her instructions that forbade an attack upon Lisbon, though the military contingent looks over-large for any lesser objective and the main Spanish naval forces were there. Yet in 1589 only success in Portugal could excuse failure to go to Santander at all; and it seems quite clear that the failure in Portugal was due chiefly to the commanders' own errors. In 1595 there was still the possibility of heavy commitments in France to keep Henry in the war. In 1596 Cadiz could have provided a base, second only to Lisbon itself, for sustained operations against Spanish shipping. The decision to abandon it was that of the commanders on the spot, Raleigh prominent among them. In 1597 it was Essex (with Raleigh as his rear-admiral) who dismissed his troops, ignored the Ferrol fleet, abandoned his own carefully thought out plan, and went off on a cruise to the Azores. It was the Queen who on these occasions kept her eye steadily upon the first, essential, objective—the destruction of the enemy fleet. It was her men of war who let their gaze be distracted or their purpose falter. Her lack of control over them is, indeed surprising. Of course, being a woman, she could hardly command in person, and in those days respect for the royal authority diminished rapidly with distance from the royal presence. In 1589 even Lisbon was a good deal more remote than Northumberland, which only twenty years before could be said to know no prince but a Percy. Further the wedding of purposes of state to enterprises for private profit, made necessary by the inadequacy of the royal revenues, also weakened the Queen's control over her commanders. Yet can we imagine Henry VIII not demanding heads for such disobedience as that of Drake and Norris in 1589 or of Essex in 1597?

We need not, however, blame the men of war too severely for their errors of judgment. They were experimenting with a novel theory, and a very novel instrument, of war. Sea power had never before been used as an independent arm operating over vast distances of ocean. Because it was so novel, its potentialities were too optimistically estimated and the difficulties of its employment very inadequately foreseen. Such things, as twentieth-century air staffs were to discover, could only be learned from actual experience in war. And if the air staffs of the twentieth century seem to have learned more rapidly than Elizabeth's advisers, we must remember that in Elizabeth's day organized general staffs and regular planning organizations were things of the distant future. Nevertheless, when we compare their achievements with their hopes, it is perhaps a little remarkable that a Queen so renowned for her hesitations should have listened to her men of war as readily as she did, learned from them as quickly, and given them as many chances. For, when the chances came, we cannot fairly say that she 'did all by halves'. 1589, 1596, and 1597 at least in size and purpose, were no 'petty invasions'. On these occasions the Queen gave her men of war the tools: it was they who did not finish the job.

We could hardly expect Raleigh to admit this, but it has been recognized by most modern critics of Elizabeth's strategy.[1] Where their picture looks more out of focus is in its over-emphasis on the offensive side of the war, on the war at sea. Now, it may be that the sea war launched England decisively out upon the oceans and on the pathway to empire. Yet because great oaks from little acorns grow, we should not forget that this particular acorn was comparatively little. For the Elizabethan war with Spain was not primarily a struggle for dominion over the ocean or for empire overseas. The peculiar vulnerability of Spain's sea communications made the ocean the obvious theatre for offensive operations. But Spain's strength on land made Europe the theatre where the danger of total disaster was gravest and most immediate. Thus the war was first and foremost a European war and its vitally important theatres were the Channel and the Channel ports, the Low Countries and Brittany and Ireland. Elizabeth, who saw the war whole, grasped this and allocated her strength accordingly, first to home defence, then to the defence of those vital areas. Yet she saw clearly enough that she could not win the war there and she kept these defensive efforts to the bare minimum in the hope of having something to spare for winning strokes by sea. It was her misfortune that the weakness of her allies and the power of her enemy left her with so little to spare and so few opportunities to use it. When the rare opportunities came, she tried to seize them in no half-hearted fashion, but neither she nor her men of war learned quickly enough how their new weapon of sea power could be most effectively employed. Her strategy was dictated by cautious common sense, with all the merits and limitations that this implies. Two things in particular she lacked. One was that genius for war which not only sees the goal but also knows instinctively and at once the surest and simplest way to it. The other was the control over her commanders that would have kept their eyes upon the true objectives and might have helped them to find the true way for

[1] e.g. Cheyney, op. cit., i, 551; Corbett, *Successors of Drake*, i, 407.

her. She was not one of England's great war leaders and she only half achieved her aims. Yet to have helped the French monarchy to its feet, to have saved half the Netherlands from Spanish 'tyranny', to have kept the other half out of French possession, and England itself out of bankruptcy, was a fair achievement against the Spain of Philip II.

XIII

The Succession Struggle in Late Elizabethan England

JOEL HURSTFIELD

'GOD bless you on earth' wrote Lord Burghley in March 1598, a few months before his death, to his son Robert, 'and me in heaven, the place of my present pilgrimage'.[1] What blessings awaited Lord Burghley in heaven we do not know; but certainly the next few years brought a whole series of blessings to Robert Cecil on earth. 'I think you happy for your great and honourable fortune' his elder brother could write to him in September 1602, 'and happier that the Lord has given you grace and judgement.'[2]

By the end of Queen Elizabeth's reign Robert Cecil, although not yet forty, had emerged as the undisputed leader of the government; and it was he who presided over the transfer of power from the Tudors to the Stuarts. Indeed, within a year of Burghley's death a correspondent, writing from London, could declare that the Queen was entirely under the direction of Robert Cecil 'who now rules all as his father did'.[3] So there grew up, even in his own day, the legend that by a marvellous combination of skill and intrigue—mostly intrigue—Cecil had by 1603 destroyed or driven into impotence all the men who stood in his way. Since this legend has survived for so long, and in recent years acquired some interesting accretions, it is time that it was tested against the background of the bitter struggle for power during the closing years of the Queen's regime. In essence there were two succession struggles during the period: one for the throne itself on behalf of rival claimants, the other for the immense concentration of power which Burghley had enjoyed for four momentous decades.

The long years of her personal rule had by this last crucial

[1] *Cal. S.P. Dom.* 1598–1601, 33. [2] Ibid. 1601–3, 240.
[3] Ibid. 1598–1601, 251.

period left the Queen a tired woman. In the summer of 1599 it was reported of her that 'when she rideth a mile or two in the park, which now she seldom doth, she always complaineth of the uneasy going of her horse; and when she is taken down her legs are so benumbed that she is unable to stand'.[1] These were the words of an unfriendly critic; but early in the next year Thomas Windebank, her clerk of the signet, recorded the inner conflict which at times paralysed the Queen's power of decision.[2] He was writing at a moment of great tension, after the earl of Essex's precipitate return from Ireland; but it was precisely at such times that a cool head at the centre of power was essential. Instead there was weakness and divided counsel: and in such an atmosphere double-dealing and corruption flourished. 'The people' said Bishop Goodman, looking back from the reign of Charles I, 'were very generally weary of an old woman's government.' He could remember, as a small boy, cheering the Queen in Armada year; but at the end of the reign he found things different.[3] When Thomas Holland, Regius Professor of Divinity at Oxford, printed in 1601 his accession-day sermon of two years earlier, he found it necessary to preface it with 'An Apologetical Discourse' against those who opposed the celebration of 17 November as a Holy Day.[4] At the opening of her last parliament, in 1601, the Queen showed the unmistakable signs of physical and spiritual fatigue.[5]

A decade ago, in a famous article, Sir John Neale drew our attention to the decay of government in the declining years of Queen Elizabeth.[6] It was moreover particularly tragic, in political terms, that the Queen and her lord treasurer grew old together; for thereby continuity of government was gravely imperilled. There was no obvious person who could transmit the established concepts of government into the new age. She frankly acknowledged her deep dependence upon him. In the last year of his life she sent him a cordial with her best wishes for his recovery. She added that 'she did intreat heaven daily for his longer life—else would her people, nay, herself, stand in need of cordials too'.[7]

[1] Ibid. 252. [2] Ibid. 394.

[3] G. Goodman, *The Court of King James I* (ed. Brewer, 1839), i, 97, 163.

[4] M. MacLure, *The Paul's Cross Sermons*, 220–1.

[5] J. E. Neale, *Elizabeth I and her Parliaments, 1584–1601*, 375.

[6] *The Elizabethan Political Scene* (Brit. Acad. Raleigh Lecture in History), reprinted in *Essays in Elizabethan History*, 59–84.

[7] John Harrington, *Nugae Antiquae* (ed. Park, 1804), i, 237.

Thomas Wilson, a sour commentator on the contemporary scene, wrote a couple of years later in less flattering terms. The factious grip upon power, the advancement of second-rate men at the expense of men of ability, all this 'was first brought by the old treasurer of whom it was written', he said, quoting Spenser, 'that he was like an aged tree that lets none grow which near him planted be'. That policy, he concluded, was being faithfully carried on by his son, Robert Cecil.[1]

Certainly Burghley had nothing to learn in the arts of faction and patronage; but the source of faction—as of authority—lay not in Burghley but in the Queen. No one minister was allowed to be the custodian of all her secrets or the delegated authority of all her power. Against Burghley there was Leicester; against Robert Cecil, Essex. But, said Wilson, this division went right through the administration and even reached into the Tower of London itself where the lieutenant of the Tower and the master of ordnance were not on speaking terms. The same conditions prevailed, he added, between the lord deputy of Ireland and the governor of Munster; and such had always been the case.

It did not need Thomas Wilson to point out the peculiarly grave perils of faction in these closing years of the sixteenth century. 'The jarrs continue as they did, if not worse by daily renewing', wrote John Chamberlain from London, 'and our music runs so much upon discords that I fear what harmony they will make of it in the end. Many things pass which may not be written.'[2] He was referring of course to the growing bitterness of the Essex-Cecil rivalry which, two years later, was to fester and burst into rebellion. But it is unfortunate that the dramatic character of this personal struggle has diverted attention from the larger struggle which underlay the whole situation: namely the struggle for the succession. Here indeed was something 'which may not be written'. There had been a thorough—and embarrassing—ventilation of the subject as long ago as 1566.[3] In 1571 an act had imposed severe penalties upon the publication of any claims to the royal succession, other than what was to be 'established and affirmed' by parliament.[4] But parliament, inhibited

[1] T. Wilson, 'The State of England, Anno Dom. 1600' (ed. F. J. Fisher Camd. Soc. 3rd ser. lii), 42–43; cf. R. Naunton, *Fragmenta Regalia* (1808 edn.), 178–9. [2] *The Letters of John Chamberlain* (ed. McClure, 1939), i, 67–68.
[3] J. E. Neale, *Elizabeth and Parliament, 1559–81*, 129–64. [4] 13 Eliz. c. 1.

by the Queen, had established and affirmed no successor, so Peter Wentworth's *Pithie Exhortation* on the subject, and his speech in the Commons, had won him a sojourn in the Tower from 1593 until his death four years later. Finally, at the time of the parliament of 1601, a bill was drafted to prohibit the writing or publishing of books about the succession on the grounds that they bred faction and inspired traitorous acts against the Queen.[1]

The English succession at this stage provided the happy hunting ground for the mischief makers of international politics. The centuries of dynastic marriage had indeed created a situation in which most of the crowned heads of Europe could claim each others thrones with some degree of plausibility. But in England the position was made more complex by the matrimonial infelicities of Henry VIII. As the result of divorces and marriages there had been provided in the last fourteen years of his reign three different acts laying down the succession, as well as Henry's last will in which, under statutory authority, Henry himself declared who were in line to succeed. Since, however, the will was alleged to be technically faulty and, in any case, was for a time mislaid (although its contents were known) the whole issue was criss-crossed with uncertainties. What was clear, however, was that the will had excluded the Stuart line and, in effect, left the crown after Elizabeth's death to the dubious claims of the House of Suffolk.

There were, in effect, about a dozen people who in the 1590s could present themselves, with varying degrees of optimism, as the future occupants of Elizabeth's throne. (Henry IV of France added one more candidate with the polite observation that, since a bastard of Normandy had succeeded to the English throne in 1066, he could not see why a bastard of his own should not do the the same thing when Elizabeth died.)[2] But of all the candidates for promotion we need only consider a short list of five. Under the law of primogeniture, James VI of Scotland had the best claim since he was descended from Margaret, the elder daughter of Henry VII. But James was a foreigner and those who opposed him could therefore allege that this barred the way. If that were so then Lady Arabella Stuart, the next senior descendent of this elder daughter, took his place. But if Henry VIII's will was valid, this claim was set aside since he had shifted the succession to Mary, the

[1] *Cal. S.P. Dom.* 1601–3, 115–16. [2] Ibid. 148.

younger daughter of Henry VII. But her marriage to the duke of Suffolk was itself of doubtful validity, as was that of her elder daughter, Catherine Grey. The Grey line need not seriously detain us here except to notice that, if Catherine's marriage were in doubt, the inheritance passed through her younger sister to the earl of Derby, married to a niece of Robert Cecil. If all these claimants were set aside, then a whole new series came up for consideration, including Philip II of Spain (descended from John of Gaunt) and, if he should stand aside, his daughter, the Infanta.

'Thus you see' wrote Thomas Wilson, 'this crown is not like to fall to the ground for want of heads that claim to wear it, but upon whose head it will fall is by many doubted.' Out of all these, three candidates received the particular attention of the succession speculators and the chanceries of Europe, namely James VI of Scotland, Arabella Stuart, and the Infanta. 'But I do assure myself' Wilson himself believed, 'that the King of Scotland will carry it, as very many Englishmen do know assuredly. But to determine thereof is to all English capitally forbidden, and therefore so I leave it.'[1] Thomas Wilson prudently acknowledged the Queen's hostility to all this speculation.

But Father Robert Parsons, as leader of the English Jesuits abroad, laboured under no such inhibition; and, from his itinerant exile on the continent of Europe, he felt free to speculate as he pleased about the Queen's successors. Where exactly Parsons himself stood became clear quite early in the debate; for, soon after the execution of Mary queen of Scots, he was engaged in manufacturing genealogical tables to establish Philip II's claim to the throne.[2] His conclusions, under the title *Conference about the Next Succession*, were published in 1594. Whether or not the essay was to be treated as a serious discussion of that delicate problem, it could certainly be expected to sow discord among the Queen's subjects. It proved also something of a boomerang for it helped to make a sharp cleavage inside the Catholic priesthood. True, to some priests it confirmed their beliefs that an anti-national, pro-Spanish policy was at this time the only way of making England safe for Catholicism. In others, the English party—or the 'Appellants' as they came to be known—it strengthened their hostility to the Spanish party and emphasized the need to break

[1] T. Wilson, 'The State of England', 5.
[2] A. O. Meyer, *England and the Catholic Church under Queen Elizabeth*, 381.

out of this entanglement and to negotiate direct with the English government some *modus vivendi* for their co-religionists. Certainly Robert Cecil, who had read the *Conference*, and no less certainly read the logic of the situation, showed himself to be an astute politician in his handling of it. In the ensuing battle of wits—in essence between Cecil and Parsons—some of the basic problems of English Catholicism were brought into the open. In the process we get also the first pointer to their ultimate solution.

It is impossible, of course, to do justice to the polemical skill of so experienced a propagandist as Robert Parsons; but for our purpose his arguments may be briefly summarized. There were numerous claimants to the English succession; but their lines were tainted with illegitimacy or heresy, or disputed over by conflicting directions of royal will or parliamentary statute. Only one candidate stood out from the rest with an incomparably superior claim: the Infanta of Spain. To her rights by inheritance she added the additional qualification of the impeccable orthodoxy of her faith.

It would not be necessary to tarry long over the unrealistic speculations of an *émigré* were it not that it was seriously alleged at about this time, for example at the trial of the earl of Essex—and repeated in modern historical studies—that these views about the succession were shared by so hard-headed a politician as Sir Robert Cecil, at that time Elizabeth's secretary of state. Cecil was not normally responsive to the persuasion of Father Parsons; but it has recently been argued again that there is a considerable body of evidence from various sources which sustains this thesis.[1] Some of this evidence can be dealt with briefly. Mrs Carmichael Stopes, who is first cited, turns out in effect to have produced a speculation of the most fantastic kind. Essex, she believed, had probably received 'some hint' that Cecil was a Spanish pensioner. However, he did not wish to incriminate others so, at his trial, he referred to the pension only in an indirect way by saying that Cecil had spoken in support of the Infanta. In short, Essex allowed his whole defence to collapse rather than state what he believed to be true about Cecil. Moreover, she continued, Cecil took a pension from the king of Spain and secret presents 'during

[1] The most recent presentation of this view is in L. Hicks, 'Sir Robert Cecil, Father Persons, and the Succession, 1600–1' (*Arch. Hist. Soc. Iesu*, xxiv), 95–139, from which the evidence discussed in the following pages is taken.

the whole life of James' (*sic*)[1] so 'it is much more than likely he had begun to do so even towards the close of Elizabeth's reign'. This time, apparently 'was a much more fitting period for the Spanish king to begin to tempt the English courtiers than the commencement of the reign of her legitimate and approved heir'. There is very little comment to be made upon this 'more than likely' explanation except to say that it carries us not an inch further than a straightforward invention of the facts.

To reinforce these guesses we are now offered additional material which, it is said, clearly establishes Cecil's involvement in this Spanish succession plot. The argument is as follows. The bitter rivalry between him and Essex, damped down during the last decade of Burghley's rule, finally flared up into a life and death struggle as soon as the old statesman was in his grave. Essex, by one device or another, had gained the ear of James VI who now looked to him as the rising statesman of the new age. With the intention of making himself doubly secure, Essex warned James of Cecil's hostility and of the latter's plot to frustrate the Stuart succession by bringing over the Infanta of Spain. Cecil, for his part, blackened Essex's name in the eyes of the Queen and took also more practical steps to discredit his rival by trapping him into accepting the impossible task of subjugating Ireland. Once Essex was there, Cecil completed the manœuvre by sabotaging the Irish campaign through inadequate provision of men and supplies.

This is a familiar accusation but with all its details we are not here concerned. Since, however, we are now offered 'a revealing letter' which purports to show one more link in the guilty chain of Cecil's duplicity, it deserves a little attention. In May 1599, Sir William Knollys, uncle of Essex, wrote to Cecil about Ireland to draw his attention to the danger arising from shortage of supplies. Part of one sentence from that letter has been quoted to indicate what was afoot, of which this is the correct version as given in the Historical Manuscripts Commission's *Report*:[2]

'I am not of opinion you have reason to hearken to any new demand, though he [Essex] shew a necessary reason touching the carriage horses which are not there to be had, and without which he will not be able

[1] I cite this as given by Father Hicks. Mrs Stopes in fact said 'during his whole life under James I': *The Third Earl of Southampton*, 212.

[2] Hist. MSS. Com. *Salisbury*, ix, 188. The problem of the supply of carriage horses is discussed in L. W. Henry, 'The Earl of Essex and Ireland, 1599' (*Bull. Inst. Hist. Res.* xxxii), 1–23.

to march, but unless you keep touch with him *in the agreements concluded on*, both for his number and the timely supplies, he may allege the same excuses that former governors have done, and *in the end that state must perish of a consumption, and it cannot but so infect England as it may grow into the like danger.*'

Apart from minor errors, the quoted extract has left out the last part of the sentence and one significant expression in the middle. (I have italicized the omitted passages.) As a result, it looks as though Knollys is simply telling Cecil to ignore these urgent demands. It is even more significant that the letter as a whole, from whose context this part of a sentence has been torn, is a strong appeal to Cecil that the government should fulfil its commitments to Essex. 'Truly', wrote Knollys, 'if it be not done in his due time, it were as good not at all, for it is so much treasure and victual lost and Her Majesty's state there growing to be worse and worse.' These needs, in other words, must be fulfilled in the national interest and for that reason 'I am not of opinion you have reason to hearken to any *new*[1] demand'. In essence he is saying that commitments must be met, in respect of 'the agreements concluded on', rather than new demands entertained. His letter includes a renewed appeal for action or '*in the end that* [*Irish*] *state must perish of a consumption and it cannot but so infect England as it may grow into the like danger.*'[2] What we are told is a piece of advice to betray Essex turns out on investigation to be an appeal to give Essex the full aid that has been promised. Since the cited extract, implying that Knollys was betraying Essex, has been used to impugn Knollys' evidence at Essex's trial, it has been necessary to establish first what in fact Knollys was saying.

But far more important than this is the new evidence, now brought forward, of Cecil's plans to replace James VI by the Infanta as Elizabeth's successor. First we are reminded of the promise by a certain Italian, Filippo Corsini, of the secret, speedy dispatch to Cecil of a portrait of the Infanta and her husband the Archduke.[3] Whether this was for himself or the Queen we cannot say; but the purchase of portraits of foreign notables was a widespread practice and it is dangerous to draw from this any conclusions other than that it represents the natural desire of a leading English statesman to have a portrait of a claimant to the throne.

[1] My italics. [2] My italics.
[3] Hist. MSS. Com. *Salisbury*, ix, 345, 391, 440.

That Cecil was interested in the Infanta there can be no question. She had, after all, been strongly urged by Father Parsons and might well be supported by English Catholics abroad—or even at home. She might indeed be raised also as a bargaining counter in the Anglo-Spanish peace negotiations which opened in 1599. Here was a perfectly good reason for the speedy dispatch of the portrait which would, especially at this time, have to be done secretly. The request is therefore no more than a sign that the English government took seriously the claims being put forward on behalf of the Infanta.

But shortly after this, in April 1600, Father Parsons began to receive letters from a correspondent in England which purported to shed light on Cecil's policy about the succession. Who the correspondent was is not stated, nor have the original letters survived. But Spanish translations of them, sometimes with comments by Parsons, were sent to Philip III of Spain (who had succeeded Philip II in 1598), having been passed on by his ambassador in Rome; and these papers are now at Simancas. The correspondent, it is claimed, 'was in contact with the party of Cecil'. The Cecilians, he said, had their own claimant in the person of Anne, daughter of the fifth earl of Derby. Since this group was not ill-affected to the Catholic religion, the Cecilians might be able to carry many of the Catholics with them. It was therefore necessary to get an indication of his views from the king of Spain so that English Catholics might know where they stood. His Majesty, however, would at this stage go no further than a vague promise of support for a Catholic, and then left Father Parsons to his own (diplomatic) devices.

By the autumn of 1600, Parsons' correspondent had, apparently, obtained from the Cecilians a more precise declaration of where their interests lay. They had, he claimed, abandoned any hope that an English subject could possibly succeed. The choice lay therefore between the king of Scots and the Infanta; and it was known that they hated and feared James VI. If, however, they received no guidance from the king of Spain, they would, the report continued, be bound soon to make terms with the king of Scots. At once this brought from Parsons his urgent plea that Philip III should act with all speed. So, at last, in February 1601, Philip acquiesced and declared himself for the Infanta; but he added the strong request that the knowledge of this decision should be withheld from everyone save those 'who can be trusted to promote its successful issue'. If Philip at last began to move, the others involved continued to drag their heels. The Infanta received the proposal coolly. The Pope, who looked with great alarm at any increase of Spanish power and feared the Catholic king of Spain more than the heretical king of Scotland, had his own reasons therefore for holding aloof. He had also to consider the king of France with whom the delicate ties of friendship might easily be snapped if it became known that the pope was supporting a Spanish candidate. 'No woman', said the disillusioned Spanish ambassador, was 'more careful not to arouse suspicion in her husband than was the Pope as regards the French King.' But the best comment on the situation in general had come earlier from a disappointed Catholic, writing in August 1600. 'The Spanish King's council', he said, 'have often inquired if we cannot find a king of our own, temperate to Catholics, and they would aid. So matters remain unresolved, and we in the briars, not knowing the way out. The Jesuits feed us with words and the Spaniards with hopes.'[1]

Who, in fact, evolved the wishful delusion of Robert Cecil engaged in ushering in the Infanta's rule of England under Spanish-Jesuit patronage we shall probably never know. It may have first taken root in Parsons' own mind since his inventive—if wayward—genius could weave fantasies with irrepressible fervour. Or it may be that his correspondent, some dim purveyor of hare-brained rumours, really persuaded Parsons that he had genuine knowledge of Cecil's political attitude. It may even be that some lesser politician in England, for reasons best known to himself, led some political innocent into a wonderland of his own. Certainly it was common enough for Cecil's enemies to accuse him behind his back of supporting the Infanta. James VI was being bombarded with such information, as earlier he had apparently been told by the earl of Leicester that Cecil's father was opposed to James.[2] Similarly, James appears to have been told that Essex was opposed to his succession;[3] while the irrepressible Father Parsons—that 'broker of kingdoms' as Camden called him—tried to persuade the earl to side with the Infanta![4]

[1] *Cal. S.P. Dom.* 1598–1601, 460. [2] C. Read, *Burghley and Elizabeth*, 291–2.
[3] Hist. MSS. Com. *Salisbury*, ix, 307–8.
[4] W. Camden, *Elizabeth* (1688 edn.), 652; *Cal. S.P. Dom.* 1598–1601, 453.

All that we have then is a vague, unsupported story (without a single scrap of concrete evidence) from some unidentified correspondent of Father Parsons. And against this must be set the repeated affirmations by Cecil that such charges were untrue, and his public refutation of them at the trial of the earl of Essex. More important still as an indication of Cecil's attitude is his behaviour after Essex was dead. Now Cecil was without his most dangerous rival and, if he had genuinely feared—as some said—that James would one day avenge himself for his mother's execution, he was in a far better position to further the claims of the Infanta. Instead he devoted all his energies and patience to procuring the peaceful accession of James VI. It seems that we must treat this latest version of Cecil's policy—based upon Parsons' documents—with the same scepticism with which it was received by the Infanta.

But if, amidst the troubled waters of international intrigue, Father Parsons was fishing with his accustomed lack of skill, it would be a mistake to dismiss the result as no more than an insignificant bubble in an extremely muddy stream. For, if we consider the timing of the episode, it has a particularly close relevance to one of the great issues of Elizabethan England, namely that of Catholic recusancy. For the English Catholics—at home and in exile—were now engaged in their own struggle over the succession. In the process the whole problem of the place of Catholics in the English polity would be thrashed out again.

By the last decade of her reign Elizabeth's relations with her Catholic subjects had reached something like deadlock. For more than thirty years her government had tried by various methods to bring them, at least nominally, within the framework of her church settlement. In her early years it seemed—at least to the Catholic exiles—that she might be succeeding; that the broken, leaderless remnant of their followers might before very long disappear into the anonymous, enveloping folds of the Church of England. But, as long as the Queen's religious policy was ambiguous, there remained among the optimists some slender hope that she might yet revert to the Roman jurisdiction. To us, looking back, the idea seems unrealistic but to contemporaries it was much more easy to conceive. A return to Rome would not necessarily mean for Elizabeth the abandonment of all that had been gained by the English Reformation: papal authority could be more flexible than its more authoritarian *dicta* might lead some to believe. After all, the Valois kings of France had negotiated a concordat which gave them something like control over a national church and had won their victory without having to fight for it. Philip II had gained the same thing. His dynastic imperialism was often hostile to papal intentions but he remained, albeit with difficulty, a powerful king of Spain at the same time that he was a faithful adherent of the Church.[1] His dynastic interests usually predominated: hence, in the context of his anti-French hostility, he had for more than a decade shielded Elizabeth from the due chastisement of a heretic.

But by 1570 the papal *Curia* had decided that it must follow a line of its own, without giving too close attention to the diplomatic manœuvres of Philip II. The bull of excommunication and deposition, issued against Elizabeth in that year, and the vigorous missionary policy which in due course followed, combined to give to Catholicism in England a political significance of grave and growing dimensions. That situation was exacerbated by the peculiar role which Mary queen of Scots assigned to herself. In face of this the government, under parliamentary pressure, responded with intensified penal legislation. By the 1580s Catholicism was a proscribed religion and its priests were being hunted down as traitors.

It is not necessary to rehearse that legislation here. In 1581 and 1585 it took on its most savage form: non-attendance at church was to be punished at the rate of £20 a month and priests were *ipso facto* to be deemed traitors. But what followed in the next decade should not be under-rated. For the act of 1593 alleviated, if only by a little, the further penalties now proposed against Catholics. A priest, who refused to answer as to his identity, could be sent to prison but did not, as proposed, in virtue of this refusal automatically become subject to the death penalty.[2] It was a small alleviation; but it was a sign of the times.

In one sense this was an acknowledgement of deadlock: the government had gone as far as it was able towards eliminating the Catholic resistance to its policy of *gleichschaltung*—and it would go on exacting the heavy penalty of £20 a month for recusancy

[1] For a discussion of this see Dr. J. Lynch's forthcoming article on 'Philip II and the Papacy' in *Trans. R.H.S.*

[2] 35 Eliz. c. 2; J. E. Neale, *Elizabeth and Parliament, 1584–1601*, 295–6.

where it could—but the small hard core of Catholicism would remain. In the north of England it was much more than this. The evidence as it began to come in, for example from Lancashire in the 1590s, drew an alarming picture of the infiltration of Catholic missionaries from top to bottom of Lancastrian society, from the family of the earl of Derby himself down through the commission of the peace, the gentry and the rest.[1] The Lancastrian recusants, said the bishop of Chester, 'despise authority . . . and are fed by their priests with hopes of a better time shortly'.[2] On the other side of England, Yorkshire had its share of Catholic resistance, probably less than in Lancashire; but in the city of York, for example, headquarters of the court of high commission, the brother of the lord mayor himself was known to be a recusant.[3] The ecclesiastical commissioners, said the Queen, behave 'as though the laws were instituted not for punishment [of recusants] but to enrich' commissioners. The instructions that 'we have sent hitherto have been written in water'.[4] In Hampshire recusancy was significant.[5] In Sussex Lord Montagu and other leading figures were Catholics. In London, the Clink, intended as a prison for active Catholics, had become a propaganda cell for the whole capital.[6] The periodic purges of the commissions of the peace, the martyrdom of priests, the heavy fines and imprisonments, if they had kept the Catholic problem within bounds, had none the less failed to break through the strategically powerful defences of Catholicism in the shires.

In that sense, then, the slight alleviation of 1593 was a recognition that the Catholic revival was too sturdy a movement to be broken by legislation, especially as that legislation was aided only by a rudimentary and corrupt police system and resisted in many places by thoroughly hostile local officials. But this more temperate mood was a sign also of something else. Mary queen of Scots had been executed; the Armada was defeated. Yet, at two such delicate moments for English security, nowhere in the country had

[1] J. S. Leatherbarrow, *The Lancashire Elizabethan Recusants*, 112–15.

[2] *Cal. S.P. Dom.* 1598–1601, 389–90.

[3] A. G. Dickens, 'The first stages of Romanist recusancy in Yorkshire, 1560–1590' and 'The extent and character of recusancy in Yorkshire, 1604' (*Yorks. Arch. J.*), xxxv, 157–81 and xxxvii, 24–48.

[4] *Cal. S.P. Dom.* 1598–1601, 276.

[5] J. E. Paul, 'Hampshire Recusants in the reign of Elizabeth I' (Southampton Univ. Ph.D. thesis, 1958).

[6] J. Gerard, *The Autobiography of an Elizabethan* (ed. Caraman), 79–80.

a single Catholic done anything to hinder the government in its defence precautions. By 1590 it had thus become certain that, although in terms of religion the Catholic movement was invincible to the Queen, in terms of politics it was invincible to her enemies. The significance of this was not lost either on the Queen's government or on the more aggressive of the Catholic missionaries. So the 1590s in effect saw the struggle for the soul of English Catholicism between the government—and more especially Robert Cecil and Richard Bancroft, the bishop of London—and the Jesuit missionaries, led with such resource and imagination by Robert Parsons. One scene of that struggle was the castle of Wisbech in Cambridgeshire.

Since 1580 this relatively isolated, decaying building on the Isle of Ely had been used as an internment centre for Catholic priests. The total number gathered there was never very large, at most about 35, but they included some notable scholars as well as some lively missionaries. After 1585 the government could, if it wished, have executed newly captured priests as felons; but the moral effect of these martyrdoms had been to inspire rather than terrify the reviving Catholic movement. Executions went on; but some of the most distinguished of the priests were spared the scaffold and sent to Wisbech. Here the conditions of confinement were, at first, probably severe. But as the community grew the prisoners were allowed, within measure, the modest amenities of communal life. They dined together, held discussions, were in some cases allowed servants and could receive guests—as well as gentlemen's sons, sent to them for their education—and were free to go into the neighbouring town. So in time Wisbech developed a character of its own and became a combination of hostel, school, postgraduate seminar in ecclesiastical studies and a propaganda discussion centre. Propaganda, like charity, begins at home; and one of the minor successes of Wisbech was the conversion of the gaoler's daughter to Roman Catholicism. Her father was a virulent puritan.[1]

But conditions were far from good. Moreover, in spite of the concentration of such diverse talent under one roof—or perhaps because of it—internal feuds began to develop. Such differences are not unknown in any academic community; and here as elsewhere

[1] T. G. Law, *A Historical Sketch of the Conflicts between Jesuits and Seculars*, pp. xlii–xliii.

they may have developed simply as the result of discordant temperaments being driven to extremity in the intimate stress of enforced communal life. But once the differences were openly expressed they took shape, not simply in personal attack, but in a struggle over principle. By 1595 two bitterly opposed parties existed at Wisbech which, in the course of the struggle, involved in their affairs the Jesuit order, the papacy, the king of Spain —and Sir Robert Cecil. For a good part of the time the battle was fought over organization; but it became increasingly dominated by the struggle over the succession.

Viewed superficially, the issue was at first simple enough: who was to preside over the Wisbech community? Among the early prisoners had been Thomas Watson, bishop of Lincoln under Queen Mary, and he had exercised an informal authority over his colleagues there. That authority had passed after his death in 1584 to the Jesuit, Thomas Metham, who had continued this unofficial leadership, latterly against some opposition, until his own death in 1592.[1] After this another Jesuit, William Weston, exercised considerable influence; but by now the friction between the two main groups had burst out into open conflict. Father Weston accordingly withdrew from the communal arrangements and he was shortly joined by eighteen other priests and the one layman incarcerated with them. In the opposing group were twelve priests led by Christopher Bagshaw and Thomas Bluet. According to the latter group Weston's withdrawal had been voluntary and he had allured or bribed others to join him.[2] According to the Jesuits, Bagshaw had forced Weston and his followers to withdraw. The exact details of these factional moves are, however, less important than the efforts of Weston's followers to obtain his official appointment as 'a judge, corrector and censurer'. This office Weston was apparently reluctant to accept; but his supporters prevailed upon Father Garnett, Provincial of the Jesuits in England, who accordingly appointed Weston but was careful to restrict his powers to moral leadership only. The opposition just the same regarded this step as nothing less than a success for the Jesuits in their efforts to impose their will on their fellow Catholics in England.

Even so, the quarrel might have blown over had it not become

[1] P. Renold, *The Wisbech Stirs* (Cath. Rec. Soc. li), pp. xii–xiv.
[2] Ibid. p. xiv and text; T. G. Law, op. cit. pp. liii–liv.

involved with a comparable struggle in the English college in Rome and, indeed, with the whole question of the Jesuit role in European affairs. For at least a decade there had been intermittent dissension among the English students in Rome, arising in part from hostility against the discipline administered by the Jesuits. But in 1595 the new outburst was the most bitter of all, involved as it was with principle as well as behaviour. That this internal movement in the English College had, as was alleged by the Jesuits, personal links with the dissidents at Wisbech there is no reason to doubt. But it is the date itself which is of the most significance. A year had passed since the publication of Parsons' book on the succession, and the debate among Catholics had taken on a more vigorous form. These dissidents, said the rector of the English College in 1596, 'speak frequently and sharply against the book on the succession to the English throne and against its author . . . I know not whether they hate the Society [of Jesus] on account of the Spaniards, or the Spaniards on account of the Society . . .'[1]

From now onwards the issue of the succession was to the fore and gave a more acute definition to the existing causes of conflict. These were in part personal, in part administrative. The Jesuits, with heroic self-sacrifice and masterly discipline, sought with characteristic devotion to carry the ideals of the Catholic Reformation, speedily and forcefully, into the lives of priest and layman alike. They carried many of the secular priests with them in these aims; but others resisted. Those who resisted also had their ideals. But what divided them from the Jesuits was their belief that the Protestant settlement in England was, after forty years, secure; that the best way to improve the lot of English Catholics was, therefore, not to attempt to overthrow the Protestant system but somehow to negotiate terms with it. They believed that there were more roads open to English Catholics than the straight and narrow one imperiously pointed out by the Jesuits. Some English Catholics were in essence becoming insular, but not separatist. They believed—ahead of their time as it turned out—that it was better for Catholicism to seek to become a tolerated minority religion than to hurl itself in vain against the established Church. They had imbibed also, along with their Protestant fellow countrymen, the insular patriotic emotions which it seems to have been

[1] C. Dodd, *The Church History of England* (ed. Tierney), iii, Appendix, lxxv.

the especial task of Philip II of Spain to intensify. In short, they hated the Spaniards more than they hated Elizabeth I of England —or James VI of Scotland.

It is unfortunate that this central issue has been obscured in recent historiography by those who have taken at its face value the volume of abuse which the controversy generated in its own day. Much of it was simply the stock-in-trade of contemporary propaganda methods. There is in fact little utility in basing arguments upon the unedifying catalogue of unnatural vice which was drawn up by both sides. For example, whatever his faults, there is no doubt as to the heroic devotion of Father Parsons in a cause to which he gave a lifetime of unremitting service and a variety of skills. On the other side, William Gifford, who rose ultimately to be a respected archbishop of Rheims, can hardly be dismissed as an irresponsible trouble-maker. Nor can any credence be given to the 'confession' of the unstable Robert Fisher who, after his arrest at Rome, turned against his Wisbech friends and provided Parsons, and his later defenders, with a valuable storehouse of polemical ammunition.[1] Parsons himself said: 'we will not affirm all to be true which he said.'[2] Nor shall we.

During 1598 this division among English Catholics altered its shape but not its content. It became known as the archpriest controversy and, amid changing fortunes, dragged on until the end of the reign. Again, in so far as it concerns the organization of Catholic dissent in England, it need not delay us here. Summarized very briefly, the argument now turned on whether, as some of the seculars wished, a bishop should be appointed to officiate as best he could in a heretical country; or whether, by the institution of the office of archpriest, Catholic interests would be better served. Again personal issues broke into theoretical differences of approach. Many of the seculars believed that a bishop would bring with him some measure of local self-determination—once again their approach bears the impress of their insular outlook—while an archpriest would emphasize, rather than mitigate, their dependence upon overseas direction. When, in fact, George Blackwell was appointed archpriest, and appeared from the start to operate under Jesuit guidance, the dissidents now felt themselves to be given over wholly to the dominance of their opponents, and they

[1] The confession is printed in full in P. Renold, op. cit. 230–63.
[2] Cited in T. G. Law, op. cit. 98*n*.

appealed to Rome. The Appellants, as they came therefore to be known, had possibly planned in any case to carry their dissident opinions to the *Curia*; but the establishment of an archpriest gave greater point to their discontent. In this appointment they probably over-rated the influence of Parsons;[1] and mistook the consequences of the appointment for its cause. Certainly Parsons played his part in defeating the work of the Appellants in Rome in 1598 and, in so doing, added fuel to the smouldering discontents of the Appellants. That, accompanied by the autocratic methods of Blackwell—including his condemnation of members of the opposition as schismatics—led to the second appeal to Rome of November 1600, signed by thirty-three priests.[2] Meanwhile a small group of the opposition had taken the dangerous step of opening negotiations with the Elizabethan government.

When exactly these secret talks began it is impossible to say. Contacts of some kind existed before the outbreak of the archpriest controversy; but it was not only the English government that was sounded in this connection. While the controversy was at its height, the Appellants looked also for support from the French embassy in Rome and from the university of Paris: one more move in the anti-Spanish struggle. But it was in their negotiations with Robert Cecil and Bancroft that the Appellants embarked upon a series of transactions which look at first sight like nothing less than treason to their cause.

From the autumn of 1598 Bagshaw was supplying the privy council with information about the Appellants' relations with the Jesuits.[3] Also, hostile material about the Jesuits was supplied to the council the following year by another priest, William Watson.[4] From now onwards, if not earlier, Robert Cecil was kept fully informed about the state of the archpriest controversy. At about this time also, the English ambassador in Paris, Sir Henry Neville, transmitted a report from a Catholic, Charles Paget, claiming to speak on behalf of Catholic laymen in bitter hostility to Jesuit plans for the succession.[5] However much he may have exaggerated the size of his following, his was not a solitary voice. Nor was this the only form in which opposition expressed itself. In the previous

[1] *Letters of Thomas Fitzherbert, 1608–10*, ed. L. Hicks (*Cath. Rec. Soc.*, xli), 127–8. [2] A. O. Meyer, *England and the Catholic Church*, 431.

[3] Law, op. cit. p. lxxix. [4] A. O. Meyer, op. cit. 425.

[5] *Cal. S.P. Dom.* 1598–1601, 220–1.

year another secular priest, John Bishop, had come forward and published a treatise against the papal claim to depose princes;[1] while the Appellants sought an order from the papacy prohibiting the publication, without ecclesiastical approval, of books hostile to the English government. From one viewpoint these moves may perhaps be described as a sign of the patriotic fervour of a group of English Catholics; but there can be no question that it is besmirched by personal hostility to the Jesuits and the willingness to denounce their activities to the government of Protestant England. The Appellants were, in essence, appealing to Rome and London at one and the same time. In so far as so dangerous and ambiguous a policy can be explained, the explanation lies in their resolution to prevent a Spanish succession to the English throne, and in their hopes of obtaining religious toleration under some other candidate.

They believed that the Jesuits would favour a Spanish succession; that the Jesuits, and those who shared their opinions, had no use for a toleration given by the tainted hands of the heretics. Toleration might indeed sap the will of Catholic resistance. '[As] for a toleration or liberty of conscience in England', the pope was reported by one of the Appellants to have said, 'it would do harm and make Catholics become heretics; that persecution was profitable to the church'.[2] Yet, in spite of the questionable tactics that they employed, it is possible to see in the Appellants the first overt sign that a group of English priests was seeking a way of life in which they might become patriotic Englishmen while remaining faithful Catholics. By contrast, the Jesuits believed that there could be no peace without Spain. It was a view sincerely held by them and shared by others, including so eminent a layman as Sir Francis Englefield, who had written in September 1596:

> Without the support and troops of Spain it is scarcely probable that the Catholic religion will ever be restored and established in that country [England]. Even the seminaries, powerful as they are in preparing men's minds for a change must fail to complete their object without the aid of temporal force.[3]

In face of this profound conflict of opinion within the Catholic world, the great campaign of denigration conducted by both sides soils the genuine idealism which lay at the basis of both.

[1] Meyer, op. cit. 420. [2] Law, op. cit. p. cvi. [3] Ibid. xiv *n* 3.

Here was the tragedy at the heart of English Catholicism. Because of it both sides played with the dangerous fires of treason, in one case against the state, in the other against their Church.

For the next few years Cecil and his colleagues were holding conferences with the dissidents, before whom was held continuously the bait of religious toleration. In return for this they would assume the welcome task of breaking the Jesuit hold upon English Catholicism and identify themselves with an anti-Spanish policy. In contrast, the instructions to the archpriest are significant. His task was 'not only to preserve union during the lifetime of the Queen but, much more, to procure a Catholic successor after her death, in conformity with certain briefs which His Holiness has already most prudently addressed to the Catholics'.[1] In allying himself with the opponents of the archpriest, therefore, Cecil was in effect allying himself with that wing of the Catholic movement which stood solidly against the Infanta's succession to the English throne. By 1600 that alliance, however tenuously, had been formed; and the date is important. For it was at this very time that Parsons began to receive letters from his correspondent in England implying that the Cecilians wanted a pronouncement on behalf of the Infanta. It is thus possible now to estimate the value of the evidence about Cecil's involvement in the Infanta plot. For Parsons' story is meaningless without its context of the archpriest controversy and the bitter struggle going on in Rome between the two elements of the English Catholic movement.

Parsons had, by 1600, won no permanent victory against the Appellants and their policy of seeking an understanding with Cecil. It was at this stage, therefore, that Parsons called upon his second line of defence. The Infanta theory, whatever dubious value it had amid the harsh diplomatic realities of 1600, had other services to render. For example, by claiming the Cecilians as allies of the Infanta, at the very time when Cecil was negotiating with the Appellants, Parsons would sow confusion in their ranks and damage the incipient agreement now under negotiation. He would also prove to Rome that the Appellants were a discredited minority who had no notion of Cecil's real plans and who were in fact a barrier to an effective alliance between Cecil and the Jesuits to bring over the Infanta. He would also discomfort and embarrass French diplomacy which was, at this very time, being

[1] Ibid. p. lxi.

asked to support the Appellants against the hispanophile Jesuits. Also, if the story ever reached the Queen's ears, it would discredit Cecil as well as his plan for a *détente* with the Catholics. In practice, the Cecil-Infanta story was more important as a move in the internal struggle between the Jesuits and the Appellants than as a serious proposal to the pope or the king of Spain.

It is not surprising that, at the very time when Parsons was filling the diplomatic bag of the Spanish ambassador in Rome with his report of Cecil's conversion to the Spanish cause, similar tales were being whispered in the ear of James VI. (That unfortunate king was the recipient of a number of far-fetched stories during the long years that he was waiting for his inheritance, including one—from Parsons!—that the Appellants were opposed to his succession.[1]) The Spaniards, James VI was warned by the friends of Essex, could rely upon the help of Cecil. Essex repeated the story in the streets of London when he said that the Crown of England was sold to the Spaniard, and he repeated it also at his own trial. Then at last he received the contemptuous refutation of Cecil himself: 'I have said that the King of Spain is a competitor of the crown of England, and that the King of Scots is a competitor, and my Lord of Essex I have said is a competitor; for he would depose the Queen and call a parliament and so be king himself.'[2] His own defence—as well as his actions—carries far greater conviction than the allegations of Essex or of the anonymous correspondent of Father Parsons. Certainly it convinced James VI and thereby inaugurated that secret correspondence between monarch and minister which was to last until James VI peacefully took his seat on the English throne.

The struggle between Cecil and Essex, which came into the open soon after Burghley's death in 1598 and ended only with the death of Essex two and a half years later, was not in any direct sense a struggle over the succession to the throne. It was rather a struggle for power itself during the lifetime of the Queen. As such it divided England and, then as since, aroused a good deal of sympathy for the defeated candidate. Cecil won because he was the more skilful politician; because, from the start, he held a firm hand

[1] Ibid. p. cvii.

[2] *Correspondence of James VI of Scotland with Sir Robert Cecil*, ed. J. Bruce (Camd. Soc. O.S. lxxviii), p. xxxiii.

on the government machine and enjoyed the confidence of the Queen; because the Queen blocked Essex in his desire and need for office for himself and his followers until in the end he fell into a trap of his own making by going to Ireland; because, finally, faced with bankruptcy, and in the midst of unendurable nervous tension, he called upon the London mob for aid. But at no stage during these intervening years is there any documentary evidence that Cecil himself planned the downfall of his opponent, nothing comparable to Essex's own plan to replace Sir Walter Raleigh, the captain of the guard, and Sir Robert Cecil, the secretary, by his own nominees, Sir William Russell and Sir Henry Neville (or Thomas Bodley).[1] Cecil could, of course, do his damage verbally since he had the ear of the Queen throughout while Essex was forbidden the royal presence. But if Cecil did this, it was certainly no worse than what Essex did on his behalf to James VI. In fact, the real damage had been done long before 1598, and by Essex himself, whose conduct at court had deprived the Queen of the confidence she had in him as a statesman. 'Mr Secretary [Cecil] did you good service in Council, and the queen liked it well', Sir Henry Ley had told him in 1598. But he added a warning: 'Your honour [prestige] is more dear to you than your life, yet consider that she is your sovereign, whom you may not treat upon equal conditions.'[2]

The Essex rebellion derived from the impossible situation in which Essex found himself in the last years before 1601. Denied access to the source of patronage and influence, he must either see his power sterilized and his following shrink for want of supplies, or he must break through to gain access to—if necessary control over—that source. That is what Cecil meant when he charged him with wanting to be king of England. 'It resteth with me in my opinion' noted the shrewd John Harrington of the earl of Essex before the storm broke, 'that ambition, thwarted in its career, doth speedily lead on to madness . . . His speeches of the queen becometh no man who hath *mens sana in corpore sano*.'[3] Essex in the end was caught in the ineluctable dilemma of power inherent in the existing political structure. Cecil was no doubt shrewd enough to see the consequences for Essex of such a dilemma; but it was quite unnecessary for him to invent one. That Cecil was alarmed by

[1] *Cal. S.P. Dom.* 1601–3, 2. [2] Ibid. 1598–1601, 88–89.
[3] J. Harrington, *Nugae*, i, 179.

Elizabeth I
From the effigy in Westminster Abbey

the rebellion is also clear enough: a full year after it had been crushed the government was still examining witnesses, still looking for the roots and offshoots of conspiracy.[1]

The elimination of Essex provided the opportunity for Cecil to establish contact with James VI. Now at last he could give the *quietus* to the scandalous reports, spread by his enemies, that he favoured the Infanta. But if the succession problem was in one sense eased, in another it was made more dangerous. For now Cecil had to engage in a secret correspondence with a foreign monarch. If it ever came to the notice of the Queen, whose opposition to announcing a successor was still unshakeable, it might lay Cecil open to the charge of disloyalty—or something worse.

There is, of course, a good deal to be said, especially in the earlier part of her reign, in favour of Elizabeth's policy of refusing to acknowledge a successor. The only feasible one then, in spite of her notorious performance as queen of Scots, would have been Mary Stuart. To have acknowledged her might well have prompted rebellion on behalf of an English candidate against a Catholic Scot. After Mary's death in 1587 Elizabeth did not change her policy; she was still anxious, perhaps, not to rouse an anti-Scottish faction which might have tried to make things impossible for James—and for Elizabeth. Whatever the political reasoning behind it, in this policy Elizabeth was consistent throughout her life. Mingled with it there were, of course, the understandable personal feelings of an old and popular Queen who hated to see her own shadow lengthen while the sun rose in Scotland. But it was a dangerous policy, for the risk was always present that James might ally with some political irresponsible who promised him present joys rather than distant prospects. That surely was what the friends of Essex were doing when they invited him to save Essex—and England—by bringing an army south in 1600.[2] Fortunately, James had none of the adventurous spirit of his mother and, at the last, shrank back from what would have been an act of war. But it was a near thing. And it was not the first time that there were rumours that James VI 'would attempt to gather fruit before it is ripe'.[3]

Long before, in the summer of 1592, James had drawn up a clear statement of his views on the English succession. At this

[1] *Cal. S.P. Dom.* 1601–3, 152–3.
[2] D. H. Willson, *King James VI and I*, 151.
[3] *Cal. S.P. Dom.* 1589–1601, 201; cf. ibid. 343.

stage, he said, he did not contemplate invading England to obtain his inheritance. Scotland itself was not at peace; and he could not move south leaving a disorderly baronage to wreak havoc behind him. Accordingly, he continued, 'in the meantime I will deal with the Queen of England fair and pleasantly for my title to the Crown of England after her decease'. If his title was recognized—'as it is not impossible, howbeit unlikely'—'we have attained our design without stroke of sword'. If not, then he would bide his time and—after notifying the king of Spain!—would obtain the English Crown without waiting.[1]

This wild scheme was never put into practice. In 1600, when it might have been, James was eight years older and had grown either more shrewd or more cautious. But even in 1601, when Cecil had established contact with James VI, a dangerous situation remained. Looking back at it, years afterwards, Cecil defended his policy of backstage negotiation with James. 'For what could more quiet the expectation of a successor', he asked, 'so many ways invited to jealousy, than when he saw her ministry, that were most inward with her [the Queen], wholly bent to accommodate the present actions of state for his future safety, when God should see his time?' But this plan of his carried dangers too. However much the Queen trusted him, he said, 'if Her Majesty had known all I did . . . her age and orbity, joined to the jealousy of her sex, might have moved her to think ill of that *which helped to preserve her*'.[2]

Very conscious of these dangers, Cecil went so far as to dismiss Simon Willis, his private secretary, 'partly for his pride' but 'principally because I was loath he should have come to some discovery of that correspondency which I had with the king our sovereign, which without great difficulty I could not have avoided'. Hence 'he might have raised some such inferences thereof as might have bred some jealousy in the queen's mind'.[3]

So Cecil, from the spring of 1601, bent himself to two tasks: to instruct James in the duties which would one day await him in London and, secondly, to ensure that James was never again tempted to seize power before his time.[4] He urged him to pay no serious attention to the 'pamphlets and projects of priests and

[1] Willson, op. cit. 111.
[2] A. Collins, *Sidney Papers*, ii, 326; my italics.
[3] Ibid. [4] See e.g. *Secret Correspondence of James VI*, 12–14.

fugitives, who are always labouring to set up one golden calf or other'. Now James began to sing a different tune. 'Yea, what a foolish part were that in me', he wrote, 'if I might do it to hazard my honour, state and person, in entering that kingdom by violence as an usurper'. Rather than climb over hedges to pick unripe fruit, he said, earlier in the letter, he would prefer to enter the garden by the gate 'and enjoy the fruits at my pleasure, in the time of their greatest maturity'.[1] How different this was from his speech to the Scottish parliament in 1599! Then he had declared that 'He was not certain how soon he should have to use arms; but whenever it should be, he knew his right and would venture crown and all for it'.[2]

This change, in so short a space of time, was a tribute to Cecil's statesmanship. And, although the king later on forgot his debt, his peaceful succession was the clearest manifestation of Cecil's achievement. But new problems arose for Cecil as Sir Walter Raleigh, his friend and collaborator, began to play the Essex in a separate correspondence with James VI. The exact nature of this new intrigue has never been fully explained, nor is it known why the breach came in the first place. Raleigh may have had an understandable suspicion that Cecil was barring his entry to the privy council. Since government was still conducted on a personal basis, with a good deal of the discussion between monarch and minister unrecorded, it is impossible to say what influence Cecil exerted in this matter. In a letter to Sir George Carew, Cecil did say that he would oppose the promotion of Raleigh to the council unless he gave up the captaincy of the guard to Carew.[3] But this was not a declaration that he would or could veto Raleigh's promotion; nor did he in fact possess any such powers. Elizabeth had indeed, years before, barred Raleigh's entry to high office and, even allowing for the undoubted greatness of that errant genius, she was probably right. But, to Raleigh and his friends at Durham House, it seemed that Cecil was destroying an alliance which had held so fast during the Essex rebellion. And certainly, in his correspondence with James VI, Cecil under provocation wrote harshly of his old friend. He thought fit to remind that virtuous monarch that Raleigh held dangerous views on religion, and that he and his

[1] Ibid. 62. [2] Ibid. p. xlv.

[3] *Letters from Sir Robert Cecil to Sir George Carew*, ed. J. Maclean (Camd. Soc. O.S. lxxxviii), 86.

friends were just 'gaping crabs'.[1] It was a squalid business, the more so as it was conducted amidst an outward show of friendship between the two sides; and nobody emerged from it with his hands clean. The situation derived from the feverish, nerve-strung conditions of these closing years, and from the discordant temperaments of the two rivals. It led ultimately to the destruction of Raleigh's political career. Elizabeth had, in any case, judged him incapable of the highest office; so did James. So probably did Cecil. Whatever may be said about the tragedy of Raleigh in personal terms, in the matter of public affairs the two monarchs and Cecil were probably right. Apart from this, if Raleigh stood in the way of mutual confidence between James and Cecil, and the plans for an easy and peaceful succession, then Raleigh must be dropped. Once Cecil had reached this conclusion, it was not in his nature to allow personal friendship to stand in his way, or to move him to save a falling colleague.

Nothing in this article has argued that Robert Cecil was a man of virtue or unchallengeable integrity. From other evidence at our disposal it is clear that he was afflicted as much as any man with the weaknesses of the time: a taste for intrigue and a greed for wealth and power. But the evidence that we have examined so far does establish that in his political skills, in his judgment of the diplomatic scene, in his supreme sense of the possible, this little, crippled statesman—her pygmy, as Queen Elizabeth elegantly described him—stood head and shoulders above his contemporaries. Only his statesmanship, cool, patient, flexible, saved England from the dangers which threatened the nation in the closing years of the old Queen. Above all, he saw clearly what was necessary to achieve a peaceful transfer of power. Without passion—perhaps without feeling—he pursued this single aim.

In the process he went a long way towards restoring unity to a factious realm. If his negotiations with the Catholics were basically political in aim, namely to draw the teeth of the Spanish wing, there was possibly present also a genuine desire for accommodation, for some working agreement with the moderate Catholics. The outcome of the long discussions was at first sight disappointing; and only thirteen priests felt that they could accept the conditions of the Queen's proclamation of 5 November 1602. That

[1] *Secret Correspondence of James VI*, 18; Helen G. Stafford, *James VI of Scotland and the Throne of England*, 267–73.

proclamation publicly rejected all notion of religious toleration but it hinted that some consideration would be given to the priests who took the oath required.[1] This consideration could not possibly mean very much; but the thirteen who declared their allegiance at the end of January 1603 believed that they had found a means of serving God and Cæsar. They were a tiny minority. Even some of those who had hitherto taken part in the negotiations withdrew before what they felt was too great a victory for Cæsar. Yet it remains true that these thirteen pointed a way to the solution which was adopted by their fellow Catholics when the intense feeling of the Counter-Reformation era had died down.

It may be that the thirteen priests were in too much of a hurry. Had all Catholics done the same at that time the Jesuits' fears might have been fulfilled: that is, having come to terms with the English State, the Catholics might have been tempted to come to terms with the English Church. The Jesuits undoubtedly played their part in maintaining the integrity of English Catholicism. But when their work had borne its fruit the heirs of the Appellants showed how it could be enjoyed in peaceful relations with the secular government. Whether or not Robert Cecil cared or thought about this distant prospect, he did at least play his part in the more immediate task of limiting the help that a Spanish candidate for the succession could expect from Catholics in England. 'I will affirm truly unto you' he wrote to James VI, 'that most of them do declare their affection absolutely to your title, and some of them have learnedly written of the validity of the same.'[2]

Meanwhile, amid all the complex negotiations about the succession, Cecil was immersed in the urgent economic questions of these years of depression, as the Queen's reign drew to a close. Since these questions are not directly involved in the struggle over the succession, the policies Cecil favoured are not considered here. When more is known about them it may be that they will be seen as part of a general programme of national reconstruction to which he had directed his mind. We know that new policies were evolved for fiscal feudalism;[3] new methods were planned for

[1] R. Steele, *Tudor and Stuart Proclamations*, no. 930; *Cal. S.P. Dom.* 1601–3, 260–1. [2] *Secret Correspondence of James VI*, 35.

[3] J. Hurstfield, *The Queen's Wards*, 311–25.

dealing with concealed lands;[1] even the lease of sweet wines, previously held by Essex, was given to a group of people 'to husband it for the queen'.[2] Again, none of this can be taken to mean that Cecil was prepared to become a poor man in the service of the state. He was, of course, fully alert to his private interest, but also alert increasingly to the necessities of a powerful modern state.

The last two years of the Queen's rule were indeed Cecil's years. His mind and will are seen in every policy which was tested out. But his greatest contribution was undoubtedly as the servant of the two monarchs, Elizabeth I and James VI: by a paradox a faithful servant to both yet above all to the national unity. The measure of his success is that there was no longer any doubt in England as to who would come in. Even before the Queen's health finally broke, eyes had turned to Scotland. 'I find some less mindful of what they are soon to lose than of what they may perchance hereafter get', wrote John Harrington on 27 December 1602.[3] He was no better than the rest; and there was something more than piety in his new year's gift to James with the words: 'Lord remember me when thou comest in thy Kingdom.'[4]

Three months later the Queen was dead and, within a few days, John Chamberlain was describing the undignified haste to Scotland in search of advancement:

'There is much posting that way, and many run thither of their own errand, as if it were nothing else but first come first served, or that preferment were a goal to be got by footmanship.'[5]

Many men travelled north in the first exciting days of the new reign: Cecil himself was summoned to meet his monarch, for the first time, at York. But all men were engaged on a peaceful mission. Thanks to him, more than to any man, not a single gun was fired in anger as the King made his long progress to his southern capital.

[1] *Cal. S.P. Dom.* 1598–1601, 493–4.
[2] A. Cecil, *A Life of Robert Cecil*, 139*n*.
[3] J. Harrington, *Nugae*, i, 321.
[4] Ibid. i, 326.
[5] *Letters of John Chamberlain*, i, 189.

The Historical Writings of Sir John Neale

I. BOOKS, ARTICLES AND LECTURES

1916 The lord keeper's speech to the parliament of 1592/3. *E.H.R.* xxxi, 128–37.

1919 Queen Elizabeth's quashing of bills in 1597–8. *E.H.R.* xxxiv, 586–8 (and note, ibid. xxxvi (1921), 480).

1920 The commons' journals of the Tudor period (The Alexander Prize Essay, 1919). *Trans. R.H.S.* 4th ser. iii, 136–70.
Proceedings in parliament relative to the sentence on Mary Queen of Scots. *E.H.R.* xxxv, 103–13.

1921 The authorship of Townshend's 'Historical Collections'. *E.H.R.* xxxvi, 96–99.
Parliament and the succession question in 1562/3 and 1566. Ibid. xxxvi, 497–520.
Section 'The Sixteenth Century' in the Historical Association's *Annual Bulletin of Historical Literature* (and 1922–25 inclusive).

1924 The commons' privilege of free speech in parliament. *Tudor Studies presented to A. F. Pollard,* ed. R. W. Seton-Watson (Longmans), 257–86.
Peter Wentworth. *E.H.R.* xxxix, 36–54, 175–205.

1925 The sayings of Queen Elizabeth. *History,* x, 212–33. [Reprinted in *Essays in Elizabethan History* (1958), 85–112.]

1927 Letter: The evidence of the casket letters. *History,* xii, 42–44.

1928 The diplomatic envoy. *History,* xiii, 204–18. [Reprinted in *Essays in Elizabethan History* (1958), 125–45.]

1929 The fame of Sir Edward Stafford. *E.H.R.* xliv, 203–19. [Reprinted in *Essays in Elizabethan History* (1958), 146–69.]

1930 Elizabeth and the Netherlands, 1586–7. *E.H.R.* xlv, 373–96. [Reprinted in *Essays in Elizabethan History* (1958), 170–201.]

1931 Three Elizabethan elections. *E.H.R.* xlvi, 209–38.

1934 *Queen Elizabeth* (Jonathan Cape, 402 pp.). Book Society choice; awarded James Tait Black memorial prize. (Also published by Harcourt Brace (New York, 1934) and The Reprint Society

(London, 1942); reissued as *Queen Elizabeth I* in The Bedford Historical Series (London, 1952), Doubleday Anchor books (New York, 1957) and Penguin books (London, 1960); translated into Danish, Swedish, Norwegian, Italian, German, Hungarian, Spanish, French.)

1935 *English Local Government: A Historical Retrospect* (privately printed for the National Association of Local Government Officers). [Reprinted in *Essays in Elizabethan History* (1958), 202–24.]

1937 Coronations in the past. *Overseas*, Jan., pp. 27–31.

1943 *The Age of Catherine de Medici* (Jonathan Cape, 111 pp.).

1946 More Elizabethan elections. *E.H.R.* lxi, 18–44.

1948 *The Elizabethan Political Scene* (British Academy Raleigh lecture; Geoffrey Cumberlege, 23 pp.), reprinted from *Proc. Brit. Acad.* xxxiv, 97–117. [Also reprinted in *Essays in Elizabethan History* (1958), 59–84.]

1949 *The Elizabethan House of Commons* (Jonathan Cape, 455 pp.).
Albert Frederick Pollard. *E.H.R.* lxiv, 198–205. [Reprinted in *Essays in Elizabethan History* (1958), 238–47.]

1950 Sir Nicholas Throckmorton's advice to Queen Elizabeth on her accession to the throne. *E.H.R.* lxv, 91–98.
The Elizabethan acts of supremacy and uniformity. Ibid. 304–32.

1951 *The Elizabethan Age* (The Creighton lecture, 1950; Athlone Press, 22 pp.). [Reprinted in *Essays in Elizabethan History* (1958), 21–44.]
John Stow. *Trans. London and Middlesex Arch. Soc.* n.s. x (pt. 3), 276–9.
The biographical approach to history. *History*, xxxvi, 193–203. [Reprinted in *Essays in Elizabethan History* (1958), 225–37.]

1952 Parliament and the articles of religion, 1571. *E.H.R.* lxvii, 510–21.

1953 *Elizabeth I and her Parliaments, 1559–1581* (Jonathan Cape, 434 pp.).
The accession of Queen Elizabeth I. *History Today*, iii, no. 5, 293–300. [Reprinted in *Essays in Elizabethan History* (1958), 45–58.]

1955 Elizabeth I and her cold war. *Saturday Review*, 1 Oct., pp. 11–12, 47–49. [Reprinted under the title, The via media in politics: a historical parallel, in *Essays in Elizabethan History* (1958), 113–24.]

1957 *Elizabeth I and her Parliaments, 1584–1601* (Jonathan Cape, 452 pp.).
New light on Queen Elizabeth's dilemma. *Listener*, 24 Jan., pp. 147–9.

1958 *Essays in Elizabethan History* (Jonathan Cape, 255 pp.).
England's Elizabeth. A lecture delivered at the Folger Shakespeare Library on 17 Nov. 1958, the fourth centenary of the accession of Queen Elizabeth I (The Folger Shakespeare Library, Washington, 20 pp.).
Choice artist in kingship. *The Times*, 15 Nov.

1959 The state of Elizabethan studies after four hundred years, and The Tudor heritage in Stuart England, in *Tudor and Stuart History* (The Folger Shakespeare Library, Washington), 9–11, 26–27.

1960 Introduction to fascimile reprint of *The Quenes Maiesties Passage through the Citie of London to Westminster the Day before her Coronacion*, ed. J. M. Osborn (Yale Univ. Press for the Elizabethan Club).

II. REVIEWS

1921 H. F. Westlake, *Westminster* (*History*, vi, 134).

1922 C. Wittke, *The history of English parliamentary privilege* (*E.H.R.* xxxvii, 277–81). E. Cammaerts, *Belgium: from the Roman invasion to the present day*; H. van der Linden (trans. Sybil Jane), *Belgium: the making of a nation*; L. van der Essen, *A short story of Belgium*; P. Geyl, *Holland and Belgium: their common history and their relations*; L. van der Essen with F. L. Ganshof, J. Maury and P. Nothomb, *Atlas de géographie historique de la Belgique* (*History*, vi, 273–5). *Calendar of State Papers, Foreign, 1585–1586* (ibid. vii, 134–5).

1923 J. R. Tanner (ed.), *Tudor constitutional documents* (*E.H.R.* xxxviii, 144–5). F. C. Dietz, *English government finance*, 1485–1558 (ibid. 279–81). J. H. Pollen, *Mary Queen of Scots and the Babington plot*; A. F. Steuart (ed.), *Trial of Mary Queen of Scots* (ibid. 443–6).

1924 Hist. MSS. Com. *Salisbury*, xiv (*History*, ix, 140–1). Gladys Scott Thomson, *Lords Lieutenant in the sixteenth century* (*E.H.R.* xxxix, 309). R. H. Mahon (ed.), *The indictment of Mary Queen of Scots* (ibid. 310). E. W. Dormer (ed.), *Gray of Reading* (ibid. 632–3).

1925 *Calendar of Patent Rolls, Edward VI*, i, ii (*E.H.R.* xl, 283–5). R. H. Mahon, *Mary Queen of Scots* (ibid. 308–9).

1926 R. S. Rait, *The parliaments of Scotland* (*History*, xi, 60–61). M. St. Clare Byrne, *Elizabethan life in town and country* (ibid. 158–9). Hist. MSS. Com. *De L'Isle and Dudley*, i (*Economic Journal*, xxxvi, 492–5).

1927 Conyers Read, *Mr Secretary Walsingham and the policy of Queen Elizabeth* (*E.H.R.* xlii, 127–34). E. P. Cheyney, *A history of England from the defeat of the Armada to the death of Elizabeth*, ii (ibid. 430–3). W. Notestein, *The winning of the initiative by the house of commons* (British Academy Raleigh lecture) (*History*, xi, 358). J. A. Muller, *Stephen Gardiner and the Tudor reaction* (ibid. xii, 73–74).

1928 *Calendar of State Papers, Rome, 1572–1578* (*E.H.R.* xliii, 261–2) A. W. Reed, *Early Tudor Drama* (*History*, xiii, 86). J. A. Williamson, *Sir John Hawkins* (ibid. 263–5). Irene L. Plunket, *Queen Elizabeth and Tudor England* (ibid. 281).

1929 Lytton Strachey, *Elizabeth and Essex* (*Manchester Guardian*, 1 Jan.). A. F. Scott Pearson, *Church and state: political aspects of sixteenth century puritanism* (*E.H.R.* xliv, 494). D. L. W. Tough, *The last years of a frontier. A history of the Borders during the reign of Elizabeth* (ibid. 679–80). P. O. de Törne, *Don Juan d'Autriche and les projets de conquête de l'Angleterre*, ii (ibid. 680).

1931 *Calendar of Patent Rolls, Edward VI*, iii–vi (*E.H.R.* xlvi, 298–9). M. P. Janelle, *Obedience in church and state* (ibid. 492–3). Gladys Scott Thomson, *Two centuries of family history* (ibid. 682). Hist. MSS. Com. *Salisbury*, xv (ibid. 684–5).

1932 *Calendar of State Papers, Foreign, Jan.-June 1588* (*E.H.R.* xlvii, 499–501).

1934 H. Brugmans (ed.), *Correspondentie van Robert Dudley Graaf van Leycester en andere documenten betreffende zijn Gouvernement-Generaal in de Nederlanden, 1585–1588* (*E.H.R.* xlix, 520–1). J. A. Williamson, *The observations of Sir Richard Hawkins in his voyage into the South sea, anno Domini 1593* (*History*, xix, 280).

1935 G. B. Harrison (ed.), *The letters of Queen Elizabeth* (*Sunday Times*, 6 Oct., 20 Oct.). V. H. Galbraith, *An introduction to the use of the public records* (*History*, xx, 287). Hist. MSS. Com. *Salisbury*, xvi (*E.H.R.* l, 178–9).

1936 R. Dudley Edwards, *Church and state in Tudor Ireland* (*History*, xxi, 185).

1937 W. Notestein, F. H. Relf and H. Simpson, *Commons' debates, 1621* (*E.H.R.* lii, 330–2). J. B. Black, *The reign of Elizabeth* (ibid. 515–18). Hist. MSS. Com. *Index of persons, A–Lever* (ibid. 723–4).

1938 *Calendar of State Papers, Foreign, July-Dec. 1588* (*E.H.R.* liii, 137–8). E. K. Chambers, *Sir Henry Lee* (ibid. 163). Hist. MSS. Com. *De L'Isle and Dudley*, iii (ibid. 712–13).

1939 C. H. Garrett, *The Marian exiles* (*E.H.R.* liv, 501–4). R. Chauviré, *Le secret de Marie Stuart* (ibid. 726–7). Hist. MSS. Com. *Index of persons, Lever–Z* (ibid. 742–3). M. M. Knappen, *Tudor puritanism* (*History*, xxiv, 146–7).

1941 *Calendar of Patent Rolls, Philip and Mary, 1553–1558* (*E.H.R.* lvi, 494–7).

1943 N. E. McClure, *The letters of John Chamberlain* (*E.H.R.* lviii, 230–3). J. U. Nef, *Industry and Government in France and England, 1540–1640* (*Ec.H.R.* xiii, 119–20). J. M. Aitken, *The trial of George Buchanan before the Lisbon Inquisition* (*History*, xxviii, 116).

1944 *Calendar of Patent Rolls, Elizabeth, 1558–1560* (*E.H.R.* lix, 115–16). E. H. Harbison, *Rival ambassadors at the court of Queen Mary* (ibid. 272–3).

1946 E. St. John Brooks, *Sir Christopher Hatton* (*Times Litt. Supp.*, 27 July, p. 354).

1947 E. St. John Brooks, *Sir Christopher Hatton* (*E.H.R.* lxii, 126–7).

1949 *Calendar of Patent Rolls, Elizabeth, 1560–1563* (*E.H.R.* lxiv, 520–3). J. S. Leatherbarrow, *The Lancashire Elizabethan recusants* (*History*, xxxiv, 285–6).

1950 D. M. Brodie (ed.), Edmund Dudley's *The Tree of Commonwealth* (*History*, xxxv, 154). G. Dickinson (ed.), *Mission de Beccarie de Pavie, Baron de Fourquevaux, en Ecosse, 1549* (ibid. 155).

1951 W. G. Zeeveld, *Foundations of Tudor policy* (*History*, xxxvi, 255–6).

1952 A. L. Rowse, *The England of Elizabeth* (*History*, xxxvii, 58–59). G. P. Rice, *The public speaking of Queen Elizabeth* (*Amer.H.R.* lvii, no. 3, 729–30). W. Croft Dickinson (ed.), John Knox's *History of the Reformation in Scotland*; C. D. Cremeans, *The reception of Calvinistic thought in England* (*History*, xxxvii, 164–5).

1953 A. Peel and L. H. Carlson (ed.), *Cartwrightiana* (*E.H.R.* lxviii, 473–4). P. Caraman (tr.), *John Gerard* (ibid. 475). G. Anstruther, *Vaux of Harrowden* (ibid. 642).

1954 T. M. Parker, *The English Reformation to 1558* (*History*, xxxix, 145–6). E. T. Davies, *Episcopacy and the royal supremacy in the church of England in the XVI century* (ibid. 146).

1956 C. Morris, *The Tudors* (*History*, xli, 222).

1957 *Calendar of State Papers, Spanish, 1554–1558* (*E.H.R.* lxxii, 113–15). D. B. Quinn (ed.), *The Roanoke voyages, 1584–1590* (*History*, xlii, 148–9). R. M. Kingdom, *Geneva and the coming of the wars of religion in France, 1555–1563* (ibid. 231–2). W. P. Holden, *Anti-puritan satire, 1572–1642* (*E.H.R.* lxxii, 171). A. J. Collins (ed.), *Inventory of the jewels and plate of Queen Elizabeth I* (ibid. 538–9). C. Falls, *Mountjoy, Elizabethan general* (ibid. 539–40).

1958 C. H. McIlwain and P. L. Ward (ed.), William Lambarde's *Archeion* (*History*, xliii, 233). P. M. Dawley, *John Whitgift and the Reformation* (*E.H.R.* lxxiii, 155). C. V. Malfatti (tr.), *The accession, coronation and marriage of Mary Tudor* (ibid. 714–15).

1959 W. M. Mitchell, *The rise of the revolutionary party in the English house of commons, 1603–1629* (*E.H.R.* lxxiv, 528–9).

1960 W. A. Gatherer (ed.), *The tyrannous reign of Mary Stewart: George Buchanan's account* (*History*, xlv, 50–51). F. M. Jones, *Mountjoy, 1563–1606: the last Elizabethan Deputy* (ibid. 53).

Index

2D*